Timken Museum of Art

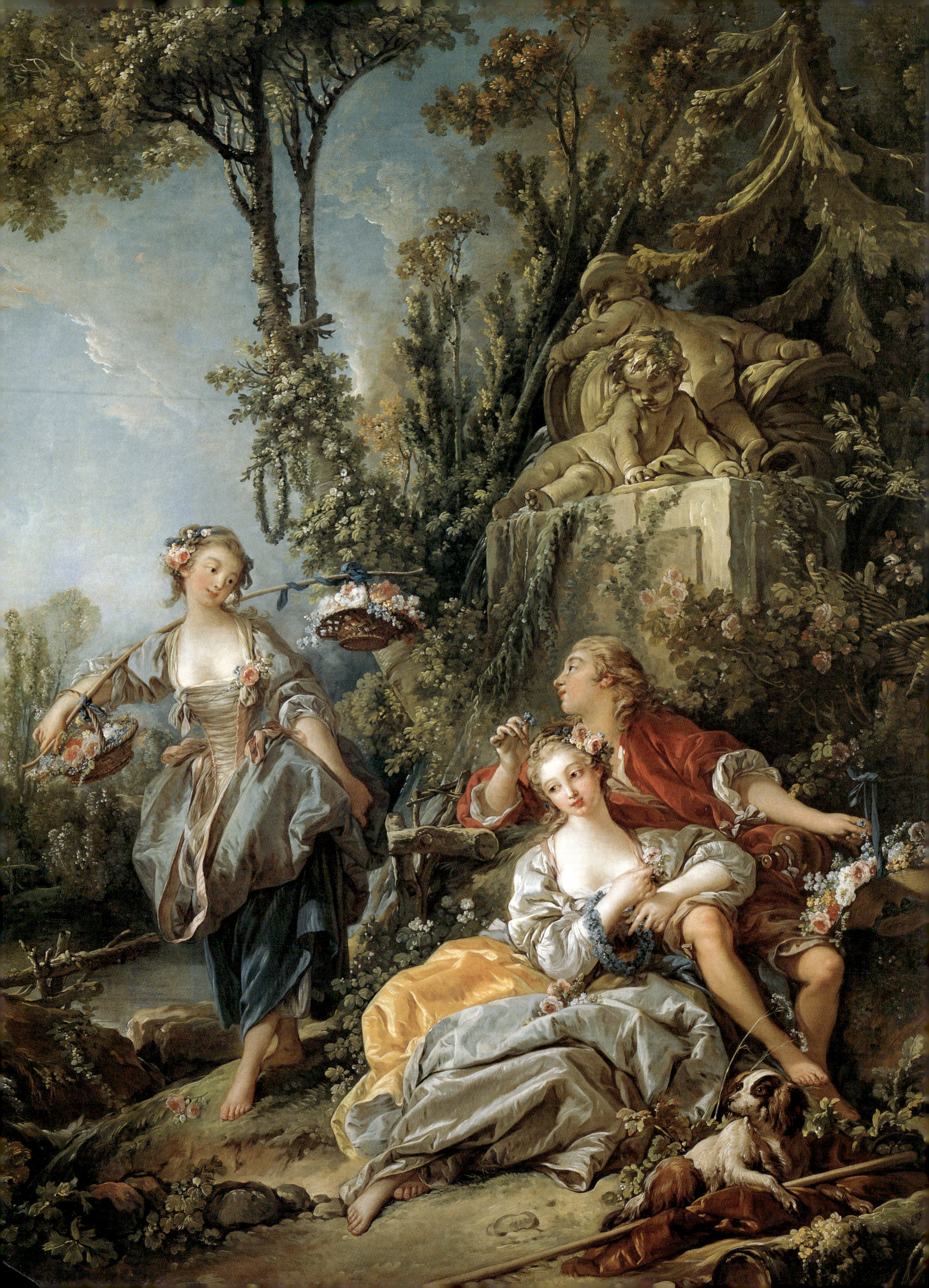

Timken Museum of Art

European Works of Art
American Paintings
and Russian Icons
in the Putnam Foundation Collection

Putnam Foundation
SAN DIEGO, CALIFORNIA

Library of Congress Cataloging-in-Publication Data
Putnam Foundation.
Timken Museum of Art : European works of art, American paintings, and Russian icons in the Putnam Foundation collection.
p. cm.
Includes bibliographical references.
ISBN 1-879067-01-3 (alk. paper)
1. Art—California—San Diego—Catalogs. 2. Timken Museum of Art—Catalogs.
I. Timken Museum of Art. II. Title.
N737.5A67 1996 96-33970
708.194′98—dc20

Hal Fischer, general editor
Fronia W. Simpson, editor
Jessica A. Eber, copy editor
Rob Vinnedge, photographer
Ed Marquand and Susan E. Kelly, designers
Produced by Marquand Books, Inc., Seattle
Printed and bound by CS Graphics, Singapore

Cover: John Singleton Copley, *Mrs. Thomas Gage,* cat. no. 35 (detail)
Frontispiece: François Boucher, *Lovers in a Park,* cat. no. 21 (detail)
P. 14: Luca Carlevarijs, *The Piazzetta at Venice,* cat. no. 2 (detail)
P. 66: Gabriel Metsu, *A Girl Receiving a Letter,* cat. no. 15 (detail)
P. 108: Philippe de Champaigne, *Christ Healing the Blind,* cat. no. 23 (detail)
P. 170: Fitz Hugh Lane, *Castine Harbor and Town,* cat. no. 39 (detail)
P. 208: *The Archangel Michael* from the *Deisis,* cat. no. 44 (detail)

Contents

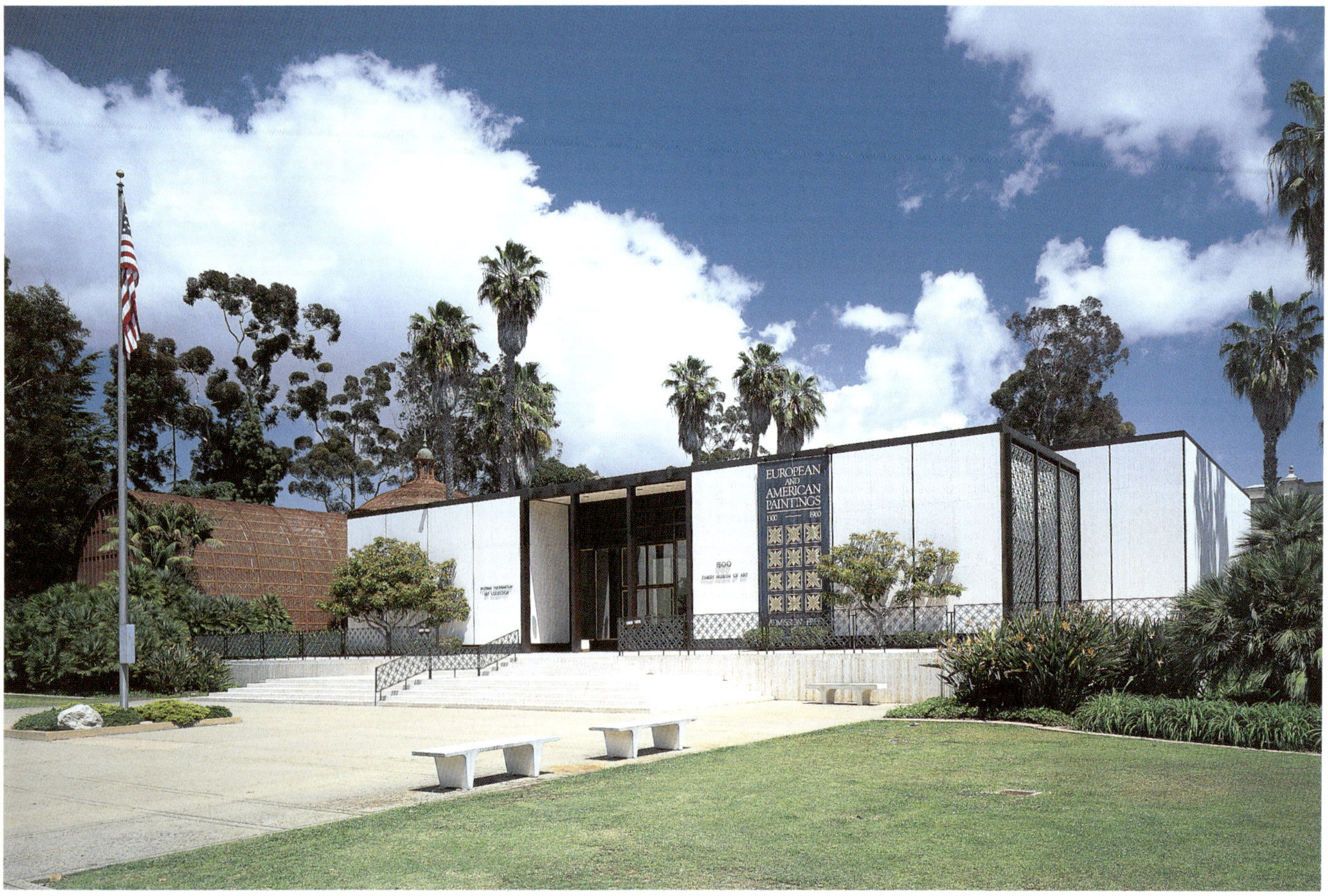
EUROPEAN AND AMERICAN PAINTINGS
1300 1900
1500

Foreword

THE BIRTH OF SAN DIEGO'S CULTURAL COMMUNITY was largely the result of the combined efforts and generosity of two families: the prominent Timken family of Canton, Ohio, and two of the Putnam sisters who arrived in San Diego with their family in the early 1900s. In 1925 Mrs. Appleton Bridges, a member of the Timken family, and her husband put forth the necessary funds for the construction of the Fine Arts Gallery (now the San Diego Museum of Art), a strikingly handsome, two-storied building, which was designed to fit the pseudo-Spanish architecture established in Balboa Park for the California-Panama Exposition of 1915–17. Upon the building's completion, its operation was assumed by the local Fine Arts Society. However, it was Mr. and Mrs. Bridges who were its principal supporters, paying the director's salary and that of the one guard employed by the society.

Soon after the death of Mrs. Bridges in 1940, the Putnam sisters, Anne (1867–1962) and Amy (1874–1958), well educated in the arts, stepped forward with generous financial support. Anne and Amy, who never married, lived close to Balboa Park in the stately family mansion at Fourth and Walnut streets. During the 1940s they began to purchase paintings of distinction, anonymously donating them to the Fine Arts Society. These gifts, for the most part, represented the Italian and Spanish schools. As a result of the sisters' generosity, the San Diego Museum of Art today maintains a distinguished collection of Spanish paintings.

In 1950 the sisters decided to establish a long-range program for the continued use of their wealth and sought the advice and counsel of their friend and attorney, Walter Ames. With his guidance they established the Putnam Foundation. In accordance with their wishes, the new foundation continued to purchase paintings of high quality. These works of art, however, were not destined to be exhibited at the San Diego Museum of Art but were to travel on loan to various institutions throughout the country. For over a decade the National Gallery of Art in Washington, D.C., New York's Metropolitan Museum of Art, Harvard University's Fogg Art Museum, and the Art Institute of Chicago exhibited Putnam acquisitions.

Although no members of the Timken family resided in San Diego after Mrs. Bridges's death, the Timkens retained an active interest in the community. Walter Ames consulted with his client Henry H. Timken, Jr., and the Timken Foundation offered to pay a substantial part of the cost of a new gallery for San Diego. Its purpose was to allow the return to San Diego of those Putnam paintings on loan to museums in the East.

The services of the architect Frank Hope were retained. He toured the nation's museums with Ames, visiting and conferring with such luminaries as James Rorimer, director of the Metropolitan Museum; John Walker, director of the National Gallery of Art; and Ernest Fiedler, administrator of the National Gallery. The end result was a building of simple elegance, designed to show the Putnam paintings to their best advantage. In October 1965 the doors of the new gallery were opened to the public. The institution was named the Timken Art Gallery because of the generous contributions the Timken family had made to the cultural life of San Diego. The formal, contemporary building of bronze, glass, and travertine marble harmonizes surprisingly well with the baroque façade of the adjacent San Diego Museum of Art. At the gallery's opening John Walker referred to the Timken as a "jewel box for the arts," a paean of praise as true today as it was some thirty years ago.

At the time of the Timken's opening, the Fine Arts Society graciously loaned twenty of the finest paintings that had been purchased for it by the Putnam sisters. These paintings hung with twenty owned by the Putnam Foundation. One gallery —lined with rich green cut-velvet cloth woven in Italy expressly for the Timken— was designed to house a unique collection of Russian icons. This collection was initiated by Amy Putnam, who had taken courses in Russian at Stanford University. Over a period of forty years she collected many Russian works of art and books, as well as more than three hundred icons. For the opening of the gallery approximately sixty of the most important icons were selected for exhibition in the Amy Putnam Icon Room.

In the years following the opening of the Timken, day-to-day operations, supervision of the staff, and selection of acquisitions were under the direction of Walter Ames, president of the Putnam Foundation, who insisted on excellence in every phase of the new museum's operations. Though Ames was educated at Stanford University as a lawyer, he had a remarkable eye for fine art, and from 1965 until his retirement in 1978 he enjoyed contacts with the foremost dealers in the art world. Mr. Ames also called on the leading art historians and scholars for advice. Several world-recognized experts were hired to spend six-month periods working at the Timken with Ames. Agnes Mongan of Harvard University and the Fogg Art Museum; Dr. A. B. de Vries, past director of the Mauritshuis in The Hague; and George L. Stout, former director of the Isabella Stewart Gardner Museum in Boston, all spent many months in San Diego offering recommendations and guidance. The present board of directors and staff have not departed from this philosophy and continue to rely on leading authorities.

The collection encompasses examples of major European old masters of the French, Dutch, Flemish, and Italian schools dating from the early Renaissance. The Foundation owns one Spanish painting, by Murillo, and a small but choice selection of American paintings. Presently the American collection includes works from the late eighteenth through the nineteenth century. French seventeenth-century tapestries are displayed on the walls of the main rotunda, and a late bronze cast of Giovanni da Bologna's *Mercury* is featured in the center of this room.

In 1969 the first catalogue of the Putnam Foundation was published, with entries written by Agnes and Elizabeth Mongan. Subsequent to publication of the first edition, significant changes were made to the collection. The twenty paintings on loan from the Timken's neighbor, the San Diego Museum of Art, were returned, and new paintings were added to the collection. For the second edition of the catalogue, published in 1983, Cecil Gould, former keeper of the collection at the National Gallery, London, created entries for European paintings acquired by the Putnam Foundation after 1969 and updated the existing entries. In addition, Michael Quick, curator of American art at the Los Angeles County Museum of Art, wrote entries for the newly established American collection.

Since publication of the last catalogue in 1983, the Timken has added three major paintings to the collection. They are *The Return of the Prodigal Son,* a late work by the seventeenth-century Italian artist known as Il Guercino; *Mrs. Thomas Gage,* painted by the America artist John Singleton Copley in 1771; and the poetic *Castine Harbor and Town,* an 1851 luminist painting by the American Fitz Hugh Lane. In an era where escalating values in the art market have severely limited the ability of museums to acquire important works of art, we are especially proud to have been able to bring three new masterworks into the Putnam Foundation Collection.

In the mid-1980s the Timken began to expand its activities. A support group, the Friends of the Timken Museum of Art, was created in 1985 to provide auxiliary support for special programs. Their first project, a monumental restoration of the *Death of the Virgin* by Petrus Christus, was successfully completed by David Bull, head of paintings conservation at the National Gallery of Art, in 1993. The restored masterwork was showcased in the exhibition *Petrus Christus: Renaissance Master of Bruges,* organized by Maryan W. Ainsworth for the Metropolitan Museum of Art in 1994.

A series of small exhibitions focusing on one painting from the Putnam Collection was initiated in 1986 with *Albert Bierstadt: "Cho-looke, the Yosemite Fall,"* curated by Nancy K. Anderson. Accompanied by small scholarly catalogues, the focus exhibitions have been an opportunity to position the Putnam paintings in contexts that have proved particularly insightful. They have also been opportunities to share our paintings with others as well. An exhibition devoted to Corot's paintings of Italy, curated by Fronia E. Wissman, traveled to the Sterling and Francine Clark Art Institute, in Williamstown, Massachusetts. Our Eastman Johnson exhibition, focusing on that artist's masterful cranberry-harvest series and curated for the Timken's twenty-fifth anniversary by Marc Simpson, traveled to the Fine Arts Museums of San Francisco, the Yale University Art Gallery, and the National Academy of Design in New York.

During this period the Timken also became more active with the loan of its paintings to museums both here and abroad. Over the past decade our Fragonard, Pissarro, Christus, Metsu, Guercino, Bierstadt, Inness, and Copley have been featured in major scholarly exhibitions. Conversely, in 1992 the Timken was the recipient of a two-year loan of thirty French decorative-arts objects from San Francisco's Fine Arts Museums when its California Palace of the Legion of Honor was closed for renovations. The generous loan of these objects, which were showcased with the Timken's eighteenth-century French paintings, was the basis for a Timken-organized exhibition entitled *The Age of Elegance: France in the Eighteenth Century.*

Concurrent with this increase in activity, the directors of the Putnam Foundation opted to change the name of the institution from the Timken Art Gallery to the Timken Museum of Art. In this way they hoped to connote the more expansive range of activities being undertaken by the institution.

Preparation for a new catalogue of the Putnam Collection began in late 1993. The process of organizing the third catalogue of the Putnam Foundation holdings was assigned to our director of exhibitions and publications, Hal Fischer. The directors of the Putnam Foundation join me in expressing our appreciation for the exacting and laborious challenge of assembling new scholars to put together this most recent and complete edition. Hal developed the format for the catalogue, which is more comprehensive than the previous editions. Some entries from previous catalogues have been retained, while others have been entirely rewritten. It was at his urging that an illustrated essay be added on the Putnam icons, and that as an aid to scholars lesser-known Putnam holdings be featured in an appendix. I wish to thank Hal for his accomplishment in creating a modern and thorough publication on the Putnam holdings, as well as for developing and managing our exhibitions over the past decade.

For their efforts on behalf of the catalogue, I want to thank James Petersen for administrative support, Nancy Andrews for research assistance, and photographer Rob Vinnedge for his superb color transparencies. We are extremely grateful to Fronia W. Simpson, who as catalogue editor saw to a myriad of details and met with consummate skill the challenges that multiple-author publications present. To Ed Marquand and the staff of Marquand Books we offer special thanks for a beautifully designed and produced catalogue.

Over the past thirty years the Timken has benefited from the wise and generous counsel of many people, whom we wish to acknowledge here: Thomas Agnew; Morton C. Bradley; Richard R. Brettell; J. Carter Brown; David Bull; James Byam-Shaw; A. B. de Vries; Lorenz Eitner; Albert Elsen; Vera B. Espinola; Everett Fahy; Ernest Fiedler; Cecil Gould; Grant Holcomb III; Evelyn Joll; Al Lank; Harold McCracken; Sir Denis Mahon; Agnes Mongan; Elizabeth Mongan; Sir John Pope-Hennessy; Richard Reilly; John Rewald; John Rorimer; David Rust; Seymour Slive; Theodore E. Stebbins, Jr.; George L. Stout; John Walker; John Walsh; Robert Wark; and John Wilmerding.

This most recent catalogue of the Putnam Foundation Collection has been an opportunity for the Timken once again to reach out to museum professionals and art historians of the highest caliber for advice and counsel. We are especially indebted to our guest authors, who have given so generously of their time, energy, and expertise: Candace J. Adelson at the Memorial Art Gallery of the University of Rochester, New York; Maryan W. Ainsworth, Laurence B. Kanter, Walter Liedtke, and Carrie

Rebora at the Metropolitan Museum of Art; Lynn Federle Orr at the Fine Arts Museums of San Francisco; Dawson Carr at the J. Paul Getty Museum; Patrick Matthiesen of the Matthiesen Gallery; Richard Rand at the Hood Museum of Art, Dartmouth College; and Vera B. Espinola; Marc Simpson; and Fronia E. Wissman.

To the Friends of the Timken Museum of Art, who provided principal funding for this publication, we extend our most sincere appreciation. Through their generous contribution to the catalogue, Mr. and Mrs. Howard F. Ahmanson, Jr., and the Ahmanson Foundation have once again demonstrated their support and friendship.

The board and staff of the Timken Museum of Art dedicate this edition of the Putnam Collection catalogue to Mr. W. R. Timken, who passed away in 1995. Mr. Timken spent fifty-one years with the Timken Company of Canton, Ohio, helping to build the family business, which was established in 1889, into a multinational enterprise. Until his death he oversaw the activities of the Timken Foundation, which was established in the 1930s and which over the past six decades has made significant contributions to charitable organizations. Mr. Timken was a loyal supporter of the Timken Museum of Art who urged us always to strive for excellence in every phase of our activities.

Nancy Ames Petersen
DIRECTOR EMERITUS

Friends of the Timken Museum of Art

THE DIRECTORS OF THE PUTNAM FOUNDATION gratefully acknowledge the following Friends, who have generously supported publication of this catalogue.

Mr. and Mrs. Howard F. Ahmanson, Jr.
Mr. and Mrs. Arnold Kirkeby

Mr. and Mrs. Robert Ames
Dr. and Mrs. Arthur Austin
Mr. and Mrs. James Bashor
Mr. and Mrs. Michael Bernique
Mr. and Mrs. John Bloomberg
Ms. Mary Boehm
Mrs. Dolores Clark
Mr. and Mrs. J. Dallas Clark
James S. Copley Foundation
Mr. and Mrs. F. P. Crowell
Dr. and Mrs. Charles C. Edwards
Mr. and Mrs. Lee Estep
Mr. and Mrs. Michael Farrior
Mrs. Henry G. Fenton
Mr. and Mrs. William Field
Mr. Walter Fitch III
Mrs. Robert Forbis
Mr. and Mrs. Milton Fredman
Mrs. Henri R. Ghilbert
Mrs. Dori Gibson
Mrs. Robert Golden
Mr. and Mrs. Kenneth Hill
Mr. and Mrs. Robert Hoehn
Mr. and Mrs. John K. Hucko
Mr. and Mrs. Charlie Jones
Mr. Maurice Kawashima
Mr. P. M. Klauber
Mr. and Mrs. Thomas Ladner
Mr. and Mrs. James Milch
Mrs. Alice K. Miller
Mr. and Mrs. Richard C. Mitchell
Mrs. J. Duncan Munro
Mr. and Mrs. Don L. Nay
Mr. and Mrs. Josiah Neeper
Mr. and Mrs. Phillip M. Prophett
Ms. Katherine Razook
Mr. Edward H. Richard
Mr. and Mrs. Donald Roon
Mrs. Dorothy O'F. Ross
Mr. and Mrs. George W. Rowe
Mr. and Mrs. Frederick Sargent
Mrs. Donna Sefton
Mr. and Mrs. Harley Sefton
Mr. and Mrs. Herbert Solomon
Mr. and Mrs. Fred C. Stalder
Mrs. Ralph Staver
Mr. and Mrs. James Stiven
Mr. and Mrs. Jose Tasende
Mr. and Mrs. John W. Thiele
Mrs. H. H. Timken, Jr.
Ms. Therese Truitt Whitcomb
Mr. and Mrs. Joe R. Williams, Jr.
Mr. R. Bruce Underwood
Mr. and Mrs. Al Vasques
Dr. and Mrs. George Walker
Mrs. Mary G. Walker
Mr. and Mrs. Louis Weinstock
Mr. and Mrs. Thomas R. Wilkinson
Mr. and Mrs. Harold B. Williams
Mr. and Mrs. Joe R. Williams
Dr. Richard P. Wunder

Contributors to the Catalogue

C. J. A.	Candace J. Adelson
M. W. A.	Maryan W. Ainsworth
D. C.	Dawson Carr
V. B. E.	Vera B. Espinola
C. G.	Cecil Gould
L. B. K.	Laurence B. Kanter
W. L.	Walter Liedtke
P. M.	Patrick Matthiesen
A. M. AND E. M.	Agnes Mongan and Elizabeth Mongan
L. F. O.	Lynn Federle Orr
M. Q.	Michael Quick
R. R.	Richard Rand
C. R.	Carrie Rebora
M. S.	Marc Simpson
F. E. W.	Fronia E. Wissman

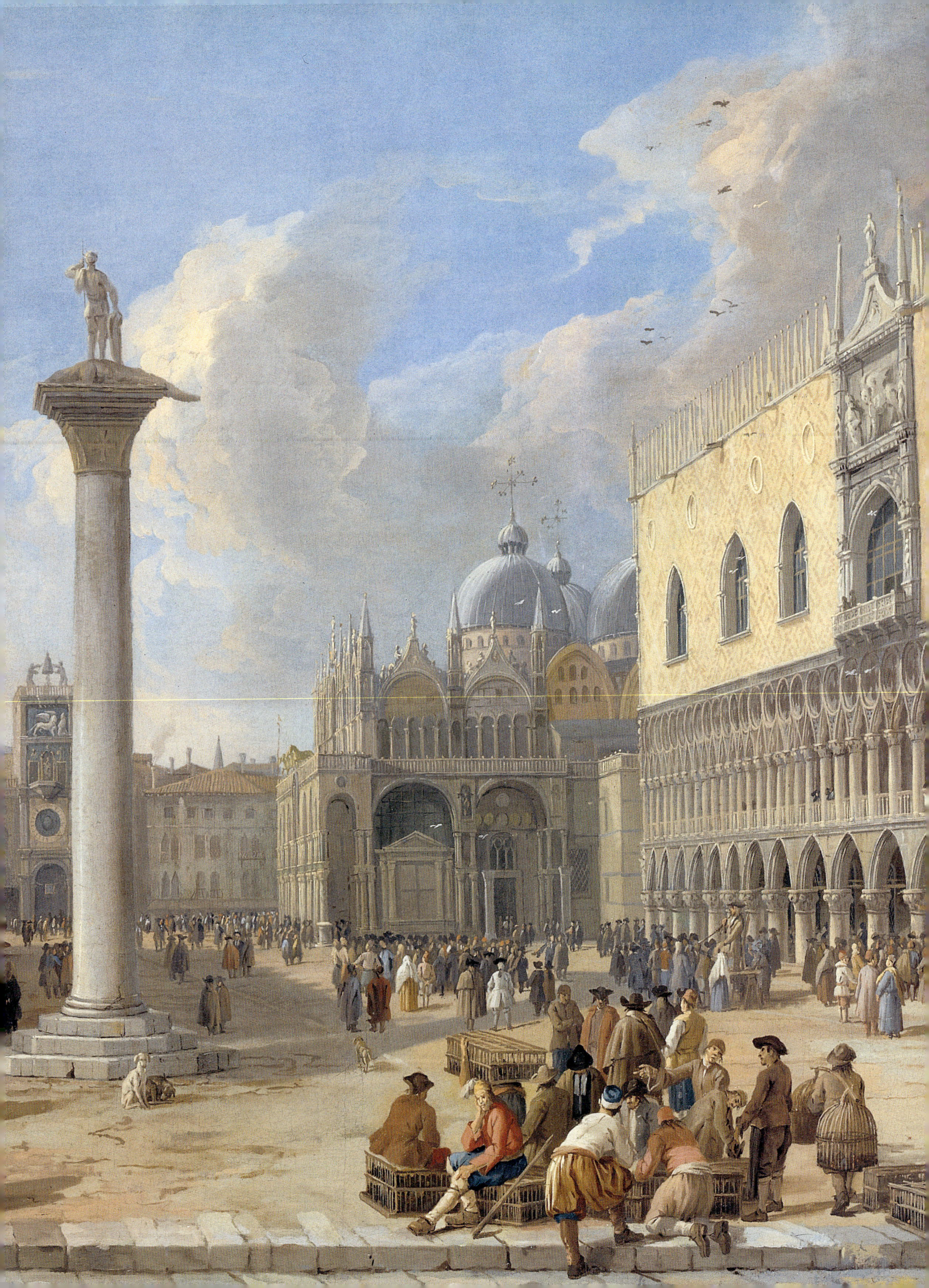

Italian and Spanish Paintings

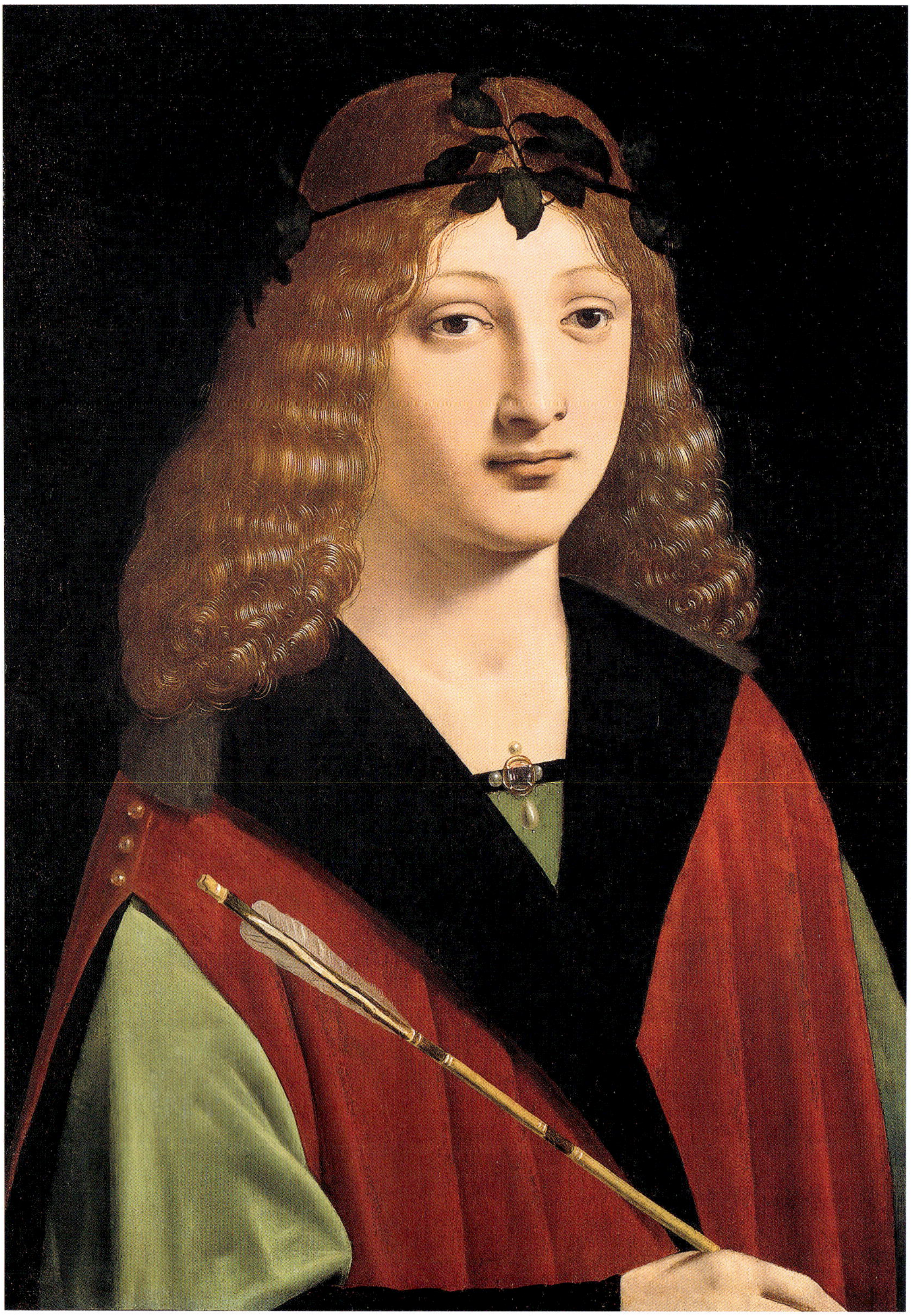

Giovanni Antonio Boltraffio
(1467–1516)

Born in Milan of a noble family in 1467, Boltraffio entered the school of Leonardo in 1491. The latter mentioned Boltraffio in a note in his *Second Book on Anatomy*. Boltraffio remained with Leonardo until about 1498–99. In 1500 Boltraffio went to Bologna, where he painted a *Madonna and Saints* for the Casio family. He painted an altarpiece at Lodi in 1508, now in Budapest, and shortly thereafter assisted in the fresco decorations of San Maurizio in Milan, where he died in 1516.

1 *Portrait of a Youth Holding an Arrow*, ca. 1500–1510
Oil on panel, 19⅝ × 14 in. (49.7 × 35.4 cm)

The young man represented half-length faces the spectator, his long golden hair bound by a fillet intertwined with laurel leaves. The fletching and shaft of an arrow are visible at center. A jewel is pinned at the opening of his cloak.

When purchased by Lord Elgin, this portrait was described as "Portrait of François de Melzo, who appears here in the costume of Apollo, by Leonardo da Vinci." Not only was the attribution to Leonardo in error, but the name of the sitter was also dubious, as a comparison with Boltraffio's presumed portrait of Melzo in the Heller Foundation, Bern, would indicate. It has been suggested that the subject might be Girolamo Casio, a well-known Bolognese poet who was a close friend of the artist. Yet the features in the Timken picture do not resemble in the slightest the portrait of Girolamo Casio in the Brera Gallery, Milan (no. 139). But our young man is closely related in features, costume, and general stylistic treatment to a portrait now at Chatsworth given to Boltraffio (see Suida 1929). It may also be related to the *Portrait of a Young Girl* by Boltraffio from the collection of Gianni Mattioli, Milan.[1]

The languid, somewhat androgynous figure suggests an allegorical theme rather than a realistic portrait. The genesis of the painting may be found in the silverpoint *Head of Young Bacchus* (fig. 1), probably by Boltraffio after a lost Leonardo drawing. Young men crowned with vine leaves or with other allegorical symbols are found in the drawings of Leonardo's circle. Leonardo's influence can be detected as well in the very genre of this painting. The idealized head, in which the style of the artist had

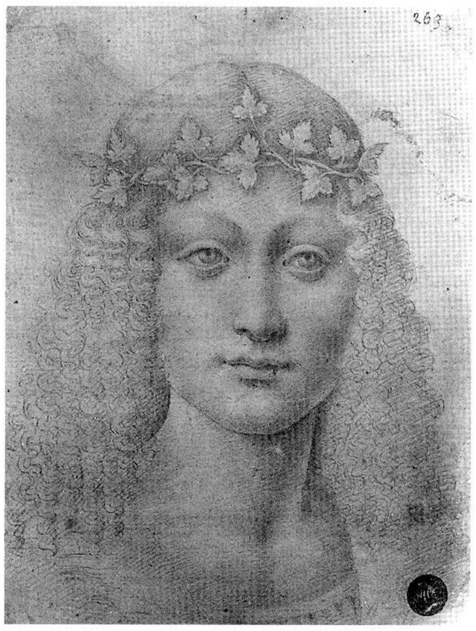

Fig. 1. Giovanni Antonio Boltraffio, *Head of Young Bacchus*. Silverpoint on paper. Venice, Galleria dell'Accademia, no. 263. Courtesy of Ministero per i beni culturali e ambientali.

precedence over the actual appearance of the sitter, if there even was one, enjoyed favor in Milan at the end of the fifteenth century.

In the Timken painting the original chiaroscuro and subtle tonal gradations have doubtless been somewhat diminished by modern restoration.

—A. M. AND E. M.

NOTE

1. See Los Angeles County Museum, 1949, *Leonardo da Vinci, Loan Exhibition,* cat. by W. R. Valentiner, pp. 23, 92, no. 43, ill.

PROVENANCE

The marquis de Gallo; purchased in Paris in 1806 by the seventh earl of Elgin; earls of Elgin and Kincardine; acquired by the Putnam Foundation, 1964.

LITERATURE

G. F. Waagen, *Galleries and Cabinets of Art in Great Britain* (supplement to his 1854 *Treasures of Art in Great Britain*), 4 vols. (London, 1857), 4:444; Bernard Berenson, *North Italian Painters of the Renaissance* (New York, 1907), p. 172; Gardner Teall, "Giovanni Antonio Boltraffio," *International Studio* 85 (October 1926): 25; Wilhelm Suida, *Leonardo und sein Kreis* (Munich, 1929), p. 287, as a half-figure of a youth; *Italian Art: An Illustrated Souvenir of the Exhibition of Italian Art at Burlington House London* (London, 1930), p. 54, no. 91, ill.; Enrico Mauceri, "Dipinti di raccolte inglese alla mostra d'arte italiana a Londra," *Dedalo* 10 (May 1930): 755, 758, ill.; Agnes Mongan and Elizabeth Mongan, *European Paintings in the Timken Art Gallery* (San Diego, 1969), pp. 28, 29, 109–10, no. 6, ill.; Burton Fredericksen and Federico Zeri, *Census of Pre-Nineteenth-Century Italian Paintings in North American Public Collections* (Cambridge, Mass., 1972), pp. 30, 524, 632; Martin E. Petersen, "Three Centuries of European Paintings, 1300–1600," *Apollo* 115 (June 1982): 447, fig. 11; *Timken Art Gallery: European and American Works of Art in the Putnam Foundation Collection* (San Diego, 1983), pp. 16–17, 115, no. 1, ill.

EXHIBITED

Manchester, England, 1857, *Catalogue of Art Treasures of the United Kingdom,* p. 23, no. 143, as Leonardo da Vinci but with the notation, "the work, most probably, of Antonio Boltraffio"; London, Burlington Fine Arts Club, 1898, *Illustrated Catalogue of Pictures by Masters of the Milanese and Allied Schools of Lombardy,* no. 47, pl. X, attributed to Leonardo da Vinci; London, Royal Academy of Arts, Burlington House, 1930, *Exhibition of Italian Art, 1200–1900,* p. 186, no. 320; London, Royal Academy of Arts, Diploma Gallery, 1952, *Leonardo da Vinci Quincentenary Exhibition,* p. 70, no. 256.

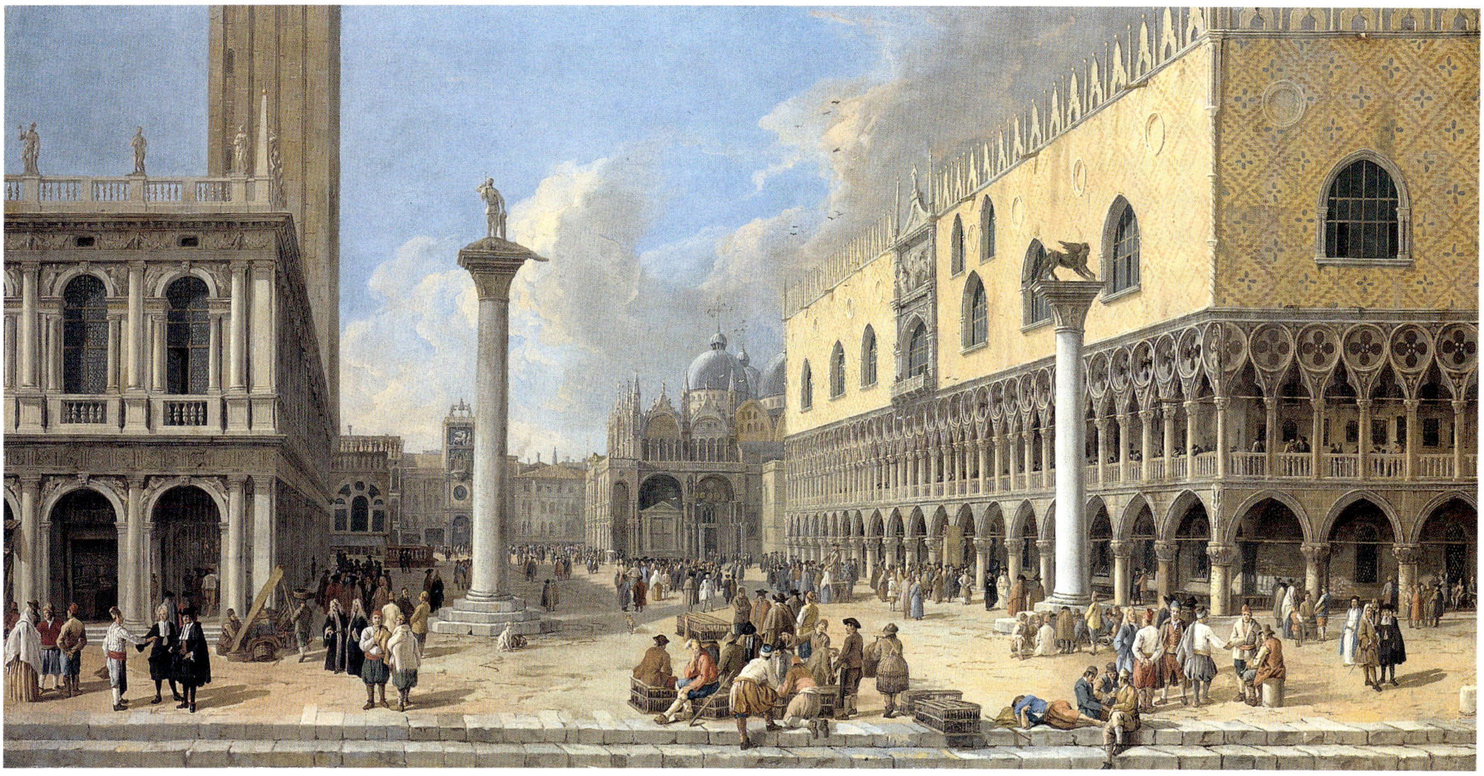

Luca Carlevarijs
(1663–1730)

Carlevarijs was born at Udine (Friuli) in 1663, but he lived and worked in Venice. He was thirty-four years older than Canaletto, forty-nine years older than Guardi. Therefore, he may count as the first specialist painter of the Venetian scene, though the Netherlander Gaspar van Wittel, known as Vanvitelli, had painted a few Venetian scenes before 1700. Carlevarijs also published, in 1703, a book of etchings of Venice. He died there in 1730.

2 *The Piazzetta at Venice*
Oil on canvas, 38 × 76⅞ in. (96.5 × 195.3 cm)

The scene is the Piazzetta, looking north toward the Piazza of St. Mark. On the left is the library designed by Jacopo Sansovino, with part of the Campanile showing above it. Farther on is the side of the Loggetta, and farther still, the clock tower partly obscured by the column of St. Theodoric. To the right are seen, next to the clock tower, the south side of St. Mark's, the Doge's Palace, and the column of St. Mark. The buildings shown, though not architecturally accurate in certain small details, remain virtually unchanged to this day, but the wings that flank the clock tower were made higher in the mid-eighteenth century.

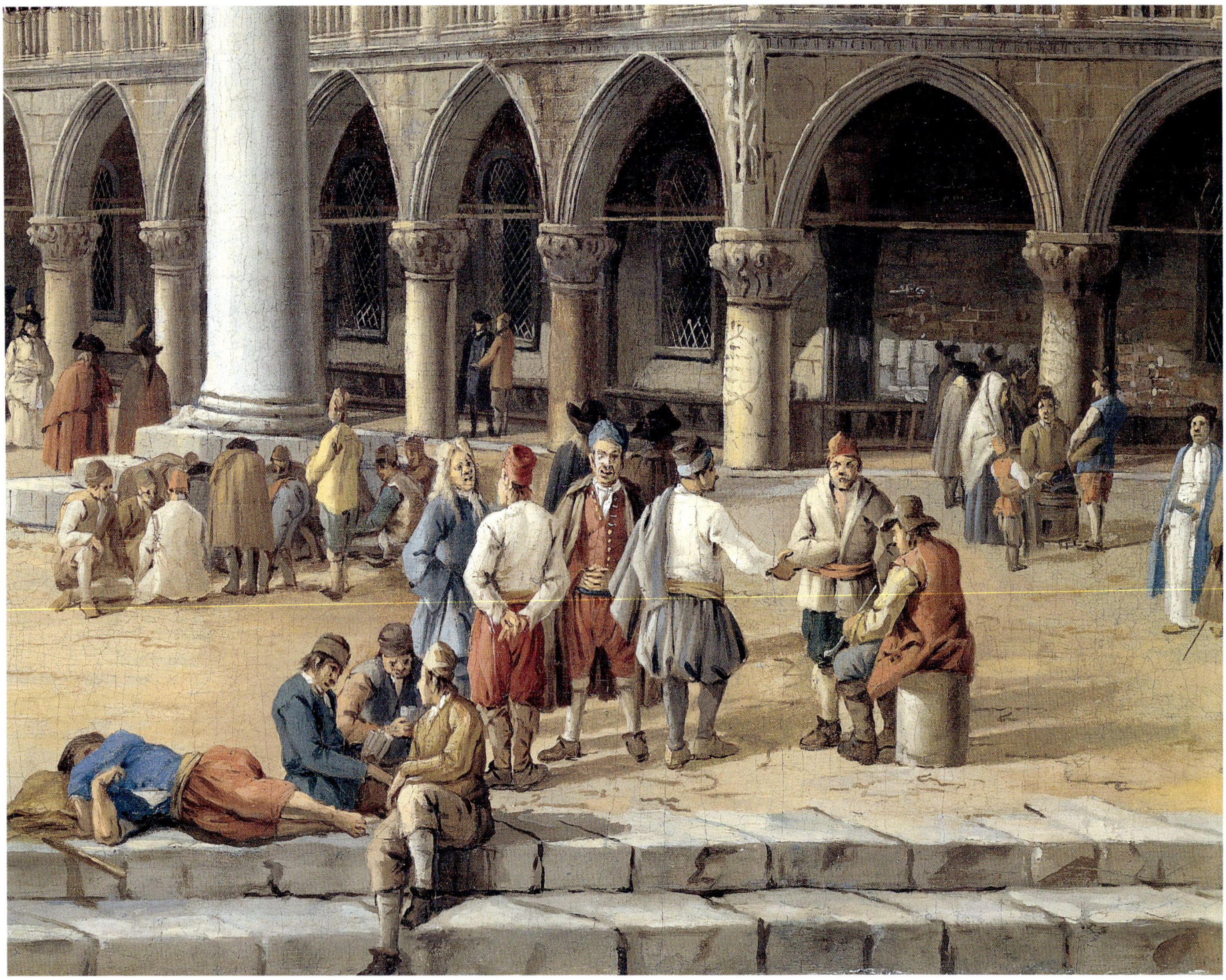

Detail of Plate 2

Rizzi (1967) pointed out that the fowl market was held in the Piazzetta on Friday mornings. Though the present picture includes, in the center, a number of cages, the market is not in progress, and the direction of the shadows—from the southwest—indicates that the time is afternoon. The market is therefore already over.

A similar view by Carlevarijs is in the Los Angeles County Museum of Art. An oil sketch that was apparently used by the artist for the figure in the center, with his left foot on the lower step, his right elbow on his right knee, is included in the Carlevarijs sketchbook in the Victoria and Albert Museum in London.[1]

—C.G.

NOTE

1. Reproduced as fig. 43 in the *Bozzetti* section of Rizzi 1967.

PROVENANCE

Arturo Grassi, New York, 1948; Sabatello, Rome; Bruschi, Florence; Paul Drey, New York; acquired by the Putnam Foundation, 1979.

LITERATURE

Fabio Mauroner, *Luca Carlevarijs* (Padua, 1945), p. 58; Antonio Morassi, "Una mostra de settecento veneziano a Detroit," *Arte Veneta* 7 (1953): 56; Carlo Donzelli, *I pittori veneti del settecento* (Florence, 1957), p. 54; Aldo Rizzi, *Luca Carlevarijs* (Venice, 1967), p. 92, pl. 139; Rodolfo Pallucchini, "Miscellanea piazzettesca," *Arte Veneta* 22 (1968): 106–30; *Timken Art Gallery: European and American Works of Art in the Putnam Foundation Collection* (San Diego, 1983), pp. 24–25, 116, no. 5, ill.

EXHIBITED

Louisville, Ky., J. B. Speed Art Museum, 1948, *A Gallery of Eighteenth-Century Venetian Paintings*, no. 4; The Detroit Institute of Arts, and Indianapolis, John Herron Art Museum, 1952, *Venice, 1700–1800*, no. 18. The painting is wrongly identified in the catalogue as one of four paintings commissioned from Carlevarijs by the English traveler Christopher Crowe. These pictures were in fact still in the possession of Crowe's descendants at the time of the Detroit exhibition, but the mistake persisted (e.g., in Rizzi's book); Udine, Loggia del Lionello, and Rome, Gabinetto Nazionale delle Stampe, 1963–64, *Disegni, incisioni e bozzetti del Carlevarijs*, cat. by Aldo Rizzi, pl. XXXII.

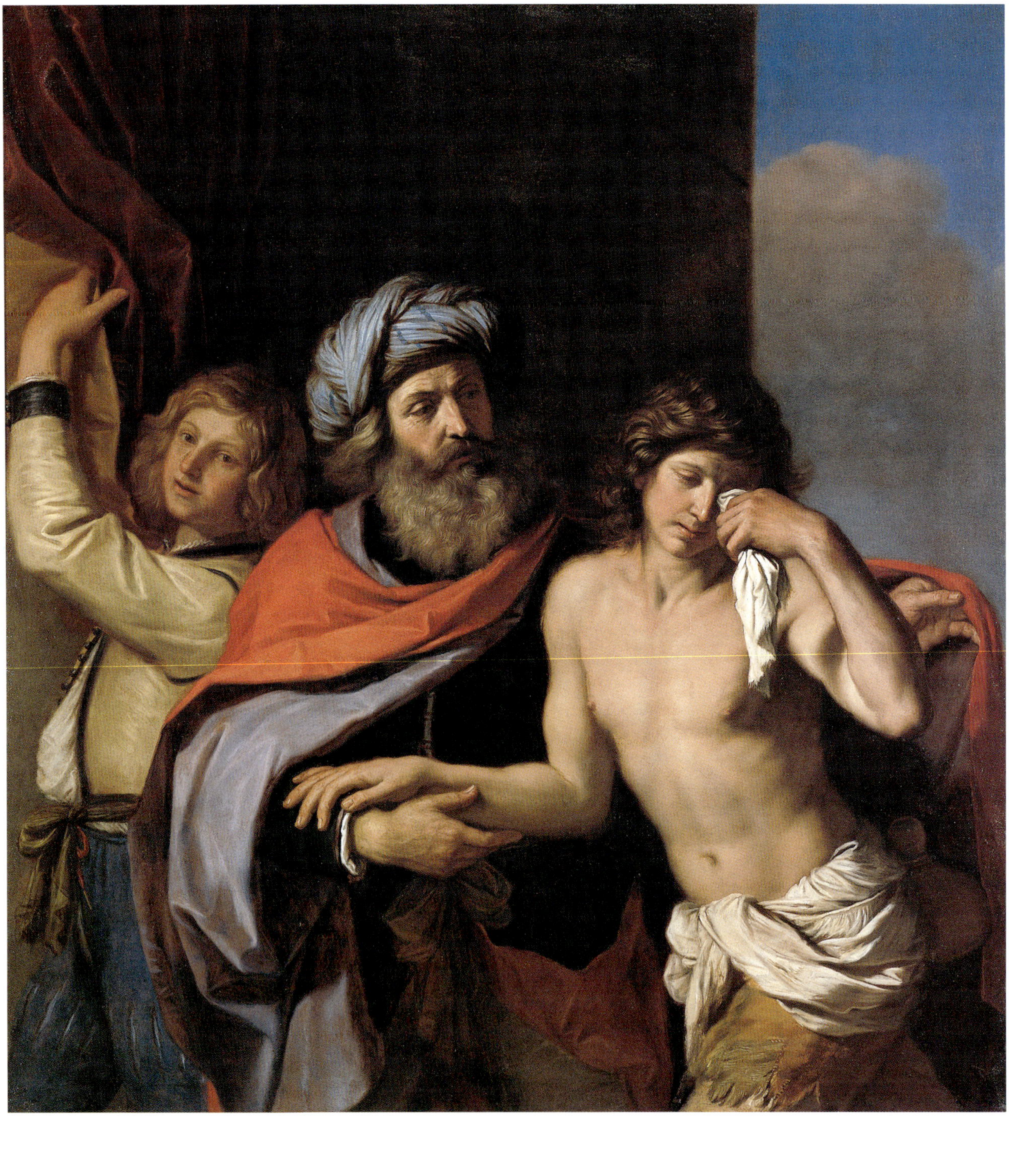

Giovanni Francesco Barbieri, called Il Guercino

(1591–1666)

Giovanni Francesco Barbieri, called Il Guercino (his nickname means "Squint-eyed") was born in Cento, a small town lying almost midway between Ferrara and Bologna. The principal artists of these neighboring towns, Scarsellino and Ludovico Carracci, were to exert the greatest influence on Guercino's early style, which associated the strong chiaroscuro of Caravaggism with the naturalism of Bologna. Late in the second decade of the seventeenth century, a visit to Venice and knowledge of Titian were to lead to a softening of Guercino's outlines and a more luminous and delicate palette. His 1616 *Virgin with Saints* (Brussels, Musées Royaux des Beaux-Arts de Belgique) heralds a more spacious and moving style, which culminates in such early masterpieces as *St. Sebastian Treated by St. Irene,* 1619, and *The Investiture of St. William of Aquitaine,* 1620 (both Bologna, Pinacoteca Nazionale). In 1621, commissioned by Pope Gregory XV to paint the *Aurora* for the ceiling of the Casino Ludovisi, Guercino produced one of the finest pieces of illusionistic baroque decoration. His *Burial of St. Petronilla,* painted for the church of St. Peter in 1622–23 (now Rome, Capitoline Museum), shows a new idealistic tension in the forms, which, however, are still naturalistically defined. Returning to Cento on the death of the pope in 1623, he set up a studio, but after the death in 1642 of Guido Reni, his chief Bolognese competitor, he transferred his studio to Bologna and became the head of the Bolognese school of painting. His later post-Roman works are characterized by a progressive sweetening and softening of the imagery, a deepening of the perspective, and a lighter, more classicizing and delicate palette. He died in Bologna in 1666.

3 *The Return of the Prodigal Son,* 1654–55
Oil on canvas, 61¼ × 57½ in. (155.6 × 146.1 cm)

The parable of the Return of the Prodigal Son, taken from the New Testament (Luke 15:11–32), is the one most frequently represented in Western art as teaching the twin virtues of repentance and forgiveness. A father with two sons divided his estate between them; the younger left home, squandering his portion in riotous living until finally, impoverished, he was reduced to tending pigs and eating their slops. The present picture shows the moment of his penitent return home, where he is joyfully received by his father, who dispatches the servant, to the left of the composition,

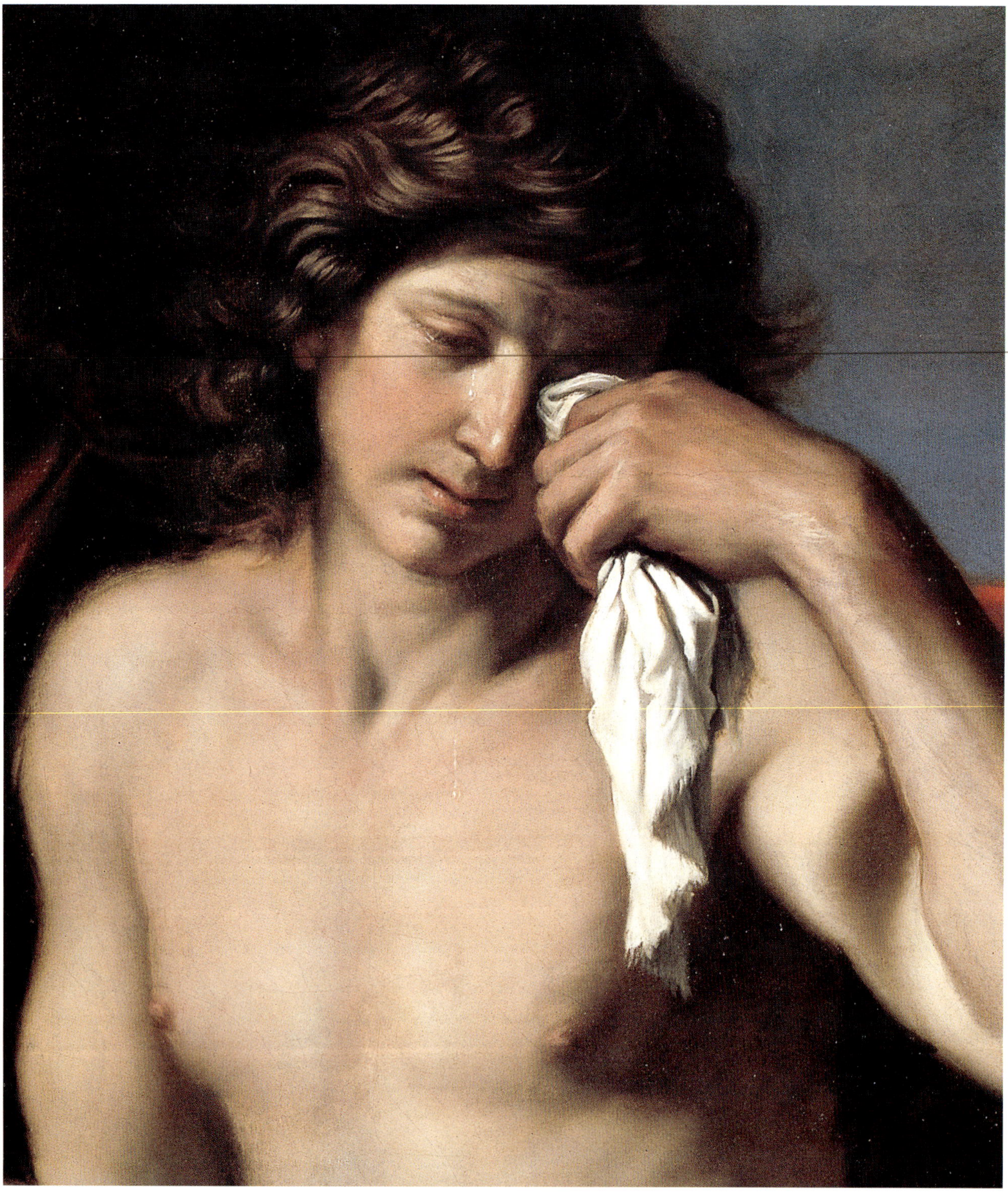

Detail of Plate 3

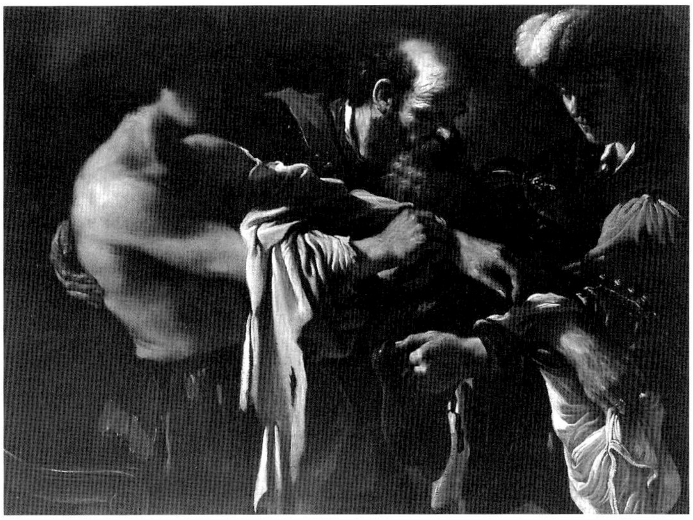

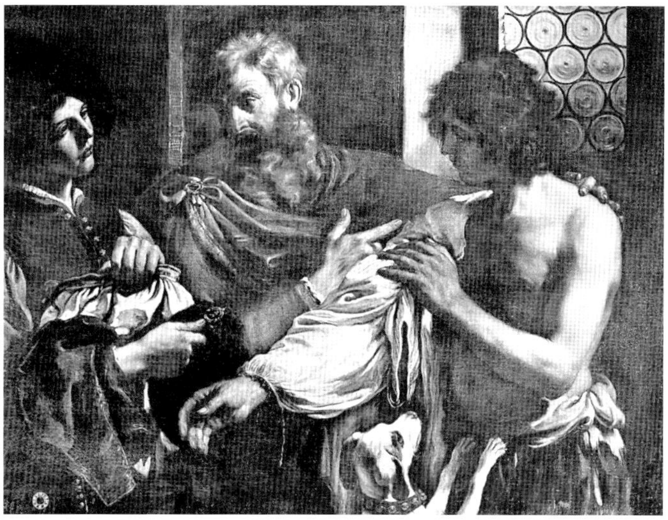

to fetch fine clothes and kill a fatted calf to make a feast. The elder son returns and, angry, has to be mollified by the father, thus underlining the act of forgiveness: "Thou art ever with me, and all that is mine is thine . . . for this thy brother was dead, and is alive again; and was lost, and is found."

Sir Denis Mahon has shown that the Timken *Prodigal Son* is the picture recorded by Malvasia in *Felsina pittrice* as having been commissioned by the archbishop of Bologna, Girolamo Boncompagni, in 1654–55 and later donated to Prince Colonna (see London 1981). This date corresponds to the style of the painting, and it seems that Boncompagni, who had become archbishop in 1651 and was later made a cardinal in 1664, took a long time to pay, for Guercino's own account book records the final payment on April 16, 1660.[1] The prelate left Bologna for Rome a month after the painting was completed, and the picture must have followed him, as it later appears both in a Colonna inventory of 1714 and again in the 1783 published catalogue of the Colonna pictures (see Literature).

The Colonnas began to sell to English collectors toward the beginning of the Napoleonic Wars, so that the painting probably reached Landsdowne House by 1830. It was certainly in the Landsdowne collection by 1844, when it was seen there by Mrs. Jameson, and shortly thereafter, in 1854, Dr. Waagen listed the picture as being in the Landsdowne House library.

Guercino painted the subject of the Return of the Prodigal Son on at least six occasions, using his favorite format of half-length figures. A seventh picture, but with full-length figures, commissioned by the Ludovisi in 1617, is now in the Galleria Sabauda, Turin.

At the height of his career, Guercino painted the earliest of his Prodigal Son works in 1619 for Cardinal Serra. The third painting he executed for this patron, it shows three figures in interlocking poses, strongly accented by dramatic contrasts of light and color (fig. 1). The power of the imagery suggests to the onlooker that the scene is unfolding there and then before his eyes. This is also the first example of the half-length-figure format Guercino was to reuse on countless occasions throughout

Fig. 1. Guercino, *The Prodigal Son*, 1619. Oil on canvas, 42⅛ × 56⅜ in. (107 × 143.2 cm). Vienna, Kunsthistorisches Museum. Photograph courtesy of Bridgeman/Art Resource, New York.

Fig. 2. Guercino, *The Prodigal Son*, 1627–28. Oil on canvas, 49¼ × 64⅛ in. (125.1 × 162.9 cm). Rome, Galleria Borghese. Photograph courtesy of Alinari/Art Resource, New York.

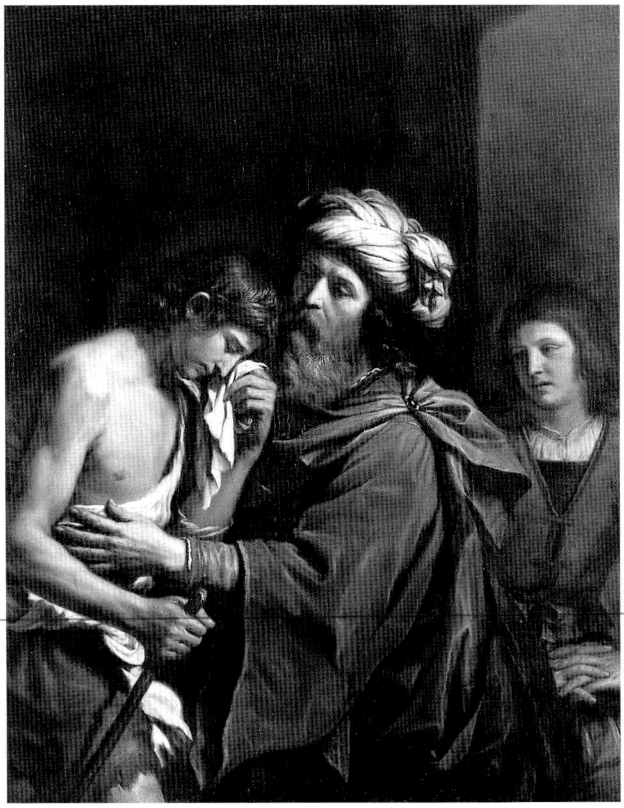

Fig. 3. Guercino, *The Prodigal Son,* 1651. Oil on canvas. Włocławek, Poland, Diocesan Museum.

his career. A comparison with Guercino's second *Prodigal Son,* of 1627–28, now in the Borghese Gallery, Rome, clearly shows his development (fig. 2). In the latter picture, the three figures are more soberly detached and arranged with greater symmetry, although still in somewhat friezelike fashion. However, the powerful spontaneity of the earlier picture is to some degree compromised. The Borghese picture represents a moment of transition.

From Malvasia (pp. 265 and 323), we know that Guercino did paint two further versions of the Prodigal Son, which are again half-length compositions. The first was commissioned by Prince Taddeo Barberini, given to Pope Urban VII, and was paid for on June 21, 1642. The second, ordered by Father D. Gregorio Maffone, was paid for on October 12, 1642. The whereabouts of both these pictures remains unknown.

Malvasia lists yet a further composition of the Prodigal Son (pp. 269 and 332), which was commissioned by the Venetian nobleman Giovanni Nani. This painting, executed only three years before the Timken picture, in 1651, is now in the Diocesan Museum, Włocławek, Poland (fig. 3). A comparison between these two pictures is useful on account of their stylistic similarities. The 1651 Włocławek composition is smaller than the 1654–55 Timken example, and therefore the restrictions of size constraining the former allowed Guercino in the later picture more space for developing and expanding the rhythm of the composition. However, both the qualities and the virtues apparent in the two pictures are extremely similar. The essential elements of the drama taking place are condensed into a representation of moving simplicity. Compared with the earlier pictures, the composition is less friezelike and arranged in depth along a diagonal. The result is a scene that, while perhaps less aggressive and more classicizing, is filled with a gentle sense of pathos. Compared with the earlier renderings of the Prodigal Son, the colors are softer and more delicate, silvery or almost pastel in tone, while the imagery suggests characteristics that Salerno (1988, p. 60) has suggested foreshadow the neoclassicism of Pompeo Batoni in the eighteenth century.

Whereas Guercino's early works are typical of the upsurge of spiritual confidence sustained by the Counter-Reformation, with compositions of unidealized naturalism, strong chiaroscuro, and a total revolt against the confused forms of late mannerism, his later works represent a tenderness of handling and a mobility of form and imagery, which are both more classical and reminiscent of the imagery and color balance of Correggio and Raphael.

—P. M.

NOTE

1. Malvasia 1841, p. 270; id., Guercino's account book, *Libro dei conti,* April 16, 1660, p. 340, which states: "Adi 16 Aprile 1660. Dall'ill.mo Sig. Co. Bonfigliolo si e riceuto Dobble n.[0] quoranto, per il Fagliol Prodigho che fu fatto a in[s]tan[c]ia del Sig.[r] Archivescovo Buon Conpagno, e questo quadro Fu donato al Sig.[re] Pren: Colonna, il denar[o] fano L 600-fano Scudi 150."

PROVENANCE

Archbishop Girolamo Boncompagni; the princes Colonna; the marquis of Landsdowne, his sale, Christie's, London, March 7, 1930, lot 443; private collection; Matthiesen Fine Art, London, 1981; acquired by the Putnam Foundation, 1983.

LITERATURE

Colonna Inventory of 1714, Rome, Colonna Archives; *Catalogo dei Quadri, e Pitture esistenti nel Palazzo dell'Eccellentissima Casa Colonna a Roma* (Rome, 1783), p. 29, no. 178; F. W. B. von Ramdohr, *Ueber Mahlerei und Bildhauerarbeit in Rom,* 3 vols. (Leipzig, 1787), 2:80–81.7; C. C. Malvasia, *Felsina pittrice: Vite de' pittori bolognesi,* 2 vols. (Bologna, 1841), vol. 2, pt. 4, p. 270; ibid., vol. 2, pt. 4, *Libro dei conti,* April 16, 1660, p. 340; Mrs. Jameson, *Companion to the Most Celebrated Private Galleries of Art in London* (London, 1844), p. 303, no. 21; G. F. Waagen, *Treasures of Art in Great Britain,* 3 vols. (London, 1854), 2:152; L. Salerno, *I dipinti del Guercino* (Rome, 1988), p. 377, no. 310.

EXHIBITED

London, Matthiesen Gallery, 1981, *Important Italian Baroque Paintings, 1600–1700,* pp. 74–77, no. 27, ill.; Bologna, Museo Civico Archeologico, 1991, *Giovanni Francesco Barbieri, Il Guercino, 1591–1666,* pp. 370–71, no. 143, ill.; Frankfurt, Schirn Kunsthalle, 1991–92, *Giovanni Francesco Barbieri, Il Guercino, 1591–1666,* pp. 328–29, no. 77, ill.; Washington, D.C., National Gallery of Art, 1992, *Guercino, Master Painter of the Baroque,* pp. 85, 298, no. 53, ill.

Luca di Tommè
(d. after 1390)

The earliest preserved notice of Luca di Tommè, recording payment for minor decorative work in Siena cathedral, dates from 1357, the same year in which he painted a book cover for the office of the Biccherna, the Sienese Treasury (Siena, Archivio di Stato). In 1362 he sat on a committee advising the cathedral authorities on the temporary removal of Duccio's *Maestà* from the high altar, and in the same year he collaborated with an older and more established master, Niccolò di Ser Sozzo, on the altarpiece of St. Thomas now in the Pinacoteca Nazionale, Siena. Three signed and dated altarpieces of 1366 (Pisa, Museo Nazionale di San Martino), 1367 (Siena, Pinacoteca Nazionale, no. 109), and 1370 (Rieti, Museo Civico) firmly establish the artistic identity of Luca di Tommè in the later part of his career. His relative seniority among Sienese painters of this period is affirmed by the appearance of his signature in the third position, following only Lippo Vanni and Jacopo di Mino del Pelicciaio, on the list of artists appended, sometime between 1378 and 1386, to the 1356 statutes of the painters' guild, and in the second position (after Jacopo di Mino) in the list of 1389. Also in 1389, Luca di Tommè accepted a commission for an altarpiece jointly with Bartolo di Fredi and his son, Andrea di Bartolo. The last known notice of Luca di Tommè dates from 1390, and it may be presumed that he died shortly afterward.

4 *The Trinity and the Crucifixion, with Scenes from the Life of Christ,* ca. 1355

The Resurrection, the Annunciation, the Nativity, the Adoration of the Magi, the Mocking of Christ, the Lamentation

Triptych, tempera on panel: center panel, 22¼ × 10⅜ in. (56.5 × 26.4 cm) overall, 20 × 9 in. (50.8 × 22.8 cm) picture surface; left wing, 22⅛ × 5¼ in. (56.2 × 13.3 cm) overall, 18⅛ × 3⅞ in. (46 × 9.8 cm) picture surface; right wing, 22½ × 5⅛ in. (57.2 × 13 cm) overall, 18¾ × 3¾ in. (47.6 × 9.5 cm) picture surface

The center panel is occupied by an unusual representation of the Trinity as a single figure with three heads and trunks but only two arms and feet, seated in a blue mandorla placed inexplicably off-center to the left beneath a flattened arch made of hardened gesso, called *pastiglia*. Beneath and before the Trinity and portrayed on a slightly smaller scale is Christ on the cross, with smaller figures of the mourning

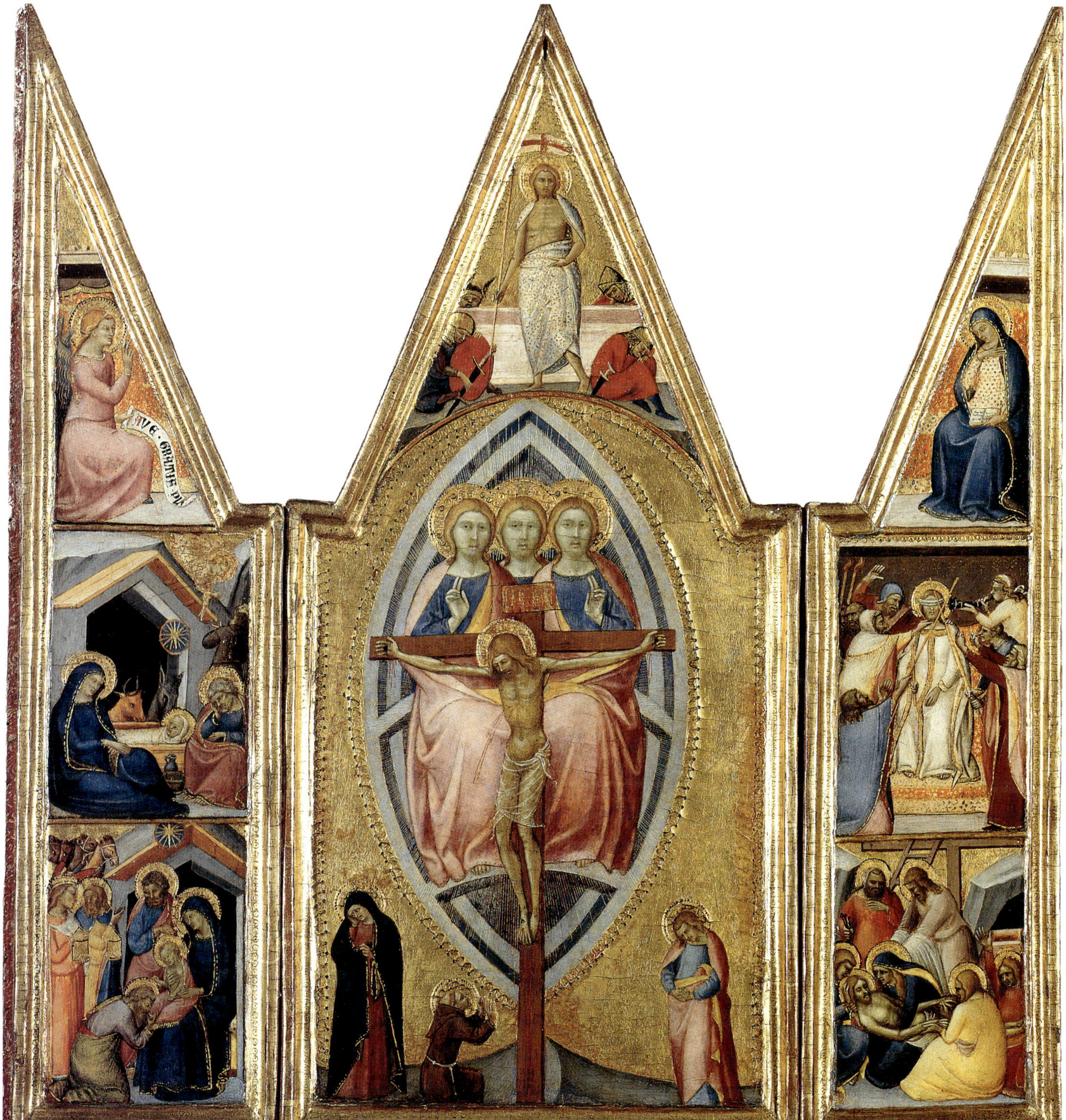
AVE · GRATIA · PL

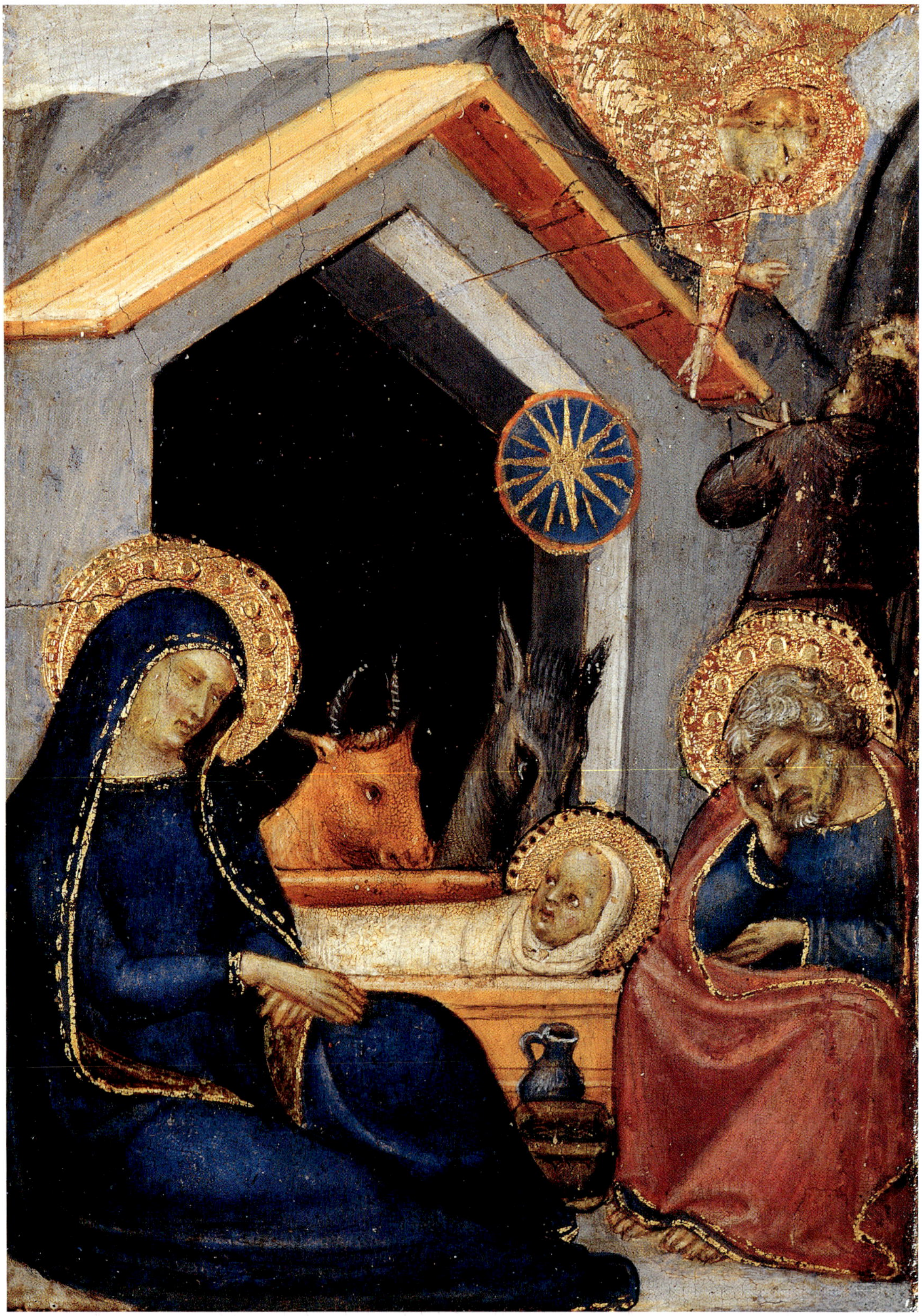

Detail of Plate 4

Virgin and St. John the Evangelist filling the corners of the panel below and an even smaller figure of St. Francis kneeling at the foot of the cross. In the pinnacle above, the resurrected Christ stands triumphantly before his empty tomb, as four Roman soldiers, one at each corner of the sarcophagus, are seated on the ground asleep.

The wings are each divided into three scenes by narrow *pastiglia* moldings. In the left wing at the top is the Angel of the Annunciation, kneeling before a cloth of honor in an open gallery, holding a scroll in his left hand inscribed "Ave gratia pl[ena]" (Hail [Mary], full of grace). Below him is a scene of the Nativity, with the Christ Child, swaddled in white, laid in a crib set before the square-cut mouth of a cave protected by a shed roof mounted on the rock face. The Virgin and St. Joseph are seated on the ground before the crib, while the ox and ass peer out from the cave behind. The star of Bethlehem hovers improbably above the Child's head in front of the mouth of the cave. In the upper right corner of the scene, an angel announces the miraculous birth to two shepherds. The lowest scene in the left wing shows the Adoration of the Magi, set before the same cave and shed roof as in the preceding scene. The Virgin is seated at the right in front of the cave, holding the Child on her lap with St. Joseph standing behind. The eldest of the magi kneels at the left, bareheaded, to kiss the feet of Christ, while the other two kings stand behind him holding gilt jars containing their gifts to the newborn. Once again, the star of Bethlehem hovers over the head of the Christ Child, and the heads of four camels and a retainer complete the upper left corner of the composition.

In the upper compartment of the right wing is the Virgin Annunciate, seated before the same cloth of honor and open gallery portrayed behind the Annunciatory Angel opposite. Beneath her is a scene of Christ enthroned, blindfolded, and mocked by a crowd of tormentors who pull his beard, slap and beat him with sticks, blow a trumpet in his ear, and insult him with obscene gestures. The lowest scene in the right wing shows the dead Christ laid across the laps of his mother and the three Holy Women. At the right the Magdalene, dressed in red and supporting Christ's feet, throws her hands in the air in grief. Behind her appears the open mouth of a cave with a glimpse of Christ's sarcophagus visible within. At the left above the Virgin, who leans forward to embrace the body of her son, stand Nicodemus and Joseph of Arimathea holding the shroud and three nails. A partial view of the cross and the ladder used to lower the body of Christ close off the composition behind.

This triptych is remarkable in being a compendium of narrative motifs—most of which are normally encountered in the predelle to large altarpieces—rather than of iconic images more typical of portable tabernacles on this scale. Two separate narrative cycles are encompassed in the complete structure. The Annunciation and, in the left wing, the Nativity and the Epiphany, or Adoration of the Magi, are commonly found among scenes of the birth and infancy of Christ, symbolizing the mystery of incarnation. The right wing and center panel, by contrast, contain four scenes from the Passion—the Mocking of Christ, the Crucifixion, the Lamentation, and the Resurrection—all concerned with the miracle of redemption. An exact program explaining the selection of these scenes and their unusual grouping in a single complex has not yet been found, but a clue linking them to Franciscan spirituality and the theology of St. Bonaventure may be offered by the inclusion in the center panel of a diminutive figure of St. Francis kneeling in prayer at the foot of the cross.

The most singular aspect of the iconography of this triptych is the portrayal of the Trinity in the main scene of the center panel, which is in effect a conflation of three separate images. The Throne of Grace, one of the most popular medieval representations of the Trinity, is normally conceived as God the Father enthroned behind and above the crucified Christ—symbolically accepting his Son's sacrifice—with the dove of the Holy Spirit linking the two figures. In this case, the figure of God the Father has been replaced by the three-headed divinity *(vultus trifons)*, which is otherwise usually employed as an independent symbol of the Trinity.[1] Finally, the addition of mourning figures of the Virgin and St. John, as well as the kneeling St. Francis, establish the scene not only as an iconic image of the Trinity but also as a devotional image of the Crucifixion, completing the narrative sequence of Passion scenes occurring in the right shutter and central pinnacle.

The approximate chronology of Luca di Tommè's mature career has been reasonably well established on the basis of three dated altarpieces painted between 1366 and 1370, while differences of opinion concerning the nature and extent of his participation in the altarpiece of 1362 signed jointly with Niccolò di Ser Sozzo—Luca may have been responsible for little or nothing more than the predella—have resulted in persistent confusion over attributions to the two artists and over discussions of Luca di Tommè's probable early works. However, the evident maturity of Luca's Biccherna cover of 1357 and its resemblance to the predella panels from the 1362 altarpiece (now divided between the Pinacoteca Vaticana, Rome, and the collection of the earl of Crawford and Balcarres) clearly define the artist's style at that moment of his career. The Timken triptych must slightly predate these works, though it closely resembles the 1357 Biccherna cover. It is unlikely to have been painted as early as a small *sacra conversazione* formerly in the Minneapolis Institute of Arts (sold Sotheby's, New York, May 19, 1995, lot 6, incorrectly ascribed to Niccolò di Ser Sozzo), or as any of the panels attributed to the fictitious Master of the Magdalene Legend[2]—not to be confused with the Magdalene Master, an artist active in Florence in the late thirteenth century (see cat. no. 5), all of which probably date close to 1350. A date for the Timken triptych around 1355 seems reasonable.

—L. B. K.

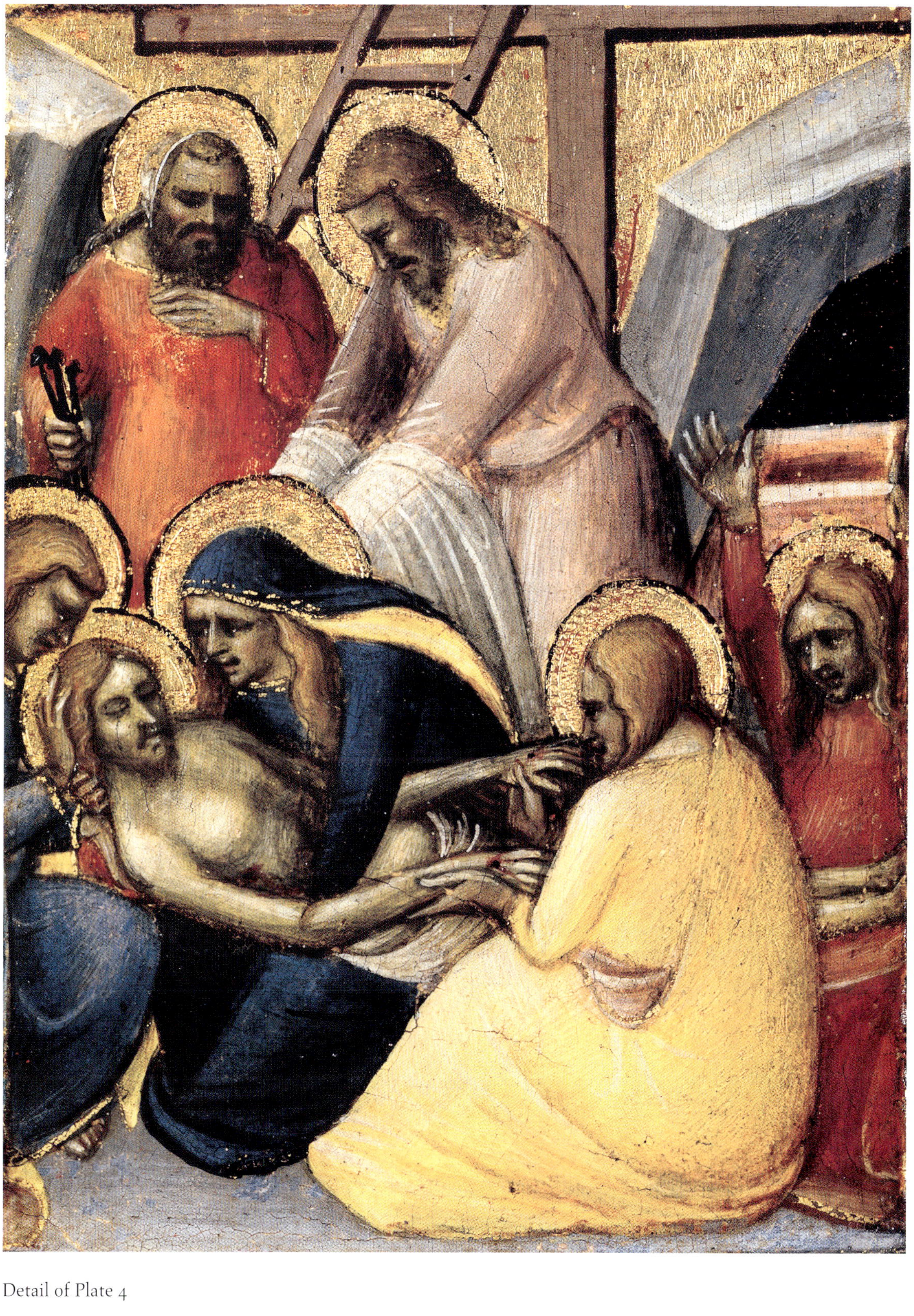

Detail of Plate 4

NOTES

1. Braunfels 1954, passim; d'Achille 1991, pp. 49–73. The representation in the Timken triptych of the *vultus trifons* with three torsos as well as heads is likely to be a matter of artistic exigency rather than doctrinal significance or iconographic innovation.

2. Meiss 1963; Sherwood A. Fehm, Jr., "Luca di Tommè's Influence on Three Sienese Masters: The Master of the Magdalen Legend, the Master of the Panzano Triptych, and the Master of the Pietà," *Mitteilungen des kunsthistorischen Institutes in Florenz* 20 (1976): 333–50. See also Federico Zeri, "Sul problema di Niccolò di Ser Sozzo Tegliacci e Luca di Tommè," *Paragone* 105 (1958): 14–16, where the Magdalene panels were first recognized and attributed to Luca di Tommè as his earliest known efforts.

CONDITION

The picture surface is in a near-perfect state of preservation except for minor losses scattered across the gold ground and along the bottom edge in the center panel. The frame moldings, which are engaged and original, have been regessoed and regilt, and all trace of the original hinges has been lost.

PROVENANCE

Duveen; T. S. Hyland, Greenwich, Conn.; acquired by the Putnam Foundation, 1967.

LITERATURE

Millard Meiss, *Painting in Florence and Siena after the Black Death* (Princeton, 1951), pp. 34–45, fig. 50; Wolfgang Braunfels, *Die Heilige Dreifaltigkeit* (Düsseldorf, 1954), p. xli, fig. 42; Millard Meiss, "Notes on Three Linked Sienese Styles," *Art Bulletin* 45 (1963): 47–48; Bernard Berenson, *Italian Pictures of the Renaissance: Central Italian and North Italian Schools,* 3 vols. (London, 1968), 1:226; H. W. van Os, *Marias Demut und Verherrlichung in der sienesischen Malerei, 1300–1450* (The Hague, 1969), pp. 68 nn. 94, 96, p. 71 n. 109; Agnes Mongan and Elizabeth Mongan, *European Paintings in the Timken Art Gallery* (San Diego, 1969), pp. 22–23, 107, no. 3, ill.; Burton Fredericksen and Federico Zeri, *Census of Pre-Nineteenth-Century Italian Paintings in North American Public Collections* (Cambridge, Mass., 1972), pp. 113, 268, 272, 284, 291, 295, 297, 302, 360, 632; Sherwood A. Fehm, Jr., *The Collaboration of Niccolò Tegliacci and Luca di Tommè* (Malibu, Calif., 1973), p. 30; Cristina de Benedictis, *La pittura senese, 1330–1370* (Florence, 1979), pp. 48, 67, 88, fig. 90; Enzo Carli, *La pittura senese del trecento* (Milan, 1981), p. 225; Martin E. Petersen, "Three Centuries of European Paintings, 1300–1600," *Apollo* 115 (June 1982): 441, fig. 3; *Timken Art Gallery: European and American Works of Art in the Putnam Foundation Collection* (San Diego, 1983), pp. 56–57, 120, no. 19, ill.; J. Gellrich, *The Idea of the Book in the Middle Ages: Language Theory, Mythology, and Fiction* (Ithaca, N.Y., 1985), p. 58, pl. 4; Sherwood A. Fehm, Jr., *Luca di Tommè: A Sienese Fourteenth-Century Painter* (Carbondale, Ill., 1986), pp. 11–12, 61–65, ill.; John T. Paoletti, "The Strozzi Altarpiece Reconsidered," *Memorie Domenicane,* n.s., no. 20 (1989): 279–300, ill.; Anna Maria d'Achille, "Sull'iconografia trinitaria medievale: La Trinità del Santuario sul Monte Autore presso Valletpietra," *Arte Medievale,* ser. 2, 5, no. 1 (1991): 57, fig. 14.

EXHIBITED

Baltimore, The Walters Art Gallery, 1962, *The International Style,* cat. by Philippe Verdier and Dorothy Miner, no. 17, pl. IX; Hartford, Wadsworth Atheneum, 1965, *An Exhibition of Italian Panels and Manuscripts from the Thirteenth and Fourteenth Centuries in Honor of Richard Offner,* p. 28, no. 32.

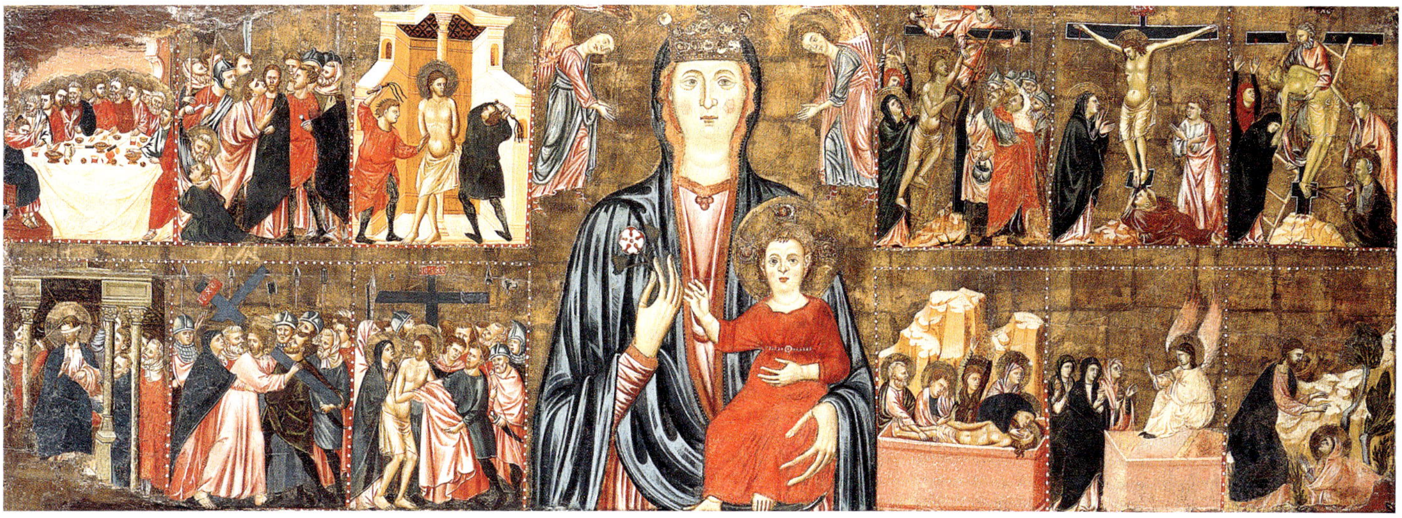

The Magdalene Master and an Unknown Florentine Painter

(end 13th–early 14th century)

5 *Madonna and Child and Two Angels, with Twelve Scenes from the Passion,* ca. 1310

The Last Supper, the Arrest in the Garden, the Flagellation, the Mocking of Christ, the Via Crucis, the Disrobing of Christ, Christ Mounting the Cross, the Crucifixion, the Deposition, the Entombment, the Three Marys at the Tomb, Noli me tangere

Tempera on panel, 26½ × 70⅝ in. (67.3 × 179.4 cm) overall, 24 × 67¾ in. (61 × 172.1 cm) picture surface

The Timken dossal (originally an ornamental cloth hung above and behind an altar, but now also understood to be a painting of similar size and shape) has long been recognized as a key element in the reconstruction of the artistic climate of Florence at the turn of the fourteenth century, but scholarly opinion has been sharply divided over its place among the achievements of Giotto's precursors and early contemporaries. The attribution of the central image of the Madonna and Child to the Magdalene Master, first proposed by Richter, in 1930, and later by Coor-Achenbach, in 1947, is widely and correctly accepted, and there is indeed nearly universal consensus that it must have been among that artist's (or workshop's) last efforts, datable probably around 1290 (Boskovits 1984, Tartuferi 1986) but possibly as much as twenty years later (Richter 1930, Garrison 1946, Coor-Achenbach 1947). The cast of the Virgin's features and the patterns created by her hands and draperies, as well as the types and attitudes of the two angels in attendance at the upper corners, correspond most closely to a full-length image of the Madonna and Child with two angels by the Magdalene Master in the church of San Donato ai Torri at Compiobbi, while the soft,

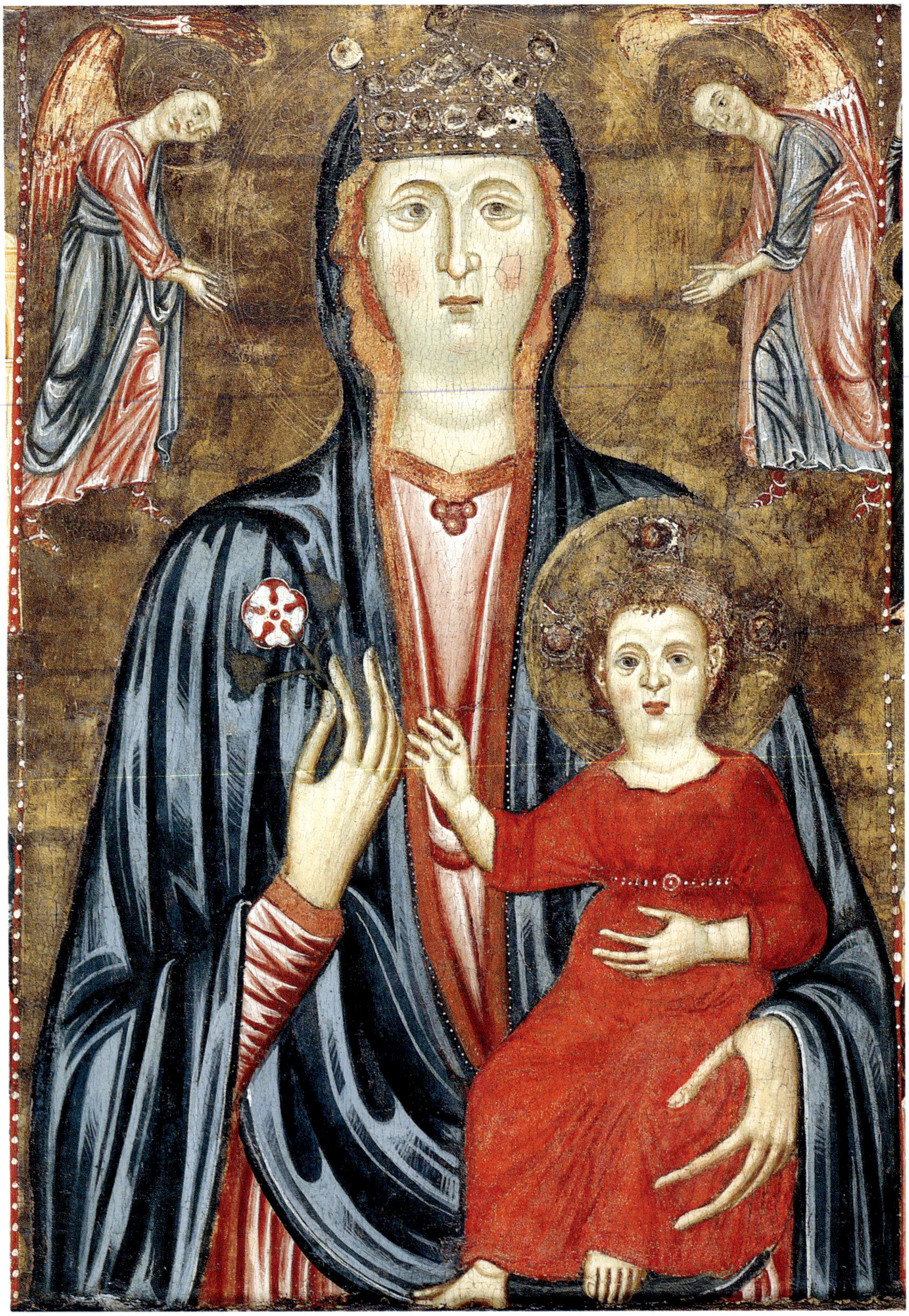
Detail of Plate 5

open modeling of the faces of all four figures exceeds even that in the artist's name piece in the Galleria dell'Accademia, Florence. That the Timken dossal may be the latest painting reasonably attributable to this artist need not be doubted, but no external evidence allowing it to be precisely dated, either shortly before or shortly after 1300, exists.

The attribution and appraisal of the twelve scenes of the Passion at either side of the Madonna and Child in the Timken dossal have been the subject of little scholarly agreement, beyond the cursory admission that they are certainly by a Florentine painter. Offner (1946?) and Garrison (1946) were the first to discuss them as by a hand different from that of the central image, a hand the latter characterized as a "Romanizing Florentine"—related to but not identical with that apparent in a small group of other panels including a tabernacle in the Christ Church gallery at Oxford, a triptych in the Bode Museum, Berlin, and an altarpiece from the convent church of San Gaggio now in the Accademia, Florence. Longhi (1948), contending that the Roman influences described by Garrison are to be understood instead as a native Florentine, pre-Giottesque tendency, pronounced all the panels in this group, plus a few other loosely related works, to be by a single artist whom he christened the Master of San Gaggio. Subsequent scholarship has been largely concerned with expanding[1] or contracting[2] the list of paintings associated with the Master of San Gaggio and with defining his art-historical significance and the period of his probable activity. At one extreme of this spectrum, Garrison saw the authors of the Christ Church tabernacle and the Timken dossal as charming and lively but derivative painters possibly active as late as 1320—well into the period of Giotto's ascendancy—characterizing them as slightly older and less talented or innovative contemporaries of Pacino di Bonaguida (act. ca. 1300–1340). For Boskovits, on the other hand, the Master of San Gaggio began his career a full generation earlier, about 1275–80, as a distinguished follower of Cimabue, developing into one of Giotto's most significant precursors. Boskovits dates the Timken dossal about 1290—for him the height of the artist's maturity—viewing it as an isolated instance of active collaboration between the Master of San Gaggio and the Magdalene Master.

Boskovits's enthusiastic estimation of the importance of the San Gaggio Master is based on the attribution to him of a relatively large group of works which appears to be only superficially homogeneous. Two triptychs, in the Dahlem Museum (Berlin) and in the collection of the earl of Crawford and Balcarres, for example, on the basis of which Boskovits has advanced the intriguing suggestion of identifying the San Gaggio Master with the painter Grifo di Tancredi named in a document of 1295,[3] betray a sophistication of conception and handling as well as an archaism of design—both works are purely Cimabuesque in culture—that are completely at odds with the naiveté of expression and almost coarse execution of either the Timken or the Christ Church panels. Furthermore, where the Christ Church tabernacle and the other paintings of the San Gaggio group faithfully transcribe narrative, decorative, and spatial formulas common in Florentine painting since the mid-thirteenth century, numerous scenes in the Timken dossal find parallels only among Sienese works

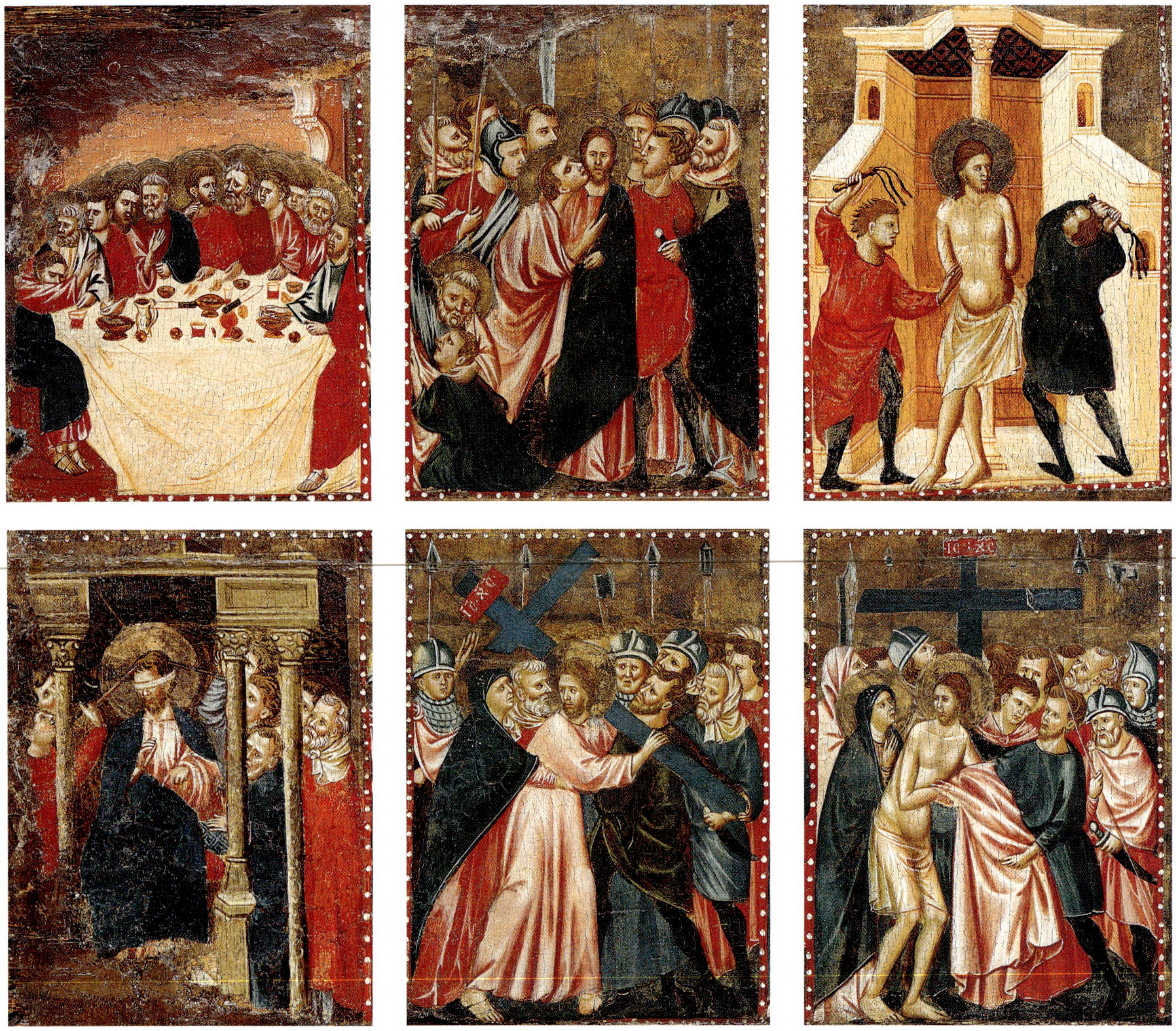

Top, left to right: The Last Supper, the Arrest in the Garden, the Flagellation; bottom, left to right: the Mocking of Christ, the Via Crucis, the Disrobing of Christ.

of the early fourteenth century by Duccio and Pietro Lorenzetti, or among Roman frescoes of the late dugento such as the Passion scenes in the Basilica di San Francesco at Assisi, which were the probable source of inspiration for these great Sienese masters. The remarkable composition of the scene of the Flagellation in the Timken dossal can only be explained by reference to the architectural backdrops in mature works by the St. Cecilia Master, a further possible connection to the Assisi frescoes, or Lippo di Benivieni, while parallels to the latter's animated figure types and system of modeling and foreshortening suggest a probable date around or shortly after 1310 for completion of the Timken dossal. Finally, the differences of figure style (note especially the idiosyncratic rendering of eyes and placement of facial features) and technique, which can also be detected between the Timken dossal and other panels attributed to the Master of San Gaggio, would appear to confirm Offner's conclusion that no other paintings by the author of the twelve small scenes in the Timken dossal are yet known.

Whether the Timken dossal was conceived from the first as a collaboration between artists of two different generations or was perhaps completed by one upon

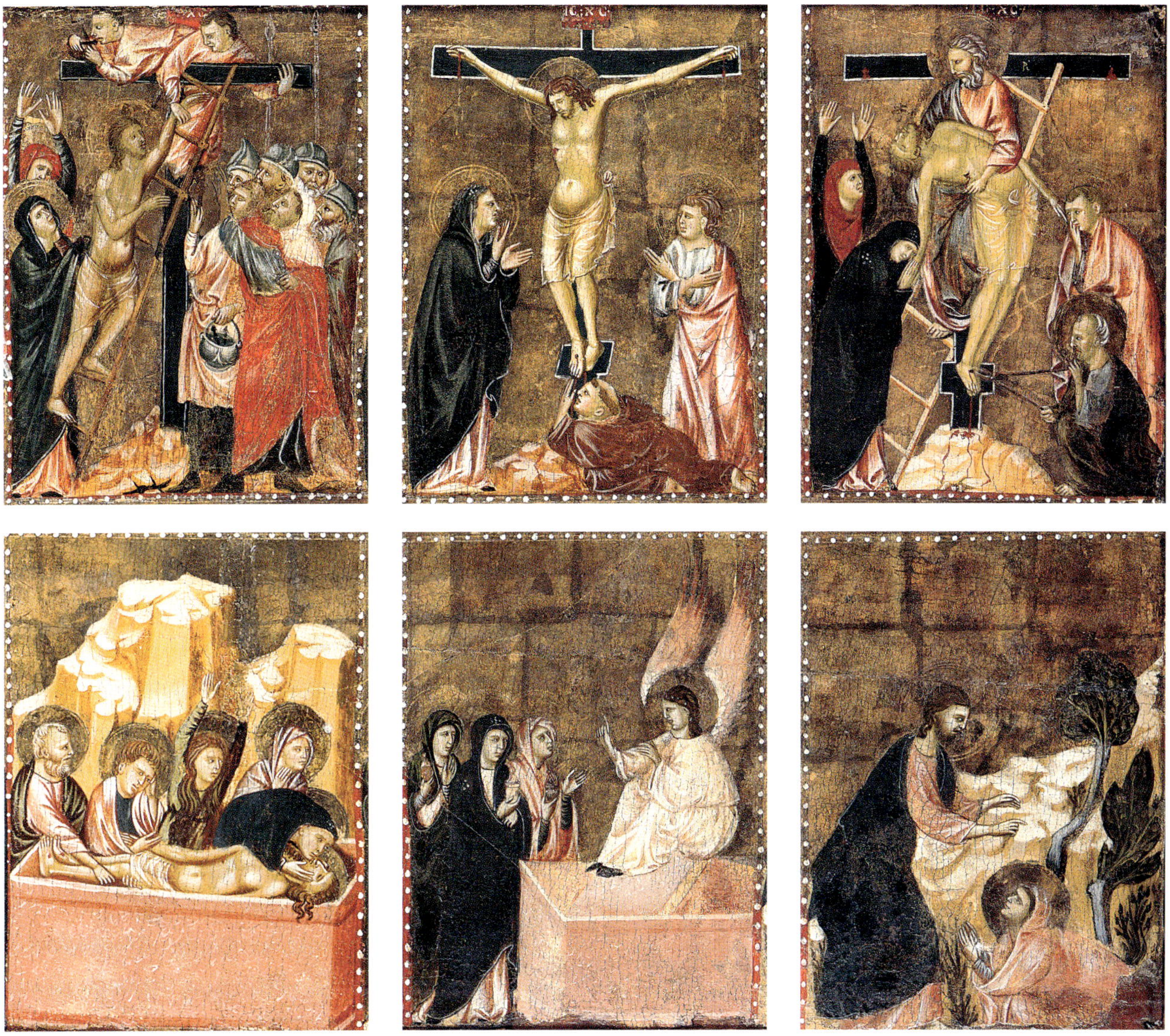

Top, left to right: Christ Mounting the Cross, the Crucifixion, the Deposition; bottom, left to right: the Entombment, the Three Marys at the Tomb, Noli me tangere.

the death of the other cannot be determined by analysis of the picture itself, nor are indications of its original provenance entirely unambiguous. Offner deduced its presence in the Augustinian convent of Santa Maria dei Candeli, Florence, by at least the third quarter of the eighteenth century, from a heavily reinforced and only partially legible inscription on the back of the panel—"opera di Cimabue e' dalla Rev.da M.re . . . fatto . . . corone d'argento è messi cristalli essendo Bad. Fra Terese Capponi"—referring to its reframing and provision with silver crowns and glass ornaments at the expense of the abbess Francesca Teresa Capponi (1705–1775). This inscription, which has been renewed at least once, was undoubtedly supplied on the occasion of the painting's transfer to a new panel support and reframing (the present frame is modern) and may imply that it had previously been the property of the Capponi family, who would have donated it to Santa Maria dei Candeli. The presence of a diminutive figure of St. Francis kneeling at the foot of the cross in the Crucifixion scene suggests that the panel originally may have been a Franciscan, not Augustinian, commission.

—L. B. K.

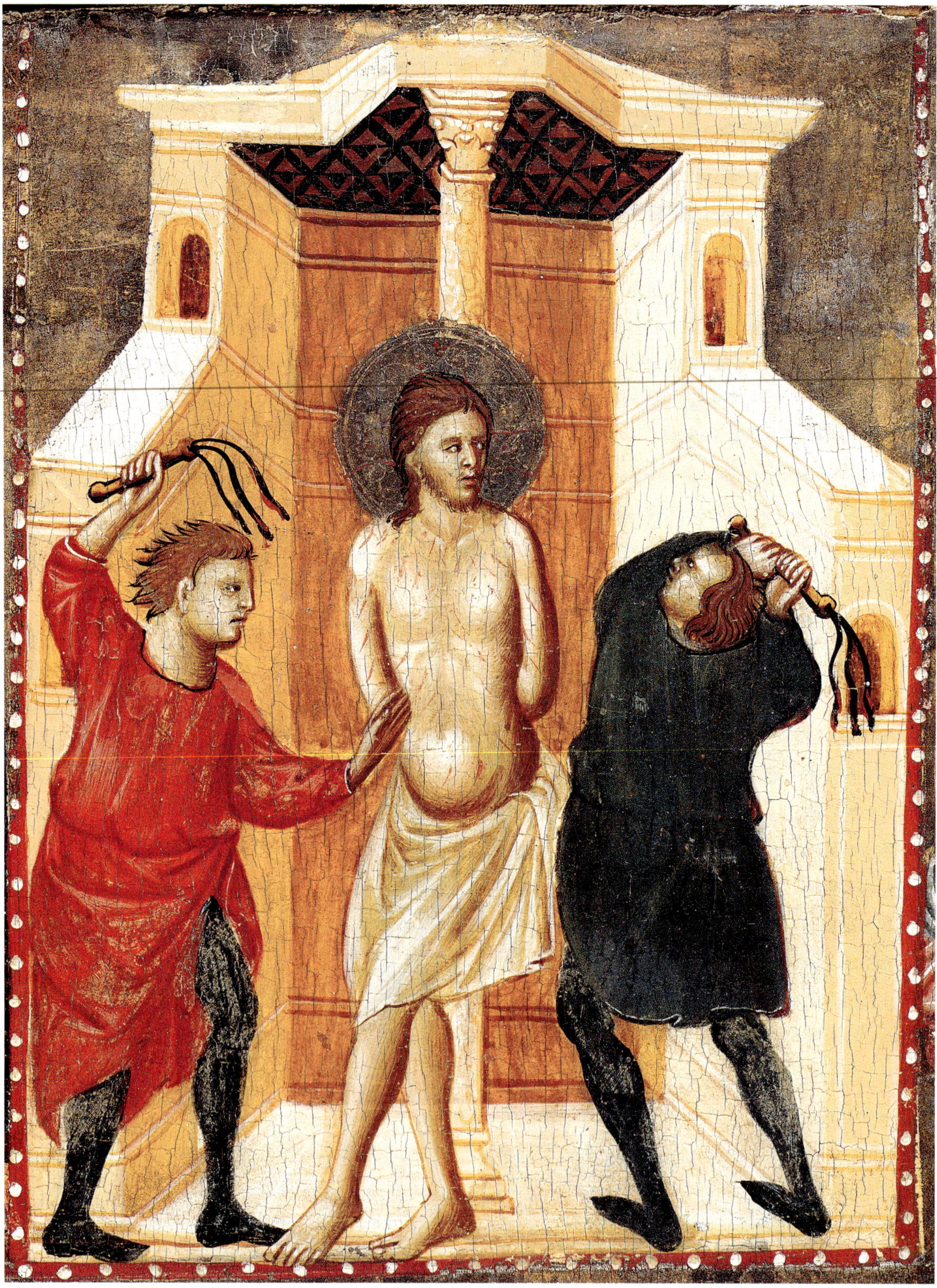

Detail of Plate 5

NOTES

1. Luciano Bellosi, *Buffalmacco e il trionfo della morte* (Turin, 1974), pp. 77–78; Tartuferi 1986; Boskovits 1988.

2. John Pope-Hennessy, "Proporzioni II," *Burlington Magazine* 90 (1948): 360; Zeri 1972.

3. Boskovits 1988; Gaetano Milanesi, *Nuovi documenti per la storia dell'arte toscana* (Florence, 1901), no. 10.

CONDITION

The paint surface and its original linen and gesso base have been transferred, probably in the late eighteenth century (see above), to a new panel support comprising a single plank of soft wood (fir or pine). Three vertical battens are affixed to the back of the panel with large claw nails, which have pushed out small paint losses on the front. A layer of gesso applied to the support beneath the linen and gesso of the painting has isolated the latter from movements in the former, minimizing paint losses along a discontinuous split in the panel running its full length along the center. Damages to the paint surface otherwise occur primarily along the edges of the panel, especially the much-consumed left edge, where large areas of the scenes of the Last Supper and the Mocking of Christ are lost. A light overall abrasion has affected mostly the dark pigments, while denser pigments, especially reds and whites, are in beautiful condition. The silver ground is largely corroded and rubbed away, surviving mostly in small islands of leaf preserved beneath missing flakes of paint. The scene of the Entombment to the right of center has been disfigured by a minor candle burn.

PROVENANCE

Santa Maria dei Candeli, Florence (?); Mr. F., 1930 (per Richter 1930); Piero Tozzi, New York (per Garrison 1946); Jacob Hirsch, New York, by 1946; T. S. Hyland, Greenwich, Conn.; acquired by the Putnam Foundation, 1967.

LITERATURE

George Martin Richter, "Megliore di Jacopo and the Magdalen Master," *Burlington Magazine* 57 (November 1930): 230 n. 13, 235; Edward B. Garrison, "The Oxford Christ Church Library Panel and the Milan Sessa Collection Shutters: A Tentative Reconstruction of a Tabernacle and a Group of Romanizing Florentine Panels," *Gazette des Beaux-Arts* 29 (June 1946): 321–46, fig. 27; Richard Offner, *An Early Florentine Dossal* (Florence, n.d. [1946?]); Gertrude Coor-Achenbach, "A Neglected Work by the Magdalen Master," *Burlington Magazine* 89 (1947): 120 nn. 7, 13; Roberto Longhi, "Giudizio sul duecento," *Proporzioni* 2 (1948): 19, 47; Edward B. Garrison, *Italian Romanesque Panel Painting* (Florence, 1949), pp. 27, 142, no. 367; Millard Meiss, *Painting in Florence and Siena after the Black Death* (Princeton, 1951), p. 129, fig. 118; Miklós Boskovits, "Un opera probabile di Giovanni di Bartolomeo Cristiani e l'iconografia della preparazione alla Crocifissione," *Acta Historiae Artium* 11 (1965): 69–94; Giovanni Previtali, *Giotto e la sua bottega* (Milan, 1967), pp. 27, 30, 133 n. 44, fig. 27 (3d ed., 1993, pp. 36, 45); Agnes Mongan and Elizabeth Mongan, *European Paintings in the Timken Art Gallery* (San Diego, 1969), pp. 18–19, 107, no. 1, ill.; Burton Fredericksen and Federico Zeri, *Census of Pre-Nineteenth-Century Italian Paintings in North American Public Collections* (Cambridge, Mass., 1972), pp. 53, 131, 281, 283–86, 288, 294, 297–98, 310, 632; Miklós Boskovits, *Cimabue e i precursori di Giotto* (Florence, 1976), p. 70 n. 4; Martin E. Petersen, "Three Centuries of European Paintings, 1300–1600," *Apollo* 115 (June 1982): 441, fig. 1; *Timken Art Gallery: European and American Works of Art in the Putnam Foundation Collection* (San Diego, 1983), pp. 58–59, 120–21, no. 20, ill.; Miklós Boskovits, *A Critical and Historical Corpus of Florentine Painting*, sec. 3, vol. 9, *The Fourteenth Century, the Painters of the Miniaturist Tendency* (Florence, 1984), p. 28 nn. 80–81; Angelo Tartuferi, "Pittura fiorentina del duecento," in *La pittura in Italia, il duecento e il trecento*, 2 vols. (Milan, 1986), 1:277; Miklós Boskovits, *Gemäldegalerie Berlin. Frühe italienische Malerei* (Berlin, 1988), pp. 116–17, 122–23; Ketti Neil, "St. Francis of Assisi, the Penitent Magdalen, and the Patron at the Foot of the Cross," *Rutgers Art Review* 9–10 (1988–89): 103–5; Miklós Boskovits, *Immagini da meditare* (Milan, 1994), pp. 206, 211 n. 21.

EXHIBITED

Hartford, Wadsworth Atheneum, 1965, *An Exhibition of Italian Panels and Manuscripts from the Thirteenth and Fourteenth Centuries in Honor of Richard Offner*, pp. 10–11, no. 2, ill.

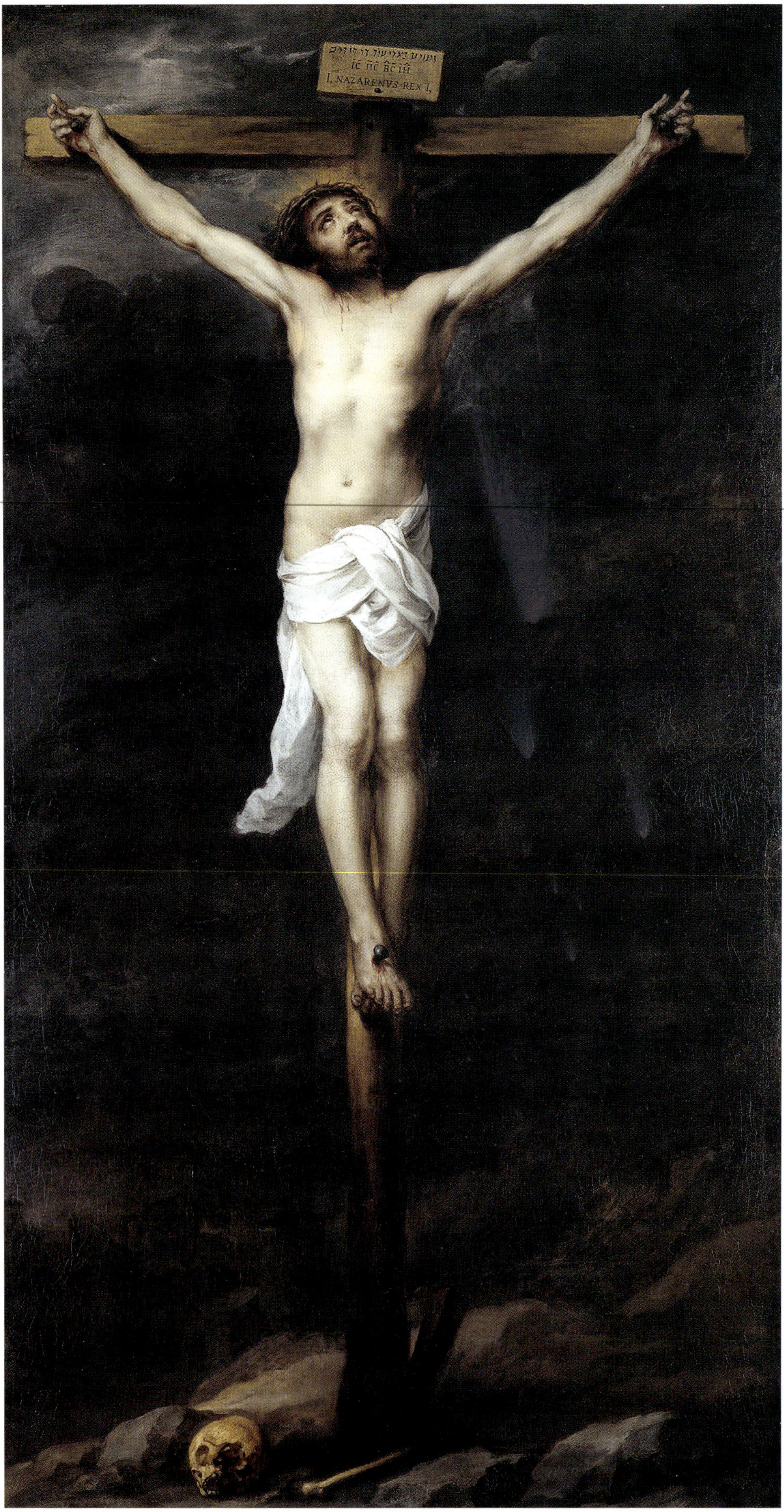
I, NAZARENVS REX I,

Bartolomé Esteban Murillo
(1617–1682)

Murillo was baptized in Seville on January 1, 1618. Orphaned at the age of ten, he entered the studio of Juan del Castillo in 1630. He was influenced when young by both Zurbarán and Ribera. In 1645–46 he painted eleven pictures for the small cloister of the Franciscan monastery at Seville. Murillo established permanent residence in Madrid in 1658. From 1646 to 1660 he was influenced by the Flemish and Venetian paintings he saw in the royal collections of Castile. According to tradition, he fell from a scaffold while working for the Capuchins of Cádiz. He was brought back to Seville, where he died in 1682.

6 *Christ on the Cross*, 1660–70
Oil on canvas, 82¼ × 44½ in. (208.9 × 113 cm)

The luminous figure of Christ extended on the cross is seen against a dark, ominous sky. An inscription at the top of the cross reads in Hebrew, Greek, and Latin versions: "Jesus of Nazareth, King of Jews." Below, at the left, in shadowy mists are discernible the outlines of the city of Jerusalem. In the foreground lie the skull and tibia of Adam, faintly touched with ocher color.

The work of Murillo is generally divided into three periods: his early manner, which is characterized as cold in color and rather dry; his middle period, called warm because of his palette; and his late style, known as misty or dark. Mayer (1913) has placed the *Christ on the Cross* in Murillo's last period, which dates from 1660 to 1670. In his introduction, he noted that Murillo painted few authentic pictures of the Passion. He mentioned this *Christ on the Cross* and two others, one in the Prado, Madrid (fig. 1), and the second, *St. Francis of Assisi Renouncing the World (Embracing the Cross),* in the Museo Provincial de Bellas Artes, Seville. All are very close in their representation of the crucified Christ. The Timken picture is closely related to the Prado *Crucifixion.* Here, however, Christ has not yet died.

Pierre Paris has clearly outlined the difference in Spanish mysticism between the religious paintings of Murillo and the visions of El Greco.[1] In Murillo, the figures and setting represent the material world, images the monks and prelates of the

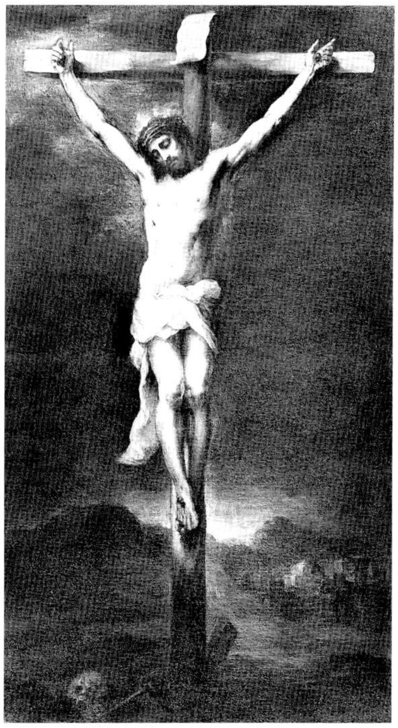

Fig. 1. Bartolomé Esteban Murillo, *Crucifixion*, 1675–80. Oil on canvas, 72 × 42⅛ in. (183 × 107 cm). Madrid, Museo del Prado. Photograph courtesy of Alinari/Art Resource, New York.

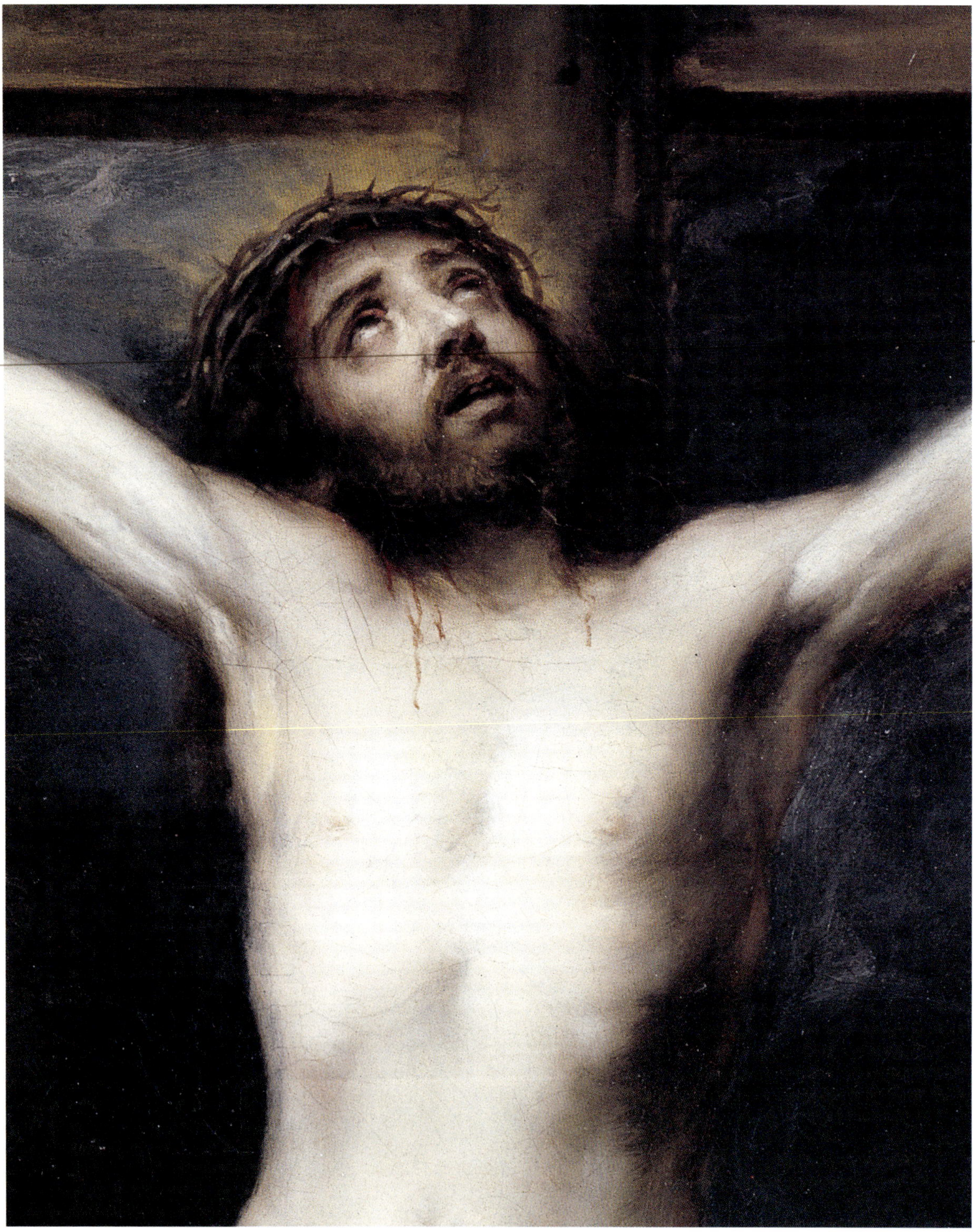

Detail of Plate 6

seventeenth century wanted for their altars. Here Murillo has surpassed himself by painting a transcendent image of the Man-God in his own Sevillian terms of Spanish Counter-Reformation understanding.

—A. M. AND E. M.

NOTE

1. *La Peinture espagnole* (Brussels, 1928).

PROVENANCE

Kaunitz collection, Vienna, ca. 1820–60; Count Czernin, Vienna; acquired by the Putnam Foundation, 1955.

LITERATURE

Luis Alfonso, *Murillo* (Barcelona, 1866), p. 219, no. 1; Carlo Justi, *Murillo* (Leipzig, 1904), p. 72; August L. Mayer, *Murillo*, Klassiker der Kunst (Stuttgart, 1913), p. 95, ill.; Karl Wilczek, *Katalog der Graf Czernin'schen Gemäldegalerie in Wien* (Vienna, 1936), p. 60, no. 48; Agnes Mongan and Elizabeth Mongan, *European Painting in the Timken Art Gallery* (San Diego, 1969), pp. 86, 87, 128, no. 32, ill.; Diego Angulo Ïñiguez, *Murillo*, 3 vols. (Madrid, 1981), 2:226, no. 268, and 3: fig. 398; *Timken Art Gallery: European and American Works of Art in the Putnam Foundation Collection* (San Diego, 1983), pp. 66–67, 124, no. 24, ill.

EXHIBITED

Sion, Switzerland, Musée de la Majorie, 1951, *La Collection Czernin de Vienne*, no. 27; Washington, D.C., National Gallery of Art, extended loan, 1957–65.

Niccolò di Buonaccorso

(d. 1388)

Niccolò di Buonaccorso was one of the most accomplished masters active in Siena in the last third of the fourteenth century. Trained probably in the 1360s in the workshop of Jacopo di Mino del Pelicciaio, he is first mentioned in a document of 1372 recording his election to public office. He registered in the painters' guild sometime between 1378 and 1386; in 1385 he painted a book cover for the office of the Biccherna (Siena, Archivio di Stato); and in 1387 he signed and dated an altarpiece formerly in the church of Santa Margherita at Costalpino. Niccolò di Buonaccorso died in 1388.

For most of the present century, only one signed work by Niccolò di Buonaccorso was known to scholars, a small panel in the National Gallery, London, representing the Marriage of the Virgin. On the basis of this painting and a number of stylistically related works, Niccolò was regarded as a charming but minor master who worked exclusively on a miniaturist scale. With the recent rediscovery of his 1387 altarpiece from Costalpino,[1] however, and the consequent identification of other monumental works by the artist, this assessment is being revised to recognize Niccolò di Buonaccorso as a leading figure of his generation, alongside his almost exact contemporary, Paolo di Giovanni Fei.

7 *The Madonna of Humility, with St. Catherine of Alexandria, St. Christopher, the Annunciation, and the Crucifixion,* ca. 1370–75

Triptych, tempera on panel: center panel, 25¾ × 10⅜ in. (65.4 × 26.4 cm) overall, 19½ × 8½ in. (49.5 × 21.6 cm) picture surface; left wing, 23¾ × 5¼ in. (60.3 × 13.3 cm) overall, 19 × 4 in. (48.2 × 10.2 cm) picture surface; right wing, 23⅛ × 5⅜ in. (58.7 × 13.7 cm) overall, 19 × 4 in. (48.2 × 10.2 cm) picture surface

In the central scene, beneath a rounded arch made of hardened gesso, or *pastiglia,* the Virgin, wearing a red-and-gold embroidered dress and a deep blue mantle clasped at the throat with a gold brooch, is seated on a gilt and tasseled cushion on a marble pavement. On her right knee she holds the Christ Child, dressed in a yellow and gold tunic with blue shadows and a rose-colored mantle lined with yellow. The Child raises his right hand in blessing, and in his left holds a short banderole bearing a now imperfectly legible inscription. Behind the Virgin an intarsia bench stretches the full width of the panel. A stand for bobbins, knitting, and knitting needles lie on the

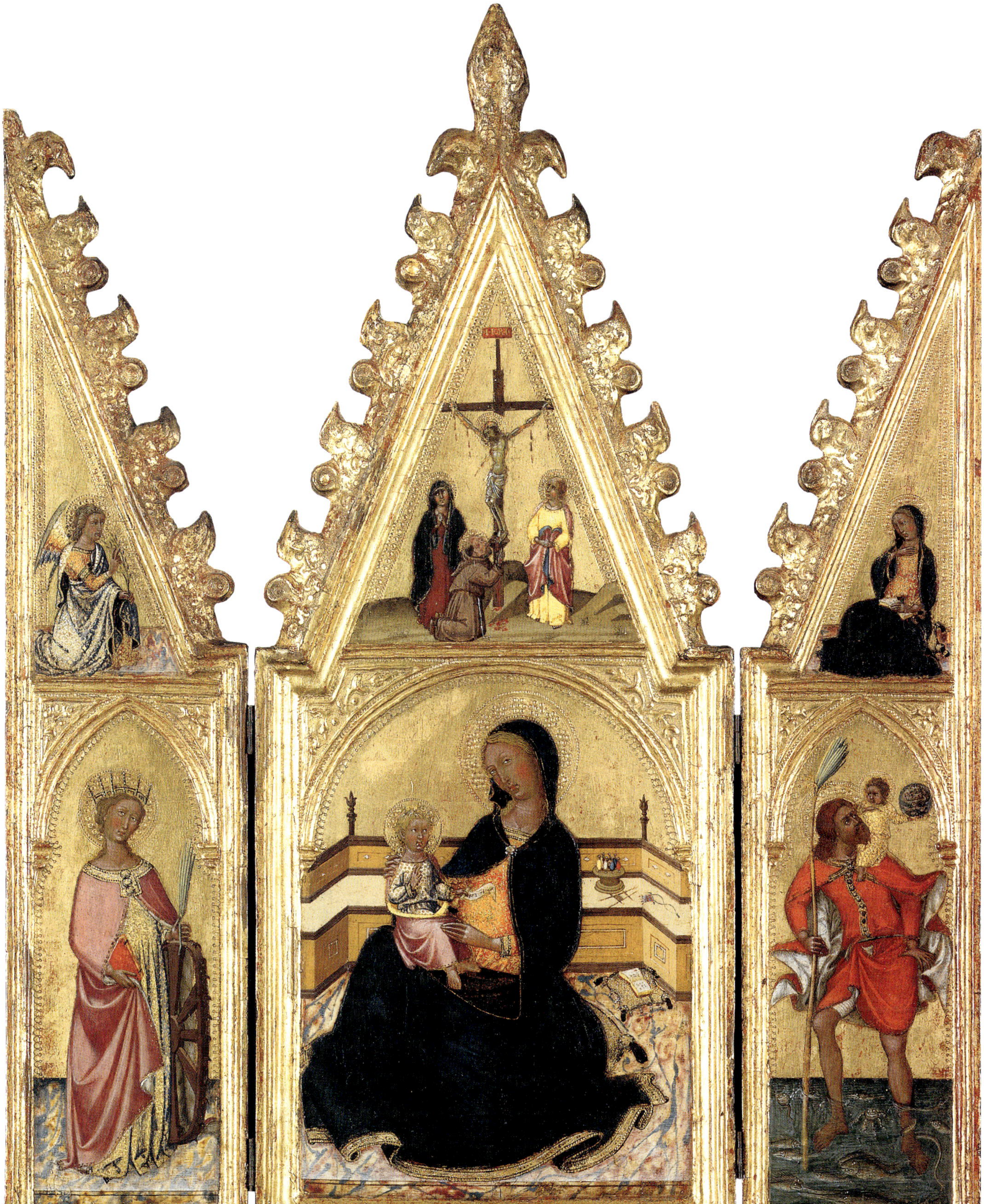

bench at the right, and an open book rests on another tasseled gilt cushion on the pavement before them.

In the left wing of the triptych, St. Catherine of Alexandria stands beneath an ogival *pastiglia* arch on a marble pavement similar to that in the central panel. She is crowned, wears a rose mantle over a yellow-and-gold brocade dress, and holds a red book in her right hand. Her left hand, holding a palm branch, rests on the symbol of her attempted martyrdom, a spiked wheel. St. Christopher in the right wing of the triptych wears a bright red tunic and a cloak lined with white, and wades through the blue-green waters of a river filled with fish. On his shoulder he carries the Christ Child, dressed in yellow and carrying a globe of the world in his left hand. The lateral pinnacles show a continuous marble pavement with the Annunciatory Angel kneeling at the left and at the right the Virgin Annunciate, dressed as she is in the central panel, seated on a gold cushion with an open book in her lap. In the central pinnacle, the crucified Christ is adored by a kneeling St. Francis, who embraces the foot of the cross, while the mourning Virgin and St. John the Evangelist stand in a barren landscape at either side.

This remarkably well preserved triptych has long been recognized as a typical work of the little-understood Sienese master Niccolò di Buonaccorso. Its exceptional condition displays the sophistication of the artist's technique at its most delicate: in the complex modeling of draperies through the use of saturate color for shadows; in the refined simulation of textile patterns and textures through sgraffito and glazed decoration over gold; and in the detailed rendering of the marble pavements in four of the six compartments, of the intarsia bench and its still life behind the Virgin in the central scene, and of the water and fish at St. Christopher's feet in the right wing. The softly drawn contours of the figures and their elongated proportions, similar to those in a pair of grisaille tabernacle shutters by Niccolò di Buonaccorso in the Alte Pinakothek, Munich, suggest a date for the Timken triptych early in the artist's short career, probably close to 1370 or 1375.

The unusual composition of the center panel of the Timken triptych, showing the Virgin seated on the ground surrounded by the tools and furnishings of domestic enterprise, was elaborated by Niccolò di Buonaccorso in a slightly later version of the subject now in the Musée du Louvre, Paris. In this second example, painted close in time to the Biccherna cover of 1385, the artist emphasized the Virgin's role as the vehicle of divine incarnation by portraying a much younger Christ Child suckling at his mother's breast and including a vision of God the Father in glory and the dove of the Holy Spirit at the top of the scene. A third and presumably still later example of the subject, painted by Benedetto di Bindo (fig. 1), follows the basic outlines of Niccolò's panel in the Louvre, reversing the cartoon of the Madonna and reducing the inlaid bench carefully rendered in perspective by Niccolò to a generic background prop.

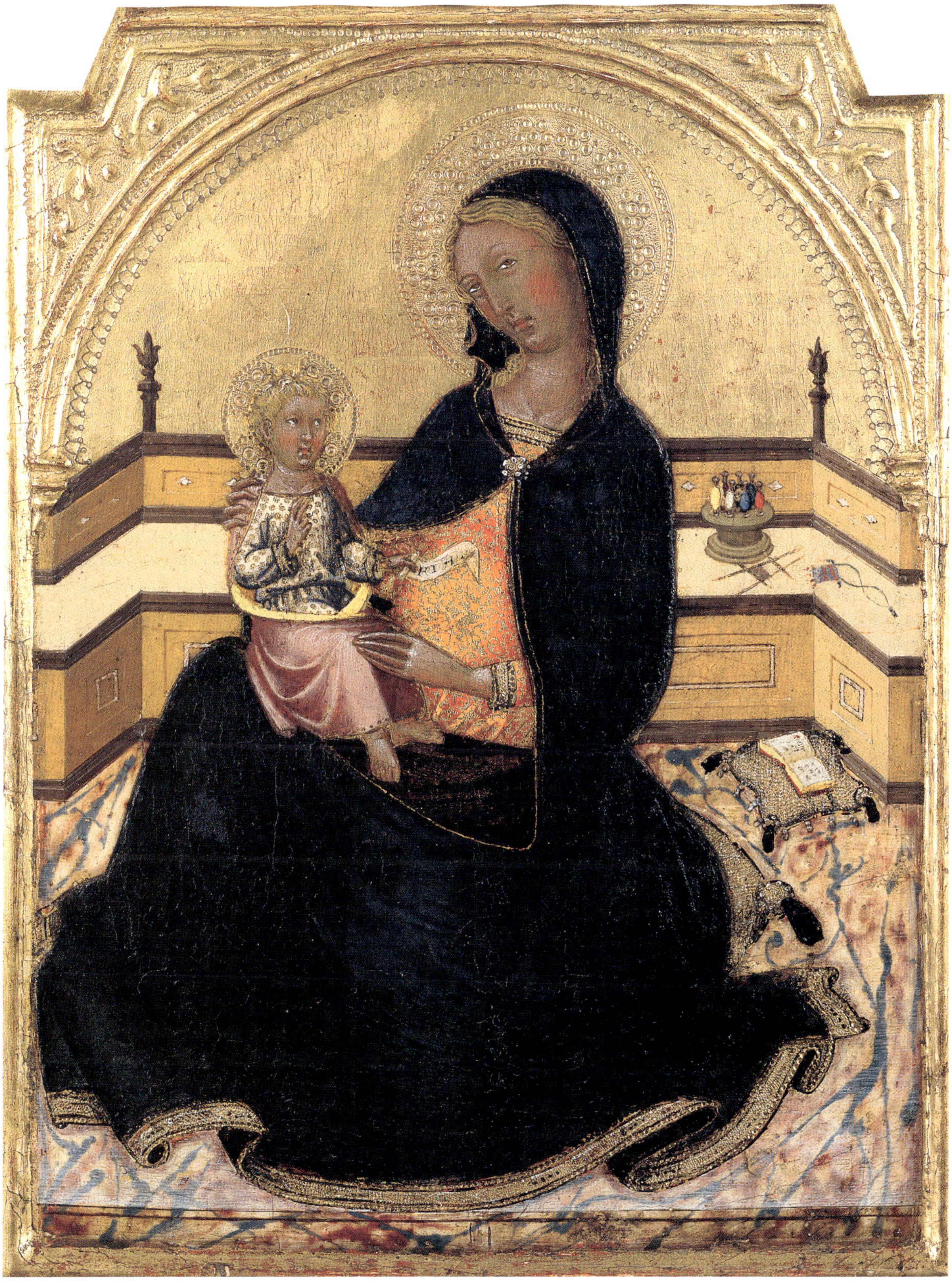

Detail of Plate 7

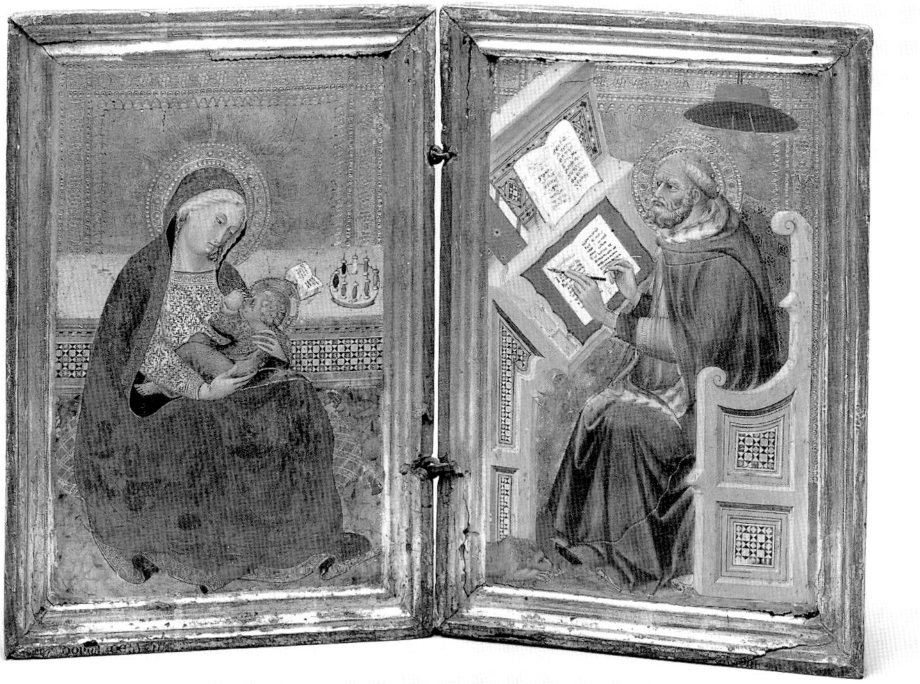

Fig. 1. Benedetto di Bindo, *The Virgin of Humility, with St. Jerome Translating the Gospel of John*, ca. 1400–1405. Tempera and tooled gold on panel, 11⅞ × 16⅝ in. (30.2 × 42.2 cm). Philadelphia Museum of Art, John G. Johnson Collection. Photograph by Graydon Wood, 1992.

A number of other fourteenth-century paintings, mostly Sienese, combine several different motifs common to these three paintings.[2] Two—a *Holy Family* possibly by Ambrogio Lorenzetti in the Abegg Stiftung, Riggisberg, and a *Virgin of Humility* by Vitale da Bologna in the Museo Poldi Pezzoli, Milan—also include sewing implements as an attribute of the Virgin. The precise significance of this detail has been variously explained as a reference to the virtues of chastity (Mary was thought to have been, before her marriage to St. Joseph, one of the virgins chosen to weave a veil for the temple) and poverty, and connected with passages in the *Meditations* of the Pseudo-Bonaventure and the apocryphal gospel of the Pseudo-James.[3] That the motif may find a specific tie to Franciscan reform spirituality, which is largely concerned with the virtues of chastity and poverty, is suggested by the presence in the Timken triptych of a diminutive St. Francis kneeling at the foot of the cross in the central pinnacle.

It is likely that the selection of saints Catherine and Christopher for portrayal in the wings of the Timken triptych is related to the identity of the painting's original owner. It is also possible, however, that St. Christopher was meant to be invoked here not as a namesake but in his role as protector of travelers, appropriate to the portable nature of the triptych itself. Representations of St. Christopher—frequently paired with St. Anthony Abbot—are disproportionately common in the wings of Sienese triptychs from the second half of the fourteenth century. Niccolò di Buonaccorso included him in the right wing of a triptych at Konopiste and another, heavily repainted, formerly in the McCormick collection, Chicago. The Master of Panzano, an artist closely related to Niccolò di Buonaccorso at one stage of his career, includes St. Christopher in the wing of a triptych formerly belonging to the Contrada dell'Istrice in

Siena (now in the collection of the Monte dei Paschi), and, in grisaille, on the reverse of a triptych shutter in the collection of the San Diego Museum of Art, to name only two instances. Further examples in the Pinacoteca Nazionale, Siena, include two triptychs by unknown masters (nos. 292, 159) and one by Taddeo di Bartolo (no. 128). All of these paintings, as well as the best-known example of the subject, Taddeo di Bartolo's fresco of 1408 in the antechapel of the Palazzo Pubblico, Siena, follow approximately the same compositional formula, suggesting that they may all derive from a single prototype lost today that established the iconic model for representations of the saint. Given the relative agitation of his pose, with its structurally complicated contrapposto, and the abundant naturalistic details of marine life in the river bed, it may be speculated that this prototype was painted by Ambrogio Lorenzetti.

—L. B. K.

NOTES

1. Miklós Boskovits, "Su Niccolò di Buonaccorso, Benedetto di Bindo, e la pittura senese del primo quattrocento," *Paragone,* nos. 359–61 (1980): 3–22.

2. Among these are a *Holy Family* (whereabouts unknown) incorrectly attributed to Simone di Gheri by Cristina de Benedictis, *La pittura senese, 1330–1370* (Florence, 1979), fig. 59; a *Virgin of Humility* by Bartolomeo Bulgarini in the Rijksmuseum, Amsterdam; and a copy of that painting by an unknown Sienese master in the Berenson collection at Villa I Tatti (H. W. van Os et al., *The Early Sienese Paintings in Holland* [Florence and The Hague, 1989], pp. 38–42, figs. 7, 8); and another *Virgin of Humility Suckling Her Child* by Niccolò di Buonaccorso, in the Indiana University Art Museum, Bloomington (Bruce Cole and Adelheid Medicus Gealt, "A New Triptych by Niccolò di Buonaccorso and a Problem," *Burlington Magazine* 119 [March 1978]: 184–87. The authors inexplicably describe the bench behind the Virgin in this painting as a set of stairs, misidentify the Benedetto di Bindo panel in Philadelphia as a work of Niccolò di Buonaccorso, and omit the Timken triptych from their list of examples with related compositions).

3. Robert L. Wyss, "Die Handarbeiten der Maria," in *Artes Minores,* ed. Michael Stettler and Mechthild Lemberg (Bern, 1973), pp. 113–88; H. W. van Os, "Mary as Seamstress," reprinted in *Studies in Early Tuscan Painting* (London, 1992), pp. 277–86.

CONDITION

Both the panel support and the paint surface are in a remarkably pure state of preservation. The Virgin's robe in the central scene has suffered minor losses, and minor flaking losses of pigment over the gold ground scar the tops of all four heads in the Crucifixion scene in the central pinnacle. The hinges connecting the wings to the central panel are modern. Two holes drilled in the outer bottom edge of the center panel may have accommodated pegs securing it to a now-missing base.

PROVENANCE

Frederick Mont, New York, as Paolo di Giovanni Fei; T. S. Hyland, Greenwich, Conn.; acquired by the Putnam Foundation, 1967.

LITERATURE

K. Ames, "An Annunciation by Niccolò di Buonaccorso," *Wadsworth Atheneum Bulletin* 2, no. 2 (1966): 24; Bernard Berenson, *Italian Pictures of the Renaissance: Central Italian and North Italian Schools,* 3 vols. (London, 1968), 1:294; H. W. van Os, *Marias Demut und Verherrlichung in der sienesische Malerei, 1300–1450* (The Hague, 1969), p. 117, pl. 56; Agnes Mongan and Elizabeth Mongan, *European Paintings in the Timken Art Gallery* (San Diego, 1969), pp. 24–25, 108, no. 4, ill.; Burton Fredericksen and Federico Zeri, *Census of Pre-Nineteenth-Century Italian Paintings in North American Public Collections* (Cambridge, Mass., 1972), pp. 149, 291, 302, 314, 381, 388, 632; Martin E. Petersen, "Three Centuries of European Paintings, 1300–1600," *Apollo* 115 (June 1982): 441, fig. 2; A.-M. Dore, "Niccolò di Buonaccorso," in *L'Art gothique siennois,* exh. cat., Avignon, Musée du Petit Palais (Florence, 1983), pp. 261–62; *Timken Art Gallery: European and American Works of Art in the Putnam Foundation Collection* (San Diego, 1983), pp. 68–69, 122, no. 25, ill.; Marvin Eisenberg, *Lorenzo Monaco* (Princeton, 1989), p. 56 n. 56; G. Freuler, *Bartolo di Fredi Cini* (Disentis, Switzerland, 1994), p. 494; Laurence B. Kanter, *Italian Paintings in the Museum of Fine Arts, Boston,* vol. 1, *Thirteenth–Fifteenth Century* (Boston, 1994), p. 106.

EXHIBITED

Baltimore, The Walters Art Gallery, 1962, *The International Style,* cat. by Philippe Verdier and Dorothy Miner, no. 25, pl. XV; Hartford, Wadsworth Atheneum, 1965, *An Exhibition of Italian Panels and Manuscripts from the Thirteenth and Fourteenth Centuries in Honor of Richard Offner,* p. 28, no. 32.

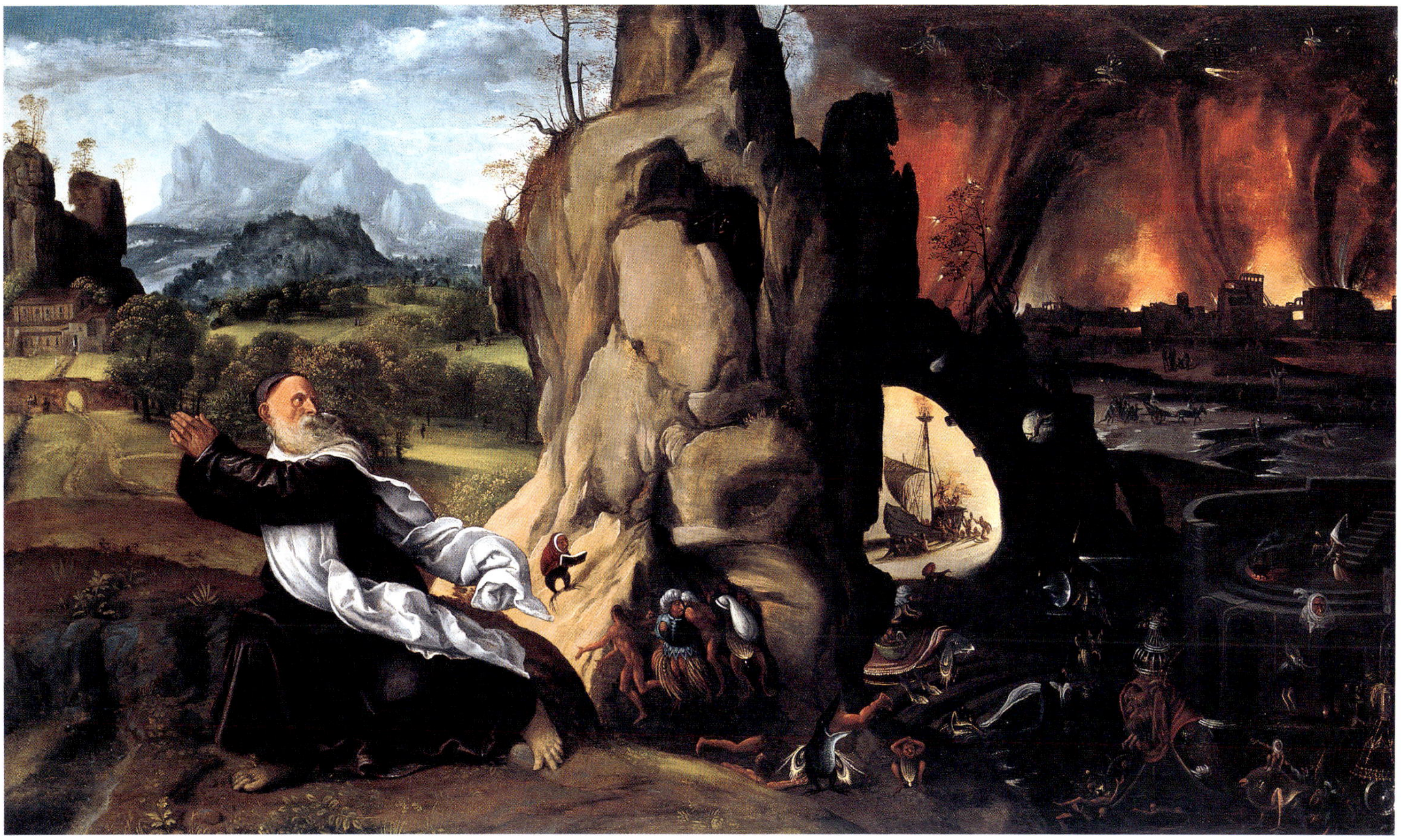

Giovanni Girolamo Savoldo
(act. 1508–after 1548)

Even though Savoldo is today acknowledged as one of the most appealing masters of the Venetian Renaissance, relatively little is known about his life. Born in Brescia, perhaps as early as 1480, he is first documented in Florence in 1508, when he entered the painters' guild. He subsequently spent most of his career in Venice, where he was active until about 1548, when he is mentioned for the last time. Savoldo's career was largely unsuccessful, both commercially and critically, in part because it coincided with Titian's dominance of Venetian painting. Savoldo's art stands apart from the mainstream, although his use of sensuous and luminous color is clearly derived from Venetian style. He is particularly remembered as a pioneer in the painting of nocturnal scenes, but it is the realism of his humble characters that most sets his work apart from that of his contemporaries. Probably inspired by Flemish examples, Savoldo's frank, sympathetic portrayal of everyday types anticipates the revolutionary art of Caravaggio at the end of the century. Although Savoldo did not enjoy the success of Titian, some of his pictures were clearly in demand because they are known in multiple versions, including autograph replicas.

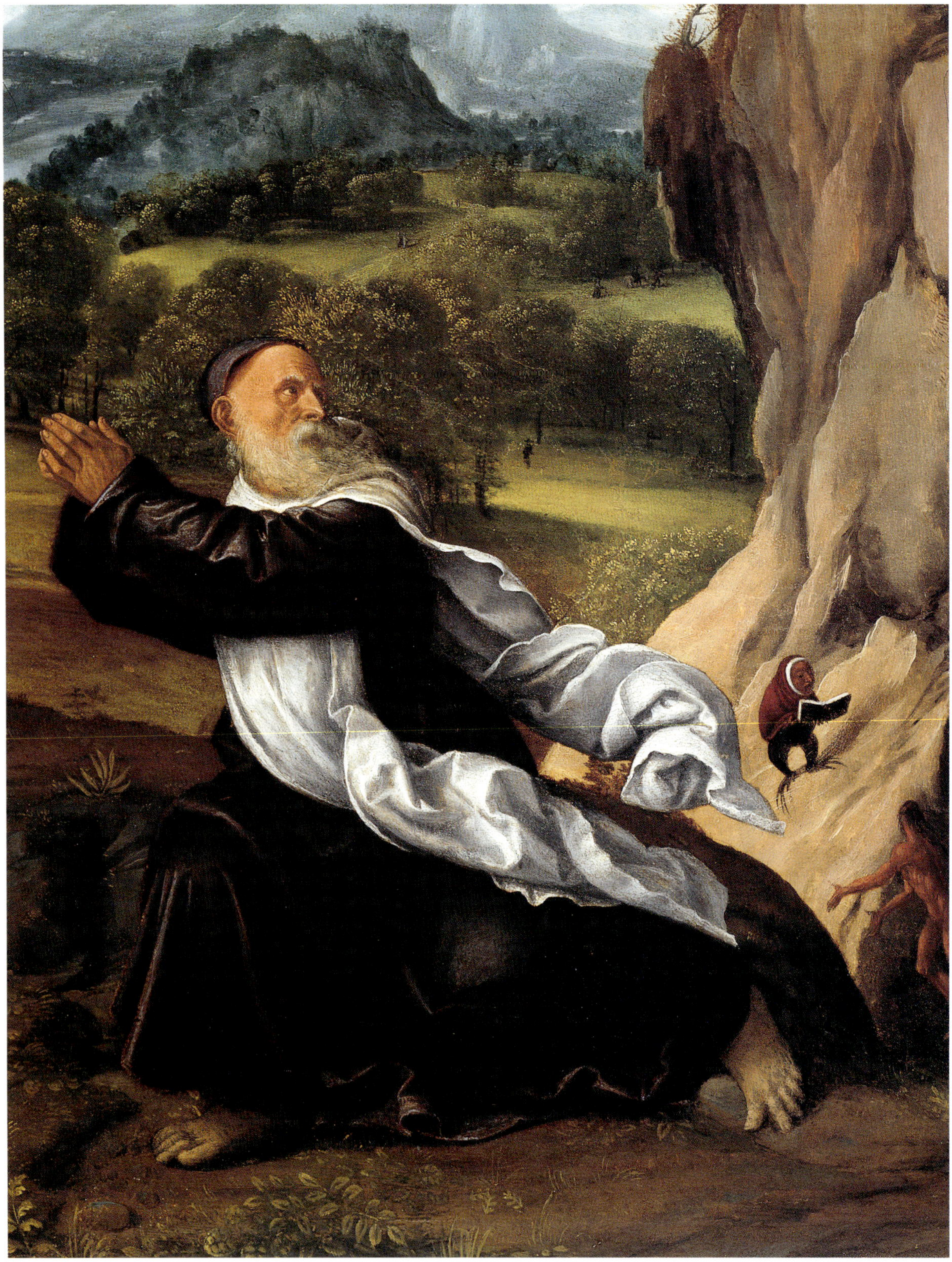

Detail of Plate 8

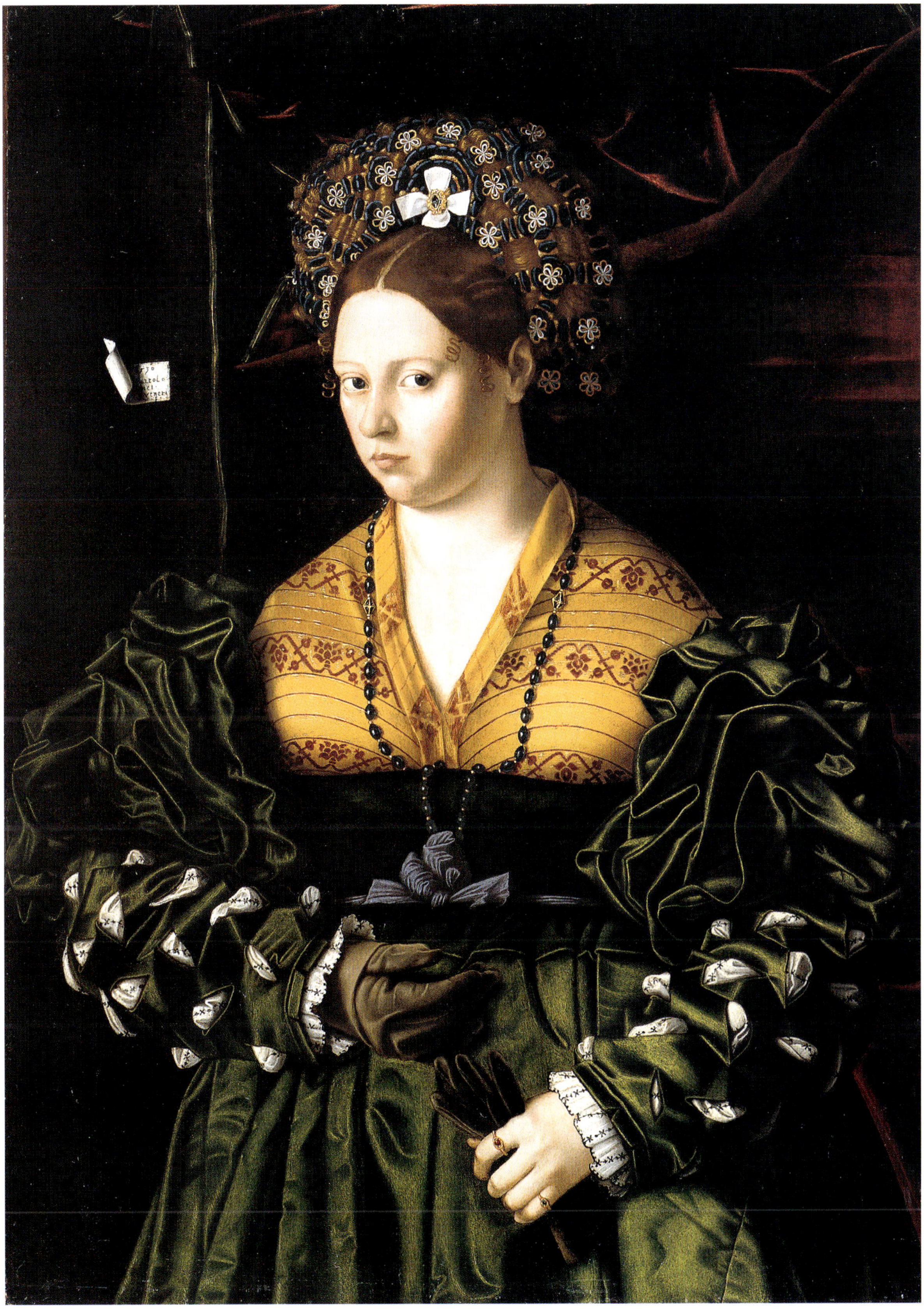

PROVENANCE

Manfrin collection, Venice; Mr. Barker (according to Crowe and Cavalcaselle 1912); fifth earl of Rosebery, Mentmore Towers, by 1884, his sale, Sotheby's, Mentmore Towers, May 25–26, 1977, lot 2407; acquired by the Putnam Foundation, 1979.

LITERATURE

London, National Gallery, MS of 1851, "Inventory and Valuation of Pictures Made from the Manfrin Collection at Venice," no. 52; F. Zanotto, *Nuovissima guida di Venezia* (Venice, 1856), p. 342; *Mentmore,* 2 vols. (Edinburgh, 1884), 1:68, no. 14; J. A. Crowe and G. B. Cavalcaselle, *A History of Painting in North Italy,* 3 vols. (London, 1912), 1:299; Bernard Berenson, *Italian Pictures of the Renaissance: Venetian School,* 2 vols. (London, 1957), 1:12; Creighton Gilbert, "Bartolommeo Veneto and His *Portrait of a Lady,*" *National Gallery of Canada Bulletin* 22 (1973): 3, 7, 12 n. 5, 15 n. 16, fig. 3; *Timken Art Gallery: European and American Works of Art in the Putnam Foundation Collection* (San Diego, 1983), pp. 78–79, 124, no. 30, ill.

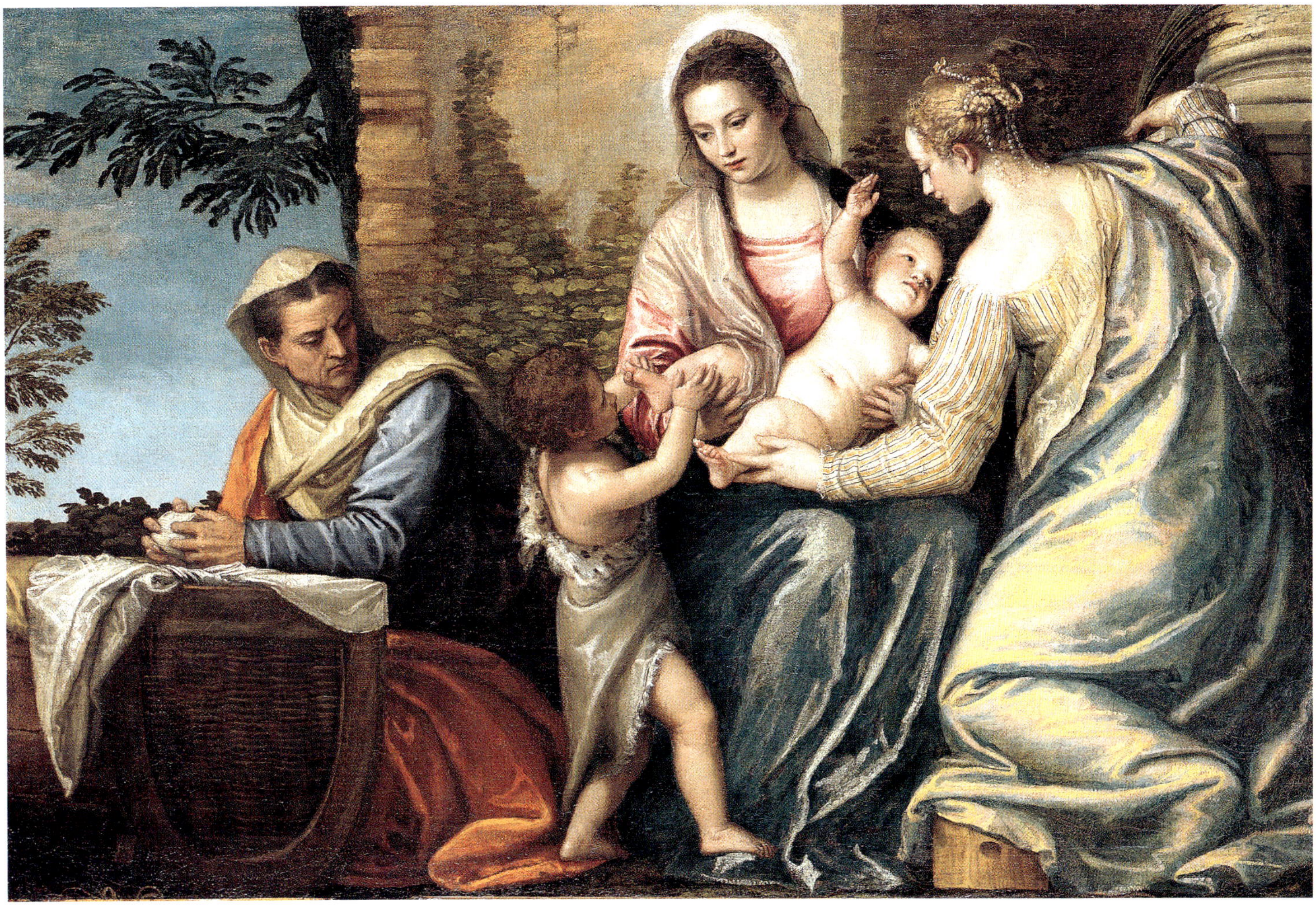

Paolo Caliari, called Veronese

(1528–1588)

The artist's nickname was derived from Verona, the city of his birth, but his fame as a painter was determined mainly in Venice, where he was active from about 1551. Along with Tintoretto, he dominated Venetian painting in the generation after Titian, receiving numerous major commissions from the state and ecclesiastical hierarchies. He won particular fame as a decorator, creating vast illusionistic scenes that celebrate the golden age of Venice. His abilities to orchestrate huge crowds of figures, enhancing the pageantry with rich color and light, are nowhere better displayed than in the *Triumph of Venice* on the ceiling of the Council Hall in the Doge's Palace, executed about 1585. He was also adept at more intimate, lighthearted decoration, notably the frescoes in the Villa Barbaro at Maser, executed not long after his first visit to Rome in 1560. Veronese's love of pageantry got him into trouble with the Inquisition for introducing irrelevant figures into a grandiose depiction of the Last Supper. The painter staunchly defended his right to artistic license, but ultimately had to alter the subject to a Feast in the House of Levi to satisfy the tribunal. His easel paintings include religious, mythological, and allegorical compositions as well as fine portraits. His influence on Venetian painting was great, particularly in the eighteenth century, when his example inspired Tiepolo and other painters in a revival of grand decoration.

10 *Madonna and Child with St. Elizabeth, the Infant St. John the Baptist, and St. Justina*, 1565–70
Oil on canvas, 40⅞ × 62¼ in. (103.8 × 158.1 cm)

Images like this one were created to celebrate a favored saint. Here, Justina, a patroness of Padua and Venice, is shown in the company of the Holy Family. The Virgin Mary and Christ are depicted along with his cousin, St. John, and his mother, St. Elizabeth, who sits before a cradle, rolling swaddling clothes. The infant Christ turns to embrace Justina, demonstrating the favor in which she was held, and thus her powers as an intercessor for the faithful. Such pictures were sometimes created for a church or a chapel dedicated to the saint, but might also have been commissioned by one of the saint's devotees, perhaps someone who shared the same name.

Very little is known about St. Justina, even when she lived. The earliest record of her cult, dating to the fifth century, notes her Paduan origin and that she died a virgin, martyred for her faith in Christ. In Venice in the sixteenth century, Justina was thought to have been the daughter of King Vitiliano and Queen Perpedigna of Padua, baptized by St. Prosdocime, the first bishop of the city.[1] Thus, Veronese depicts her dressed in sumptuous clothes with pearls festooned in her hair. However, the life of the saint on which this is based was later shown to be a medieval invention.

Justina was greatly venerated in Padua and Venice. The Paduans consecrated a splendid church to her in the sixteenth century, for which Veronese created the *Martyrdom of St. Justina* in 1574–75, which is still in situ. Another, smaller, version of this subject by Veronese is today in the Uffizi, Florence (no. 589). In Venice, a church, a square, and a bridge were named for Justina. The church, twice rebuilt by 1594, was closed in disrepair in 1810. It is possible that the Timken painting was made for this church.

Both the Virgin Mary and St. Elizabeth are lost in thought, perhaps musing on the divine nature of their children and their ultimate demise at the hands of their fellow man. Their faces show the classical dignity and pathos that Veronese could bring to his figures.

The disposition of the figures against a brick wall that opens onto a landscape is a basic Venetian compositional formula of the sixteenth century. The arrangement of figures is typical of Veronese, who establishes a stately flow of interconnecting forms across the picture plane. Justina's broad gesture echoes that of the Christ Child. Equally characteristic of the artist is the palette, perfectly balanced between warm and cool colors unfolding in syncopated progression. The play of light richly models the forms, highlights flickering across the garments, created with virtuoso brushwork.

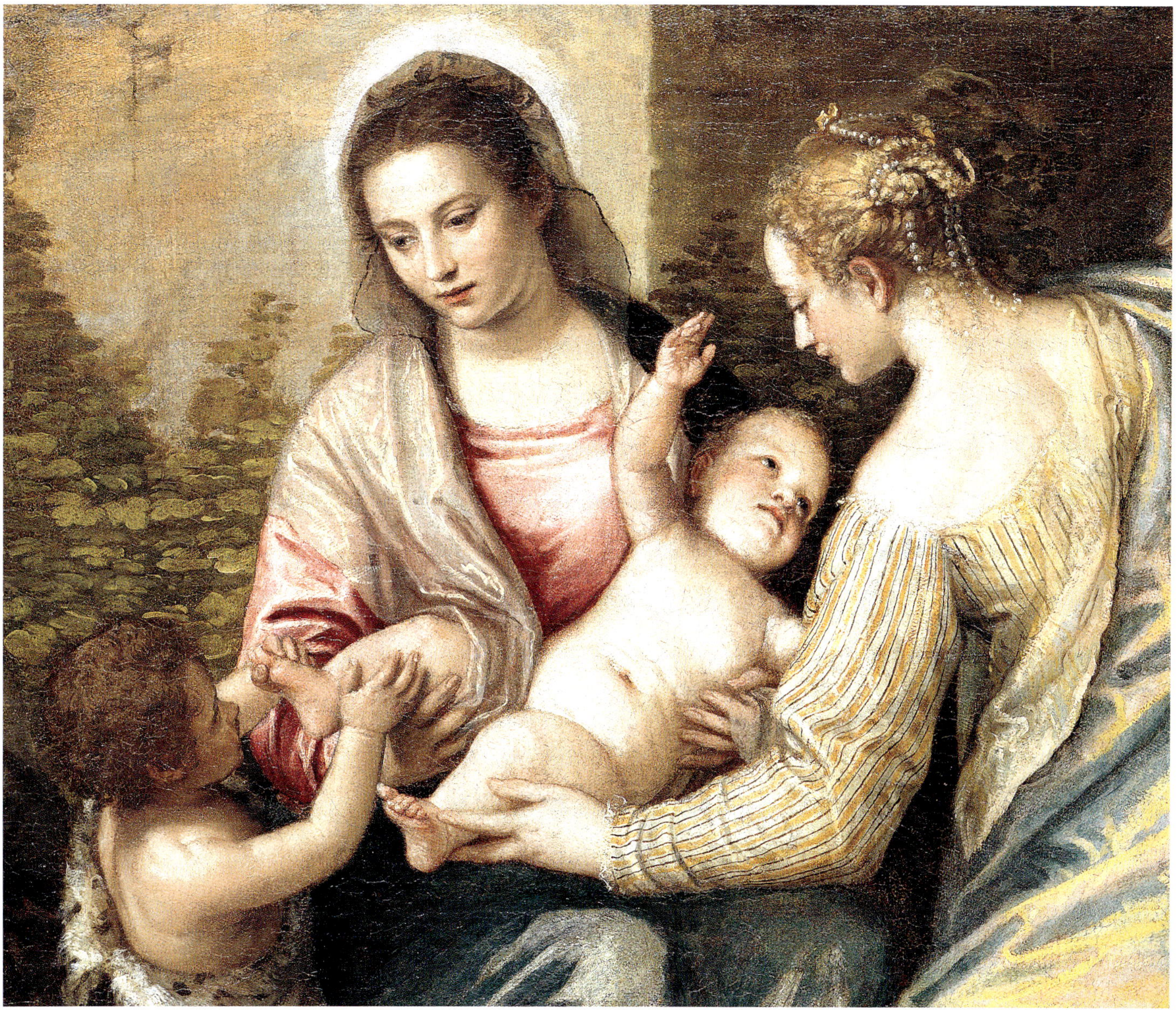

Detail of Plate 10

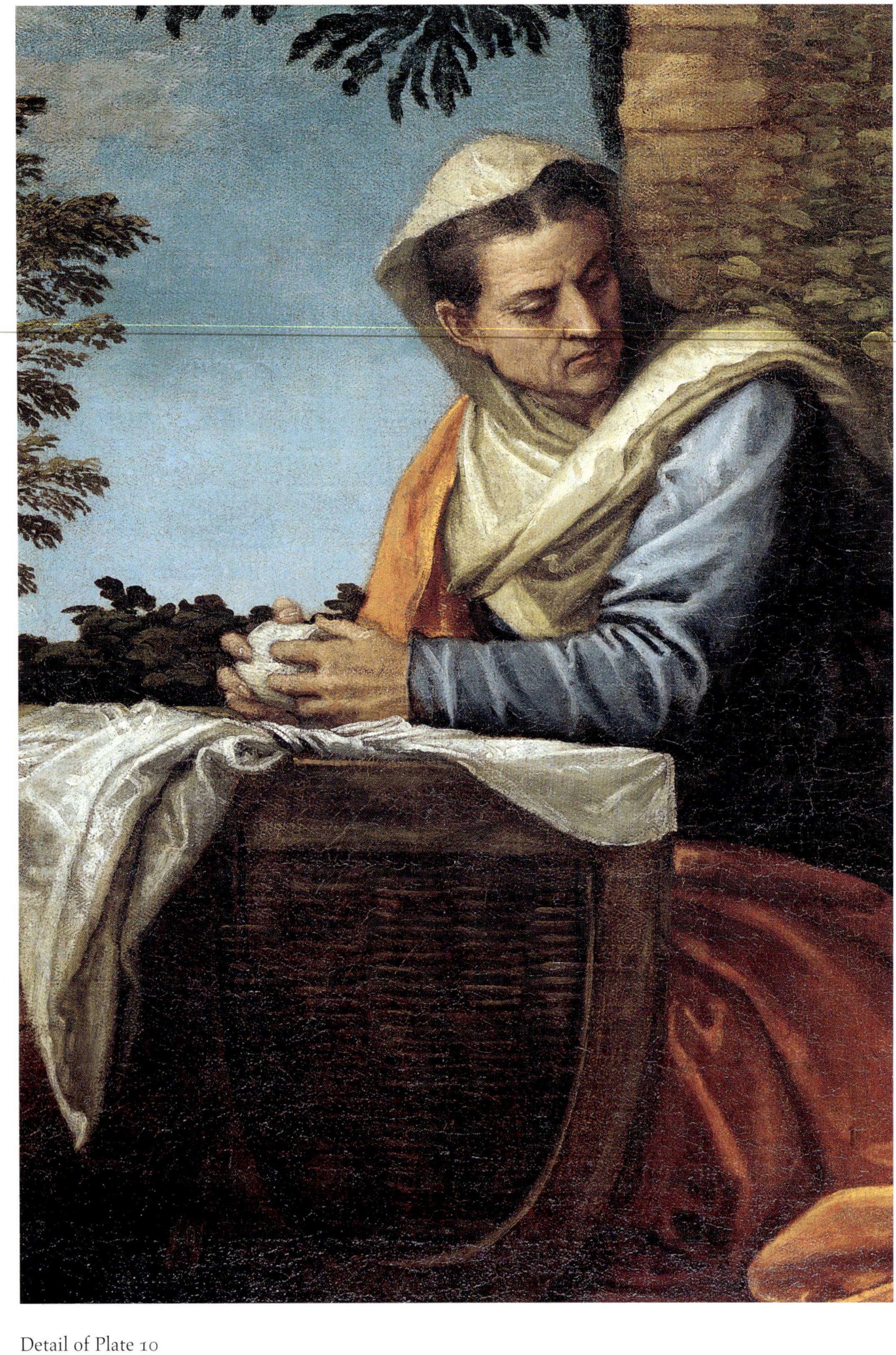

Detail of Plate 10

Based on a comparison with an engraving after the painting made by Giovanni Vendramini in the late eighteenth or early nineteenth century, the painting would seem to have been slightly reduced at the top and bottom. However, it should be noted that printmakers sometimes added to compositions that seemed too cramped.

— D. C.

NOTE

1. See her biography in *Legendario delle vite dei santi* (Venice, 1594).

PROVENANCE

Possibly mentioned by Ridolfi as in the possession of the heirs of Veronese; according to Cicogna (1824–53), the work belonged to Abbott Celotti; Bondon, Paris, until 1831, his sale, Paris, June 8, 1831 (Lugt 12689), no. 10; Quantock; Norman Clark Neill, Cowes, as of 1925; Mrs. H. F. Buxton, London; acquired by the Putnam Foundation, 1956.

LITERATURE

C. Ridolfi, *Le maraviglie dell'arte ovvero le vite degl'illustri pittori veneti e dello stato . . .* (1648), ed. D. von Hadeln, 2 vols. (Berlin, 1914 and 1924), 1:344; E. Cicogna, *Delle iscrizioni veneziane,* 6 vols. (Venice, 1824–53), 4:235; Percy H. Osmond, *Paolo Veronese* (London, 1927), p. 32; "Country-wide Loans from California," *Art News* 55 (November 1956): 33, ill.; Bernard Berenson, *Italian Pictures of the Renaissance: Venetian School,* 2 vols. (London, 1957), 1:135; Remigio Marini, *L'opera completa del Veronese,* introduction by Guido Piovene (Milan, 1968), p. 135, no. 392; Agnes Mongan and Elizabeth Mongan, *European Paintings in the Timken Art Gallery* (San Diego, 1969), pp. 36–37, 111, no. 10, ill.; Pierre-Jean Mariette, *Ecoles d'Italie: Notices biographiques et catalogues des oeuvres reproduites par la gravure,* Les Grands Peintres, no. 1 (Paris, 1969), p. 302; Burton Fredericksen and Federico Zeri, *Census of Pre-Nineteenth-Century Italian Paintings in North American Public Collections* (Cambridge, Mass., 1972), pp. 40, 348, 632; Paolo Ticozzi, "Le incisioni da Paolo Veronese nel museo Correr," *Bolletino dei Musei Civici Veneziani* 20, nos. 3–4 (1975): 46, no. 130; Terisio Pignatti, *Veronese,* 2 vols. (Venice, 1976), 1:125–26, no. 129, and 2: fig. 373; Paolo Ticozzi, *Paolo Veronese e i suoi incisori,* exh. cat., Museo Correr (Venice, 1977), p. 32, under no. 88; Martin E. Petersen, "Three Centuries of European Paintings, 1300–1600," *Apollo* 115 (June 1982): 441, fig. 6; *Timken Art Gallery: European and American Works of Art in the Putnam Foundation Collection* (San Diego, 1983), pp. 84–85, 124–25, no. 32, ill.; Terisio Pignatti and Filippo Pedrocco, *Veronese: Catalogo completo dei dipinti,* I gigli dell'arte, no. 18 (Florence, 1991), p. 334, no. 68A.

EXHIBITED

London, Burlington Fine Arts Club, 1925–26, *Winter Exhibition Catalogue,* no. 61; Washington, D.C., National Gallery of Art, extended loan, 1956–65.

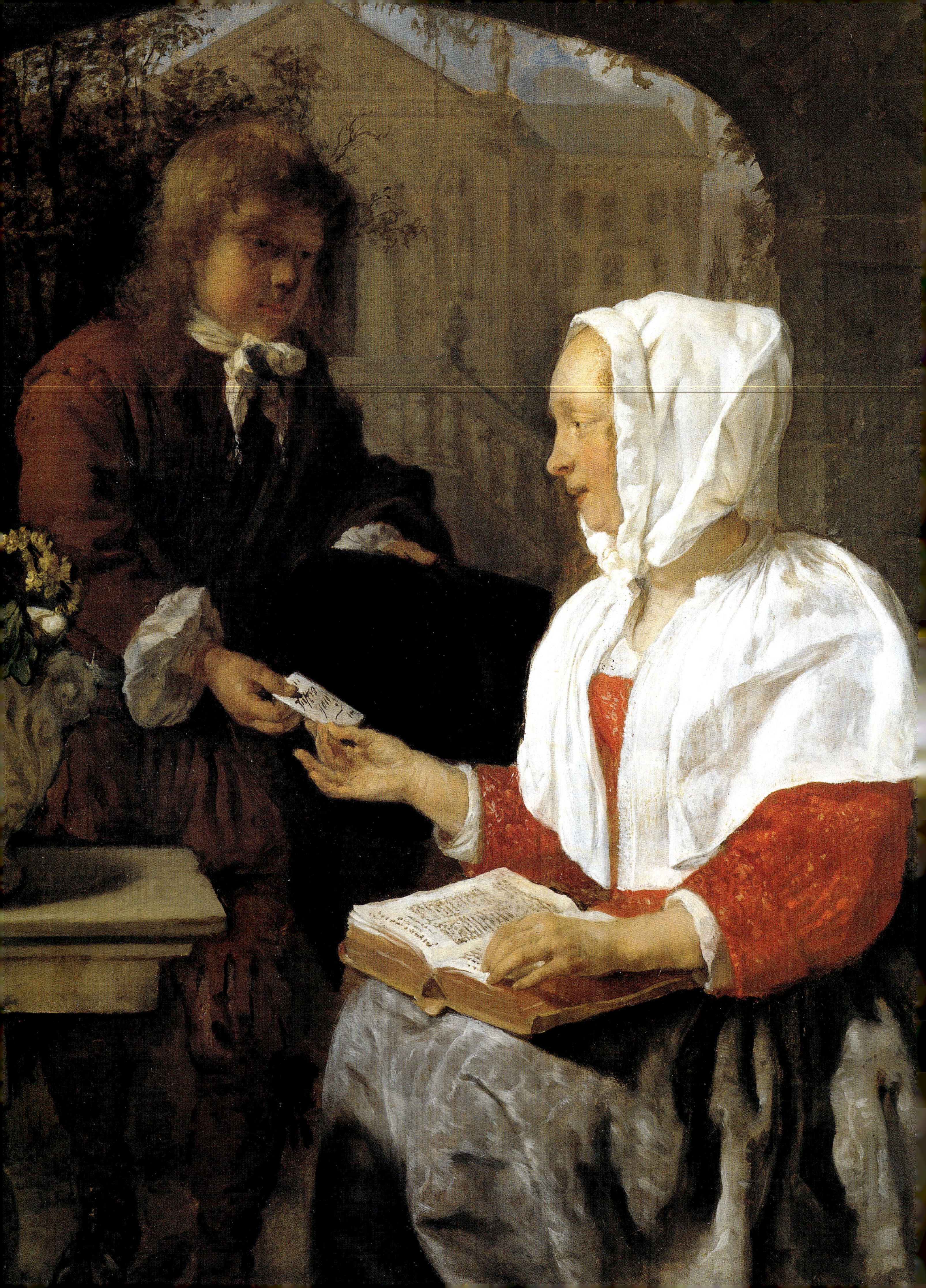

Dutch and Flemish Paintings

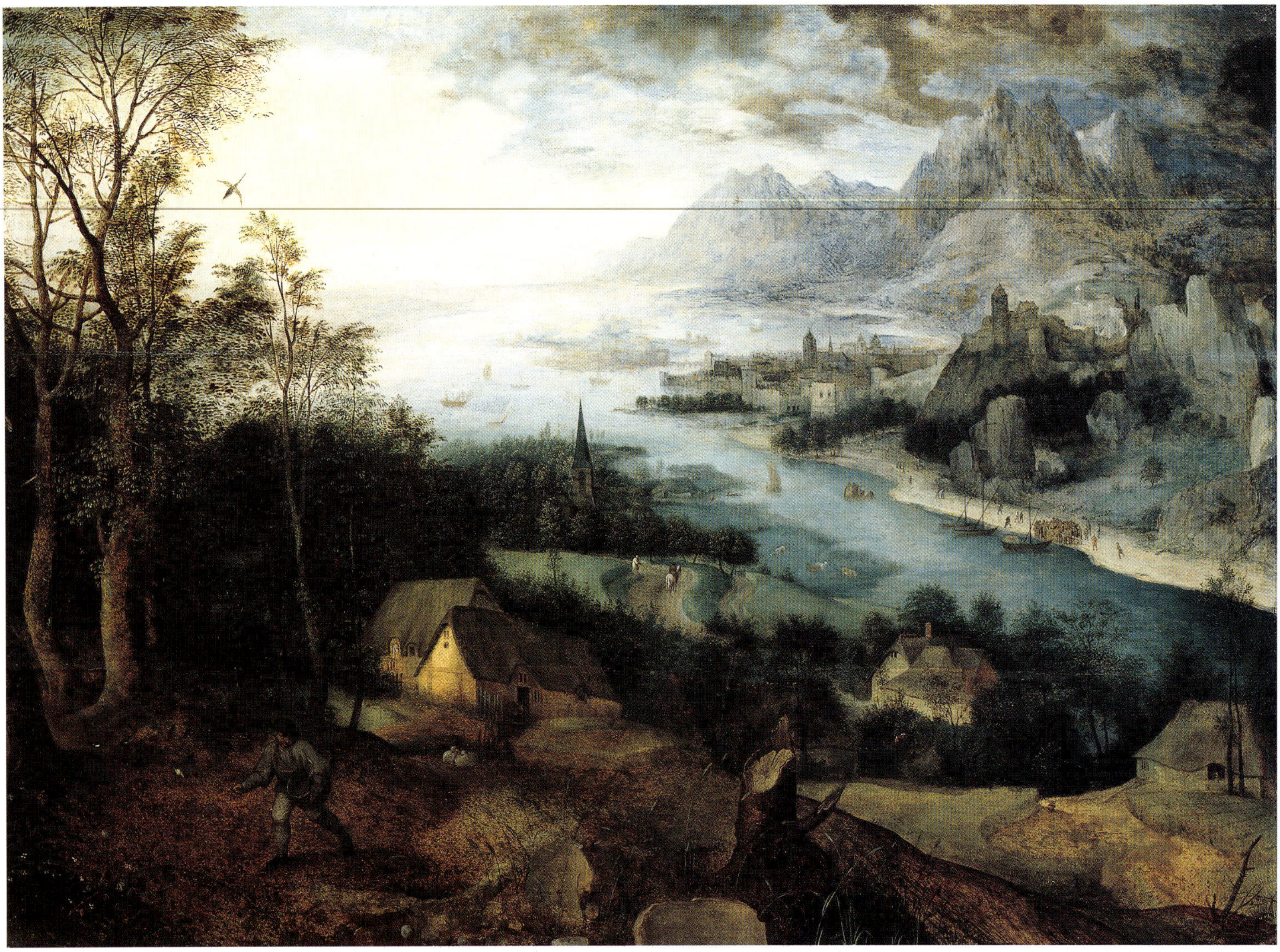

Pieter Bruegel the Elder

(ca. 1525–1569)

Bruegel was born about 1525, possibly in Breda. He was a pupil of Peter Coeck van Aelst in Antwerp, and in 1551 he was enrolled as a master in the Guild of St. Luke in that city. In 1553 he traveled to Rome, where he collaborated with the miniaturist Giulio Clovio. Bruegel then returned to Antwerp, where he supplied drawings for prints published by Hieronymus Cock. In 1563 he moved to Brussels, where he married. He died there in 1569.

11 *Parable of the Sower*, 1557
Oil on panel, 29 × 40½ in. (73.7 × 102.9 cm)
Signed and dated lower right: *Brueghel / 1557*

In the left foreground, a peasant scatters seed on a small upland pasture. In accordance with the text from Matthew (13:3–13), fowl are devouring the seed, thorns are flourishing, and there are stony places. Below to the right and in the middle distance near a chapel is the "good ground," where the seed has multiplied, thirty-, sixty-, and a hundredfold. A river flows diagonally from the right middle distance into a broad estuary. Three small boats are moored on the right bank of the river. Near the first one, a small crowd gathers to hear Jesus preaching. Further along on the right bank is a small fortified town on a hill; below, a little to the left, is a larger town dwarfed by Alpine crags.

The picture first came to notice when it was bought by Fernand Stuyck at public auction at the Fievez Gallery, Brussels, in 1924. It was then catalogued simply as Flemish school, seventeenth century. In December of that year, when it was cleaned by the elder Mr. Buesco, conservator for the Belgian royal family, the signature *Brueghel* and the date *1557* were revealed. The painting came to the United States just before World War II. It was then shown in San Francisco and Washington, D.C. Two known replicas of the painting exist, both attributed to Bruegel. One was owned in 1932 by Cloots, the director of the Gallery Alice Marteau, Paris; the other is in the Prado, Madrid (no. 1964).

Friedländer (1937) considered this panel one of Bruegel's earliest signed paintings, done shortly after his designs for Cock in Antwerp. The drawings upon which the designs were based were made by Bruegel as he crossed over the Alps on his

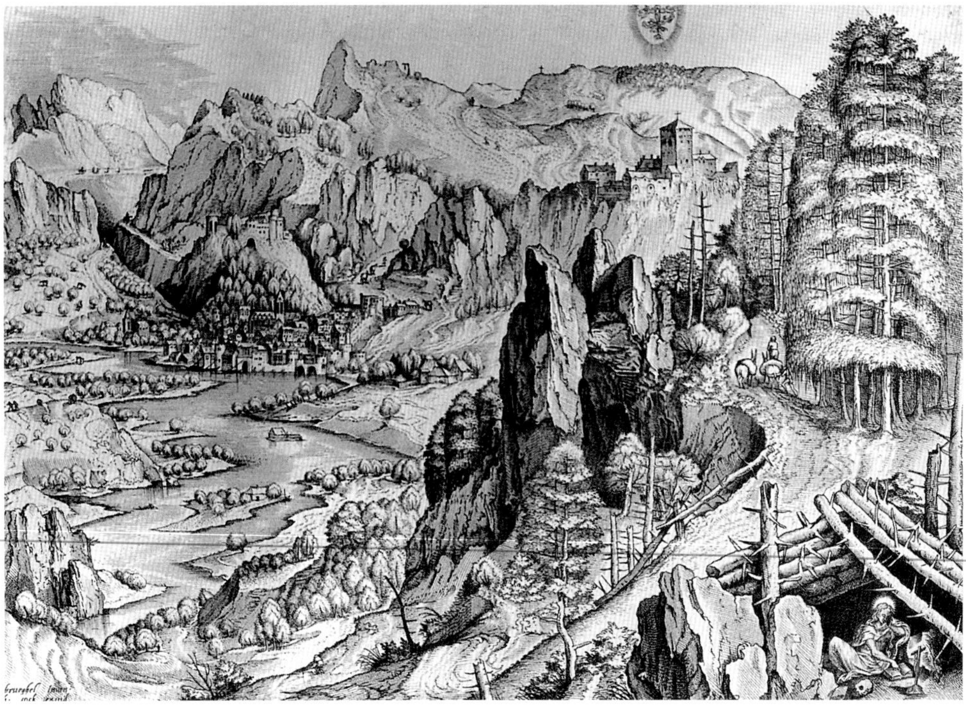

Fig. 1. Pieter Bruegel the Elder, *Penitent Magdalen.* Engraving, 12¾ × 16¹³⁄₁₆ in. (32.4 × 42.7 cm). New York, The Metropolitan Museum of Art, Harris Brisbane Dick Fund, 1926 (26.72.53).

return from Italy. They reveal the impact on the Northern artist of both the heroic spirit of the Renaissance with which he became acquainted in Rome and the austere grandeur of the magnificent mountains. His Northern eyes, with their inherited inclination toward detail and exactitude, looked with awe upon the scenes, which his genius, broadened by his Italian experience, recorded in a series of drawings unique in their breadth and detail. From them came the etched landscapes that were published in Antwerp in 1555–57. A careful comparison of the Putnam picture with details in Bruegel's etched landscapes is revealing. Fortified hill towns situated on similar steep rocky bluffs are to be found in the *Plaustrum Belgicum,* the *Euntes in Emmaus,* and the *Penitent Magdalen*[1] (fig. 1).

The aerial perspective of the painting, the sentiment of landscape, and the manner in which it is composed all confirm the early date inscribed on the panel, a date before Bruegel's departure for Brussels. The subject matter is Bruegel's earliest treatment of the theme of a parable, a subject he took up often in later years.

—A. M. AND E. M.[2]

NOTES

1. See R. van Bastelaer, *Les Estampes de Pierre Bruegel l'Ancien* (Brussels, 1907), nos. 11, 14, and 8, respectively.

2. The editor thanks Walter S. Gibson for his review of the Literature.

PROVENANCE

Fernand Stuyck del Bruyère, Antwerp, 1924; acquired by the Putnam Foundation, 1957.

LITERATURE

Max J. Friedländer, "Neues von Pieter Bruegel," *Pantheon* 7 (February 1931): 58; Edouard Michel, "A propos de Bruegel le Vieux," *Gazette des Beaux-Arts* 7 (February 1932): 126–32, ill.; Charles de Tolnay, *Pierre Bruegel l'Ancien* (Brussels, 1935), pp. 75–76, fig. 143; Leo van Puyvelde, *Pierre Bruegel l'Ancien à l'exposition d'art ancien de Bruxelles* (Brussels, 1935); Gustav Glück, *Pieter Brueghel, the Elder* (London, 1936), p. 24, no. 6, ill.; Max J. Friedländer, "Pieter Bruegel," in *Die Altniederländische Malerei,* 14 vols. (Berlin and Leiden, 1924–37), 14:11, pl. IV; Gotthard Jedlicka, *Pieter Bruegel: Der Maler in seiner Zeit* (Erlenbach, 1938), p. 513, pl. 3; Leo Bruhns, *Das Bruegel Buch* (Vienna, 1941), p. 14, no. 6, ill.; Gustav Glück, *Das grosse Bruegel-Werk* (Vienna, 1951), p. 40, ill.; Robert Genaille, *Bruegel l'Ancien* (Paris, 1953), p. 26; Charles de Tolnay, "An Unknown Early Panel by Pieter Bruegel the Elder," *Burlington Magazine* 97 (August 1955): 239; F. Grossman, *Bruegel: The Paintings* (London, 1955), pp. 18, 190, pl. 5; Robert L. Delevoy, *Bruegel* (Geneva, 1959), p. 30, ill.; Valentin Denis, *All the Paintings of Pieter Bruegel* (London, 1961), pp. 13, 26, 27, pl. 2; Leo van Puyvelde, *La Peinture flamande au siècle de Bosch et Brueghel* (Paris, 1962), p. 81; Piero Bianconi, *The Complete Paintings of Bruegel* (New York, 1967), pp. 88, 90, no. 10, ill.; Bob Claessens and Jeanne Rousseau, *Our Bruegel* (Antwerp, 1969), p. 33, pl. 5; Marguerite Kay, *Bruegel* (London, 1969), pp. 16, 32, pl. 3; Roger H. Marijnissen, *Bruegel* (Brussels, 1969), pp. 38, 86–87, no. 5, ill.; Agnes Mongan and Elizabeth Mongan, *European Paintings in the Timken Art Gallery* (San Diego, 1969), pp. 54, 55, 116–17, no. 18, ill.; Wolfgang Stechow, *Pieter Bruegel the Elder* (New York, [1969]), pp. 19, 21, 52, pl. 1; R[oger] Marijnissen and M. Seidel, *Bruegel* (New York, 1971), p. 38, no. 5, pls. on pp. 86–87; Keith Roberts, *Bruegel* (London, 1971), p. 6; F[ritz] Grossman, *Pieter Bruegel: Complete Edition of the Paintings,* 3d ed. (London, 1973), p. 190, pl. 22; Walter S. Gibson, *Bruegel* (New York, 1977), pp. 38, 42–43, 156, fig. 19; Tiziana Frati, *Bruegel: Every Painting* (New York, 1979), pp. 4, 13, fig. 3; Alexander Wied, *Bruegel* (London, 1979), pp. 40–41, 85, 90, 185, no. 4, ills.; Martin E. Petersen, "Three Centuries of European Paintings, 1300–1600," *Apollo* 115 (June 1982): 445, fig. 8; *Timken Art Gallery: European and American Works of Art in the Putnam Foundation Collection* (San Diego, 1983), pp. 20–21, 115–16, no. 3, ill.; Walter S. Gibson, *"Mirror of the Earth": The World Landscape in Sixteenth-Century Flemish Painting* (Princeton, 1989), p. 66.

EXHIBITED

Brussels, Exposition universelle et internationale, 1935, *Cinq Siècles d'art,* 1:63, no. 133, and 2: pl. LVIII, as *The Estuary;* Paris, Musée de l'Orangerie, 1935, *De van Eyck à Bruegel,* p. 15, no. 14, pl. XLI; Worcester, Mass., Worcester Art Museum, and Philadelphia Museum of Art, 1939, *Exhibition of Flemish Painting,* cat. intro. by Leo van Puyvelde, p. 54, no. 94, ill.; San Francisco, Golden Gate International Exposition, 1939, *Master Works of Five Centuries,* no. 3, ill.; Washington, D.C., National Gallery of Art, extended loan, 1958–65.

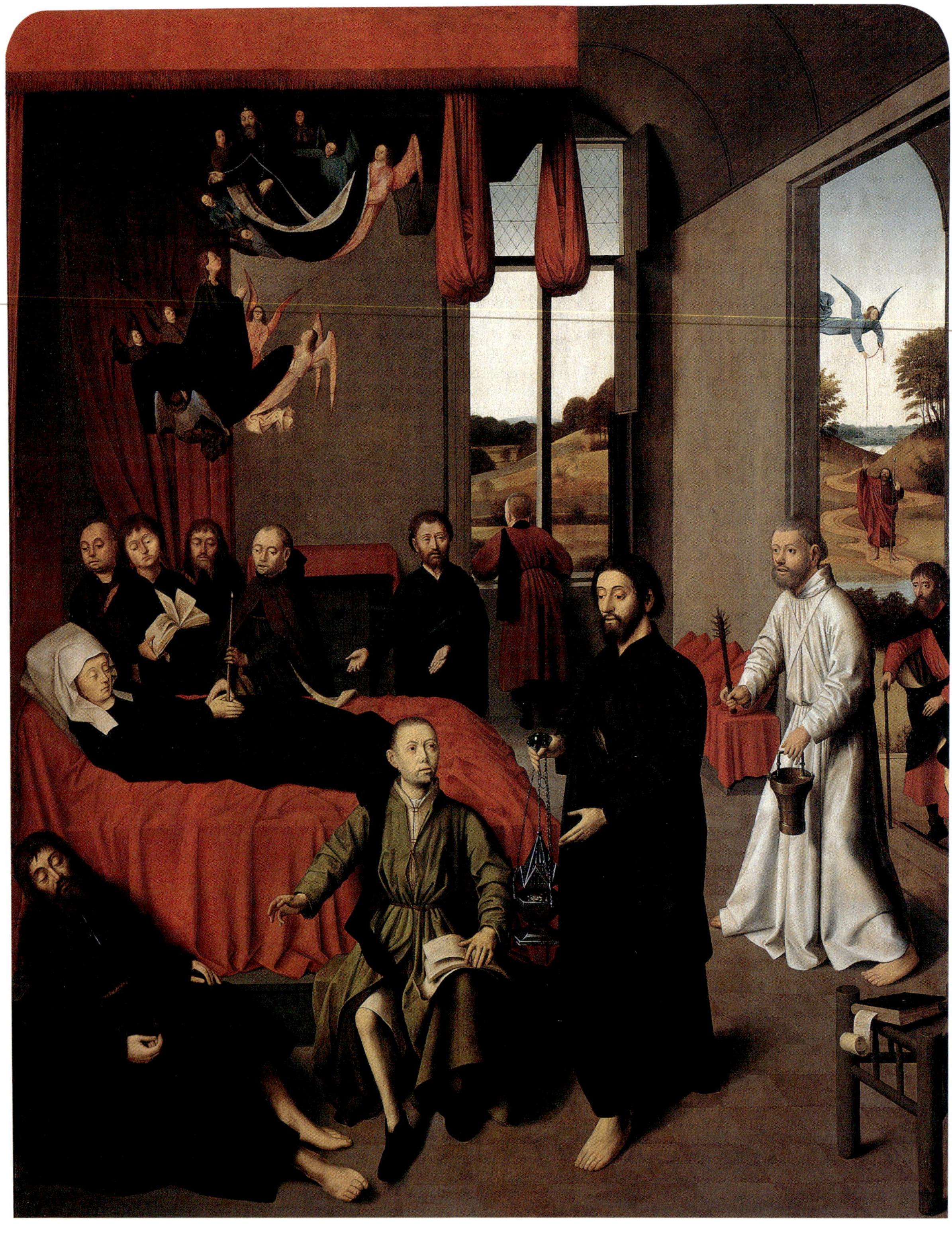

Petrus Christus

(d. 1475/76)

Petrus Christus came from Baerle, near the present Belgian-Dutch border, and lived in Bruges from 1444 until his death in 1475/76. Although he arrived too late to study with the court painter, Jan van Eyck (d. 1441), Christus was greatly influenced by that master's work. Nine panels are signed and/or dated out of a small oeuvre comprising around thirty-two paintings, three or four drawings, and one known manuscript illumination. Christus excelled as a portrait painter in works such as the *Portrait of a Lady* (Berlin, Gemäldegalerie, Staatliche Museen) or the *Portrait of a Carthusian* (New York, The Metropolitan Museum of Art), and is credited with several innovations including the introduction of one-point perspective to Northern painting.

12 *Death of the Virgin*, ca. 1460–65
Oil on oak, transferred to mahogany and cradled, 67⅜ × 54½ in.
(171.1 × 138.4 cm)

The story of the Death of the Virgin is recounted in the *Golden Legend*, where there are details of the gathering of the apostles from all over the world, summoned by an angel to witness the event.[1] Although the subject is a standard theme represented in early Netherlandish painting, Petrus Christus's rendition of it is unusual in the conflation of three episodically distinct events: the death of the Virgin, her Assumption, and the reception of the Virgin's girdle by St. Thomas (the latecomer) as proof of the Assumption. The assembled apostles prepare to administer Extreme Unction to the Virgin, bringing along a container of holy water and the aspergillum, a censer, the Holy Scriptures, and a candle, traditionally placed in the hands of the dying as a symbol of Christian faith.

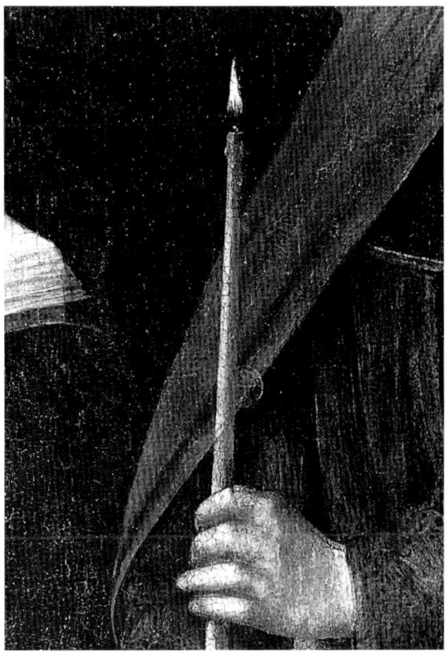

Fig. 1. Detail of eucharistic wafer.

Immediately to the right of the candle above the apostle's left hand (fig. 1) is a nearly transparent, round object with an embossed decorative border and a cross on it—a eucharistic wafer.[2] The Host here symbolizes Christ's presence at the Virgin's death, illustrating John 6:51: "I am the living bread which came down from heaven." This passage occurs in the liturgy only in the Mass for the Dead. The consecrated Host, according to Catholic doctrine, becomes the real presence and body of the Lord. Considered in this context, the presence of the Host at Mary's Dormition signals her mystical union with Christ after death. The echo of the miraculous appearance of the

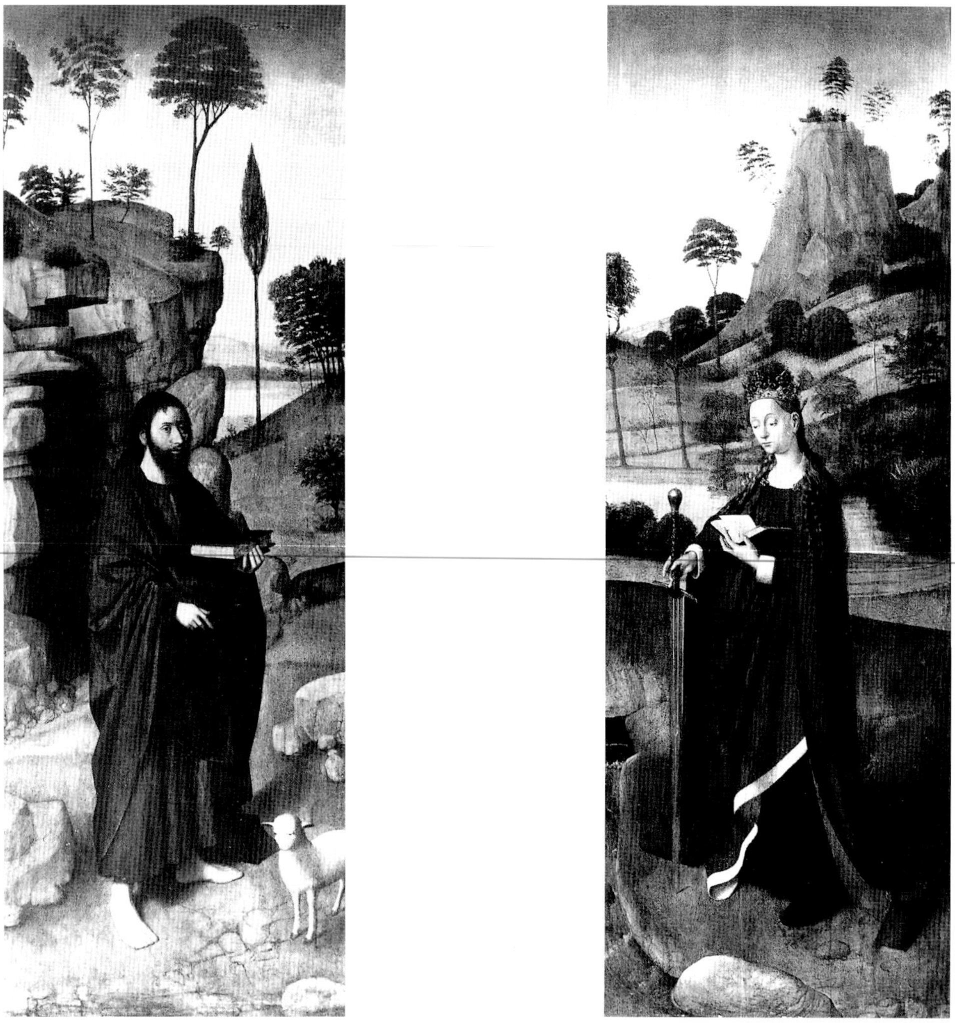

Fig. 2. *St. John the Baptist* and *St. Catherine*, ca. 1460–65. Oil on oak, each 68⅛ × 24¾ in. (173 × 62.9 cm). Destroyed during World War II; formerly Berlin, Kaiser-Friedrich-Museum.

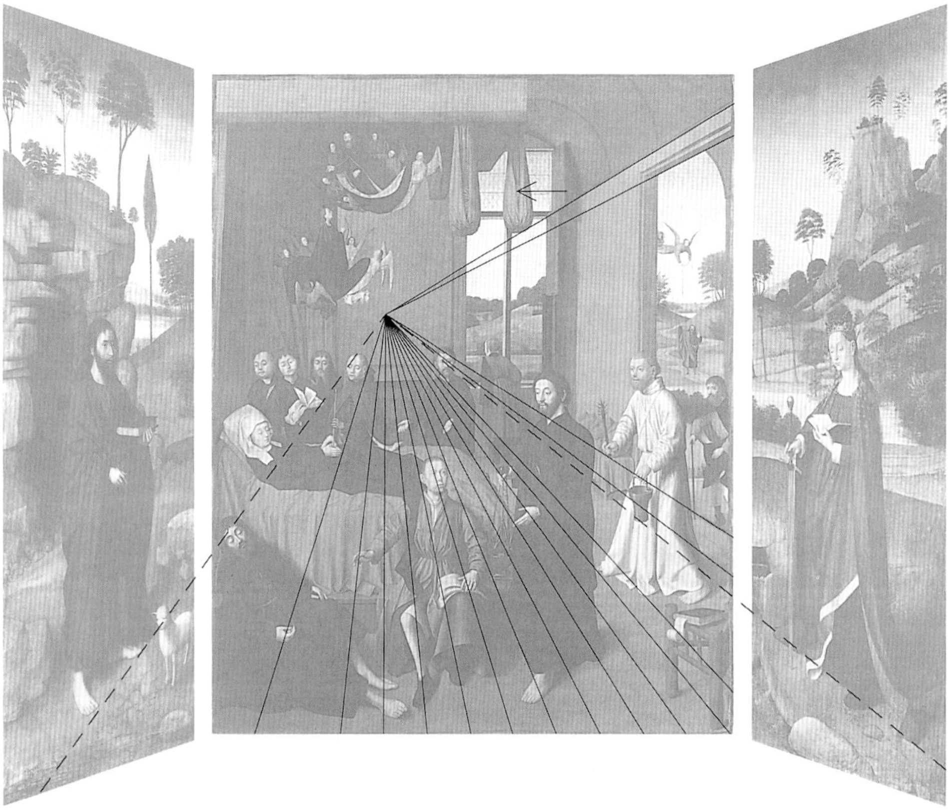

Fig. 3. Perspectival diagram, with wings.

Host is found in the background scene, where the Virgin's girdle is suddenly brought by an angel to the doubting Thomas to verify the Virgin's Assumption.

Highly unusual for a Netherlandish painting of the mid-fifteenth century are both the size of this work and its spatial presentation. It measures 67⅜ by 54½ inches (171.1 × 138.4 cm), making it the largest work in Christus's known oeuvre; half the cavernous space is taken up with the extensive height of the walls capped by a barrel-vaulted ceiling. Any discussion of the spatial representation must take into account the wings, which once formed a triptych with this panel.[3] Representing St. John the Baptist at the left and St. Catherine at the right (fig. 2), these wings were destroyed in the Flakturm fire in Berlin in 1945.[4] Only black-and-white photographs of them remain, along with color notes provided in the Berlin catalogue.

Somewhat awkward is the juncture of wings with saints that are larger in scale than the figures of the central panel (that is, except for the figure holding the censer). However, if the two wings are placed at an oblique angle to the central panel, the saints John the Baptist and Catherine serve as midway markers in the transition from the viewer's space to that of the main scene, and the orthogonals of all three panels converge at a single point on the far wall above the Virgin's bed. This is the only known instance in Christus's oeuvre in which all three panels of a triptych are coordinated in a one-point perspective scheme (fig. 3).

The *Death of the Virgin* has not always been uniformly accepted as by Petrus Christus.[5] Having suffered greatly over time, it has lost the effect of its original enamel-like surface and the fine finishing details of modeling due to severe abrasion and the transfer of the painting to another support. In addition, until its recent cleaning and restoration, the *Death of the Virgin* was obscured by a very thick yellowed varnish. All of these factors have thwarted efforts to deal effectively with the attribution of the painting. Further confusing the issue is the picture's uncommonly large size, an unaccustomed one for Christus, whose handling and execution in paint was most practiced on a far smaller scale.

Many of the features of the *Death of the Virgin*, nonetheless, indicate Christus's characteristic style and handling: the stereometrically conceived figures, seemingly boneless and in static poses, the ovoid heads with heavy-lidded eyes and pronounced triangular-shaped noses, and draperies falling in broad, flat folds. In addition to the perspective system made with incised and drawn ruled lines, also typical of Christus's working method here is the precise underdrawing in the figures and in the objects in the room, and the free, calligraphic swirls of the brush found in the landscape (fig. 4).[6]

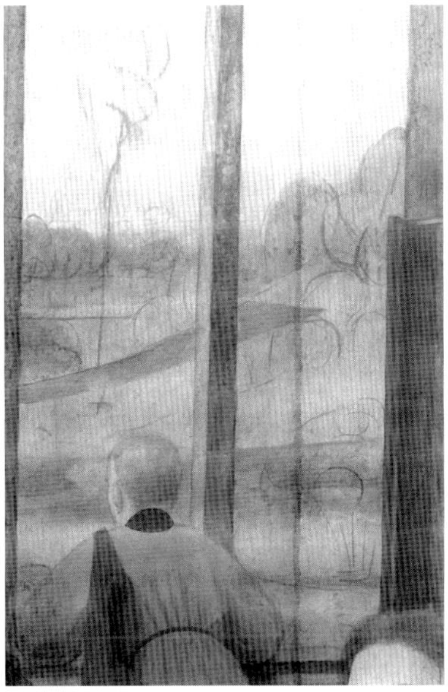

Fig. 4. Infrared-reflectography computer assembly (underdrawing of the landscape).

Perhaps soon after its completion, the large triptych was sent south to Italy, for Christus's unusual composition found no particular following in the North.[7] Roberto Longhi maintained that the *Death of the Virgin* was in Sicily all along and that it was the most important source of Antonello da Messina's knowledge of Christus and early Netherlandish painting,[8] while others suggested that it is the painting referred to in an intriguing document in the state archives of Venice.[9] The document of July 30, 1451, states that a "maestro Piero de Fiandra" was paid seventy-eight ducats for an altarpiece *(pala)* and additional expenses for transporting it to Santa Maria

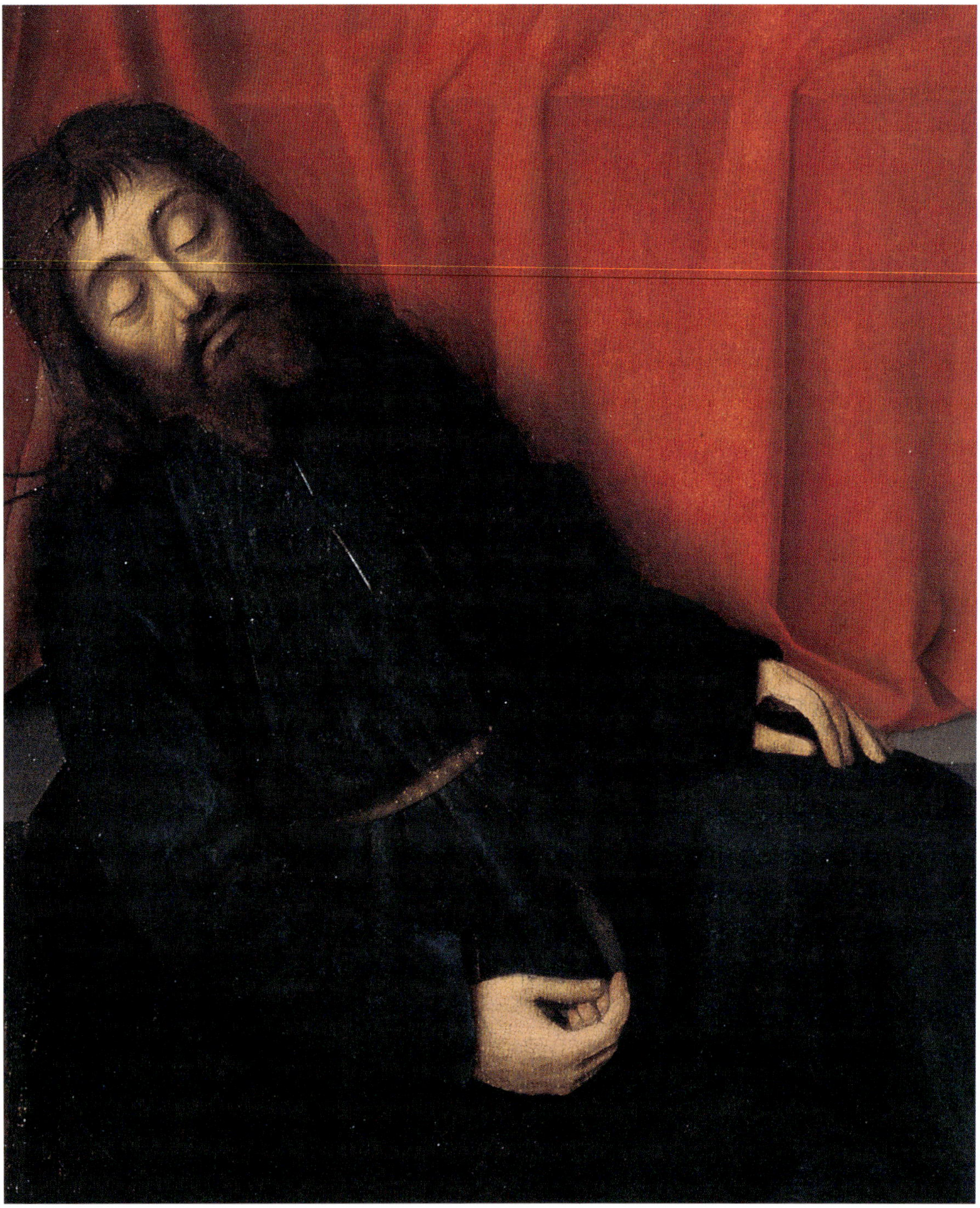

Detail of Plate 12

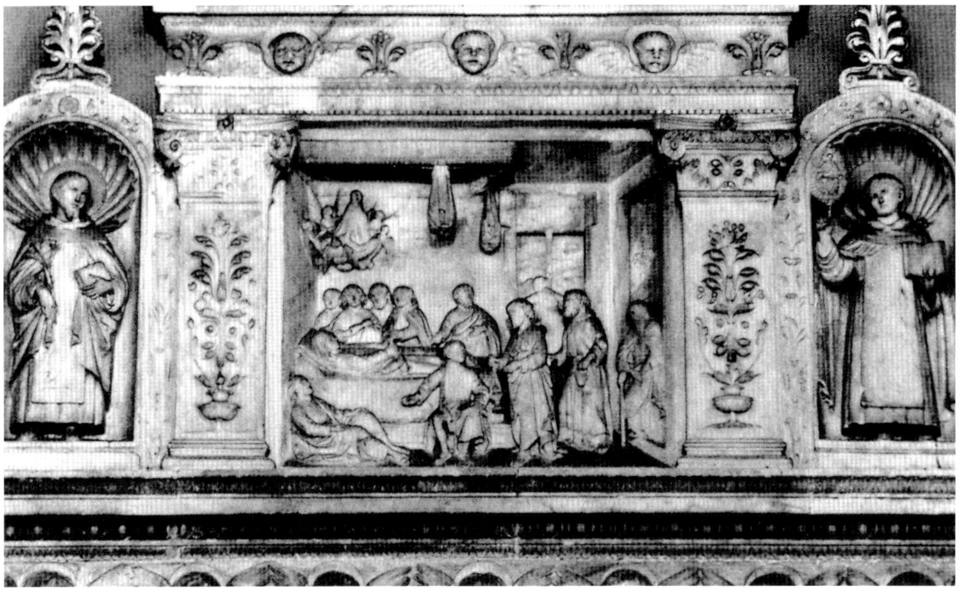

Fig. 5. Studio of Antonello Gagini, *Death of the Virgin*, ca. 1503–4 (detail of the retable). Marble. Palermo, Santa Zita.

della Carità in Venice. However, there is no evidence to prove that the "maestro Piero de Fiandra" mentioned is Petrus Christus or that he is even an artist. He could just as well have been an art dealer or ship captain responsible for transporting the altarpiece. In any case, 1451 is too early a date for the *Death of the Virgin*, which is demonstrably later.

The provenance of both the Timken painting and the destroyed wings leads back to Italy, specifically to Sicily. Although the painting was traditionally thought to have been in the Santacanale family of Palermo from the fifteenth century up until the time it was sold to Knoedler and Company in 1938, Vincenzo Scuderi has discovered that it belonged previously to the Consiglio family of Sciacca, a town on the south side of Sicily.[10] Although the original location of the large altarpiece is not known, it apparently was seen by Vincenzo degli Azani, called Vincenzo da Pavia, who was directly inspired by it for his own version of the *Death of the Virgin* for the Chiesa del Carmine in Sciacca, which he left unfinished at his death in 1557.[11]

More significant proof that the *Death of the Virgin* was in Sicily early on is the fact that an exact copy of it was executed around 1503–4 for Santa Zita in Palermo, produced by the studio of Antonello Gagini (fig. 5).[12] The Christus altarpiece need not have traveled to Palermo at this time, for the Gagini were well known to have worked on commissions in Sciacca. Although this was later, there is no reason to believe that the altarpiece traveled to the Palermo area before it was transferred over to the ownership of the Santacanale family in 1865.

As with many of Christus's paintings, theories about the date of the *Death of the Virgin* vary from the 1440s, to the 1450s, to the 1460s. It now seems clear—from the sophisticated spatial representation of the painting, its mostly uniform perspective design, and the advanced stage in stylistic development of the preparatory drawing—that the Timken painting was created late in Christus's career, about 1460–65.[13]

—M.W.A.

NOTES

1. Jacobus de Voragine, *The Golden Legend,* trans. William Granger Ryan, 2 vols. (Princeton, 1993), 2:77–97.

2. There are miniatures where Christ in Majesty holds a wafer between his fingers which is an enlarged, cross-inscribed disk, representing concurrently the globe of Christ in Majesty and the eucharistic wafer. See C. Gottlieb, "The Mystical Window in Paintings of the Salvator Mundi," *Gazette des Beaux-Arts,* 6th ser., 56 (December 1960): 316.

3. Lola Gellman, "The *Death of the Virgin* by Petrus Christus: An Altarpiece Reconstructed," *Burlington Magazine* 112 (March 1970): 147–48.

4. Wilhelm Bode purchased the wings in Florence in 1908. See H. Posse, ed., *Die Gemäldegalerie des Kaiser-Friedrich-Museums* (Berlin, 1913), pp. 103–4, nos. 529E, F, for detailed color notes on the wings.

5. Erwin Panofsky, *Early Netherlandish Painting* (Cambridge, Mass., 1953), p. 490, and Peter Schabacker, *Petrus Christus* (Utrecht, 1974), pp. 132–34.

6. For comparisons see Maryan W. Ainsworth, *Petrus Christus: Renaissance Master of Bruges,* exh. cat., The Metropolitan Museum of Art (New York, 1994), pp. 146–53 and passim.

7. The exception to this is an early work by Bartolomé Bermejo of the Death of the Virgin which appears to have been directly influenced by the Timken painting. Bermejo was known to have traveled to Flanders early in his career, and Eric Young places the artist in association with Christus and his workshop ca. 1460, allowing for direct observation of Christus's work. Eric Young, *Bartolomeo Bermejo* (London, 1975), pp. 10–16, pl. 6.

8. Roberto Longhi, "Frammento siciliano," *Paragone,* no. 47 (November 1953): 26.

9. Joel Upton, *Petrus Christus: His Place in Fifteenth-Century Flemish Painting* (University Park, Pa., and London, 1990), p. 44 n. 54.

10. Vincenco Scuderi, "La collocazione originaria della *Morte della Vergine* attribuita a Petrus Christus, gia della collezione Santacanale a Palermo e ora a S. Diego di California," in *Antonello da Messina, Atti del convegno di studi tenuto a Messina,* November 29–December 2, 1981 (Messina, 1981), pp. 101–10. Scuderi does not mention any wings for the triptych.

11. See Vincenzo Scuderi in *Soprintensenza alle gallerie ed opere d'arte della Sicilia, Palermo. VII: Mostra di opere d'arte restaurate* (Spring 1972), pp. 27–28 and pl. XXIX; Teresa Viscuro ("Scheda sulle tavolette fiamminghe di S. Caterina e S. Rocco," *XI Catalogo di opere restaurate* [Palermo, 1980], p. 56) assumed that Vincenzo copied it from the Gagini marble, which is in Palermo. However, as Sciacca was the home of the Consiglio family, who probably owned the Christus *Death of the Virgin* early on, it is most likely that Vincenzo saw Christus's painting there.

12. Hanno-Walter Kruft, *Antonello Gagini und seine Söhne* (Munich, 1980), pls. 35, 41. This connection was first noted by Ursula Panhans-Bühler, in *Eklektizismus und Originalität im Werk des Petrus Christus* (1978), p. 124.

13. See Ainsworth, *Petrus Christus,* p. 153 n. 31, for a full listing of opinions about the date of the painting.

PROVENANCE

Sciacca, Sicily, 16th century; Gaetano Consiglio, Sciacca, until 1856; Marianna Consiglio, until 1865; Giuseppe Santacanale Denti, Palermo, by 1865; Villa Santa Canale, Bagheria, Sicily; sold, Knoedler and Co., New York, 1938; acquired by the Putnam Foundation, 1951.

LITERATURE

Adolfo Venturi, *Storia dell'arte italiana* 7, pt. 4 (Milan, 1915), p. 172, fig. 100 (before cleaning), as "Maestro della Meta del'400"; Raimond van Marle, *The Development of the Italian Schools of Painting,* 19 vols. (The Hague, 1934; reprint, New York, 1970), 15:402; Doris Brian, "The Masters of Gothic Flanders," *Art News* 41 (April 15–30, 1942): 14, 16, cover ill.; "Flemish Primitives," *Magazine of Art* 35 (May 1942): 168–69, ill.; Helen Comstock, "The Connoisseur in America," *Connoisseur* 110 (October 1942): 60, ill.; Joseph van der Elst, *The Last Flowering of the Middle Ages* (Garden City, N.Y., 1944), p. 70, pl. 47; Max J. Friedländer, "*The Death of the Virgin* by Petrus Christus," *Burlington Magazine* 88 (July 1946): 159–63, ill. opp. p. 159, pl. IIc, d; Germain Bazin, "Petrus Christus et les rapports entre l'Italie et la Flandre au milieu du XVe siècle," *La Revue des*

Arts 2 (December 1952): 194–209; Erwin Panofsky, *Early Netherlandish Painting,* 2 vols. (Cambridge, Mass., 1953), 1: no. 8, p. 490 n. 5; "Countrywide Loans from California," *Art News* 55 (November 1956): 33; Josua Bruyn, *Van Eyck Problemen* (Utrecht, 1957), pp. 111, 113, 119, pl. 40; Liana Castelfranchi Vegas, "I rapporti italia-fiandra, II," *Paragone,* no. 201 (November 1966): 48, pl. 33; Giorgio T. Faggin, *Petrus Christus* (Milan, 1966), pp. 1, 4; Agnes Mongan and Elizabeth Mongan, *European Paintings in the Timken Art Gallery* (San Diego, 1969), pp. 46, 47, 114–15, no. 14, ill.; Lola Gellman, "*Death of the Virgin* by Petrus Christus: An Altarpiece Reconstructed," *Burlington Magazine* 112 (March 1970): 146–48, ill.; id., "Petrus Christus" (Ph.D. diss., The Johns Hopkins University, 1970), pp. 244–52, 450–54, no. 20A; Charles Sterling, "Observations on Petrus Christus," *Art Bulletin* 53 (March 1971): 1–3, 8, 21, fig. 1; Joel M. Upton, "Petrus Christus" (Ph.D. diss., Bryn Mawr College, 1972), pp. 159–64, 392–96, no. 26; Peter H. Schabacker, *Petrus Christus* (Utrecht, 1974), pp. 132–34, as work erroneously attributed to Christus; Ursula Panhans-Bühler, *Eklektizismus und Originalität im Werk des Petrus Christus* (Vienna, 1978), pp. 17, 34, 72–74, 123–25, 131–36, no. 76, pl. 34; James M. Collier, "The Kansas City Petrus Christus: Its Importance and Its Dating," *Nelson Gallery and Atkins Museum Bulletin* 5 (September 1979): 27, 28, 34, fig. 4; Joanne Wright, "Antonello da Messina: The Origins of His Style and Technique," *Art History* 3 (March 1980): 44, 56; Maria Grazia Paolini, "Problemi antonelliani i rapporti con la pittura fiamminga," *Storia dell'Arte,* nos. 38–40 (1980): 163–65; A. T. Lurie, "Newly Discovererd Eyckian St. John the Baptist in a Landscape," *Cleveland Museum Bulletin* 67 (April 1981): 105, 109, 118; Martin E. Petersen, "Three Centuries of European Paintings, 1300–1600," *Apollo* 115 (June 1982): 441, pl. 1; *Timken Art Gallery: European and American Works of Art in the Putnam Foundation Collection* (San Diego, 1983), pp. 30–31, 117, no. 8, ill.; Joel M. Upton, *Petrus Christus: His Place in Fifteenth-Century Flemish Painting* (London, 1990), pp. 44, 65, 71–77, fig. 64; Hans J. van Miegroet, "Petrus Christus, *The Death of the Virgin,*" in *Flemish Paintings in America* (Antwerp, 1992), pp. 60–62; id., "Afterthoughts and Challenges to Modern-Day Connoisseurship," in id., ed., *Petrus Christus in Renaissance Bruges: An Interdisciplinary Approach* (New York and Turnhout, 1995), pp. 205–14.

EXHIBITED

New York, M. Knoedler and Co., 1942, *An Exhibition of Flemish Primitives,* pp. 22, 23, ill.; Cambridge, Mass., Fogg Art Museum, 1948, *Early Flemish Painting;* Washington, D.C., National Gallery of Art, extended loan, 1952–65; New York, The Metropolitan Museum of Art, 1994, *Petrus Christus: Renaissance Master of Bruges,* cat. by Maryan W. Ainsworth, pp. 146–53, no. 15, ill.

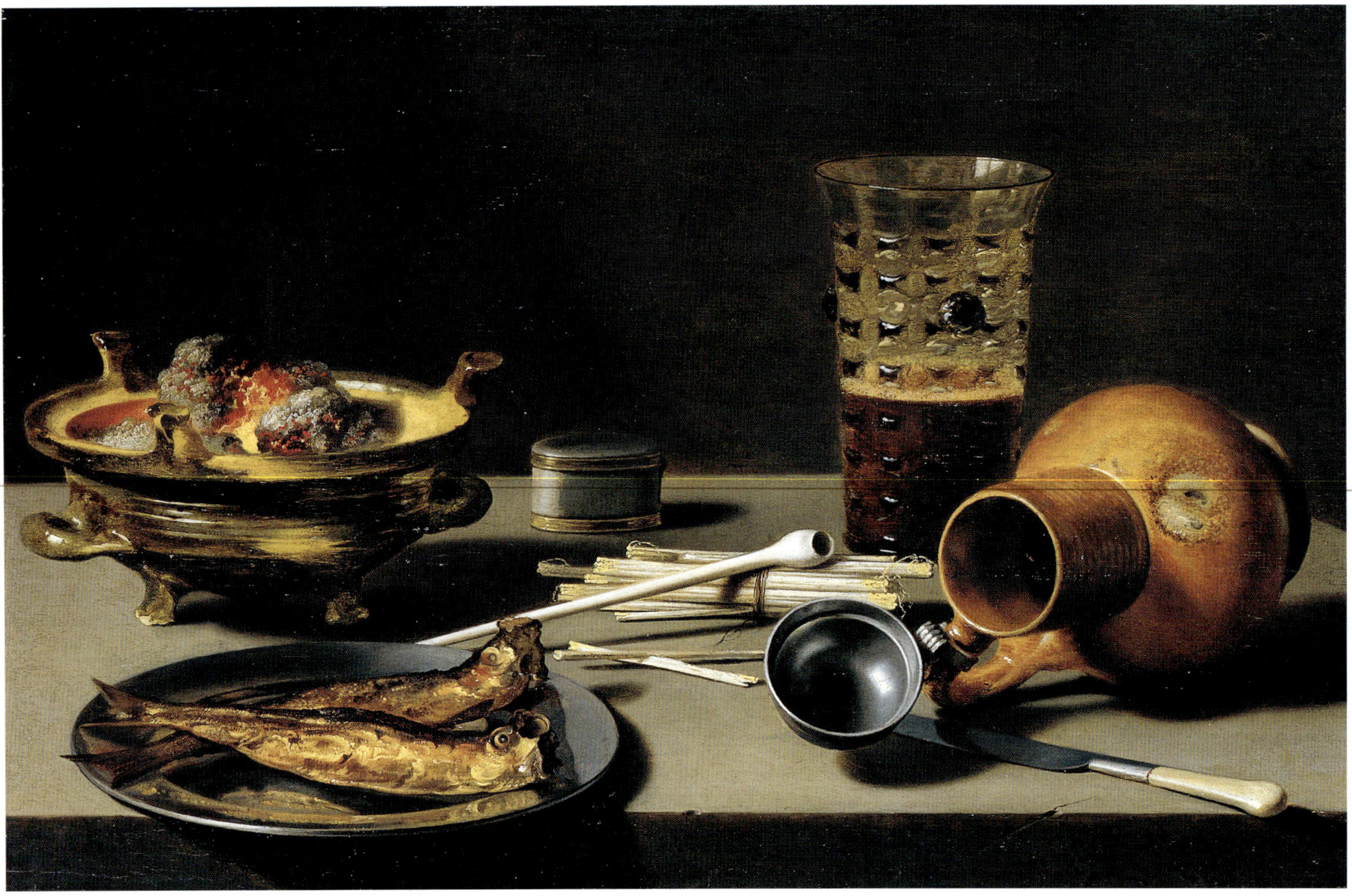

Pieter Claesz.

(1596/97–1661)

Claesz. was born in Westphalia in 1596 or 1597. He moved to Haarlem in 1617. The father of the landscape painter Nicolaes Berchem, Claesz. painted still lifes almost exclusively, displaying his originality in the form of effectively simplified compositions, usually consisting of only a few objects painted with considerable confidence and mastery in a subdued range of colors. He died in Haarlem in 1661.

13 *Still Life*, 1627
Oil on oak panel, 14¼ × 22⅝ in. (36.2 × 57.5 cm)
Signed and dated lower right: *PC Ao 1627* (PC in monogram)

The subject is a combination of the types known as breakfast pieces and smokers' requisites.[1] The type in this case consists of a pewter dish with two cooked fish, half a glass of stout, a knife, an overturned earthenware jug with the hinged metal lid open, a clay pipe, a small box for tobacco, a pot of burning charcoal, and a pile of tapers.

Before the seventeenth century, still life was not normally an independent branch of painting, though many large pictures of religious subjects included vases of flowers or open books or other still-life subjects in the background or on a ledge in the foreground.

A changed economic and social climate in seventeenth-century Holland gave rise to a new market for pictures. The lack of an aristocracy and a church that was not dependent on images for devotion, previously the sources of artistic commissions, meant that artists now often painted pictures of their own choice and then offered them for sale in the market. Claesz.'s pictures found favor with buyers, and he was able to spend much of his life devising different arrangements of domestic objects—often the same knives, jugs, and glasses. They are always painted with muted colors, and the different angles of the straight elements, such as knives or tapers, are contrasted with the curves of the glasses or jugs seen in perspective. This is well illustrated in the present picture.

—C. G.

NOTE

1. See N. R. A. Vroom, *A Modest Message: As Intimated by the Painters of the Monochrome "Banketje,"* 2d ed. (Schiedam, 1980).

PROVENANCE

Acquired by the Putnam Foundation, 1970.

LITERATURE

Timken Art Gallery: European and American Works of Art in the Putnam Foundation Collection (San Diego, 1983), pp. 32–33, 117, no. 9, ill.

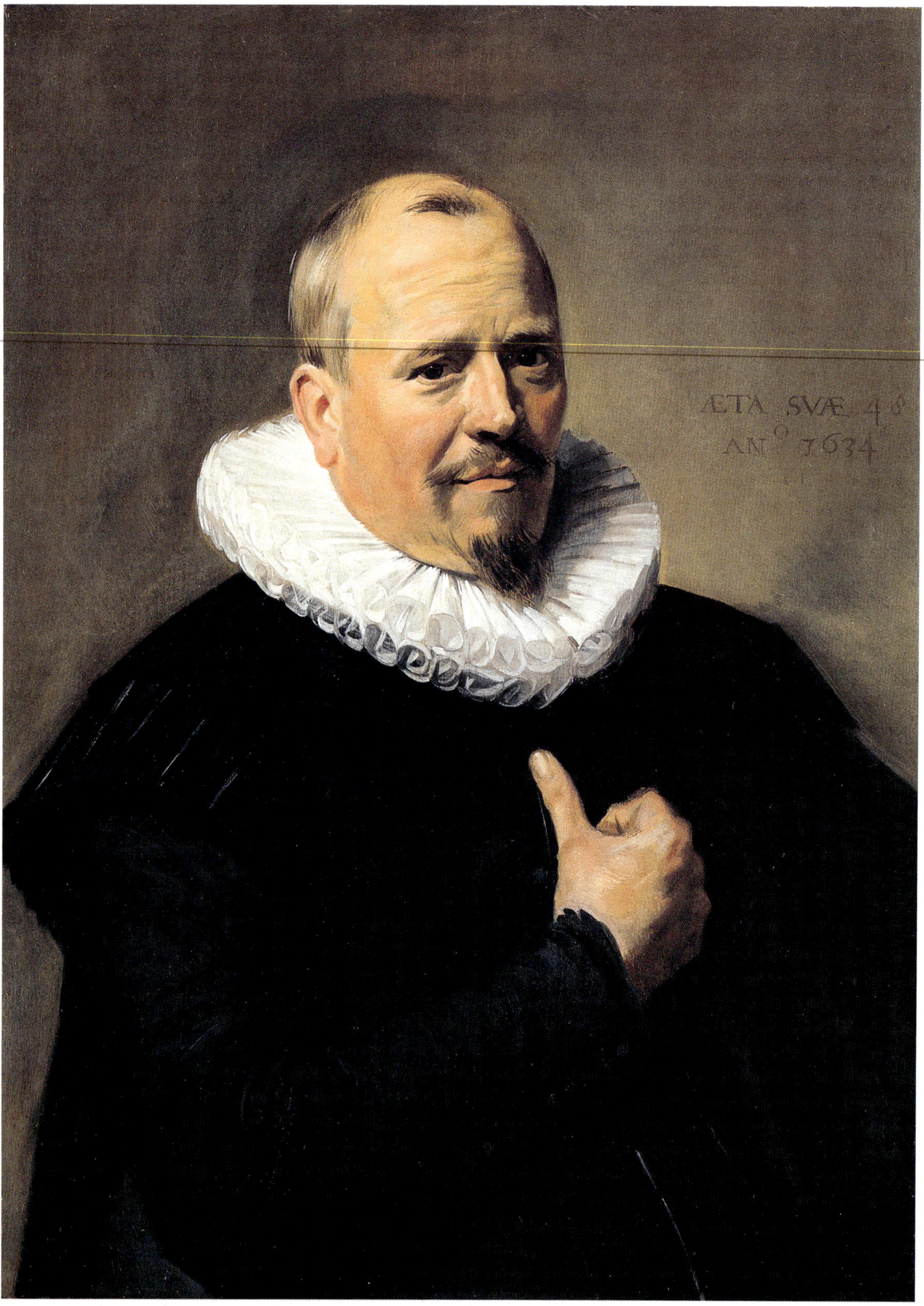
ÆTA SVÆ 46
ANº 1634

Frans Hals

(1581/85–1666)

Hals was born in Antwerp sometime between 1581 and 1585, the son of a weaver from Mechelen. He was a pupil of Karel von Mander from about 1600 to 1603. His first dated painting was a portrait of Jacobus Zafflius, done in 1611. The same year he enrolled as an associate of the Haarlem Society of Rhetoricians, De Wijn Gaertranken; his affiliation with the society lasted until 1625. By the 1620s, he was the leading portrait painter in Haarlem, which was the most important Dutch city at that time. In 1644 he served on the board of the St. Luke's Guild of Haarlem. His famous group portraits are all now in the Frans-Hals Museum, Haarlem. The artist was buried in St. Bavo's, Haarlem, in 1666.

14 *Portrait of a Man*, 1634
Oil on oak panel, 28⅞ × 22⅛ in. (73.3 × 56.2 cm)
Inscribed at upper right: *AETA SVAE 48 / ANo 1634 / FH* (FH in monogram)

A middle-aged man—the inscription gives his age as forty-eight—of slightly florid countenance with thinning hair and a light brown pointed beard is seen half-length, turned one-quarter right, silhouetted against a gray-brown background. He wears a black doublet with a white pleated ruff; a dark mantle is draped over his left shoulder. His right hand is raised to his chest.

This portrait, dated 1634, belongs to Hals's middle period. It was painted a year after the famous *Company of St. Hadrian* (Haarlem, Frans-Hals Museum). It has been suggested that there is a companion piece, inscribed *AETA SVAE 34 / ANo 1634 / FH.* That portrait, formerly in the Oppenheim collection, Cologne, is now in the Detroit Institute of Arts (fig. 1).

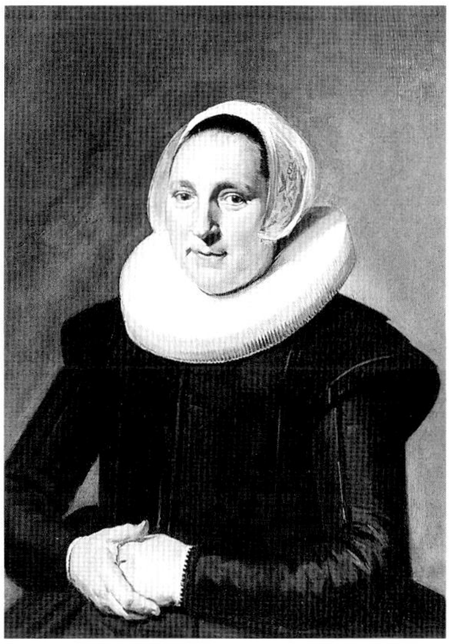

Fig. 1. Frans Hals, *A Woman*, 1634. Oil on wood panel, 28½ × 21½ in. (72.4 × 54.6 cm). The Detroit Institute of Arts, City of Detroit Purchase, 23.27. © The Detroit Institute of Arts 1994.

Seymour Slive, in the exhibition catalogue celebrating the centenary of the Municipal Museum at Haarlem,[1] noted the main characteristics of Hals's style in the 1630s, which mirrored those of Dutch art in general. Hals tended toward a greater unity and simplicity in composition. The richly embroidered clothes of the previous period are replaced by the black regent costume. The silhouettes of the figures become more regular, and there is new restraint in the use of pictorial accents.

The overall somber aspect of the painting is relieved by the penetrating eyes and the ruddy complexion of this interesting personage, whose identity remains unknown.

—A. M. AND E. M.

Eighteenth-century copies in watercolor (now in the Dayton Art Institute, Dayton, Ohio) of the present picture and of the companion portrait of a woman are inscribed as being after Johannes Verspronck (1597–1662). This is likely to be a copyist's error, as neither of the paintings resembles the style of Verspronck, nor is there any reason to question the authenticity of Hals's initials on the present picture. —C. G.

NOTE

1. (Haarlem, 1962), p. 46.

PROVENANCE

W. Unger, an artist who made an etching after the portrait, Amsterdam, 1872; Van der Willigen, Haarlem; Marczell de Nemes, Budapest and Paris, 1913; Baron M. L. Herzog, Budapest; acquired by the Putnam Foundation, 1955.

LITERATURE

Wilhelm von Bode, *Studien zur Geschichte der holländischen Malerei* (Braunschweig, 1883), p. 88; Hartung J. von Pflugk, "Hamburg, die Weber'sche Gemäldesammlung," *Repertorium für Kunstwissenschaft* 8 (1885): 82; Karl Woermann and Alfred Woltmann, *Geschichte der Malerei*, 3 vols. in 4 pts. (Leipzig, 1879–88), 3: pt. 2:599; Gerald S. Davies, *Frans Hals* (London, 1902), p. 141, no. 187; E. W. Moes, *Frans Hals: Sa Vie et son oeuvre* (Brussels, 1909), p. 106, no. 132; Cornelis Hofstede de Groot, *A Catalogue Raisonné of the Works of the Most Eminent Dutch Painters of the Seventeenth Century*, 8 vols. (London, 1908–27), 3:81, no. 280; Rudolph Lepke's Kunst-Auctions-Haus, Berlin, February 20–22, 1912, Sale Galerie Weber, Hamburg, lot 223, ill.; Francis de Miomandre, "Les Idées d'un amateur d'art (Collection Marczell de Nemes)," *L'Art et les Artistes*, no. 96 (March 1913): 254, ill.; Gabriel Mourey, "La Collection Marczell de Nemes," *Les Arts*, no. 138 (June 1913): 21, ill.; Galerie Manzi, Joyant, Paris, June 17–18, 1913, Vente Marczell de Nemes, lot 53, ill.; Wilhelm von Bode, ed., *Frans Hals: His Life and Works*, 2 vols. (London, 1914), 1:44, no. 145, pl. 85a; Wilhelm R. Valentiner, *Frans Hals*, Klassiker der Kunst (Stuttgart, 1923), p. 314, no. 124, pl. 124; id., *Frans Hals Paintings in America* (Westport, Conn., 1936), no. 46, ill.; N. S. Trivas, *The Paintings of Frans Hals* (New York, 1941), p. 41, no. 46, pl. 68; G. D. Gratama, *Frans Hals* (The Hague, 1943), pp. 39, 48, no. 48, pl. 48; Agnes Mongan and Elizabeth Mongan, *European Paintings in the Timken Art Gallery* (San Diego, 1969), pp. 64, 65, 121–22, no. 22, ill.; Seymour Slive, *Frans Hals*, 3 vols. (London, 1970), 3:56–57, no. 100, and 2: pl. 158; Claus Grimm, *Frans Hals: Entwicklung, Werkanalyse, Gesamtkatalog* (Berlin, 1972), pp. 91, 202, no. 65; E. Montagni, *L'opera completa di Frans Hals* (Milan, 1974), pp. 97–98, no. 87, fig. 87; *Timken Art Gallery: European and American Works of Art in the Putnam Foundation Collection* (San Diego, 1983), pp. 50–51, 119–20, no. 16, ill.

EXHIBITED

Düsseldorf, Kunsthistorische Ausstellung, 1904, *Katalogue*, cat. by Firmenich-Richartz, p. 133, no. 313; Düsseldorf, Kunsthalle Düsseldorf, 1912, *Katalog der aus der Sammlung des Kgl. Rates Marczell von Nemes—Budapest Ausgestellten Gemälde*, no. 41, ill.; Los Angeles Museum of History, Science, and Art, 1933, *Five Centuries of European Painting*, no. 14, ill.; San Francisco, California Palace of the Legion of Honor, 1934, no. 23; The Detroit Institute of Arts, 1935, *An Exhibition of Fifty Paintings by Frans Hals*, no. 23, pl. 3; Hartford, Wadsworth Atheneum, 1937, *Forty-three Portraits*, no. 17, ill.; Haarlem, Frans-Hals Museum, 1937, *Frans Hals Tentoonstelling*, p. 40, no. 50, pl. 51; New York, Schaeffer Galleries, 1937, *Paintings by Frans Hals*, no. 9, ill.; Providence, Rhode Island School of Design, 1938, *Dutch Paintings in the Seventeenth Century*, cat. by Wolfgang Stechow, no. 18, pl. 18; Los Angeles County Museum of Art, 1947, *Loan Exhibition of Paintings by Frans Hals, Rembrandt*, p. 17, no. 5, ill.; New York, Koetser Galleries, 1964, *Dutch Painting*, no. 12; Cambridge, Mass., Fogg Art Museum, extended loan, 1960–65.

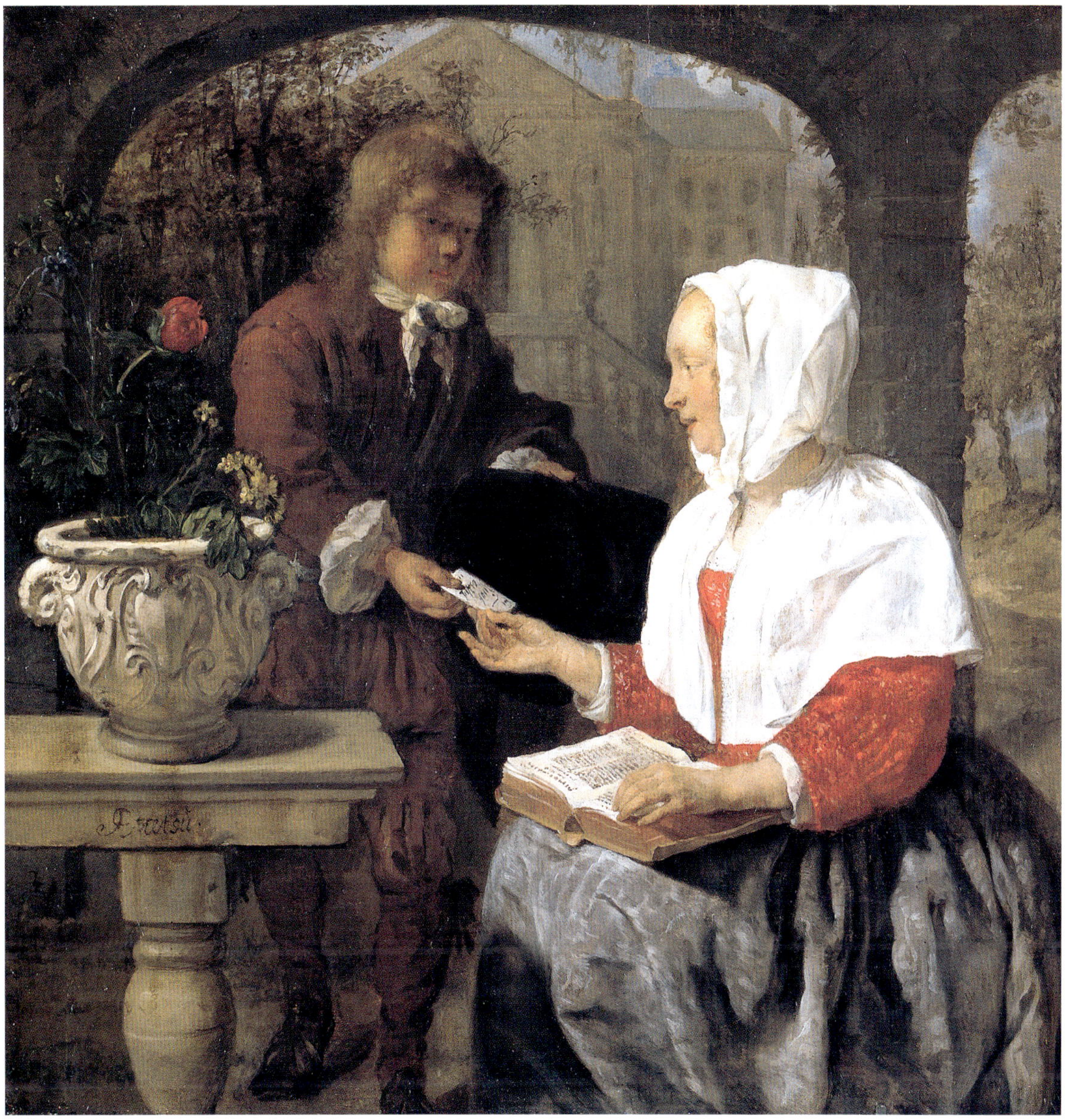

Gabriel Metsu

(1629–1667)

Little specific documentation has come to light for Gabriel Metsu's early life and training. However, the entry in the Amsterdam marriage registry recording the artist's wedding to Isabella de Wolff on April 12, 1658, establishes that Metsu was born in Leiden in early 1629. Frequent mentions in the records of Leiden's Guild of St. Luke, the painters' guild of which Metsu was a founding member in March 1648, place the painter in Leiden from the late 1640s through the mid-1650s. By 1657 Metsu had taken up residence in Amsterdam, living on the Prinsengracht near the brewery Het Rode Hert (The Red Stag). Metsu became a citizen of Amsterdam on January 9, 1659, and lived in his adopted city until his death. He was buried there in the Nieuwe Kerk on October 24, 1667.

15 *A Girl Receiving a Letter*, ca. 1658
Oil on panel, 10⅛ × 9⅝ in. (25.7 × 24.4 cm)
Inscribed lower left: *G Metsu* (possibly a later addition)

Gabriel Metsu is today celebrated for his scenes of everyday bourgeois life, quiet genre paintings realized in exquisite detail, which are the products of the last decade of his life. Because these later works resemble, both in technique and subject matter, those of the Leiden painter Gerard Dou, it has often been suggested that Metsu received his initial training with Dou in his native Leiden. However, Metsu's earliest known paintings, representing religious and mythological subjects, are fashioned in the broad style of the Utrecht artists Nicolaus Knupfer and Jan Baptist Weenix. This has led to the supposition that Metsu's absence from Leiden, around 1651–52, may have been spent in Utrecht. Once establishing himself in Amsterdam, Metsu focused increasingly on subjects drawn from everyday life, and he began to approach the minutely detailed, highly refined style of Dou and other members of the Leiden *fijnschilders*. The works from Metsu's Amsterdam period are the most accomplished of his short career, and it is from this period, about 1658, that scholars date the San Diego panel.

A diminutive work of delightful charm, the San Diego *Girl Receiving a Letter* is representative of a group of Dutch paintings dealing with the widely popular subject of the love letter. In such works, artists, including Gerard ter Borch and Johannes Vermeer, explored the theme of the love letter written and/or received. The establishment of a somewhat reliable postal system in the seventeenth century stimulated a vogue in letter writing throughout much of Europe. This fashion gave rise to a number of contemporary tracts on the craft of composing letters. Providing particular assistance with writing love letters, Jean Puget de la Serre's *Secrétaire à la mode* was translated into Dutch in 1651. Precisely at this moment, the theme enjoyed popularity with Dutch artists.

The pairing of two paintings to elaborate on the theme—one representing the letter writer, the other the letter receiver—is Gabriel Metsu's own invention. The San Diego *Girl Receiving a Letter* belongs to such a pair, its pendant being the *Man Writing a Letter* in the Musée Fabre in Montpellier (fig. 1). That Metsu conceived of these two paintings as a pair is evidenced by the similarity of their dimensions and their shared early provenance—the pictures are recorded together until they were sold in Paris in 1818. More important, the two compositions complement each other perfectly. In the Montpellier panel a man composes a letter, which the young woman in the San Diego panel receives. The two figures and their surroundings are cleverly contrasted: he works at his desk, the candle carried by the young maid countering the room's fading light; seated before a stone arcade with an airy view to a Palladian villa beyond, the young woman is interrupted by an adolescent messenger. If the two paintings were hung together as illustrated (figs. 1, 2), the main characters would be seen to be beautifully related by reciprocal pose and gesture.

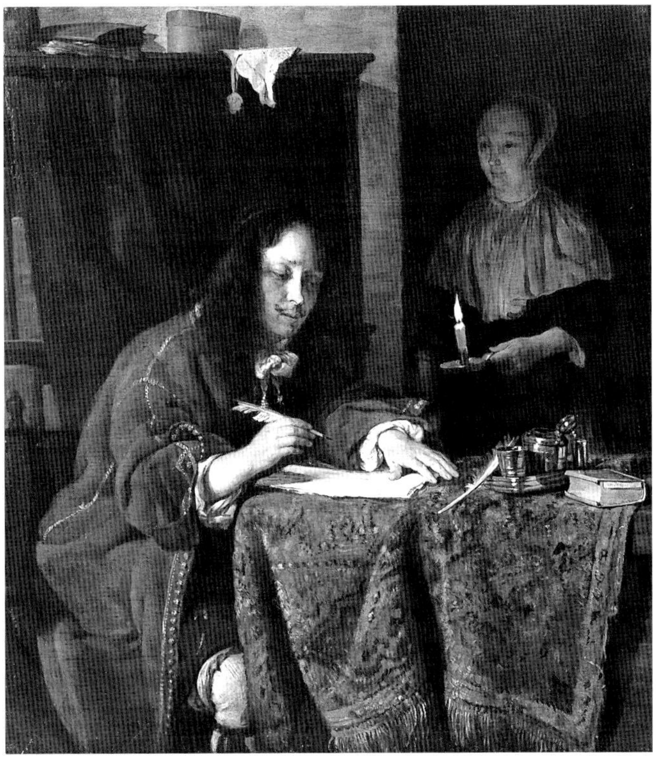

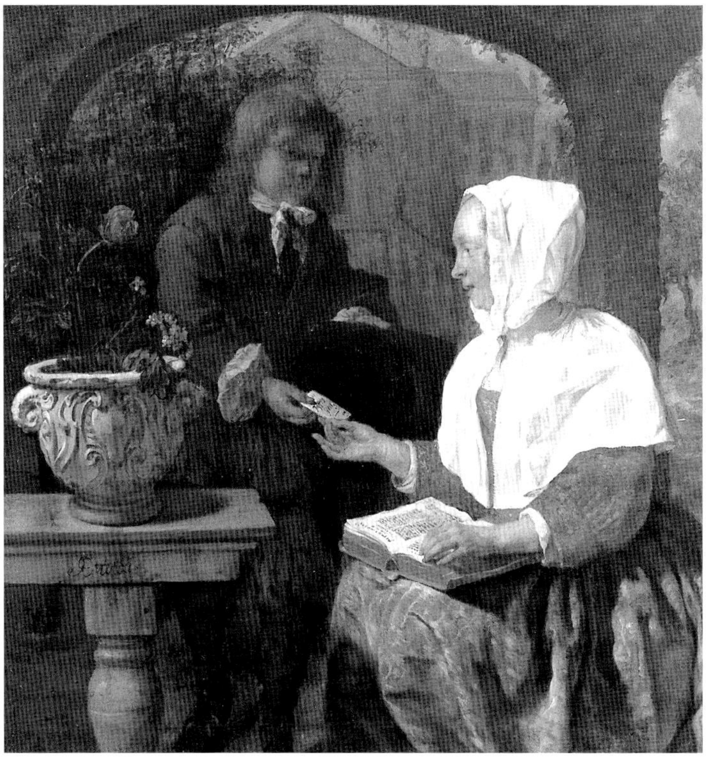

A strong physical resemblance exists between the facial features of these two figures and known portraits of Metsu and his wife, Isabella, suggesting that the artist cast himself and his spouse as the separated correspondents. The painting of paired portraits of husband and wife was popular in Holland in the seventeenth century, and Metsu ingeniously melded this portrait type with the genre theme of the love letter. Following the conventions of portraiture, Metsu placed the husband (himself) on the left and the wife (Isabella) on the right. Here, as was typical, the man is allowed a more casual, active manner, while tradition demanded that the young woman's composure be more formal and passive. Identification of the San Diego and Montpellier figures as Metsu and Isabella, whom he married in 1658—around the year that this painting is thought to have been painted—adds resonance to our understanding of the two paintings. The subject of the love letter written and received was treated by other artists, but rarely developed with such tenderness.

—L. F. O.

Fig. 1. Gabriel Metsu, *A Man Writing a Letter,* ca. 1658. Oil on panel, 10⅝ × 10⅛ in. (27 × 25.7 cm). Montpellier, Musée Fabre, no. 836-4-38.

Fig. 2. Gabriel Metsu, *A Girl Receiving a Letter.*

PROVENANCE

The Dowager Boreel, Amsterdam, her sale, Amsterdam, September 23, 1814, pp. 6–7, lot 8; Van Iperen, Amsterdam; king of Sardinia (?); Mr. Stanley, London, *The Catalogue of a Superb Collection of Truly Valuable Dutch and Flemish Cabinet Pictures . . . ,* auction cat., June 7, 1815, p. 13, lot 170; Mme Le Rouge, Paris, her sale, Paris, April 27, 1818, p. 22, no. 34; Nieuwenhuys, Brussels; Auguste-Marie-Raimond, prince of Arenberg, Brussels; duke of Arenberg, Brussels; Wildenstein & Co., New York; acquired by the Putnam Foundation, 1958.

LITERATURE

Charles Spruyt, *Lithographies d'après les principaux tableaux de la collection de A. S. Monsigneur le Prince Auguste d'Arenberg avec le catalogue descriptif* (Brussels, 1829), p. 10, no. 54; *Catalogue et description des tableaux qui forment la collection de S.A.S. le Prince August d'Arenberg* (Brussels, 1833); John Smith, *A Catalogue Raisonné of the Works of the Most Eminent Dutch, Flemish, and French Painters,* 9 vols. (London, 1829–42), 4:95, 96, no. 70; W. Bürger [Théophile-Etienne-Joseph Thoré], *Galerie d'Arenberg à Bruxelles* (Brussels, 1859), pp. 140–41, no. 36; Auguste Marguillier, "L'Exposition des maîtres anciens à Düsseldorf," *Gazette des Beaux-Arts* 32 (1904): 284; C. Hofstede de Groot, *A Catalogue Raisonné of the Works of the Most Eminent Dutch Painters of the Seventeenth Century,* 8 vols. (London, 1908–27), 1:310–11, no. 183 (cf. nos. 24, 262); Edouard Plietzsch, "Gabriel Metsu," *Pantheon* 17 (January 1936): 5, ill.; Agnes Mongan and Elizabeth Mongan, *European Paintings in the Timken Art Gallery* (San Diego, 1969), pp. 72, 73, 123–24, no. 26, ill.; Franklin W. Robinson, *Gabriel Metsu* (New York, 1974), pp. 39–40, 41, 60, 81, fig. 76, frontispiece; *Timken Art Gallery: European and American Works of Art in the Putnam Foundation Collection* (San Diego, 1983), pp. 62–63, 121, no. 22, ill.; Franklin W. Robinson, *Gabriel Metsu: The Letter* (San Diego, 1985).

EXHIBITED

Brussels, Ducal Palace, 1855; Düsseldorf, 1904, *Kunsthistorische Ausstellung. Katalogue,* cat. by Firmenich-Richartz, p. 143, no. 341; Cambridge, Mass., Fogg Art Museum, extended loan, 1960–65; The Hague, Mauritshuis, and The Fine Arts Museums of San Francisco, *Great Dutch Paintings from America,* 1990, pp. 330–33, no. 42 (San Francisco only).

Rembrandt Harmensz. van Rijn

(1606–1669)

Rembrandt van Rijn was born in Leiden on July 15, 1606. He studied in the Latin School of Leiden about 1615–19 and enrolled in the University of Leiden in 1620. Nonetheless, from about 1619 to 1622 Rembrandt served as an apprentice to the painter Jacob van Swanenburgh and then (1623?) spent half a year with the prominent Amsterdam artist Pieter Lastman. The latter experience must have opened Rembrandt's eyes to art elsewhere in the Netherlands and Europe and inspired him to treat biblical, historical, and mythological themes.

Rembrandt's development in Leiden between 1626 and 1631 was extraordinarily precocious and prolific. About fifty paintings and many etchings date from the Leiden period and reveal the influences of Lastman's circle, the Caravaggesque painters of Utrecht, and a century of printmaking, from the work of Lucas van Leyden to Hendrick Goudt's engravings after Adam Elsheimer.

In the winter of 1631–32 Rembrandt moved to Amsterdam, to which he was drawn by commissions such as that for the *Anatomy Lesson of Dr. Tulp* of 1632 (The Hague, Mauritshuis). Many single and pendant portraits by Rembrandt, ranging in scale from small bust-length to large full-length pictures, date from the 1630s. Rembrandt also became a painter of ambitious history pictures (for example, *The Capture of Samson*, 1636, Frankfurt, Städelsches Kunstinstitut). He certainly employed assistants and had distinguished pupils such as Govert Flinck and Ferdinand Bol, but the recent notion that he ran a large workshop is implausible.

In June 1634 Rembrandt married Saskia van Uylenburgh (1612–1642), the daughter of an important politician and cousin of Hendrick van Uylenburgh, an Amsterdam art dealer. Saskia's dowry and Rembrandt's success made the years 1635–40 the most comfortable of his life. An imposing house in the Breestraat became Rembrandt's home and studio in 1639. He was evidently less successful in the 1650s and 1660s but still enjoyed the support of important patrons such as Jan Six and the admiration of many pupils.

Rembrandt's work dating from after about 1650 is generally more introspective than the theatrical pictures of the 1630s. In paintings such as *Aristotle with a Bust of Homer* of 1653 (New York, The Metropolitan Museum of Art), the use of light and shade subtly suggests dramatic moments and the play of thoughts and feelings in the figures' faces. Rembrandt had always emphasized optical experience, but in his later work this evolved in the direction of broader effects, so that light, textures, and the sense of form in space are rendered by complex schemes of loose brushwork and glazes.

As a widower from 1642, Rembrandt raised his son Titus (1641–1668) with the help of a housekeeper, Geertge Dircx, and from 1650 to her death in 1663 with Hendrickje Stoffels. In 1660 Hendrickje and Titus formed a company to protect Rembrandt from his debts, which had resulted in his insolvency in 1656 and sales of his household goods and art collection in 1656 and 1658. The last decade of Rembrandt's life was plagued by personal losses, but he remained intensely productive, as in *The Syndics of the Cloth Drapers' Guild, The Jewish Bride* (both Amsterdam, Rijksmuseum), and a number of profound self-portraits. The latter complete a visual diary that began in Leiden and suggests a complicated self-awareness. Rembrandt died on October 4, 1669, and was buried in the Westerkerk in Amsterdam. Hundreds of drawings and etchings as well as about 320 paintings are known. About twice that number of pictures was assigned to Rembrandt in the early twentieth century, which attests to his effectiveness as a teacher and to the impression he made on artists of three centuries.

16 *St. Bartholomew*, 1657
Oil on canvas, 48⅜ × 39¼ in. (122.7 × 99.7 cm)
Signed and dated center left: *Rembrandt / f. 1657*

The subject of this large and dramatic picture, St. Bartholomew, is identified by his traditional attribute, a butcher's knife. Almost nothing is known of the historical figure except that he was one of the twelve apostles. Later writers credit Bartholomew with spreading the Gospel in Lycaonia, India, and in particular Armenia, where he is said to have been skinned alive.

Rembrandt painted a number of pictures of apostles in the late 1650s and in or about 1661. Valentiner in 1921 and recently Tümpel (1993) have attempted to reconstruct one or two series of canvases. A few autograph paintings dated 1661, including the *St. Bartholomew* in the J. Paul Getty Museum (fig. 1), suggest that Rembrandt may have envisioned an apostle series at that time. However, the works brought into discussion present so many problems of attribution, conflicting sizes, and contrasting compositions that the idea of an intended series remains completely hypothetical. Rubens and other Northern European artists had produced series of apostle pictures. Rembrandt, by contrast, had painted independent pictures of apostles in the Leiden period and throughout his career was inclined to approach biblical figures as individuals rather than as types or members of groups. The *St. Paul at His Desk* of about 1629–30 (Nuremberg, Germanisches Nationalmuseum) looks forward to the Timken and Getty paintings of St. Bartholomew in that it depicts the apostle as reflective and

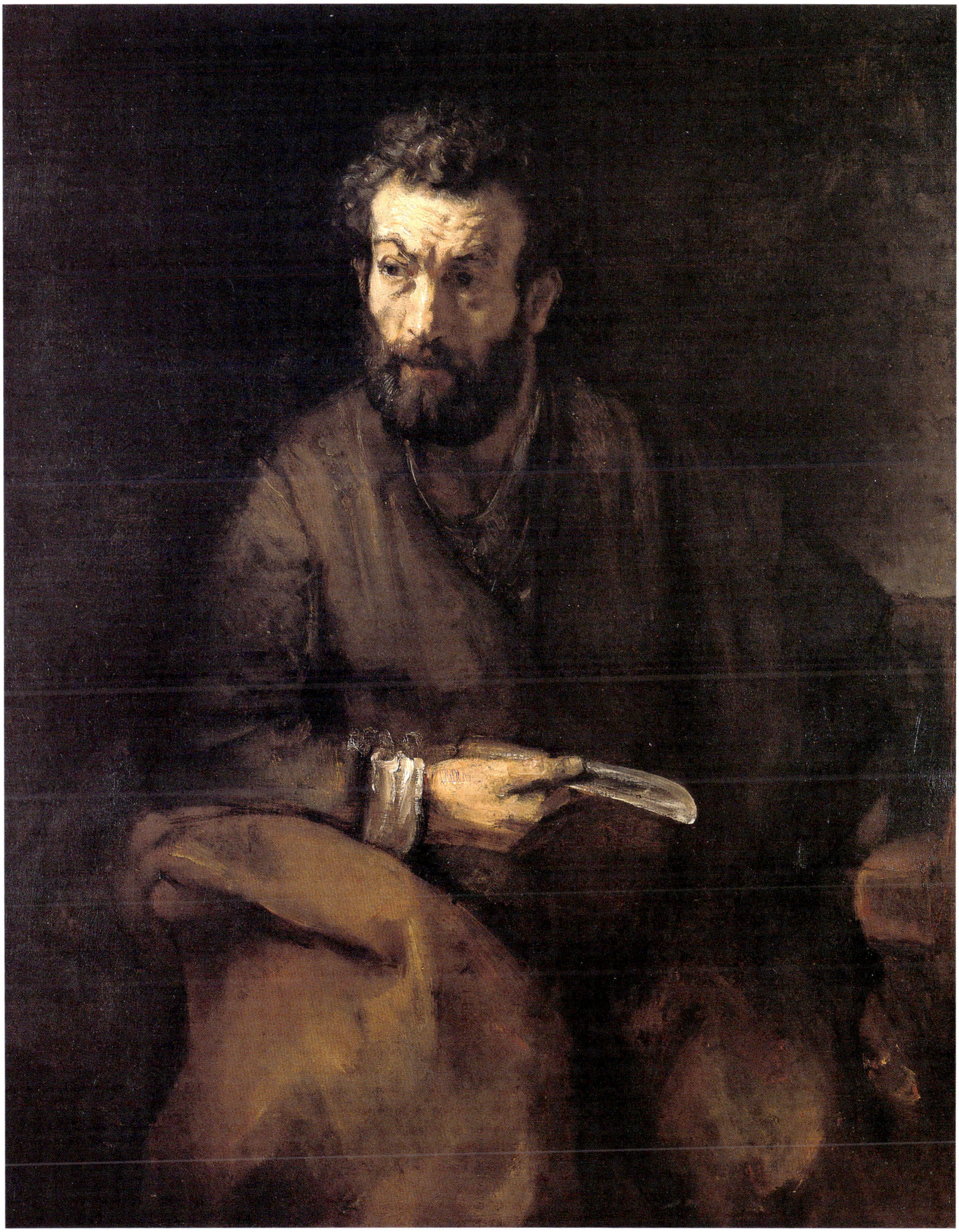

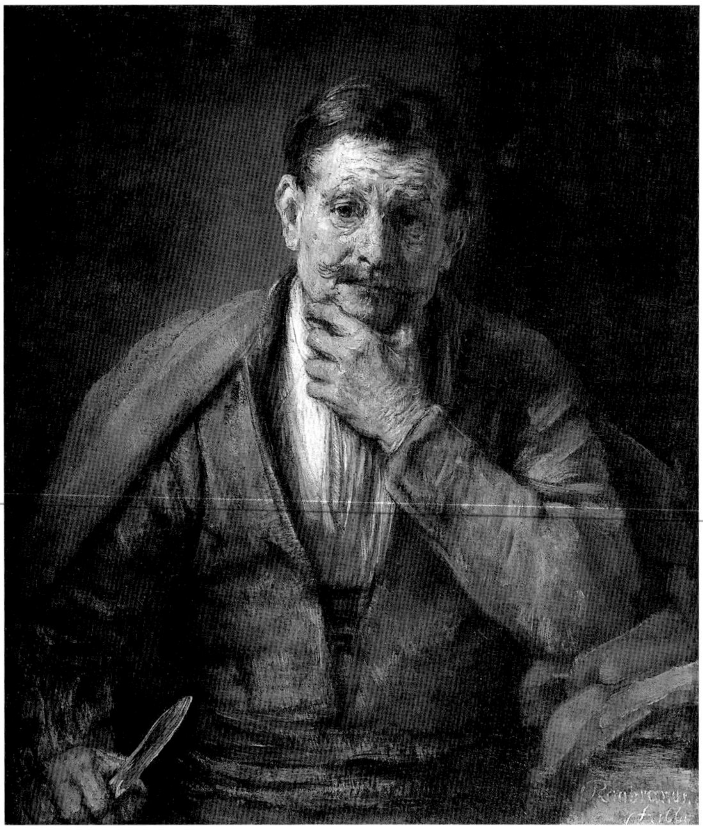

Fig. 1. Rembrandt Harmensz. van Rijn, *St. Bartholomew,* 1661. Oil on canvas, 34⅛ × 29¾ in. (86.7 × 75.6 cm). Malibu, California, Collection of the J. Paul Getty Museum.

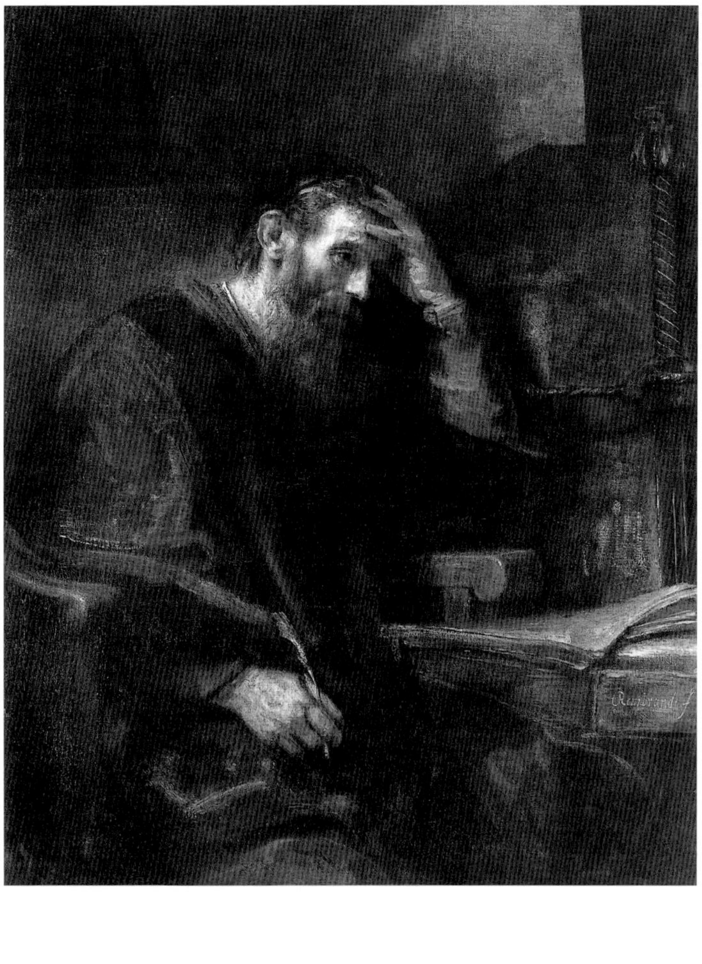

Fig. 2. Rembrandt Harmensz. van Rijn, *The Apostle Paul,* ca. 1657. Oil on canvas, 50¾ × 40⅛ in. (129 × 102 cm). Washington, National Gallery of Art, Widener Collection, 1942.9.59.

inactive, although the figure in the Timken picture is remarkable for its latent energy. Comparisons with the Getty painting, the *Apostle Simon* of 1661 (Zurich, Kunsthaus), and other pictures by Rembrandt, not to mention traditional representations of St. Bartholomew, also indicate that the knife functions mainly as an attribute (however evocative it may be for the viewer) and not as a narrative element: that is, the apostle does not contemplate his martyrdom but like all of Rembrandt's apostles is preoccupied by spiritual concerns or, more specifically, questions. As in *Aristotle with a Bust of Homer* there is a strong sense of pondering an ethical problem, which here seems to animate the eyes and forehead, the mouth, and the figure's unsettled pose. The hand with the knife (which was shifted slightly downward by Rembrandt and reveals *pentimenti* at the cuff and wrist) is an effective counterpoint to the saint's expression precisely because he, unlike the viewer, seems unconscious of what the object is.

In an earlier catalogue of the Putnam Foundation Collection (1983) it was stated that *The Apostle Paul,* a canvas of about the same size in the National Gallery of Art, Washington, D.C., is also dated 1657, and is generally regarded as a companion piece (fig. 2). In fact, the date is cut off, the picture was originally painted in a different format, and the two works are related only in that they treat similar subjects at about the same time in Rembrandt's career.

In his dissertation (Princeton, 1987) Francis Broun revealed that Sir Joshua Reynolds bought this painting at auction in 1757. The sale catalogue describes the subject as "A Man with a Knife in his Hand" (and the size as 48 × 39 in.), but Reynolds later listed it as "St. Bartholomew." In 1916 Hofstede de Groot reported that "the knife was formerly painted out and changed into a book." Broun also observes that the "Prince Lavalle" recorded in earlier literature as having taken the painting to Russia "can probably be identified with Anne-Adriaen-Pierre de Montmorency, duc de Laval, who was born in 1768 and who fled to England at the start of the French Revolution."

—W. L.

PROVENANCE

Jonathan Richardson, his sale, March 4, 1747, lot 49; Dr. Bragge, his sale, Prestage, London, February 9, 1757, lot 48; Sir Joshua Reynolds, London, from 1757; Anne-Adriaen-Pierre de Montmorency, duc de Laval, from about 1790; his daughter, Princess Troubetskoy; her daughter, Princess Davidoff; her grandson, Prince Wassili Davidoff, Kiev; Henry Goldman, New York; acquired by the Putnam Foundation, 1952.

LITERATURE

Wilhelm von Bode, "Neu entdeckte und wiedererstandene Gemälde von Rembrandt," *Der Cicerone* 4 (July 1912): 505–8, ill.; C. Hofstede de Groot, *A Catalogue Raisonné of the Works of the Most Eminent Dutch Painters of the Seventeenth Century,* 8 vols. (London, 1908–27): 6:120, no. 169; Wilhelm R. Valentiner, *Rembrandt: Wiedergefundene Gemälde,* Klassiker der Kunst (Stuttgart, 1921), p. 82, ill.; id., *The Henry Goldman Collection* (New York, 1922), no. 14, ill.; Georg Gronau, "Die Sammlung Henry Goldman," *Der Kunstwanderer* 6 (1924): 345; Frank E. Washburn Freund,

"Eine Ausstellung niederländischer Malerei in Detroit," *Der Cicerone* 17 (May 1925): 461, 463, ill.; Werner Weisbach, *Rembrandt* (Berlin, 1926), pp. 577–78, 626; W. R. Valentiner, "The Henry Goldman Collection," *Art News* 25 (May 14, 1927): 17, ill.; id., "Important Rembrandts in American Collections," *Art News* 28 (April 26, 1930): 65, ill.; A. Bredius, *The Paintings of Rembrandt* (London, 1937), p. 26, no. 613, ill.; "Countrywide Loans from California," *Art News* 55 (November 1956): 33; Kurt Bauch, *Rembrandt Gemälde* (Berlin, 1966), p. 12, no. 217, ill.; Sherman E. Lee, "Rembrandt: *Old Man Praying*," *Bulletin of the Cleveland Museum of Art* 54 (December 1967): 301 n. 7; Horst Gerson, *Rembrandt Paintings* (Amsterdam, 1968), p. 378, no. 296, ill.; Richard Hamann, *Rembrandt* (Berlin, 1969), p. 460; Paolo Lecaldano, *L'opera pittorica completa di Rembrandt* (Milan, 1969), pp. 118, 119, no. 357, ill.; Agnes Mongan and Elizabeth Mongan, *European Paintings in the Timken Art Gallery* (San Diego, 1969), pp. 66, 67, 122–23, no. 23, ill.; Otto Benesch, *Collected Writings*, ed. Eva Benesch, 4 vols. (London, 1970–73), 1 (Rembrandt): 192–93, fig. 159; Claude Roger-Marx, *Rembrandt* (Paris, 1972), p. 342; J. Bolten and H. Bolten-Rempt, *The Hidden Rembrandt* (Oxford, 1978), p. 198, no. 470, ill.; Christopher Brown, *Rembrandt: Every Painting*, 2 vols. (New York, 1980), 2:58, no. 315, ill.; Jean-Luc Bordeaux, "Baroque to Neo-Classicism," *Apollo* 115 (June 1982): 450, fig. 9; *Timken Art Gallery: European and American Works of Art in the Putnam Foundation Collection* (San Diego, 1983), pp. 70–71, 122–23, no. 26, ill.; Gary Schwartz, *Rembrandt: His Life, His Paintings* (Harmondsworth, 1985), p. 310, fig. 352; Peter C. Sutton, *A Guide to Dutch Art in America* (Washington, D.C., 1986), p. 272, fig. 408; Leonard J. Slatkes, *Rembrandt: Catalogo completo dei dipinti* (Florence, 1992), p. 150, no. 80; Christian Tümpel, *Rembrandt: All Paintings in Colour* (Antwerp, 1993), pp. 341, 401, no. 80, ill.; Walter Liedtke, "Rembrandt and the Rembrandt Style in the Seventeenth Century," in Walter Liedtke, Hubert von Sonnenburg, et al., *Rembrandt/Not Rembrandt in the Metropolitan Museum of Art*, exh. cat., The Metropolitan Museum of Art (New York, 1995), 2:31, fig. 43.

EXHIBITED

New York, The Metropolitan Museum of Art, extended loan, 1913–14; The Detroit Institute of Arts, 1925, *Catalogue of a Loan Exhibition of Dutch Paintings of the Seventeenth Century*, no. 22; The Detroit Institute of Arts, 1930, *Catalogue of a Loan Exhibition of Paintings by Rembrandt*, no. 59, ill.; New York, Wildenstein & Co., 1950, *A Loan Exhibition of Rembrandt at Wildenstein*, no. 18, ill.; Toronto Art Museum, 1951, *Rembrandt Exhibition*, no. 10; Washington, D.C., National Gallery of Art, extended loan, 1952–65.

Peter Paul Rubens

(1577–1640)

Peeter Pauwel Rubens was born to Flemish parents in Siegen, Westphalia, on June 28, 1577. Rubens's father, Jan, had been the lawyer, advisor, and lover of Anne of Saxony, William the Silent's second wife. After her husband's death in 1586, Rubens's mother moved the family back to their native Antwerp. The young Rubens and his brother Philip, who was to become a distinguished classicist, went to Latin schools and learned to love Greek and Roman literature. Rubens's mother then placed him in service as a page to a widowed countess at the court of Brussels, where the future artist acquired the rudiments of his exceptional social polish and diplomatic skills. Rubens read widely, added French to his knowledge of Dutch and German, and cultivated an interest in art, in particular by drawing after examples of famous masters.

From about the age of fifteen in Antwerp, Rubens studied with three painters, the most important being Otto van Veen. In May 1600 Rubens left for Italy, where he visited Venice and then moved to Mantua, seat of the famous Gonzaga court. Rubens served the duke of Mantua for nearly eight years but also worked in Genoa and for long periods in Rome. The most distant of his many travels in this Italian period was the trip to Spain in 1603 as the duke's goodwill ambassador. The foundations of Rubens's mature style were laid in Rome, where he passionately studied antiquity, the Early and High Renaissance, and the major talents of the moment, in particular Annibale Carracci and Caravaggio. Rubens himself became one of the most modern and successful artists in Italy.

Rubens returned to Antwerp at the end of 1608 and was kept there by extraordinary opportunities. He was appointed court painter of the regents of the Spanish Netherlands, Archduke Albert and Archduchess Isabella, but he was allowed to live in Antwerp, with freedom from regulation by the painters' guild. This enabled Rubens to organize a large workshop which was needed to redecorate the many churches that had been attacked by Protestant iconoclasts. In 1609 Rubens married Isabella Brant, whose father, Jan Brant, was a wealthy tapestry merchant and city secretary. In 1610 Rubens bought the large house that he was to transform into a model of Renaissance design and a factory of baroque painting.

Great altarpieces predominate in Rubens's oeuvre from about 1610 through the early 1620s, but he also produced designs for tapestry cycles, the oil sketches for thirty-nine ceiling paintings in the Jesuit church of Antwerp, a number of portraits, mythological and biblical pictures for private patrons, and large hunting scenes for princely collectors such as the duke of Bavaria. To spread his fame and protect his fortune Rubens supervised the production of engravings after his Antwerp designs. By the 1620s he was recognized as the foremost painter of decorative projects outside Italy and as a powerful propagandist of the church and state. Rubens and his workshop painted the Maria de' Medici cycle (Paris, Musée du Louvre), the ceiling paintings for the Banqueting House at Whitehall, London, other secular projects, and numerous altarpieces and independent religious pictures.

In 1630 Rubens married the young Helena Fourment, with whom he had five children. He painted a number of landscapes and family portraits in the 1630s, mostly for his own pleasure. The artist died on May 30, 1640. His influence on contemporary Flemish art was enormous and was decisive for the early careers of Anthony van Dyck and Jacob Jordaens. Later artists as diverse as Watteau, Fragonard, Reynolds, Géricault, and Delacroix deeply admired his work.

17 *Portrait of a Young Man in Armor*, ca. 1620
Oil on canvas (transferred from panel), 25½ × 20 in. (64.8 × 50.8 cm)

This bust-length picture of a handsome, curly-haired young man in contemporary armor, with a red sash or scarf thrown over his shoulder, has been variously dated and described (usually as a portrait), but it has never been doubted as a superb study by Rubens in a very good state of preservation. The present writer would suggest dating the painting very approximately about 1620 and regarding it as a study head (or *tronie* in Dutch) based on a live model but not intended as a portrait. The traditional title, *Portrait of a Young Captain*, captures the dashing spirit of the picture, but only the word "young" can be defended conclusively, and that by viewers who would so describe a man in his twenties.

In the first half of this century the painting was usually discussed as a "Portrait of a Duke of Mantua" and dated accordingly. Held, for example, suggested "the very end of Rubens's stay in Italy, about 1608." This view was encouraged by the listing in Charles I's collection of a "picture of the deceased young duke of Mantuas brother done in armoure to the Shouldrs by Sr Peeter Paule Rubins when he was in Italie" (see Jaffé 1961). However, the sitter bears no resemblance to Francesco Gonzaga or any other Mantuan prince, and the manner of execution is strongly reminiscent of Rubens's study heads and portraits dating from ten to fifteen years after he returned to Antwerp. A more likely possibility is that this panel is "The picture of a man in armour with a red scarfe" listed as number 129 in the *Specification*, or inventory, of paintings in Rubens's house at his death in 1640. Muller mentions a Rubensian *Head of a Warrior* in the Hermitage, St. Petersburg,[1] but that older, bearded man with a fancy hat would seem, by the *Specification*'s own standards, to be less well described by the entry than is the Timken painting.

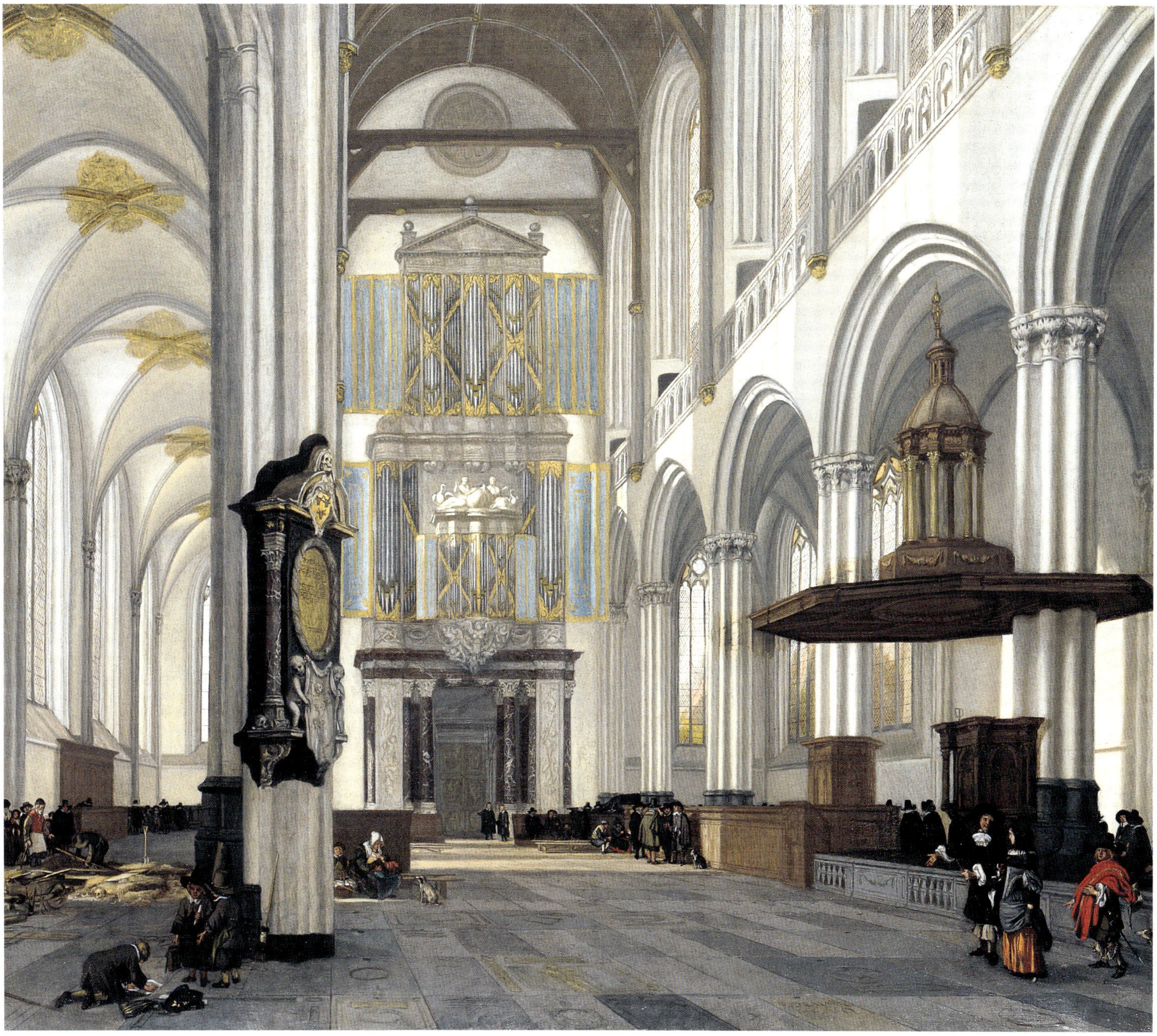

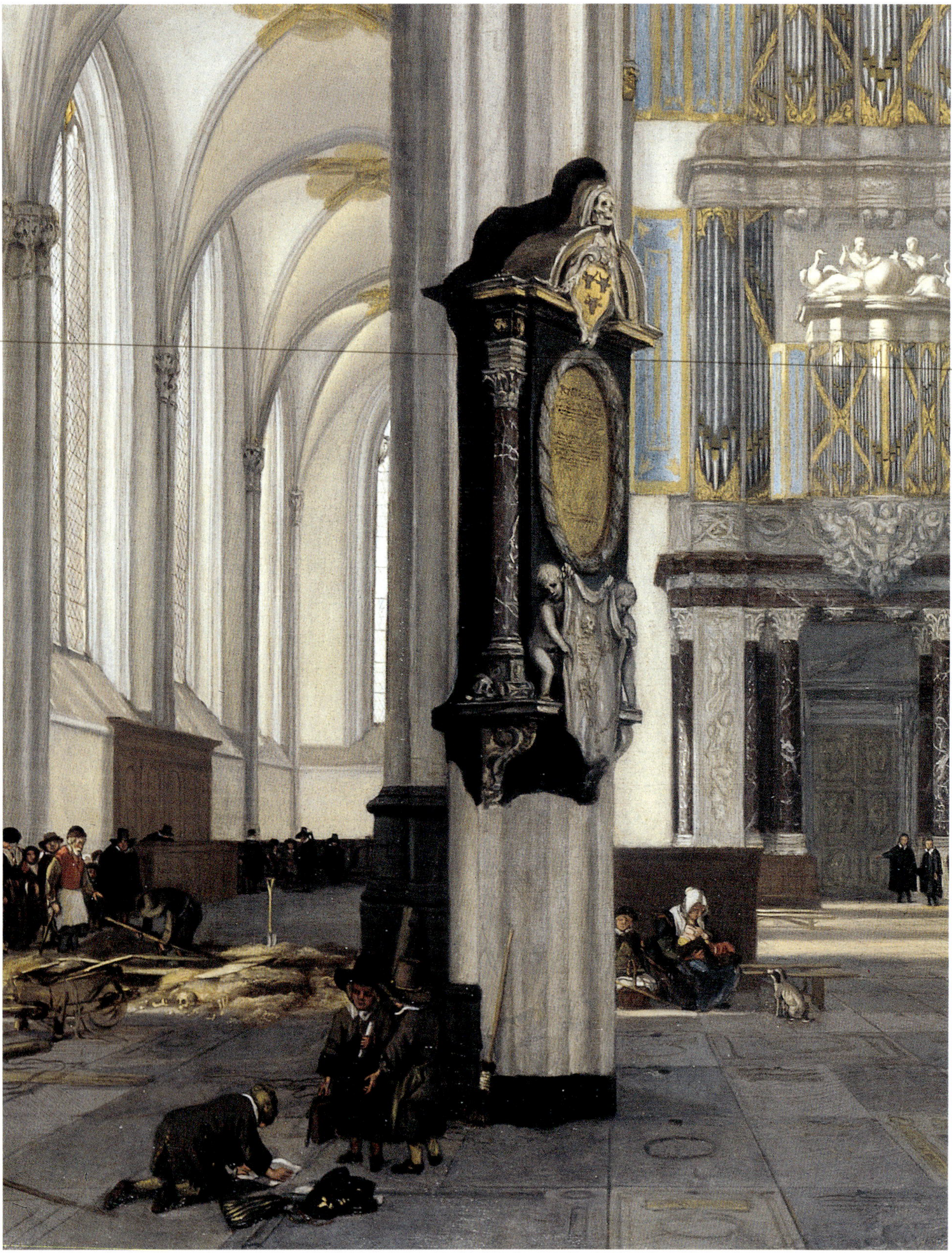

Detail of Plate 19

before 1664. The great organ, also shown here, likewise dates from after the fire of 1645. Its case was designed by the well-known architect Jacob van Campen.

The coat of arms on the monument attached to the pillar on the left was identified by Professor I. G. van Gelder (in a private communication) as that of the Coymans family. Professor Van Gelder found that the two Coymans brothers, Balthasar and Joan, both died in the year 1657, the year in which the Timken picture was painted. The brothers married sisters, Maria and Sophia, from the family Trip, a dynasty of armaments manufacturers. Portraits of members of the Trip family were painted by many of the leading Dutch painters of the day, including Rembrandt. Since Joan Coymans died at Velsen, and his brother, Balthasar, in Amsterdam, the picture more likely commemorates the latter, whose grave may be that which is being dug. In the early 1980s the Coymans monument was not where De Witte depicts it. Inquiries made at the church reveal that this monument is thought to have been dismantled before 1900 and has since disappeared. As De Witte is known to have taken topographical liberties on occasion, it is not certain if it ever appeared as it does in this painting.

—C. G.

PROVENANCE

Jean-Louis Turrentine, Geneva, ca. 1760; by descent to Mme Louis Perrot de Montmollin, her sale, Christie's, London, June 27, 1969, lot 71; acquired by the Putnam Foundation, 1970.

LITERATURE

Walter Liedtke, "Architectural Painting in Delft: Gerard Houckgeest, Hendrick van Vliet, Emanuel de Witte," *Aetas Area,* Monographs on Dutch and Flemish Painting, 3 (Doornspijk, ca. 1982), no. 239; *Timken Art Gallery: European and American Works of Art in the Putnam Foundation Collection* (San Diego, 1983), pp. 86–87, 125, no. 33, ill.

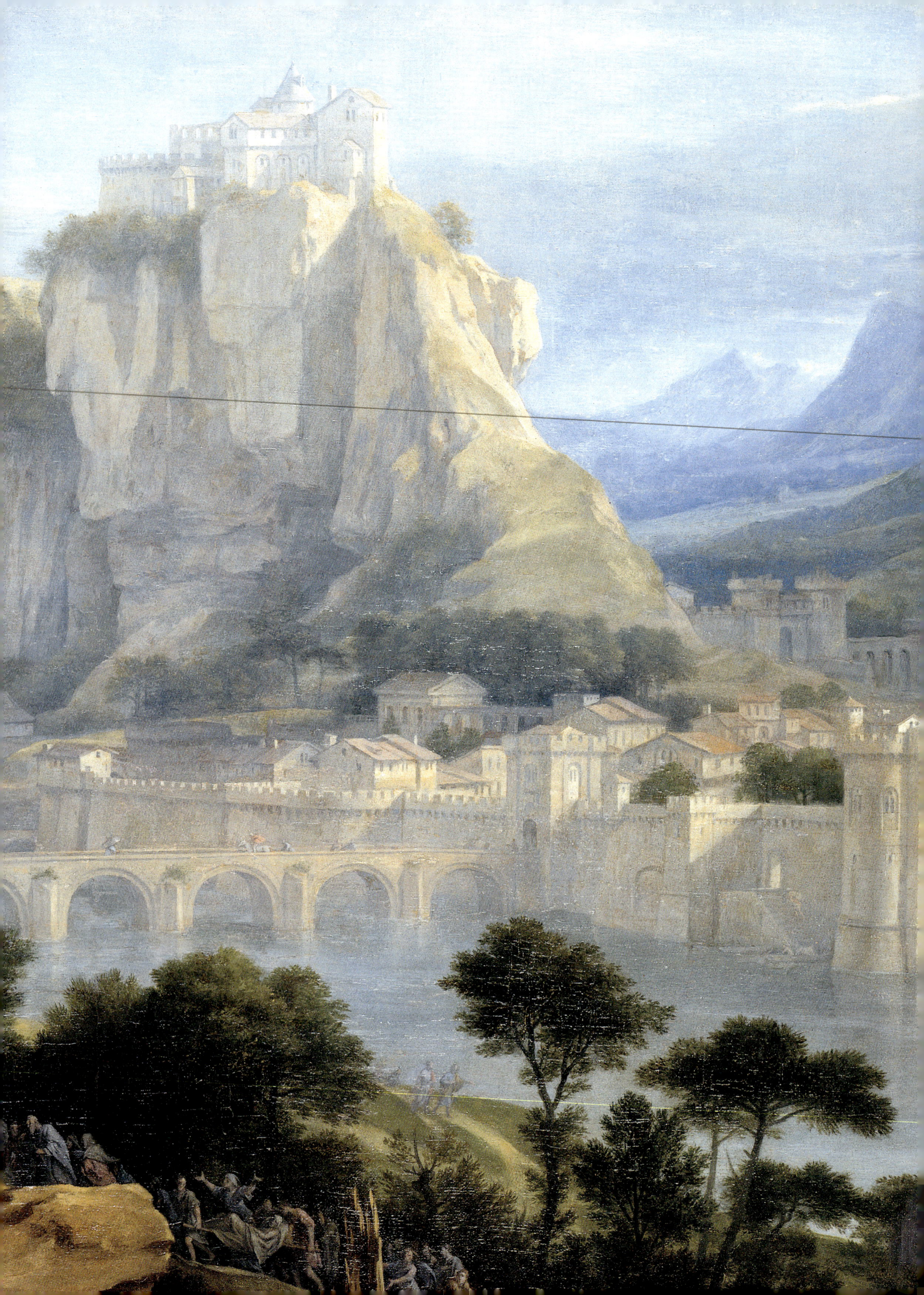

French Tapestries and Paintings

French School

20 Four *Entrefenêtre* Tapestries from the Series *Stories of Queen Artemisia*
Central designs by Antoine Caron (French, 1521–1599), France, ca. 1562–65. Border designs probably by Henry Lerambert (ca. 1540/50–1608). Cartoons by various artists, France, ca. 1600–1617. Woven by various masters in the Faubourg Saint-Marcel manufactory of Marc de Comans (Flemish, 1563–1644) and François de la Planche (Flemish, 1573–1627), Paris, ca. 1620. Slit tapestry woven on low-warp looms; warp: undyed wool threads, ca. 20 per inch; weft: dyed wool and silk threads and silver and silver-gilt metallic threads, ca. 33–45 per inch.

A. *The Requests of the Citizens (Les Requêtes du peuple)*
185 × 64 in. (469.9 × 162.6 cm)

B. *The Petitions (Les Placets)*
186 × 94 in. (472.4 × 238.8 cm)

C. *The Queen Distributing the Booty (La Reine distribue le butin)*
183 × 93 in. (464.8 × 236.2 cm)

D. *A Group of Soldiers*
186 × 94 in. (472.4 × 238.8 cm)

The Timken's four tapestries are examples of one of the most successful of all French tapestries series, the *Stories of Queen Artemisia.*[1] They are also from what was numerically the largest and one of the richest known sets of the *Artemisia* series. These eighteen or more tapestries, woven in Paris sometime between 1611 and about 1620, originally decorated the palace of Duke Charles Emmanuel I of Savoy (1562–1630) in Turin, Italy, and the remnants of at least sixteen of them are still identifiable.[2]

Charles Emmanuel, who had married the sister of King Henry IV of France (1553–1610), was active in the chess games of war and politics that rattled Europe during the late sixteenth and early seventeenth centuries, but perhaps because he was too devious, he was not the most successful player. He maintained most of his family's lands in the Piedmont (northwestern Italy) but in 1601 was forced to give up parts of Savoy (now all of Savoy is in France, just southwest of Switzerland), and his military efforts to annex other areas proved fruitless. To strengthen his political alliances, he arranged a marriage between his son Victor Amadeus I (1587–1637) and Victor's first cousin, Christina of France (1606–1663), daughter of Henry IV and Marie de' Medici. It was celebrated in February 1619, when Christina turned thirteen.

In January 1620 Charles Emmanuel's ambassador finalized purchasing the *Artemisia* tapestries at the Faubourg Saint-Marcel manufactory, which was run by the naturalized Flemish weavers Marc de Comans and François de la Planche. As similar tapestries were used at the French court, these, which went to Christina, were a fitting tribute to the Savoy's now double marriage bond with France. They would also have been a public affirmation of the duke's continued wealth and power, for tapestries were prized, and priced, far above paintings. Great painters designed tapestries and created full-scale colored models, called *cartoons*, for expert masters to weave. Calculated to magnify their owners' grandeur by their rich weaving and symbolic stories, tapestries were customarily displayed as a total environment, entirely covering the walls of a room from the floor reaching toward the ceiling. Charles Emmanuel's unusual set would have been considered all the more impressive because it was of the most expensive and prestigious quality of tapestry, with not only wool and silk but also precious silver and silver-gilt threads. So that the tapestries would conform to the Turin palace more precisely, the ambassador had included in the order at least eight *entrefenêtres*—narrow pieces without side borders, designed to fit between windows and in other small spaces—with the duke's arms added at the top. Among these were the four Timken tapestries.

By 1620 the series from which Charles Emmanuel's tapestries came, *Stories of Queen Artemisia*, had an international reputation. Its intriguing history demonstrates how historical events can modify the course of art. In the 1560s Nicolas Houel, a learned Parisian apothecary, had created an epic tale to glorify the French queen regent Catherine de' Medici (1519–1589). A male ruler could turn to numerous historical and mythological heroes for role-model propaganda, but few heroines had comparable literary traditions.[3] Houel based his Artemisia story on two historical figures, adding other, imagined, events. The two Artemisias had been queens of Caria, an Aegean island today part of Turkey, in the fifth and fourth centuries B.C. The first was known for her military prowess. The second had built the Mausoleum of Halicarnassus, one of the Seven Wonders of the ancient world, for her deceased husband, Mausolus. Houel decided to have episodes of his book illustrated for Catherine by Antoine Caron and others, with the idea that these large drawings could be models for tapestries to announce the queen's virtues to the world. The apothecary also wrote a sonnet explaining each drawing, probably meant to be woven into the final tapestry's border. But before the drawings were completed, Catherine faced civil war and a depleted treasury and was unable to order any tapestries.[4]

Over thirty years and several French kings later, the remarkable King Henry IV reestablished peace and unity in France and turned to patronage of the arts both to glorify his reign and to create new jobs. With an eye to the balance of payments, he revived tapestry production, so that the wealthy would cease buying tapestries in neighboring Flanders. He subsidized the few weavers remaining in Paris and brought in Comans and La Planche to launch the Flemish low-warp technique. In low-warp

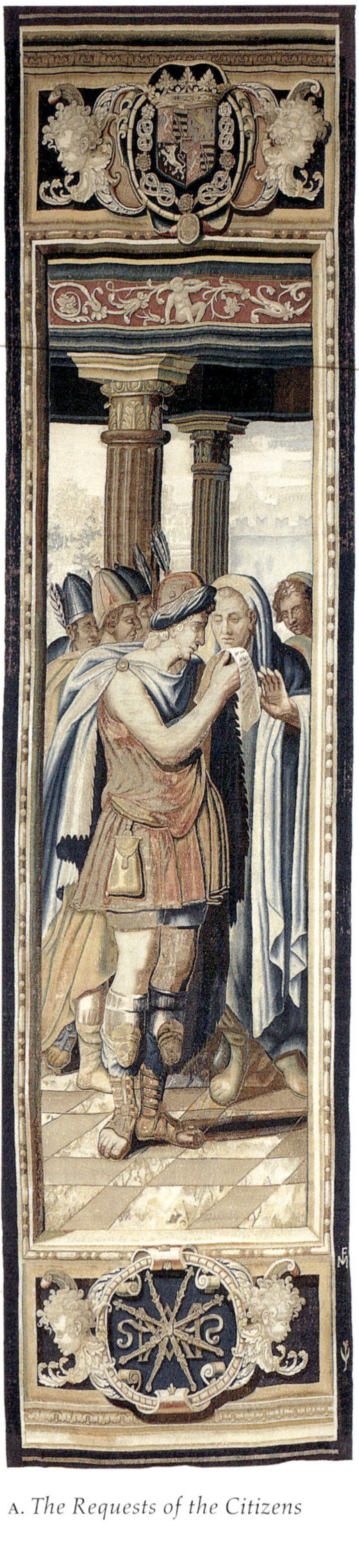

A. *The Requests of the Citizens*

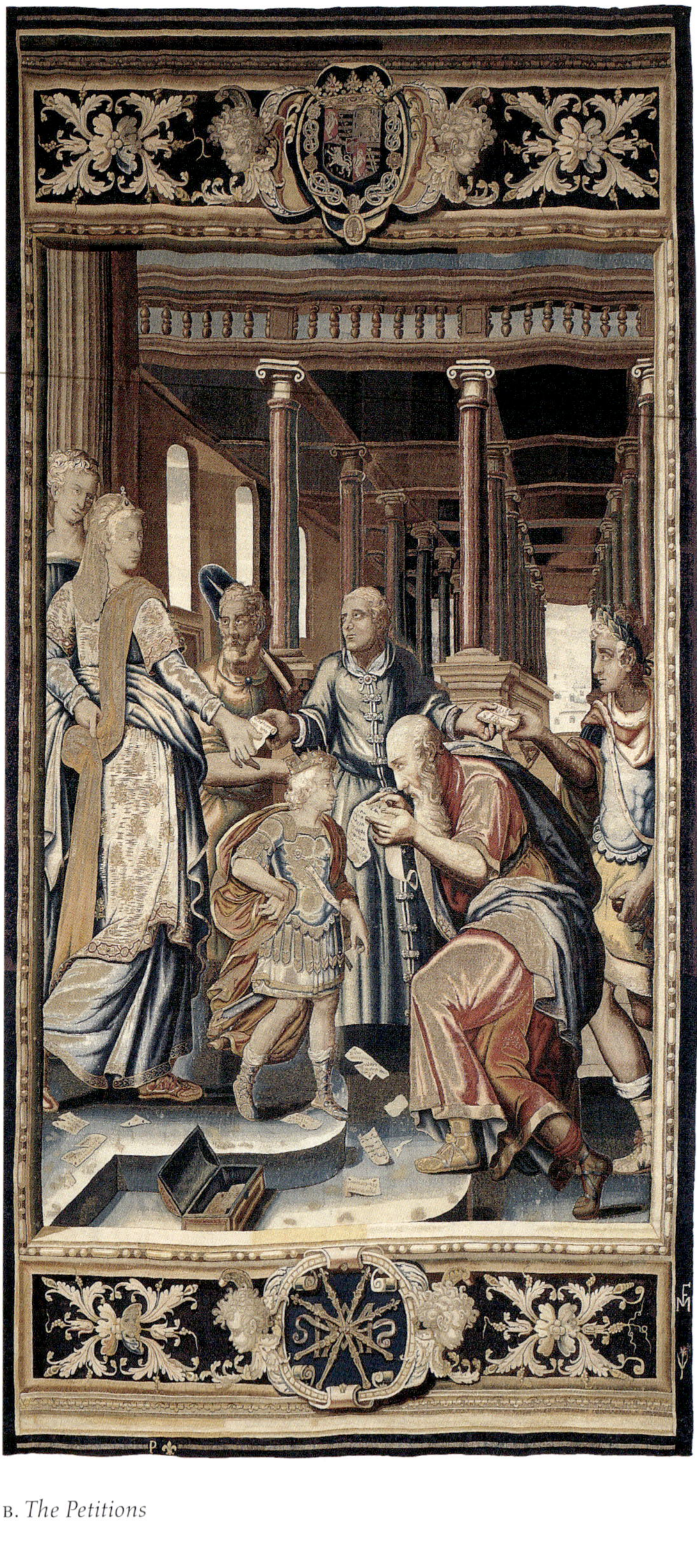

B. *The Petitions*

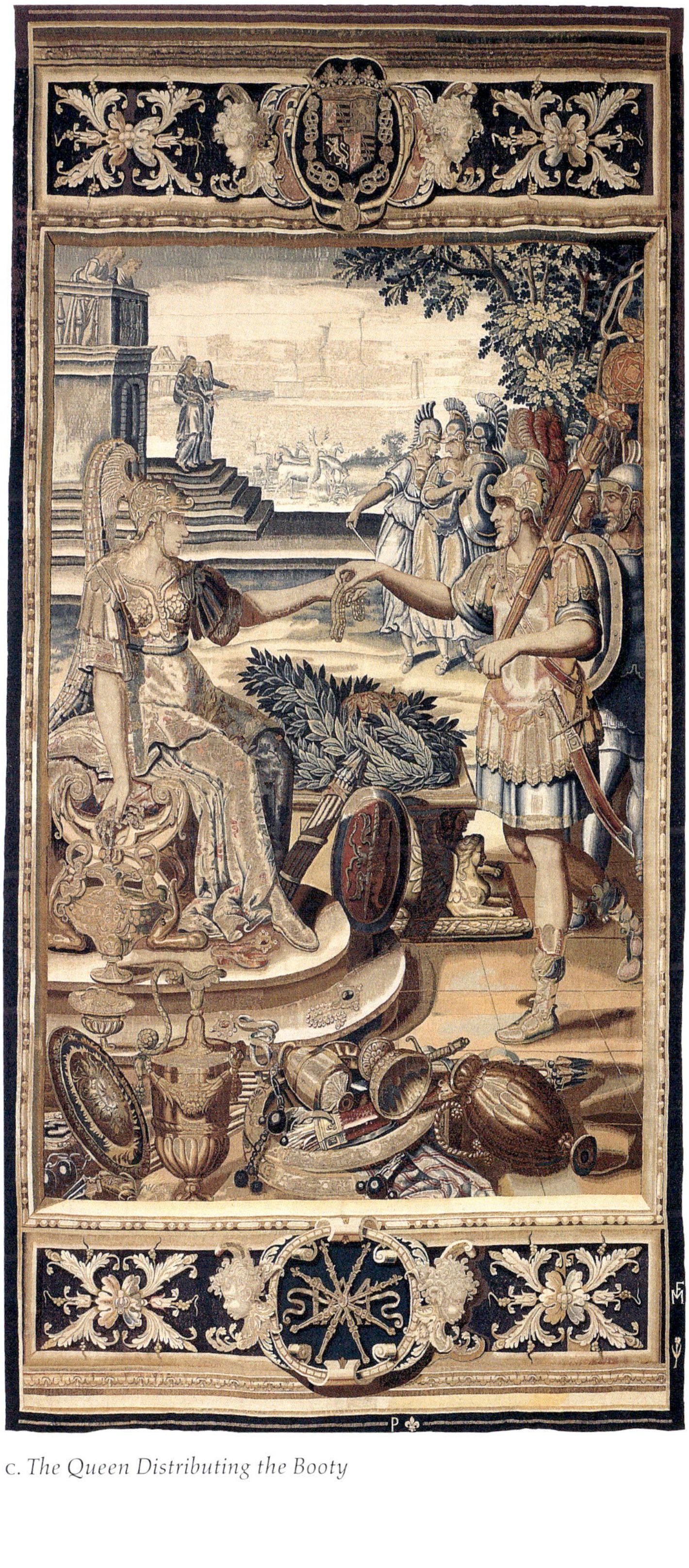

c. *The Queen Distributing the Booty*

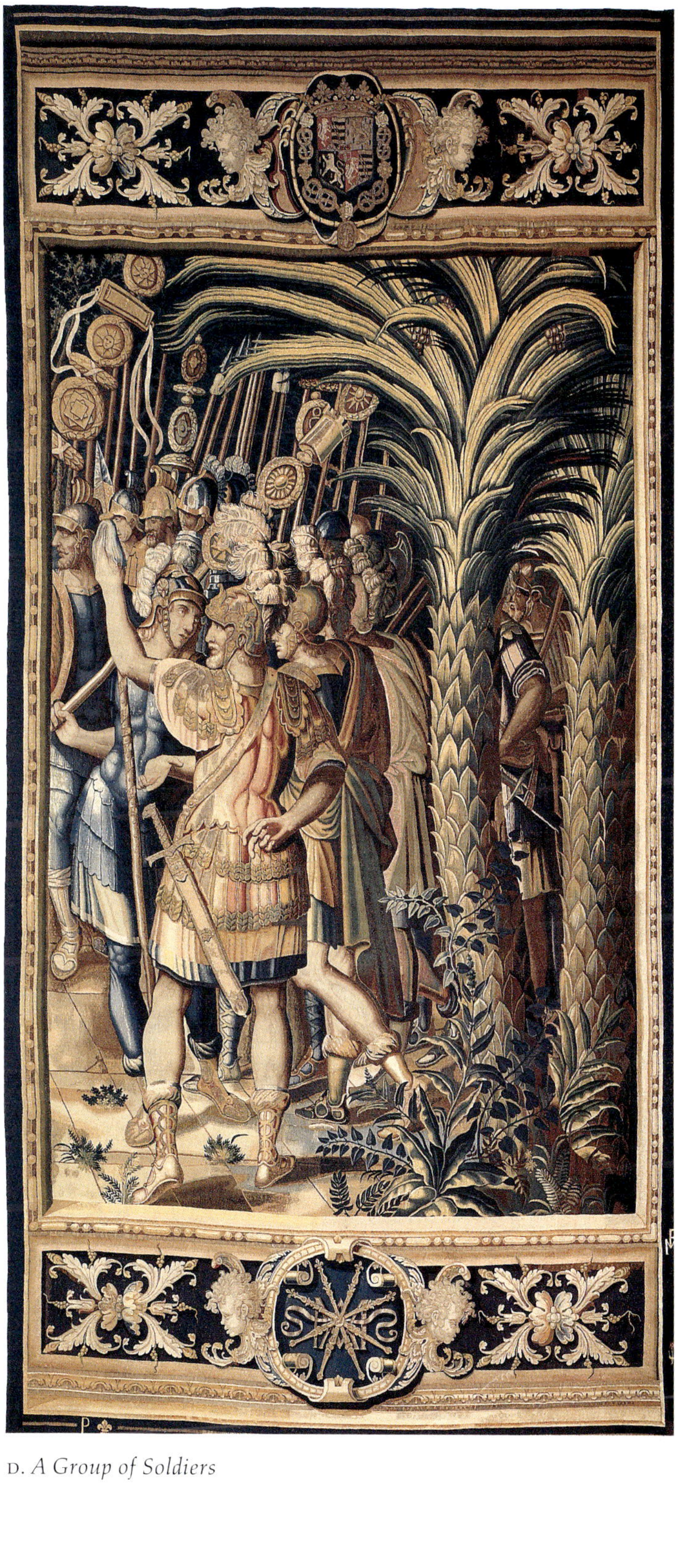

d. *A Group of Soldiers*

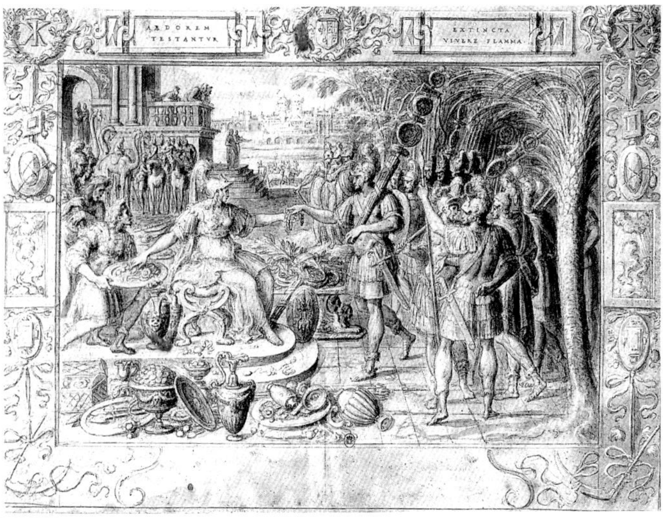

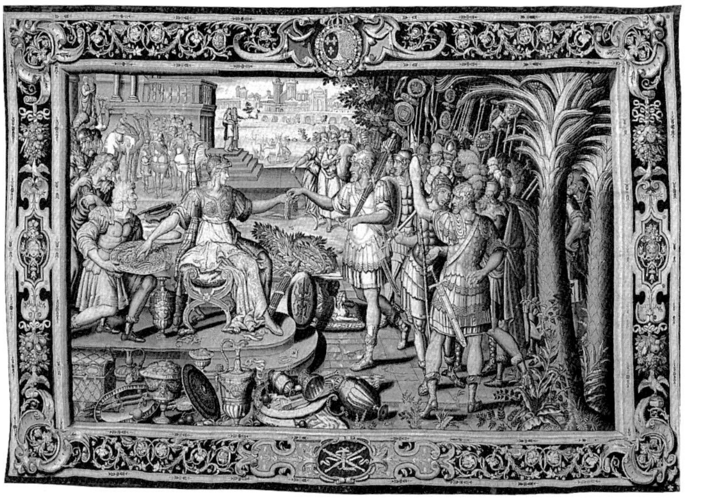

Fig. 1. Antoine Caron, *The Queen Distributing the Booty*, ca. 1562. Gray-brown pen and wash with white heightening over pencil on beige-washed paper, 16⅛ × 21⅞ in. (40.9 × 55.5 cm). Paris, Bibliothèque Nationale, Est., Rés. Ad 105, fol. 25.

Fig. 2. After Antoine Caron, *The Queen Distributing the Booty*. Weaving attributed to Lucas Wandandalle in the Faubourg Saint-Marcel manufactory of Marc de Comans and François de la Planche, Paris, ca. 1611–27. Slit tapestry, wool and silk threads, 13 ft. 5⅜ in. × 20 ft. ½ in. (410 × 611 cm). The Minneapolis Institute of Arts, The Ethel Morrison Van Derlip Fund, 43.13.10.

weaving, the warps (the first set of threads put on the loom) are parallel to the floor and the cartoon is directly below them, which speeds production and thus makes the final tapestries more economical.

To provide work for Paris's tapestry weavers and in honor of his marriage to Marie de' Medici (1573–1642), a distant cousin of Catherine's, Henry revived the *Artemisia* series and commissioned the first cartoons in about 1599–1600. Logically, he chose the drawings from Houel's album that best glorified his own reign, and his artists also added a few new designs. Houel's sonnets were not, however, included in the borders. Caron's original drawing for *The Queen Distributing the Booty* (fig. 1) was enlarged into a cartoon and woven into tapestries at this time (fig. 2). Strips of this cartoon served for weaving the Timken's tapestries *The Queen Distributing the Booty* (C), which is the center of the design, and *A Group of Soldiers* (D), which shows the soldiers at the right of the scene. Henry chose this subject because of its symbolic message, namely that a magnanimous ruler richly rewards his or her warriors, an idea explained in Houel's original sonnet.[5]

Before the Savoy set was woven, however, history once more modified the *Artemisia* series. In 1610 Henry was assassinated and Marie de' Medici found herself in Catherine's position—regent for her minor son, Louis XIII (1601–1643; the father of Louis XIV, the Sun King). Marie appreciated the ready-made propaganda in the original *Artemisia* drawings, making them the basis for a large group of new cartoons. *The Requests of the Citizens* (A) and *The Petitions* (B) were among the compositions chosen. Both are from the beginning of the second book of Houel's *Artemisia* saga, which explains how the queen regent governed the country intelligently and fairly.

One of Artemisia's first actions was to call a meeting of the country's assembly of states. She ordered that, in preparation, local judges should record all complaints and requests, even from her lowliest subjects.[6] Caron's drawing of a judge gathering the information (fig. 3)[7] served as the basis for the tapestry *The Requests of the Citizens* (fig. 4). The Timken piece on this subject (A) shows only the far left of the composition.[8]

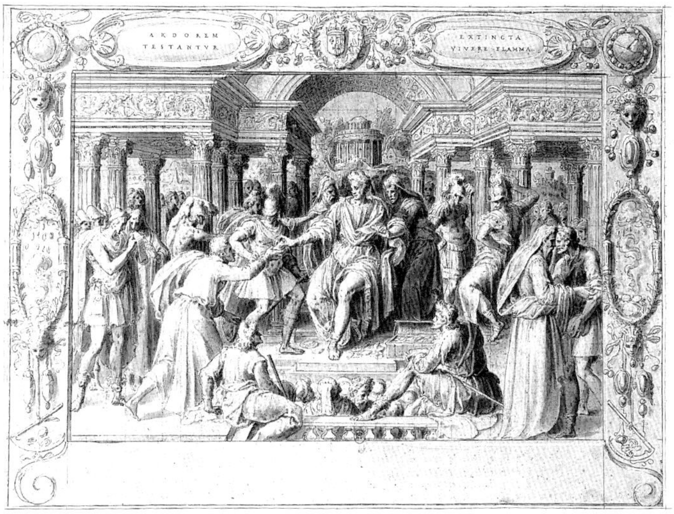

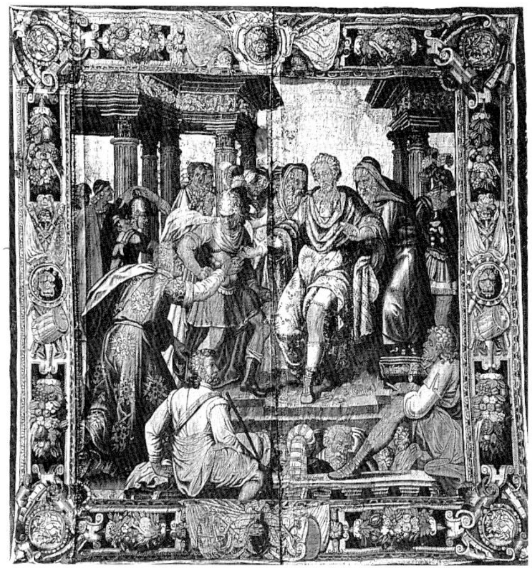

Fig. 3. Antoine Caron, *The Requests of the Citizens*, ca. 1562. Brown pen and wash and white heightening over pencil, on beige paper, squared for transfer, $11\frac{7}{8} \times 21\frac{5}{8}$ in. (40.2 × 54.8 cm). Paris, Bibliothèque Nationale, Est., Rés. Ad 105, fol. 16.

Fig. 4. After Antoine Caron, *The Requests of the Citizens*. Slit tapestry, wool and silk threads. Munich, Residenz, inv. W-72.

Artemisia then asked the assembly delegates to visit her before the meeting, to find out how well this mandate had been executed. The sonnet about this scene explains that, to the queen's satisfaction, the delegates produced copies of all the complaints and requests the judges had gathered.[9] To prepare her son Lygdamis for kingship, Artemisia included him in the session, as shown in the Timken tapestry (B) and in Caron's drawing (fig. 5). Traditionally, this composition has been called *The Petitions*. The Timken tapestry shows the left of the composition, with the queen and her son, a few delegates, and some servants at the bottom of a stairway. The right side of the composition shows a garden like the ones at royal French châteaux (fig. 6).[10]

As a result of Henry IV's enlightened patronage, Paris indeed became an important tapestry center. The *Artemisia* series, which in the end offered a selection of about 50 available cartoons, was particularly popular among the wealthy of Europe. Besides Charles Emmanuel of Savoy, Duke Maximilian I of Bavaria ordered a set, and Cardinal Antonio Barberini, nephew of Pope Urban VIII, bought another. Of the perhaps 250 pieces woven, over 100 still survive.[11]

At least nine different borders appear around *Artemisia* tapestries. Henry Lerambert, Henry IV's official tapestry cartoon painter, probably designed the borders that decorate the Savoy tapestries. In the narrow Timken *entrefenêtres*, only the central parts of the top and bottom borders appear. These imitate carved, painted frames, with central roundels flanked by ornamental foliage, on a ground that ranges from dark brown to blue. At the sides of the roundels are heads of curly-haired putti. The top roundel sports the arms of Charles Emmanuel of Savoy, while in the bottom one are four crossed scepters tied by a ribbon, in front of the monogram *AM*. The monogram letters are now thought to stand for Artemisia and her husband, Mausolus. In wide pieces with this border, other compartmented decorations continue around the tapestry.[12] This border seems to have been standard for Faubourg Saint-Marcel *Artemisia* tapestries with metallic yarns, perhaps so that sets could be made up from individual pieces in stock, according to a buyer's needs. Indeed, this is probably how Charles Emmanuel of Savoy's set was composed.[13]

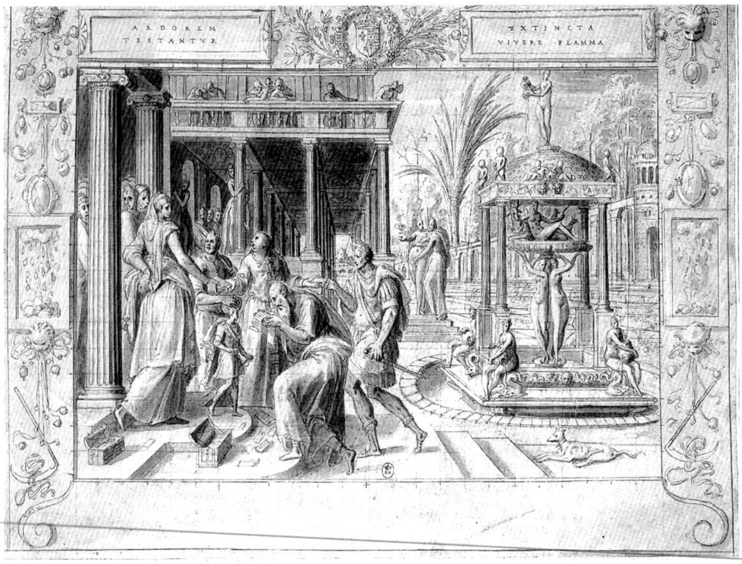

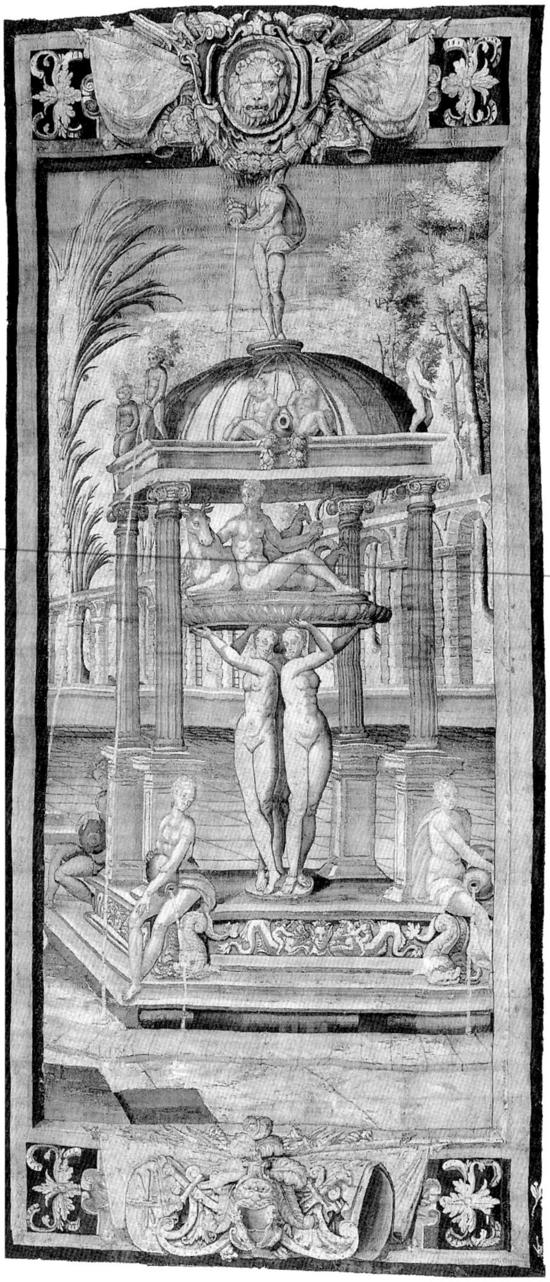

Fig. 5. Antoine Caron, *The Petitions*, ca. 1562. Brown pen and wash with white heightening over pencil, on beige paper, squared for transfer, 16⅛ × 21⅞ in. (41 × 55.6 cm). Paris, Bibliothèque Nationale, Est., Rés. Ad 105, fol. 37.

Fig. 6. After Antoine Caron, *La Fontaine d'Anet*, or *The Petitions* (*entre-fenêtre* from right side). Slit tapestry, wool and silk threads, 13 ft. 6¼ in. × 70½ in. (412 × 179 cm). The Art Institute of Chicago, Gift of Charles J. Singer, 1890.9. Photograph © 1996, The Art Institute of Chicago. All Rights Reserved.

The *P* in the bottom galloons, or colored edgings, of the Timken tapestries indicates the tapestry was woven in Paris, and the fleur-de-lis next to it indicates the workshop was licensed by the king (fig. 7). This mark was required on Paris tapestries of the time.[14] The monogram *FM* (fig. 8), seen toward the bottom of the tapestries' right galloons, appears on many of the known *Artemisia* tapestries, and the mark of a flower—a pink, or dianthus—below it (fig. 9), is on most *Artemisia* tapestries with *AM* borders. The *FM* may be a general mark identifying the Faubourg Saint-Marcel manufactory or one of its workshop groups. The flower is the mark of the unidentified head of the workshop that wove the Savoy tapestries, which specialized in fine tapestries like these with metallic threads.[15]

—C. J. A.

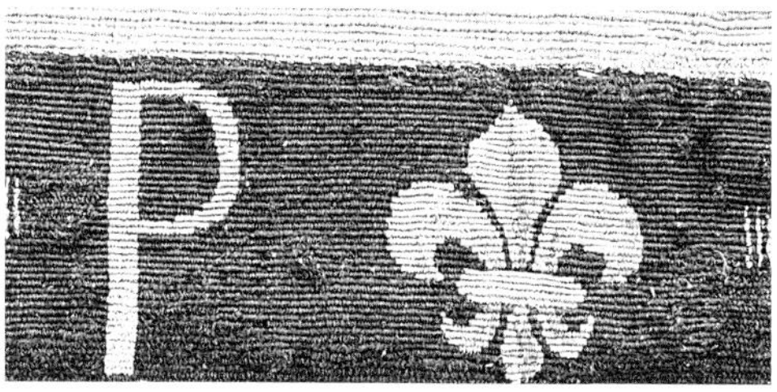

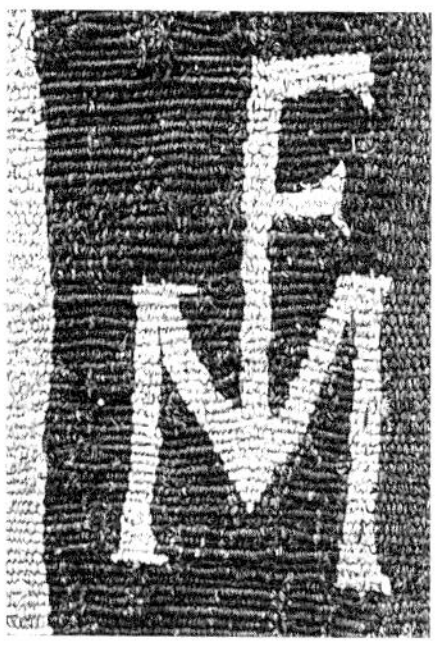

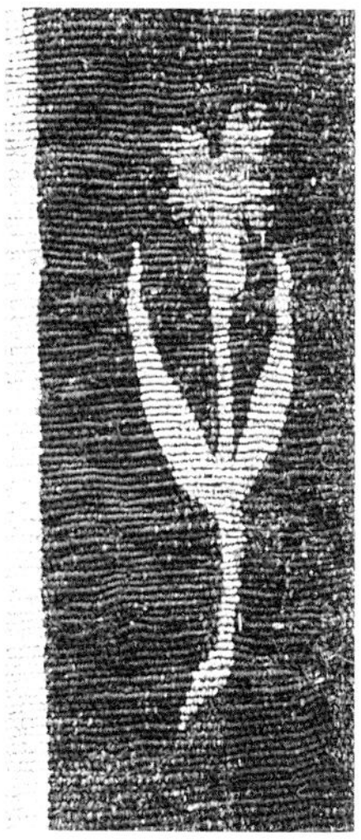

Fig. 7. Detail of the Paris mark from *A Group of Soldiers* (D).

Figs. 8–9. Details of the weaving marks from *The Requests of the Citizens* (A).

NOTES

1. On this series in general see Adelson 1994, pp. 160–288, with earlier bibliography; Candace J. Adelson and Sheila ffolliott, *Images of a Queen's Power: Royal French Tapestries in the Minneapolis Institute of Arts*, exh. cat., The Minneapolis Institute of Arts (Minneapolis, 1993); Isabelle Denis, "L'Histoire d'Artémise, commanditaires et ateliers: Quelques Précisions apportées par l'étude des bordures," *Bulletin de la Société de l'Histoire de l'Art Français* (1991 [1993]): 21–36.

2. The Savoy ambassador in Paris, Augusto Manfredo Scaglia di Verua, who had encountered problems contracting through an agent, bought the pieces directly. Ten were sent to Turin immediately; presumably the remaining pieces followed as they were finished. The 1664 inventory of Christina, duchess of Savoy, counted eighteen pieces. Besides the four Timken pieces, others are in Palazzo Chiablese, Turin (6); Museo Civico, Turin (2; one of them a fragment from one of the Palazzo Chiablese pieces); Palazzo Reale, Turin (1); church of Saint-Georges-sur-Cher, deposited at the château de Blois (1; kindly brought to my attention by Isabelle Denis); Museo Nacional de Bellas Artes, Buenos Aires (1); and in private collections (2). For these pieces see Camilla Lacey sale, Nightingale Page Bennett Knight Frank Rutley, London, November 28–30, 1922, lot 120; Heinrich Göbel, *Wandteppiche,* 3 pts. in 6 vols. (Leipzig, 1923–34), pt. 2, 1:66, 2: fig. 32; Viale and Viale 1952, pp. 93, 95–97, 147–49, nos. 94–96, pls. 82–84, with a list of eleven located pieces from the set; Jean Ehrmann, "Antoine Caron: Tapisserie et tableau inédits dans la série de la reine Artémise," *Bulletin de la Société de l'Histoire de l'Art Français* (1964): 27–29, ill.; Umberto Chierici, *Torino il Palazzo Reale* (Turin, 1969), pl. 44; *European and American Works of Art in the Putnam Foundation Collection* 1983, p. 46; Luigi Mallé, *Museo Civico di Torino, mobili e arredi lignei, arazzi e bozzetti per arazzi, catalogo* (Turin, 1972), pp. 521–23, figs. 9–10; Baudi di Vesme 1963–82, 4:1679–80; Edith A. Standen, *European Post-Medieval Tapestries and Related Hangings in the Metropolitan Museum of Art,* 2 vols. (New York, 1985), 1:274 n. 38; *Diana trionfatrice. Arte di corte nel Piemonte del seicento,* exh. cat., Palazzo Reale (Turin, 1989), p. 147; Adelson 1994, pp. 184, 198–99 n. 120, 242, 244 n. 25.

The Ville de Paris owns two unmarked *entrefenêtres* without metallic yarn and with the cartoons reversed—Savoy arms and all (Maurice Fenaille, *Etat général des tapisseries de la manufacture des Gobelins, depuis son origine jusqu'à nos jours,* 6 vols. [Paris, 1903–23], 1:212; Juliette Niclausse, *Tapisseries et tapis de la Ville de Paris* [Paris, 1948], pp. 26–27, nos. 5–6; Ehrmann 1964, p. 28, ill.). They are possibly later copies made to complete the Savoy set.

3. See Sheila ffolliott, "Catherine de' Medici as Artemisia: Figuring the Powerful Widow," in *Rewriting the Renaissance: Discourses of Sexual Difference in Early Modern Europe,* ed. Margaret W. Ferguson, Maureen Quilligan, and Nancy J. Vickers (Chicago and London, 1986), pp. 227–41, 370–76; id., "Casting a Rival into the Shade: Catherine de' Medici and Diane de Poitiers," *Art Journal* 48 (Summer 1989): 138–43; and id., "Once upon a Tapestry: Inventing the Ideal Queen," in Adelson and ffolliott, *Images of a Queen's Power,* pp. 13–19.

4. Houel's original prose book is in the Bibliothèque Nationale, Paris (Cabinet des Manuscrits, Ms. fr. 306; cited here as "Houel prose book"). Most of the early drawings are also there (Est., Rés. Ad 105, Rés. B 5), but a few are in the Musée du Louvre (Département des Arts Graphiques, filed as Antoine Caron, inv. 25138–39, RF 29728bis$^{1-4}$, RF 29752$^{1-7}$). Inscribed on the verso of each drawing is the sonnet explaining the next drawing in the original album sequence (the drawings were mounted in the album on right-hand pages, with their corresponding sonnets to the left).

5. So, having thus swiftly executed
A queen's duty, & having seen subjugated
To her power this captured city,
She wished to show her liberality.

(Donc s'estans en cela brusquement acquité,
Le devoir de la Royne, & ayant veu reduitte,
Au pouvoir de son bras ceste ville seduitte,
Elle voulut monstrer sa liberalité.

Therefore, imitating the equity of the greatest warriors,
She had all the elite soldiers called,
And all the Carians who under her command
Had merited some reward from this campaign.

And in a great square, where she had caused to be put
All the booty won, she would not allow there to be
Anything left for herself without sharing it with them;

Demonstrating by this, that whoever wishes
To solicit from a soldier his service & his life
Must also honor soldiery with presents.

Car des plus grandz guerriers imitant l'equité,
Elle fit appeler tous les soldatz d'eslite,
Et tous les Cariens que dessoubz sa conduitte,
Avoient en ceste part quelque gaing merité.

Et dans une grand place, ou elle avoit faict mettre
Tout le butin conquis, onq ne voulut permettre
Que rien luy demeurast sans leur en faire part;

Nous monstrant par cela, que cil qui a envie
De tirer d'un soldat, le service, & la vie,
Doibt par presents aussi, honorer le Soldart.)

Author's translation. The sonnet is on the back of the drawing for *The Queen's Entry into the Harbor of Rhodes* (Est., Rés. Ad 105, fol. 21v; Ulrika von Haumeder, "Antoine Caron. Studien zu seiner *Histoire d'Arthémise*" [Ph.D. diss., Ruprecht-Karl-Universität, Heidelberg, 1976], p. 297 sonnet no. 56). For other tapestries of the composition, see Adelson 1994, p. 259.

6. Houel prose book, fol. 39v, C.

7. The sonnet that originally explained this drawing does not survive, however.

8. The *entrefenêtre* from the Savoy set showing the center of the scene was in the Camilla Lacey collection (see n. 2), and a full tapestry of the subject and the right *entrefenêtre*, both also from the Savoy collection, are in the Palazzo Chiablese, Turin (Viale and Viale 1952, pp. 147–48, nos. 3, 7). A tapestry showing just the center, from Duke Maximilian I of Bavaria's set (fig. 4), is in the Residenz of Munich (Adelson 1994, p. 198 n. 114). Another, of the central and left parts of the scene, including the reading man who is in the Timken *entrefenêtre*, is in the Hall of the Knights at Hildesheim cathedral in Germany (see Adelson 1994, pp. 185, 199 n. 122). The Mobilier National, Paris, has an example of this subject (see Adelson 1994, pp. 185, 199 n. 123), and another was in the Marczell von Nemes sale, Munich, June 16–19, 1931, lot 305 (letter from Edith A. Standen, October 27, 1978, Timken Museum files; Marillier, vol. T37x, "History and Military," II, i, p. 6, ill.). Another reduced version was misidentified as Agamemnon and the messenger from Achilles (American Art Association, New York, February 13, 1932, lot 412, ill.); and an *entrefenêtre* similar to the Timken one but slightly narrower at the right was on the art market (Victoria and Albert Museum, Textile Department, photograph files).

9. But before she went to hold her assembly of states,
She sent for her delegates to be diligent
And come visit her at her pleasure retreat
Where she was resting and taking amusement.

When they arrived, she did not fail
To ask about the execution of her strict order,
To determine whether there had been any negligence,
In gathering the complaints of the lowest people.

So to demonstrate to her the care
That had been used, immediately she was shown
A large coffer filled with notebooks and writings,

Where the people's complaints had been recorded:
Which she approved, since her only desire
Was to prosper her people.

(Mais avant qu'elle vint a tenir ses estats,
Manda les deputez de faire diligence
De la venir trouver, en un lieu de plaisance,
Ou lors elle prenoit son aise, & ses esbats.

Eulx estant arrivez, elle ne faillit pas
De s'enquerir du faict de sa saincte ordonnance,
Pour sçavoir son avoit usé de negligence,
A recevoir les cris du populaire bas.

Adonc pour luy monstrer quel estoit le devoir
Dont on avoit usé, soubdain on luy fit voir
Un grand bahu rempli de cayers, et memoires,

Ou du peuple on avoit la plainte mise au net:
Qu'elle vîtt de bon oeil, n'ayant autre souhait,
Que son peuple tirer de toutes ses affaires.)

Author's translation. This is on the reverse of Caron's drawing for *The Requests of the Citizens* (Est., Rés. Ad 105, fol. 16; von Haumeder, "Caron. Studien," p. 289 sonnet no. 30; the original prose text is Houel prose book, fol. 39, C).

10. The Savoy set also included a full tapestry of this subject, now missing its right side, which is in the Palazzo Chiablese, Turin (Viale and Viale 1952, p. 148, no. 4, pl. 84, a). A tapestry with almost the same scene as in the Timken piece is in the Munich set (see n. 8), and another that adds a small part of the garden at the right is in the Louvre, on deposit from the Mobilier National (Madeleine Jarry, "Tapisseries inédites de la tenture d'Artémise," *L'Oeil* 220 [November 1973]: 6, 9–10, fig. 2). An *entrefenêtre* showing just the garden is in the Art Institute of Chicago (Jarry, pp. 7–11, fig. 3; my fig. 6).

11. For a list and further bibliography, see Adelson 1994, pp. 182–85.

12. On the interpretation of the monogram, see Adelson 1994, p. 170. For an example of the complete border, see *The Queen's Entry into the Harbor of Rhodes* in the Minneapolis Institute of Arts (Adelson 1994, pp. 278–79, color ill.). For other sets with this border and its history, see Adelson 1994, pp. 184–85.

13. Adelson 1994, pp. 350, 353 n. 61.

14. The very narrow *Requests of the Citizens* (A) has no *P* and fleur-de-lis. In Brussels, pieces below a certain size did not need a city mark. A similar rule may have applied in Paris.

15. On the interpretation of the weaving monograms, see Adelson 1994, pp. 180–82.

PROVENANCE

Duke Charles Emmanuel I of Savoy, 1620; Christina of France, duchess of Savoy (d. 1663); House of Savoy; Archduke Leopold Salvator of Austria, until ca. 1924; P. W. French and Company, New York, by 1931; acquired by the Putnam Foundation, 1964.

LITERATURE

H. D. Marillier, *Subject Catalogue of Tapestries,* manuscript, Textile and Costume Department, Victoria and Albert Museum, London, inv. T37-1946, vol. T37x, "History and Military," II, i, p. 5; Mercedes Viale and Vittorio Viale, *Arazzi e tappeti antichi,* exh. cat., Palazzo Madama (Turin, 1952), p. 177, inventory of Christina of France, 1664; Alessandro Baudi di Vesme, *Schede Vesme. L'arte in Piemonte,* 4 vols. (Turin, 1963–82), 4:1679–80, documents related to purchase, 1620; *European and American Works of Art in the Putnam Foundation Collection* (San Diego, 1983), pp. 46–48, no. 15, ill.; Candace J. Adelson, *European Tapestry in the Minneapolis Institute of Arts* (Minneapolis, 1994), pp. 198–99 n. 120, 258–59, 261 n. 11.

EXHIBITED

The Minneapolis Institute of Arts, 1931, loaned by P. W. French and Company, New York, "List of tapestries exhibited at the Minneapolis Institute of Arts. January 24 to March 2, 1931," on file at National Art Library, London, typescript 86.Y.13, pp. 2–3, nos. 15–18.

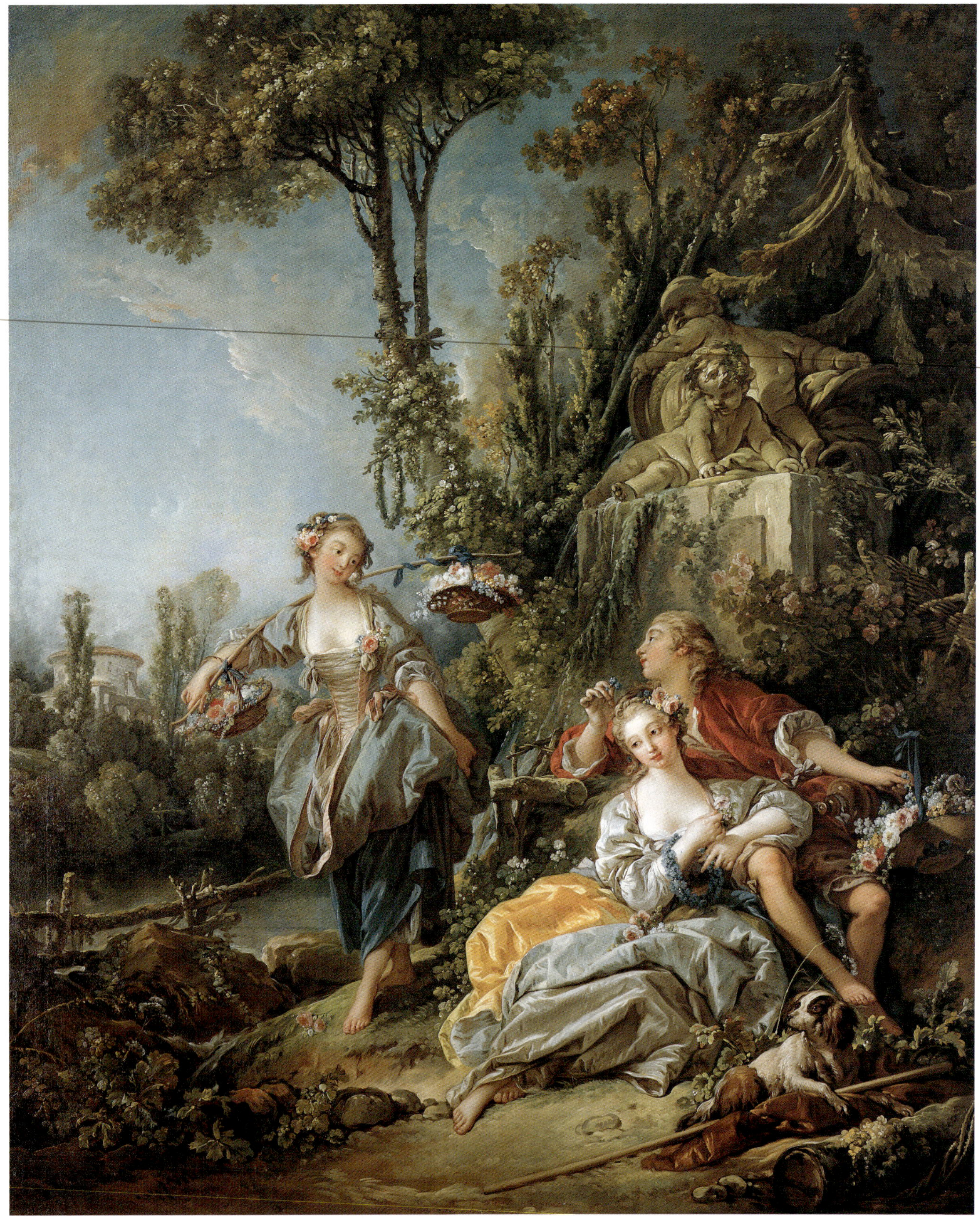

François Boucher

(1703–1770)

A native of Paris, Boucher learned the rudiments of painting from his father, Nicolas. From 1721 to 1723 he studied with François Lemoyne and won the Prix de Rome in 1723. Boucher's trip to Italy was delayed several years, however, during which time he produced numerous etchings for Jean de Jullienne's compendium of prints after compositions by Watteau. He finally traveled to Italy in 1728 and was back in Paris by 1731. That same year he was admitted into the Royal Academy of Painting and Sculpture, gaining full membership three years later with his painting *Rinaldo and Armida* (Paris, Musée du Louvre). From that followed an exceptionally successful career, as Boucher won commissions from the French crown and aristocracy and soon earned an international reputation. With Charles-Joseph Natoire and Carle Vanloo he was one of the principal exponents of the rococo, the style of art associated with the reign of Louis XV (1715–74). Perhaps best known for his mythological and pastoral subjects, Boucher also produced religious paintings, genre scenes, landscapes, and portraits. In addition to his many painted decorations and cabinet pictures, he contributed designs for the Beauvais and Gobelins tapestry works, the Sèvres porcelain factory, as well as sets and costumes for the theater. He was the favorite artist of Louis XV's mistress, Madame de Pompadour, for whom he painted some of his most impressive works, such as *The Rising of the Sun* and *The Setting of the Sun* of 1753 (London, Wallace Collection). His career was capped in 1765 when he was appointed First Painter to the King and elected director of the academy. He died in Paris in 1770.

21 *Lovers in a Park*, 1758
Oil on canvas, 91½ × 76¾ in. (232.4 × 194.9 cm)
Signed and dated lower right: *F. Boucher / 1758* (FB in monogram)

Boucher's monumental pastoral compositions are among his most characteristic, if still less appreciated, creations. *Lovers in a Park*, signed and dated 1758, is one of the finest from his later period, brilliantly displaying the painter's dazzling brushwork and splendid sense of color. On a canvas more than seven and a half feet high, Boucher conjured up a fairy-tale vision of a lush landscape peopled with graceful and sweet-tempered figures. The delicate pastel color scheme and the fluid painting technique, most vivid in the creamy folds of the seated woman's draperies and in the richly worked foliage of the trees and bushes, epitomize Boucher's rococo style, which by the 1750s had reached a level of virtuosity unparalleled by the artist's contemporaries.

The subject, such as it is, of *Lovers in a Park* is lighthearted and whimsical, in keeping with the essentially decorative character of the painting: an amorous young couple, perhaps out for a stroll with their spaniel in the countryside or grounds of a vast, overgrown estate, has stopped to rest beneath a sculpture of two *amorini.* The man has taken flowers from the woman's upturned hat and is weaving them into the hair of his lover, whose thoughts appear to wander, perhaps dreaming of the implications of her companion's actions. His attentions are distracted, however, by the appearance of a young woman—her less elaborate costume suggests she is a milkmaid or shepherdess—who walks into the scene; she has been gathering her own flowers, which she carries in baskets suspended at the ends of a pole. Boucher took unusual care in orchestrating the postures, gestures, and glances to create a balanced, though fluid, triad of interacting figures, all convincingly integrated into an enveloping landscape.

In placing his lovers in a lush garden setting, Boucher drew on a tradition that goes back to the medieval period, although he would have been more familiar with sources closer in time and spirit, like Peter Paul Rubens's *Garden of Love* (1632–34, Madrid, Prado Museum), which he could have seen in a private collection in Paris. With its doll-like figures and candy-box colors, however, *Lovers in a Park* is far removed from Rubens's robust forms and rich palette. In the Timken painting Boucher makes no pretense of portraying a believable situation. His world is rather a modern Arcadia in which a fecund and radiant nature is inhabited by cheerful country folk and pleasant, complacent lovers. The potentially uneasy encounter between the peasant girl and the elegant young couple is defused by the artist's idealizing vision and the constraints of the pastoral genre, which allowed few signs of strife or conflict. Boucher's image brings to mind the contemporary taste for the literary pastoral, such as Jean-François Marmontel's *Moral Tales* of 1761 or Jean-Jacques Rousseau's 1751 operetta, *Le Devin du village* (The village fortune-teller; a production of which featured Madame de Pompadour in the lead).[1] Indeed, the somewhat contrived composition of *Lovers in a Park* is a reminder that Boucher was active as a designer for the stage.

In keeping with their decorative function, Boucher's large-scale pastorals were often conceived in pairs or series. *Lovers in a Park* is generally thought to have a pendant, *The Fisherman* (signed and dated 1759, Hamburger Kunsthalle), a painting of like dimensions and compatible subject, if slightly later date (fig. 1). Here the encounter between a young man and two women takes place in an equally luxuriant landscape. The fisherman has made a successful catch and holds up his prize for the admiration of the women. The rather crude metaphor is softened by the nesting doves at the upper left and somewhat undermined by the rambunctious children,

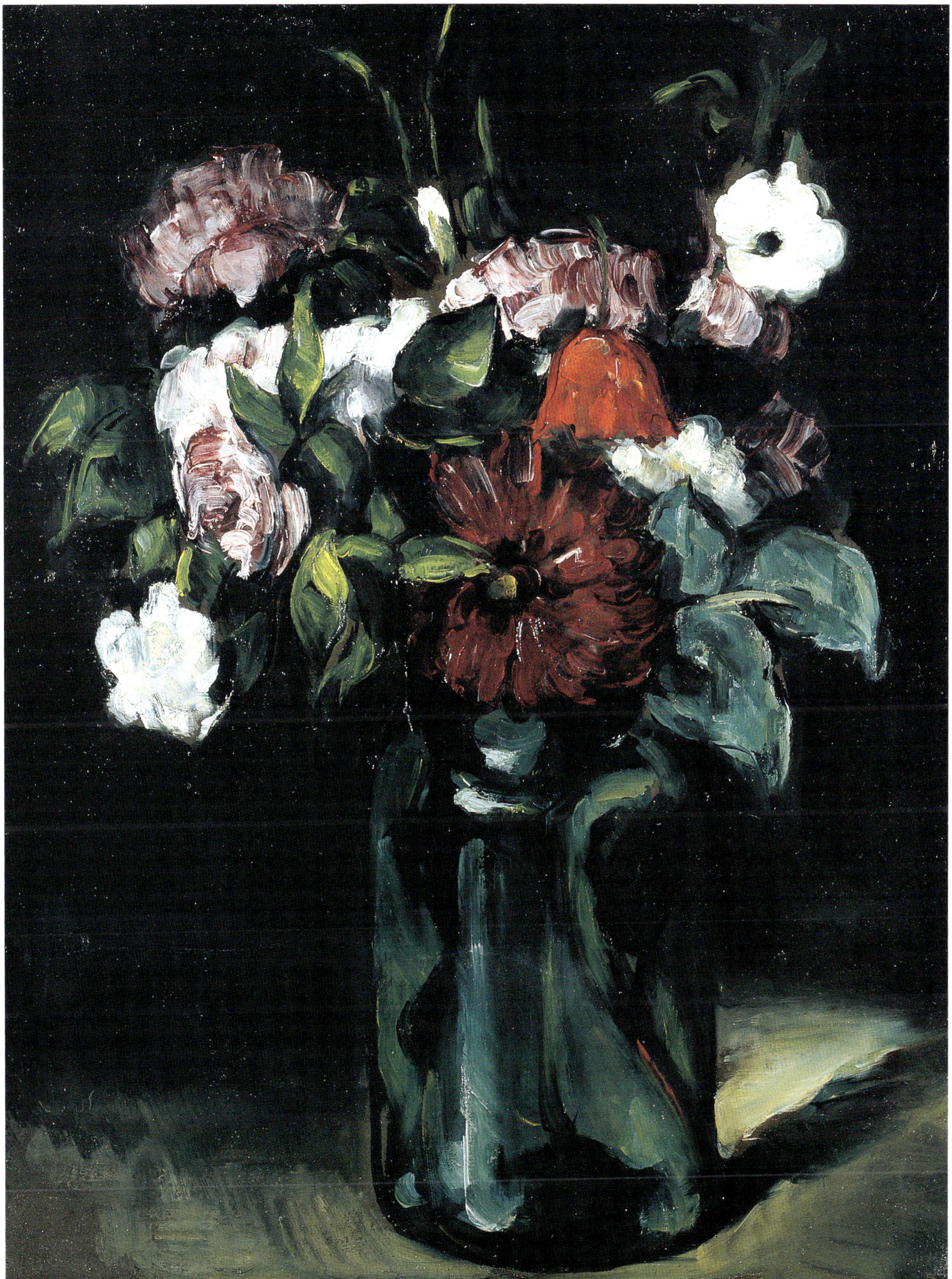

Flowers in a Glass Vase dates from the time in Cézanne's career when, in the early 1870s, he was under the influence of Pissarro, then based in Pontoise, northwest of Paris (see cat. no. 31). Pissarro's open, forgiving, and truly artistic nature allowed him to overlook Cézanne's abrasive personality in favor of his talent. At this time, Cézanne needed more than just artistic guidance. His companion, Hortense Fiquet, had given birth to their son, Paul, in January 1872. Cézanne's stormy relationship with his father prevented him from telling his parent about Hortense, much less about the child, and the three were thus forced to live on Cézanne's allowance, calculated for a bachelor's supposedly modest needs. Pissarro, taking pity on Cézanne's domestic plight, invited the young family to stay with him and his family in Pontoise. There, Pissarro helped the younger artist to see that the color of an object is relative, its perceived hue dependent on the colors and the atmosphere surrounding it. Pissarro also helped Cézanne to focus on painting pictures of things around him, especially landscapes and still lifes, rather than the imaginative, and sometimes violent and erotic, subjects he had been painting before. The growing dependence on the perceived world, under Pissarro's example, also had the effect of lightening Cézanne's palette.

It is more than likely that this small canvas was painted in the Auvers home of Dr. Gachet, an amateur artist as well as a medical man, with whom Cézanne stayed for a time in early 1873.[1] Gachet is perhaps better known for his later care of Vincent van Gogh, yet his interest in path-breaking contemporary art preceded by decades Van Gogh's expressions of personal passions. In the late 1860s Gachet had been a regular at the Café Guerbois in Paris, which was frequented by the artists Edouard Manet, Félix Bracquemond, Bazille, Fantin-Latour, Edgar Degas, Renoir, Sisley, Monet, and Pissarro, and the writers Zacharie Astruc, Edmond Duranty, Armand Silvestre, Emile Zola, and Théodore Duret, among others. By the early 1870s the doctor had begun to collect his friends' works, including Cézanne's fantasy-ridden *Modern Olympia* (1872–73, Paris, Musée d'Orsay).

Cézanne always felt uncomfortable and confined in cities, and even the market town of Pontoise was too urban in character for him. In Auvers, a small village of unpaved streets and thatched stone cottages, a few miles up the Oise river from Pontoise, Cézanne was more at ease. Gachet opened his house to Cézanne, as had Pissarro, and Cézanne flourished under the doctor's encouragement. (Printing presses in Gachet's studio allowed him to indulge his interest in etching; Cézanne's only etchings were made with Gachet's copperplates and equipment.)

Cézanne's struggle to be faithful to the motif in front of him, following Pissarro's example, can be seen in the heavily worked surface of *Flowers in a Glass Vase*. Yet, as John Rewald has noted, "[s]o intense were his impressions, so tremendous his will to penetrate the secrets of nature, so humble his attempt to retain his sensations, that even countless hours of work upon the same canvas did not destroy the naïveté and truth, the delicacy and power of his perceptions."[2] Manet's example is often evoked in discussions of Cézanne's early palette,[3] yet the careless arrangement of the red, pink, and white blooms and foliage bespeaks a temperament more nervous, more excitable, more eager than the controlled expression of Manet. The German poet Rainer Maria Rilke described in a letter to his wife of October 9, 1907, what he perceived to be the basis of Cézanne's art.

> I think there was a conflict, a mutual struggle between the two procedures of, first, looking and confidently receiving, and then of appropriating and making personal use of what has been received; that the two, perhaps as a result of becoming conscious, would immediately start opposing each other, talking out loud, as it were, and go on perpetually interrupting and contradicting each other.[4]

This internal dialogue gives Cézanne's paintings, regardless of subject, their highly individualistic character.

For Cézanne, who painted still lifes for his own purposes, the identification of the flowers was not important, as it was to an artist such as Fantin-Latour who made part of his livelihood painting floral still lifes. What mattered to Cézanne was the close harmonies of related pinks and reds, set against the richness of the black background, relieved only slightly by the reflections on the glass and the curious, almost unearthly patch of light that seems to emanate from the container itself. Rilke understood the essence of Cézanne's color. "There's something else I wanted to say about Cézanne," he wrote in another letter to his wife. "No one before him ever demonstrated so clearly the extent to which painting is something that takes place among the colors, and how one has to leave them alone completely, so that they can settle the matter among themselves. Their intercourse: this is the whole of painting."[5] Thinking of Cézanne's color in this way, as an active, almost autonomous agent, excuses the viewer from trying to determine what flowers are depicted. The brushstrokes, the carriers of the color, are applied in swishes, swirls, flourishes, and squiggles. They crisscross, abut, and efface one another.

Despite this activity of the brush, however, the bunch of flowers is structured no less architectonically than the artist's late views of Mont Sainte-Victoire. The center is established by the vertical reflection rising from the bottom of the vase. It thickens slightly in the darkest red flower, which, in its frontality, imposes an almost Byzantine sense of hierarchy. Slender shoots of what one assumes is foliage at the top complete the central axis. The white blooms at top right and lower left stick firmly to the surface. They are balanced by the axis established by the darker pink flower at the upper left, whose upward-turning petals find an answer in the downward-pointing leaves at lower right. Our first sense of a lushly painted bunch of garden flowers, picked for the artist by Madame Gachet,[6] roughly stuck in a jar (one hesitates to call it a vase), is undercut by the realization of the artifice with which Cézanne has turned the blooms into architecture.

This little painting comes from a distinguished collection. It was once owned by Louisine and Horace Havemeyer, who brought to this country some of the finest paintings by Courbet, Manet, Corot, Degas, and Monet, many of which now form part of the collections at the Metropolitan Museum of Art. It and a later floral still life (1879–80, Munich, Franz Heinz)[7] were purchased by the Havemeyers in Paris in April 1901 from the dealer Ambroise Vollard, who had a small shop on the rue Laffitte. As was their custom, the Havemeyers began their collection of Cézannes, which eventually totaled thirteen canvases, modestly, with by no means the best of the more adventurous of the artist's work available to them. (They would later buy such masterpieces as *The Gulf of Marseilles Seen from L'Estaque,* New York, The Metropolitan Museum of Art.) The impetus for their buying still lifes, rather than portraits, figure pieces, or landscapes, was most likely the influence of their advisor, Mary Cassatt, who did not care for Cézanne's other subjects. But the Havemeyers' tentative purchases in 1901 were significant in that they were among the first paintings by Cézanne to come to the United States.

—F. E. W.

NOTES

1. John Rewald, *The History of Impressionism,* 4th ed. (New York, 1973), p. 296.

2. Ibid., p. 299.

3. Mongan and Mongan 1983, no. 6, reprinted from catalogue of 1969.

4. Rainer Maria Rilke, *Letters on Cézanne,* ed. Clara Rilke, trans. Joel Agee (New York, 1985), p. 36.

5. Letter of October 21, 1907, p. 75.

6. Rewald, *History of Impressionism,* p. 296.

7. See New York 1993, p. 304, checklist no. 73.

PROVENANCE

Mr. and Mrs. H. O. Havemeyer, New York, probably bought from Ambroise Vollard in 1901, until 1907; Mrs. H. O. Havemeyer, New York, 1907–29; her son, Horace Havemeyer, New York, 1929–34; deposited with Durand-Ruel, New York, in 1931; The Denver Art Museum, given anonymously by Havemeyer in 1934; deaccessioned and sold, May 14, 1949; Knoedler and Co., New York, received on consignment from Denver, June 1949; Dr. and Mrs. David M. Levy, New York, bought from Knoedler and Co., June 1949; Adele R. Levy Fund, Inc.; assigned to the Putnam Foundation, 1962.

LITERATURE

H. O. Havemeyer Collection: Catalogue of Paintings, Prints, Sculpture and Objects of Art (Portland, Maine, 1931), p. 330; Lionello Venturi, *Cézanne: Son Art, son oeuvre,* 2 vols. (Paris, 1936), 1:107, no. 184, and 2: pl. 49; Alfred M. Frankfurter, "Cézanne: Intimate Exhibition," *Art News* 36 (March 26, 1938): 15–17, ill.; Lionello Venturi, "The Denver Art Museum," *Pacific Art Review* 2 (Summer 1942): 17, 18, fig. 3; Agnes Mongan and Elizabeth Mongan, *European Paintings in the Timken Art Gallery* (San Diego, 1969), pp. 104, 105, no. 40, ill.; Sandra Orienti, *The Complete Paintings of Cézanne* (London, 1972), p. 96, no. 225, ill.; *Timken Art Gallery: European and American Works of Art in the Putnam Foundation Collection* (San Diego, 1983), pp. 26–27, 116, no. 6, ill.; Frances Weitzenhoffer, *The Havemeyers: Impressionism Comes to America* (New York, 1986), p. 142, fig. 105.

EXHIBITED

New York, Durand-Ruel Galleries, 1938; New York, The Metropolitan Museum of Art, 1993, *Splendid Legacy: The Havemeyer Collection,* cat. by Alice Cooney Frelinghuysen et al., pp. 230, 302, no. 69, pl. 224.

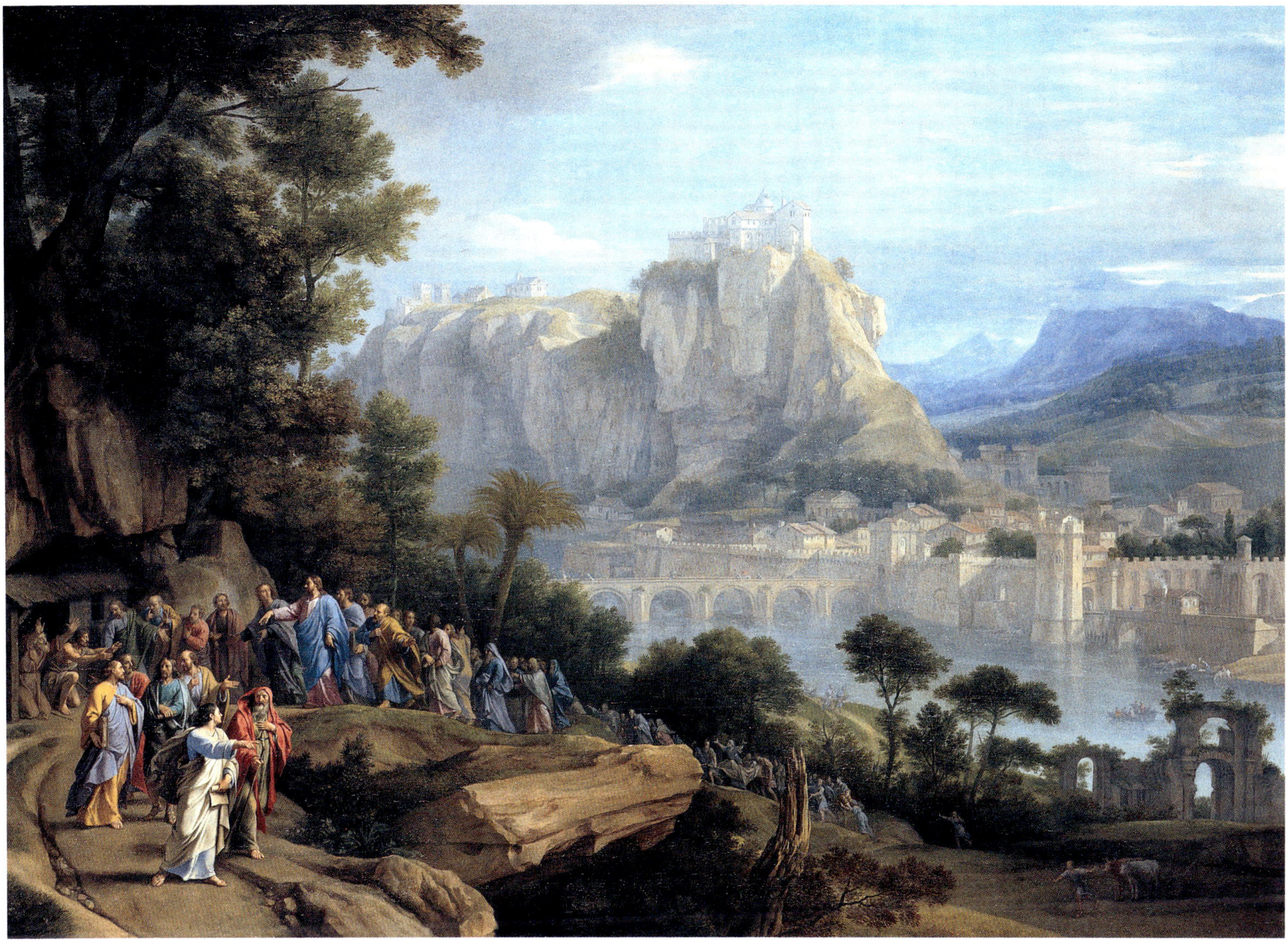

Philippe de Champaigne
(1602–1674)

Champaigne was born in Brussels in 1602. He was the pupil of Jacques Fouquières and with him, in 1621, went to Paris. Rubens's presence in Paris at this time may have been the impetus for Champaigne's move to that city. From 1622 to 1626 he painted landscapes for the Luxembourg Palace under the direction of Nicolas Duchesne. He formed a friendship with Nicolas Poussin in 1623. In 1627 Champaigne returned to Brussels but went back to Paris in 1628 and became a naturalized citizen. From 1634 to 1641 he worked for Cardinal Richelieu and Louis XIII. Champaigne's portraits of Richelieu show how he moderated the baroque idiom he had admired in Rubens toward a more linear classicism, which began to be more popular in the mid-seventeenth century. In the early 1640s he was influenced by the Jansenists, a very austere Catholic sect; his daughter became a nun at the Jansenist convent at Port-Royal. Champaigne was a founding member of the Royal Academy of Painting and Sculpture. He died in Paris in 1674.

23 *Christ Healing the Blind*, ca. 1655–60
Oil on canvas, 40¼ × 55⅞ in. (102.2 × 141.9 cm)

On a grassy mound over a grotto, the majestic figure of Christ, dressed in a violet robe with a blue mantle, stretches out his right hand toward two blind men who appear in the middle distance at the far left. A long procession, made up of apostles and followers, winds down diagonally through the foreground of the painting. In the middle distance is a broad river with a bridge, which leads to a walled town. In the far distance to the right are imposing blue mountains.

Before the exhibition of the work of Philippe de Champaigne in the Musée de l'Orangerie in Paris in 1952, the painter was chiefly known for his solemn, stately portraits and deeply religious paintings. However, a number of landscape paintings were included in that exhibition. In the words of Anthony Blunt, who reviewed the exhibition: "These paintings, which must date from the maturity of the artist, probably after 1648, show him using the classical convention of Poussin but with strong blue distances recalling the Flemish tradition."[1]

This picture seems to have been influenced by Poussin's *Christ Healing the Blind*, painted in 1650 (Paris, Musée du Louvre). Both follow Matthew 20:29–34, where Christ heals two blind men instead of one. Poussin's picture, painted for a manufacturer of silk and brocade from Lyon, named Reynon, was in the collection of the duc de Richelieu in Paris, where Champaigne could have seen it. The fact that *Christ Healing the Blind* was in the artist's studio at the time of his death would suggest a date later than the landscapes included in the Paris exhibition, probably 1655–60. The elongated figures of the apostles, similar in proportion to those in a work begun in 1657 known only through a study drawing now in the Louvre,[2] would also support the later date.

The Counter-Reformation interpretation of the parable of Christ Healing the Blind, as an example of Christ cleansing the church, must have had compelling attraction for an artist like Champaigne, who was tied firmly to the Jansenist movement, which stressed the individual's personal relationship to God, in opposition to Catholic teachings.

—A. M. AND E. M.

NOTES

1. "Shorter Notices," *Burlington Magazine* 94 (June 1952): 172–75.

2. See F. Lugt, *Inventaire général des dessins des écoles du nord: Ecole flamande*, 2 vols. (Paris, 1949), 1: no. 517, pl. XLI.

PROVENANCE

Studio of Philippe de Champaigne; inherited by his nephew Jean-Baptiste de Champaigne; Mme Gentil de Chavagnac, her sale, Paris, Galerie Labrun, June 20, 1854, pp. 37–39; the dukes of Ferrari de Galliera, near Dijon; inherited by a niece of the last duke, Mlle de la Renotière; acquired by the Putnam Foundation, 1967.

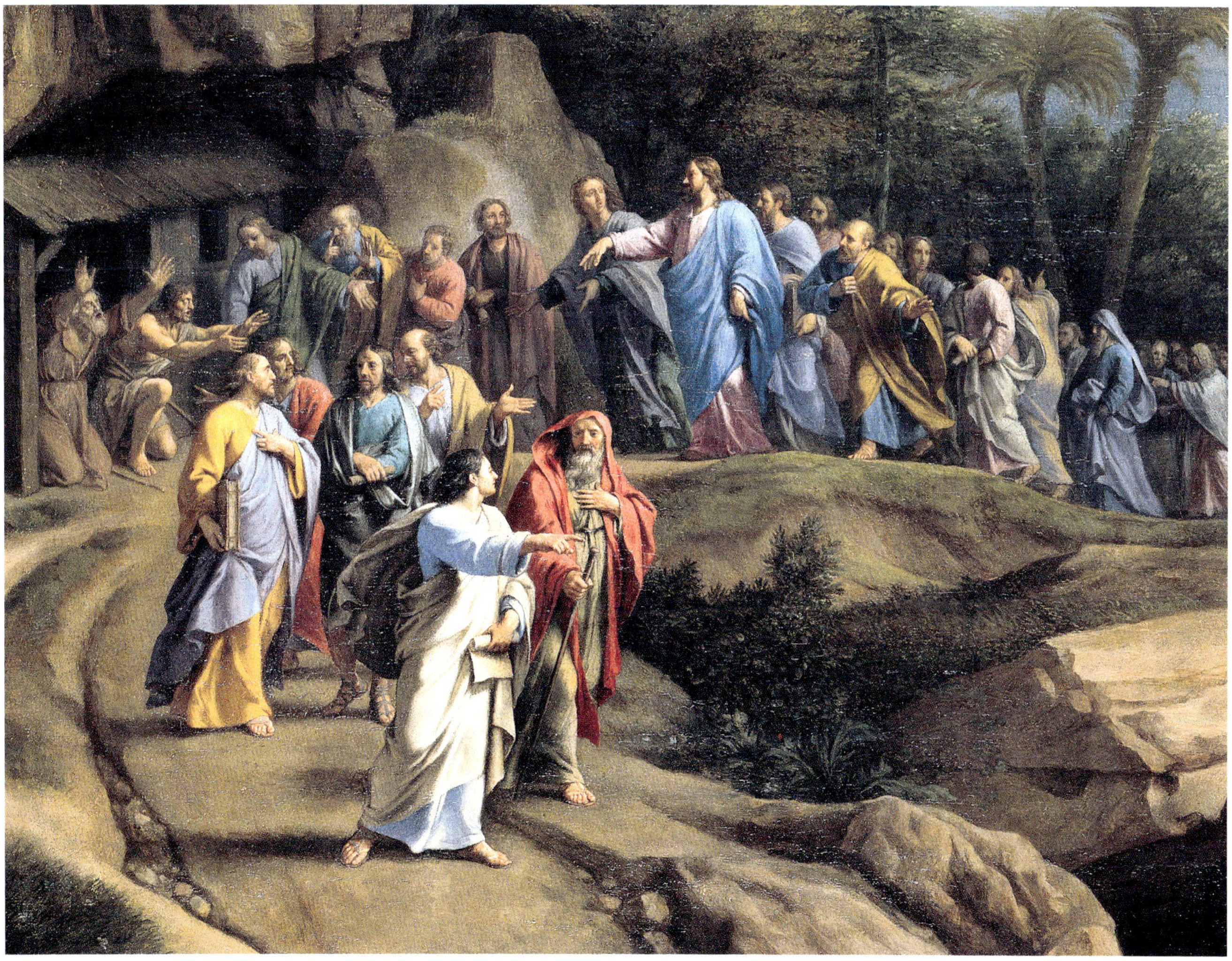

Detail of Plate 23

LITERATURE

Henri Stein, *Philippe de Champaigne et ses relations avec Port-Royal* (Paris, 1891), p. 17 n. 13; Vicomte de Groucy, "Les Peintres Philippe et Jean-Baptiste de Champaigne: Nouveaux Documents et inventaires après décès," *Nouvelles Archives de l'Art Français,* 3d ser. *(Revue de l'Art Français Ancien et Moderne)* (1892; reprint, Paris, 1973), 8:182, 196, nos. 12, 13; Agnes Mongan and Elizabeth Mongan, *European Paintings in the Timken Art Gallery* (San Diego, 1969), pp. 94, 95, 130–31, no. 35, ill.; Bernard Dorival, "Philippe de Champaigne: Chercheur d'âmes," *Connaissance des Arts,* no. 273 (November 1974): 126–33, ill.; id., *Philippe de Champaigne, 1602–1674: La Vie, l'oeuvre, et le catalogue raisonné de l'oeuvre,* 2 vols. (Paris, 1976), 1:7, 99, 121, 122, 141, 178, no. 230, and 2:128, ill.; Jean-Luc Bordeaux, "Baroque to Neo-Classicism," *Apollo* 115 (June 1982): 456, fig. 15; *Timken Art Gallery: European and American Works of Art in the Putnam Foundation Collection* (San Diego, 1983), pp. 28–29, 116–17, no. 7, ill.

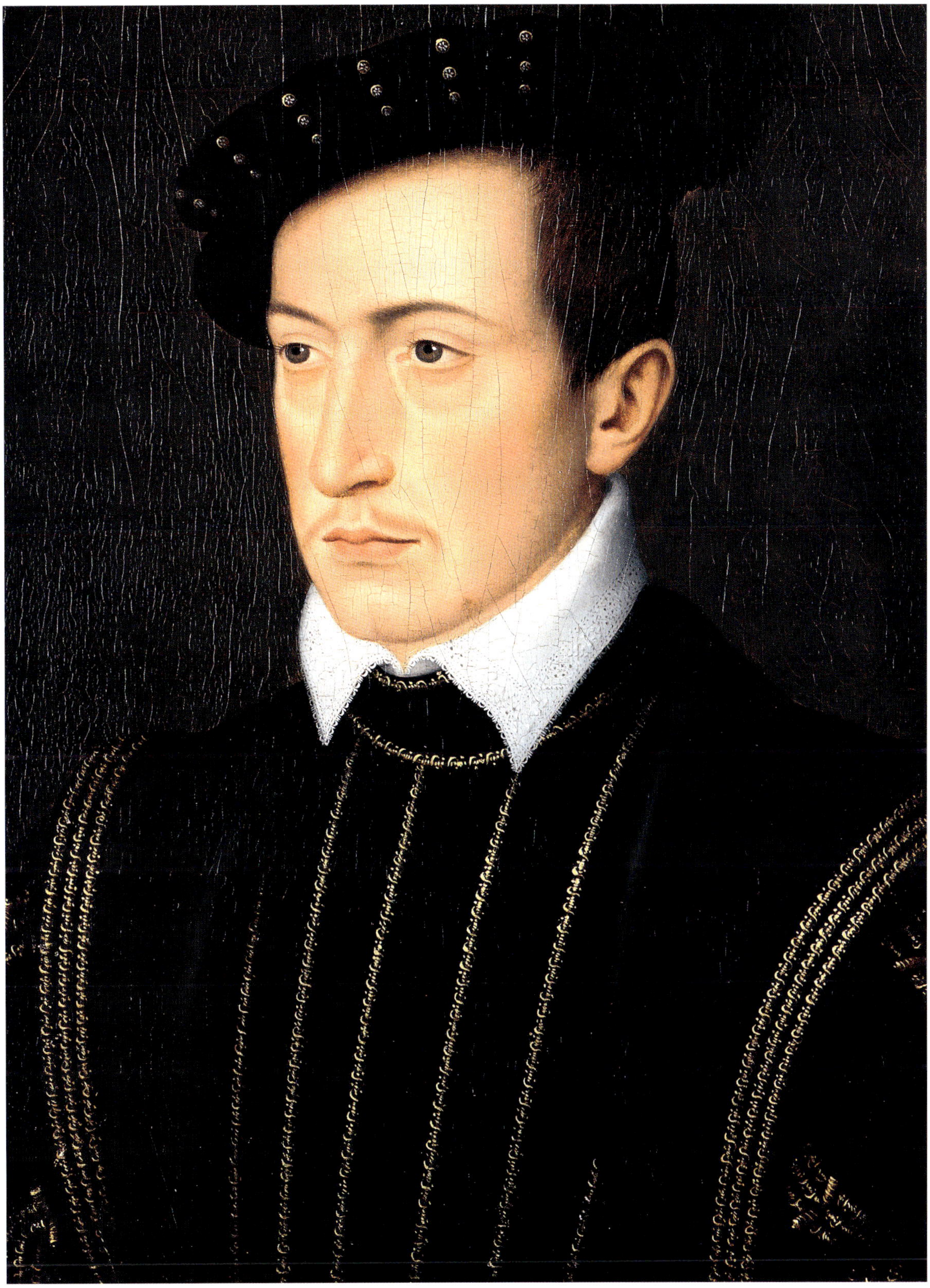

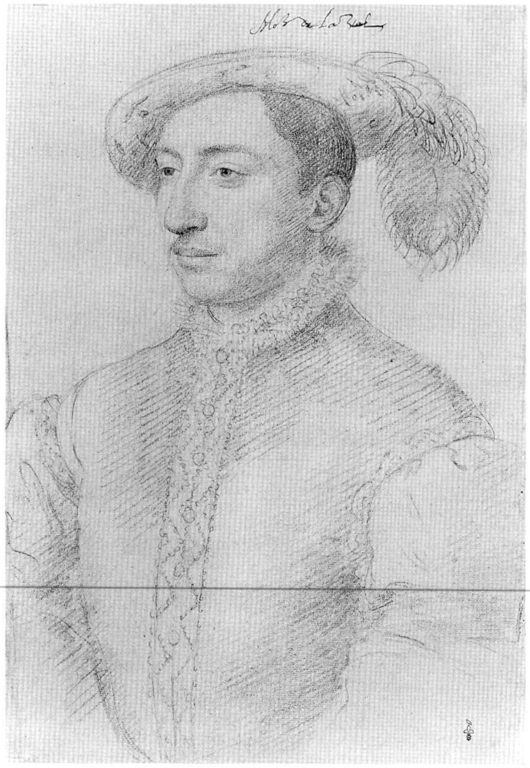

Fig. 1. *Claude, Known as Guy, Comte de Laval*, ca. 1540. Black chalk heightened with red chalk. Chantilly, Musée Condé. Photograph courtesy of Giraudon/Art Resource, New York.

and furniture to pay the debts before marrying, after only eight months of widowhood, the comte de Luxembourg, Charles de Martignes. The first child of this second marriage died. The mother died giving birth to her second child when word was received of her husband's death in 1553 at the siege of Hesdin. This ended the direct de Foix and Lautrec lines. A drawing of Claude de Foix and a painting in the Louvre reveal that the countess was somewhat hunchbacked.

This somber family history may explain why the portrait has been little known and without a name. It first appeared on the art market in the 1950s, the sitter unidentified. The identification was made by the present writers, who noticed its likeness to two sixteenth-century drawings, both with contemporary inscriptions calling him Laval: one at Chantilly (fig. 1) and one formerly in the collection of Philip Hofer, Cambridge, Massachusetts, now [as of 1969] in an English private collection.[1] The Chantilly drawing is described as representing Guy Laval at the age of eighteen.

We would like to suggest that the young man in the painted portrait is also about eighteen; that is, the portrait would have been painted in 1540. There seem to be strong reasons for assigning it to that year. Jean Clouet, who had been Valet of the Bedchamber and First Painter to the King, died in 1540/41. François I appointed Jean's son François to the posts his father had held. In 1541 the king appointed young Laval (as well as his first cousin François Montmorency) a Gentleman of the Bedchamber of the King. By an act of the Royal Will on November 3, 1540, the king also declared that, although still legally a minor, Laval was to be of age and given control of his own affairs.[2] The two acts of the king would place the youth close to the royal household and to its official artist, also newly raised to his royal office. The quality of the painting would bear out the attribution.

French court portraits of the mid-sixteenth century showed the sitters, elaborately but soberly dressed, bust-length against a neutral background. The features are recorded with exactitude and without flattery, but the sitters are withdrawn, as is this young man, in a world of their own thoughts. Later portraits by François Clouet show the artist more at his ease and more brilliant in both choice of color and technique. Here he is, at the outset of his distinguished career, somber in tone and earnest in interpretation.

—A. M. AND E. M.

NOTES

1. Reproduced in Agnes Mongan, "A Group of Newly Discovered Sixteenth-Century French Portrait Drawings," *Harvard Library Bulletin* 1 (1947): 155–75, pl. V.

2. A. Bertrand de Broussillon and P. de Farcy, *La Maison de Laval, 1020–1605*, 5 vols. (Paris, 1895–1903), 4:108.

PROVENANCE

Château de Nantilly (the seat of the bishops of Lyon); M. de Montgolfier; M. Lucien Brun, Château d'Essuly, near Lyon; private collection, Paris; acquired by the Putnam Foundation, 1955.

LITERATURE

Louis Dimier, *Histoire de la peinture de portrait en France au XVIe siècle* (Paris and Brussels, 1925), p. 25, no. 101; "Countrywide Loans from California," *Art News* 55 (November 1956): 33; Agnes Mongan and Elizabeth Mongan, *European Paintings in the Timken Art Gallery* (San Diego, 1969), pp. 92, 93, 129–30, no. 34, ill.; *Timken Art Gallery: European and American Works of Art in the Putnam Foundation Collection* (San Diego, 1983), pp. 36–39, 118, no. 11, ill. and detail.

EXHIBITED

Cambridge, Mass., The Fogg Art Museum, 1951, *Cranach and Clouet: Princely Portrait Drawings of the Northern Renaissance;* New York, The Metropolitan Museum of Art, extended loan, 1956–65.

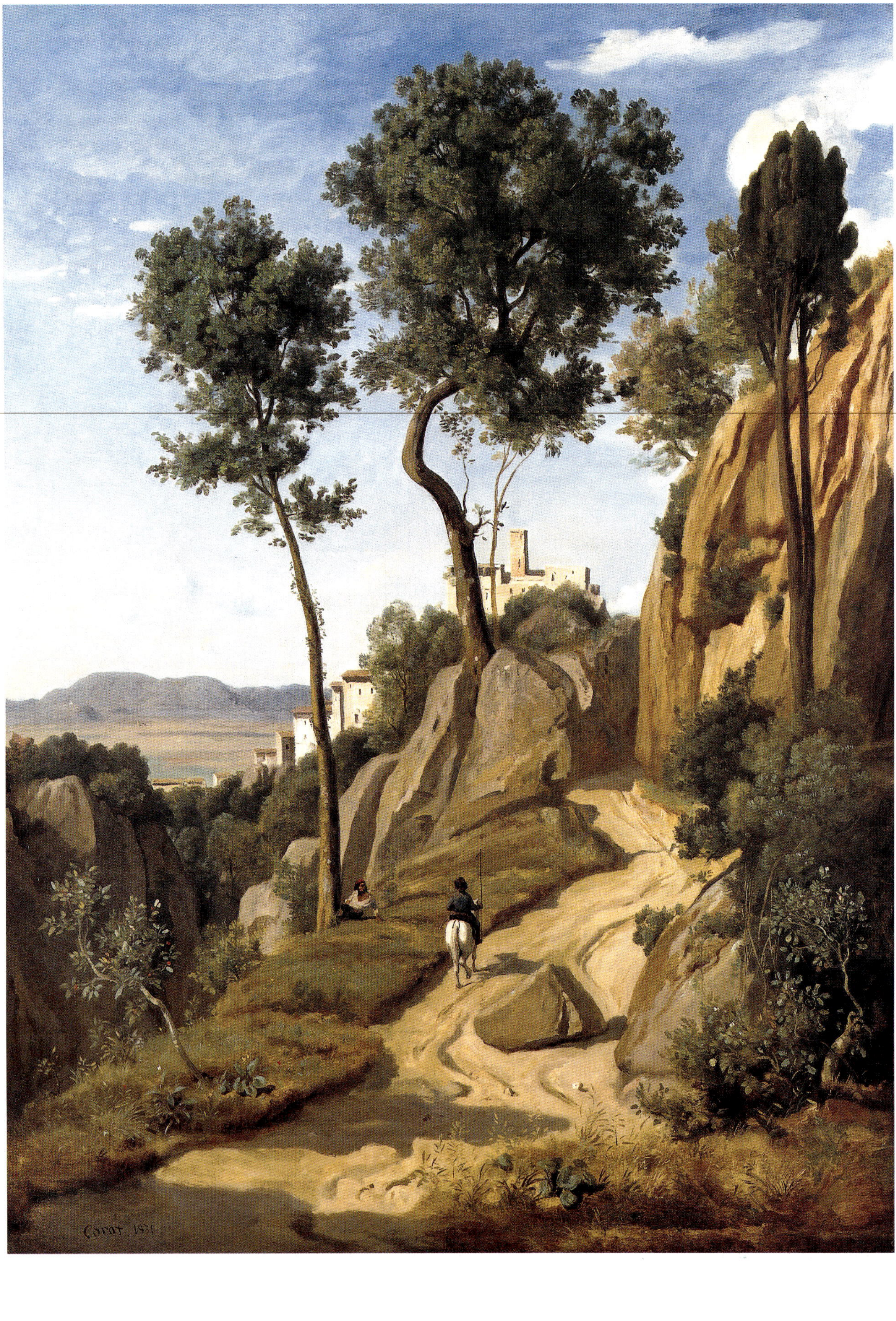

Jean-Baptiste-Camille Corot
(1796–1875)

Corot, one of the most prolific and successful landscape painters of the nineteenth century, was born in Paris in 1796. After proving himself to be unsuitable in the vocation chosen for him by his parents, that of cloth merchant, he was allowed to study painting. In 1827 he began exhibiting at the Salon, the annual or biennial art exhibition sponsored by the French government, and continued to do so until his death, in Paris, in 1875. His early production was based on the models established by French and Dutch landscape painters of the seventeenth century. Three trips to Italy—1825–28, 1834, and 1843—provided motifs that appeared in his paintings throughout his career. It was only around 1850, however, that he developed his signature style, characterized by forms and colors softened through the agents of atmosphere and memory. This style proved to be extremely popular, and Corot (and others; his work was widely forged) willingly produced replicas and variants of sought-after works for a growing middle-class market. His evident love of nature and close attention to and transcription of its moods and appearance made his work a model for much later nineteenth-century art, both in Europe and America.

26 *View of Volterra*, 1838
Oil on canvas, 62⅝ × 47 in. (159.1 × 119.3 cm)
Signed and dated lower left: *COROT 1838*

View of Volterra was inspired by the hill town southwest of Florence and northwest of Siena, which Corot visited on his second trip to Italy, in 1834. Leaving Paris in May, he had intended to join fellow painters Théodore Caruelle d'Aligny and Edouard Bertin in Rome. Corot was in Genoa by June 1; traveling on, he spent almost a month in Volterra. He found the countryside to be "magnifique" and painted at least five small oil sketches there. For unknown reasons, Corot never got as far as Rome; he was back in Paris in the early autumn.

The town that so fascinated him was perched by its fourteenth-century builders on a 1,700-foot-high rust-colored hill, on the site of earlier Etruscan and Roman cities. It was—and remains—protected by yellow sandstone walls, thirteen feet thick and forty feet high (fig. 1). It is known for the local alabaster, quarried from the hill itself and fashioned into bowls and vases. Isolated and somewhat desolate, Volterra

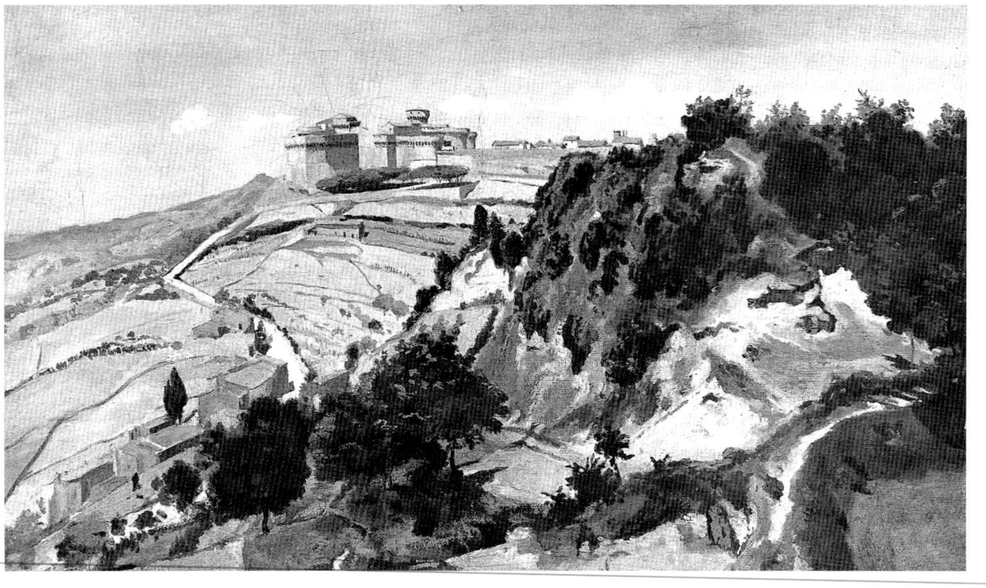

Fig. 1. Jean-Baptiste-Camille Corot, *Volterra, the Citadel,* 1834. Oil on canvas, 18½ × 32¼ in. (47 × 82 cm). Paris, Musée du Louvre. Photograph courtesy of the Réunion des Musées Nationaux.

could count a population of only around four thousand in the early nineteenth century. Contemporary descriptions of Volterra remark on its slightly forbidding character.

> Volterra is situated right on top of a mountain, like an eagle's or vulture's nest; one gets there along a very rugged and rocky path; it is surrounded by a crown of small olive trees, above which the city rises up all white.[1]

> From the towers of Volterra the view extends to the barren beaches [of the Mediterranean, visible on clear days]. The bareness of the soil is interrupted only by a few cypress and oak trees, whose dark foliage stands out against the yellowish ground of the countryside.[2]

Corot's oil sketches of Volterra, which smartly capture this feeling of barrenness, were made in the spirit of note taking. By gathering material for future paintings, he was following accepted academic artistic practice. Although he did not attend the national art school, the Ecole des Beaux-Arts, Corot had studied for several years with landscape painters and had learned from them the importance of direct observation and sketching in front of the motif. Only by working and studying out-of-doors could a landscapist hope to convey to the viewer the impression of the site. Thus, Corot's oil sketches of Volterra were useful several years later, when he painted two large, finished views of the area (the Timken's and one in Washington, D.C., fig. 2).

Given the specificity of the sketches, which show the city's distinctive walls, towers, and buildings, the large pictures are surprisingly generalized, more allusive than descriptive. Gone from the Timken picture are the imposing walls seen most prominently in figure 1; the bare cliffs take the place of the protective fortifications. The picture in Washington is even more removed from the particulars of the site. With no shining white walls, and not even a proper hill town to be seen, the Washington picture conveys only a generalized feel of Italy. While making the oil sketches,

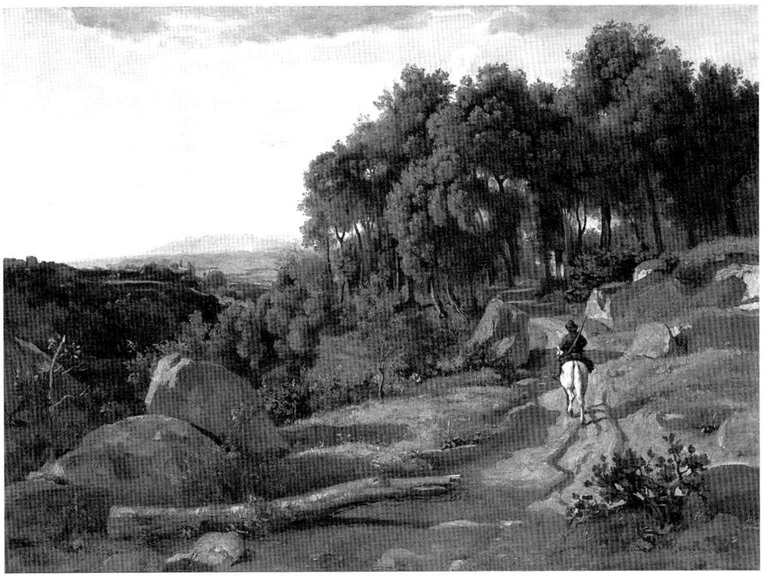

Fig. 2. Jean-Baptiste-Camille Corot, *A View near Volterra,* 1838. Oil on canvas, 27⅜ × 37½ in. (69.5 × 95.3 cm). Washington, National Gallery of Art, Chester Dale Collection, 1963.10.111.

Corot was interested in the rugged topography, the tonal relations of buildings seen in sunlight and shade, the visual leap from near to far necessitated when viewing the city at a distance. In the Timken painting, by contrast, the city is seen through the back door, as it were, uncharacteristically, informally, almost intimately. Without the walls, the city depicted here is not necessarily Volterra at all but could be any one of many hill towns in Tuscany. Not a portrait of a specific site, as the title suggests, *View of Volterra* is, instead, a *souvenir,* a memory of what Volterra felt like rather than what it actually looked like. To trigger this memory, Corot was careful to include the salient features of a hill town: the rust-colored earth, the precarious siting, the precipitous drop to the flat valley below, the answering hills on the other side. As he was to do increasingly in his later career, Corot let the magic of memory operate, evoking through suggestion the ambiance of a site or even a more generalized sense of the out-of-doors, away from urban centers.

It has been suggested that the Timken picture was shown in the Salon of 1838, but such is not the case. The dimensions of the pictures submitted to the Salon jury were recorded at the time. In 1838 Corot's *Vue prise à Volterra* measured 85 by 110 centimeters, indicating, first, that it was a horizontally oriented canvas, as is the picture in Washington. These measurements include the frame. If we assume the frame to have been of standard width, approximately three inches (fifteen centimeters) on a side, then the dimensions recorded in the Salon register correspond closely with those of the painting in Washington.

If the Timken picture was not exhibited at the Salon of 1838, why was it painted? Its size and the fact the artist signed and dated it indicate that Corot considered it a major work. The vertical orientation of the Timken work perhaps provides a hint of a different impetus. Most landscape paintings are horizontal, taking their cue from the horizon itself. The verticality of *View of Volterra,* which emphasizes the vertiginous cliffs, combined with the painting's large size, summary brushwork, and immediate impact, suggests that this view may have been intended as a decorative wall treatment, much like the scenes Corot painted for the home in Mantes of his friends the Roberts. The vertical compositions of this ensemble are *souvenirs* of the Bay of Genoa, gorges in the Tyrol, the region around Naples (the latter not dissimilar to the Timken's painting), and a view of Rome with the Castel Sant'Angelo and St. Peter's. With the exception of the Roman view, the others, although identified, are generalized, as is the Timken's, suggesting rather than describing those warmer transalpine locales.

—F. E. W.

NOTES

1. Ern[est] Legouvé, "Volterra," in *Italie pittoresque: Tableau historique et descriptif* (Paris, 1835), p. 17.

2. Saint-Germain Leduc, "Toscane," in *L'Italie* (Paris, 1834), p. 112.

PROVENANCE

Durand-Ruel, Paris; Boussac collection, Paris; Wildenstein & Co., New York; acquired by the Putnam Foundation, 1955.

LITERATURE

Alfred Robaut, *L'Oeuvre de Corot*, 4 vols. (Paris, 1905), 2:130, 131, no. 367, ill.; "Countrywide Loans from California," *Art News* 55 (November 1956): 33; Agnes Mongan and Elizabeth Mongan, *European Paintings in the Timken Art Gallery* (San Diego, 1969), pp. 102, 103, 133, no. 39, ill.; Jean-Luc Bordeaux, "Baroque to Neo-Classicism," *Apollo* 115 (June 1982): 456, fig. 17; *Timken Art Gallery: European and American Works of Art in the Putnam Foundation Collection* (San Diego, 1983), pp. 40–41, 118, no. 12, ill.

EXHIBITED

Washington, D.C., National Gallery of Art, extended loan, 1956–62; San Diego, Timken Art Gallery, and Williamstown, Mass., Sterling and Francine Clark Art Institute, 1988, *J.-B.-C. Corot: "View of Volterra,"* cat. by Fronia E. Wissman.

Jacques-Louis David

(1748–1825)

Jacques-Louis David was born in Paris, where he entered the studio of Joseph-Marie Vien in 1766. After several attempts, he won the Prix de Rome in 1774. In Rome from 1775 to 1780, he was profoundly influenced by the works of antiquity and of Poussin and was introduced to an international community of artists and scholars devoted to a revival of classicism. Back in Paris, he exhibited his *Belisarius* (Lille, Musée des Beaux-Arts) at the Salon of 1781, followed in 1783 by the even more severe *Andromache Mourning Hector* (Paris, Musée du Louvre), which gained him acceptance into the Royal Academy of Painting and Sculpture. Already attracting a coterie of devoted students, David returned to Rome to paint his seminal neoclassical masterpiece, *The Oath of the Horatii* (Louvre), which caused a sensation at the Salon of 1785. In ensuing years he exhibited a succession of innovative history paintings, such as the *Brutus* (Louvre) of 1789. Active in the Revolution, David forged a dramatic career in which his artistic and political ambitions merged. In 1790 he was commissioned by the Jacobins to paint *The Oath of the Tennis Court* (Louvre), a project that was abandoned, but he followed with a series of portraits of political martyrs, such as *The Death of Marat* of 1793 (Brussels, Musées Royaux). David organized several public festivals intended to inspire revolutionary feeling, and he led an attack on the academy, which was abolished in 1793. Imprisoned after the fall of Robespierre, he returned to the public eye in 1799 by exhibiting the large *Intervention of the Sabine Women* (Louvre). David won the favor of Napoleon, becoming First Painter to the Emperor in 1804. Besides portraits of the emperor, he produced two vast canvases on Napoleonic themes, *Le Sacre* (1805–7, Louvre) and *The Distribution of the Eagles* (1810, Musée National du Château de Versailles). After the restoration of the Bourbon dynasty in 1815 David left for Brussels, where he spent his last years painting mythological subjects and portraits. He died in Brussels in 1825.

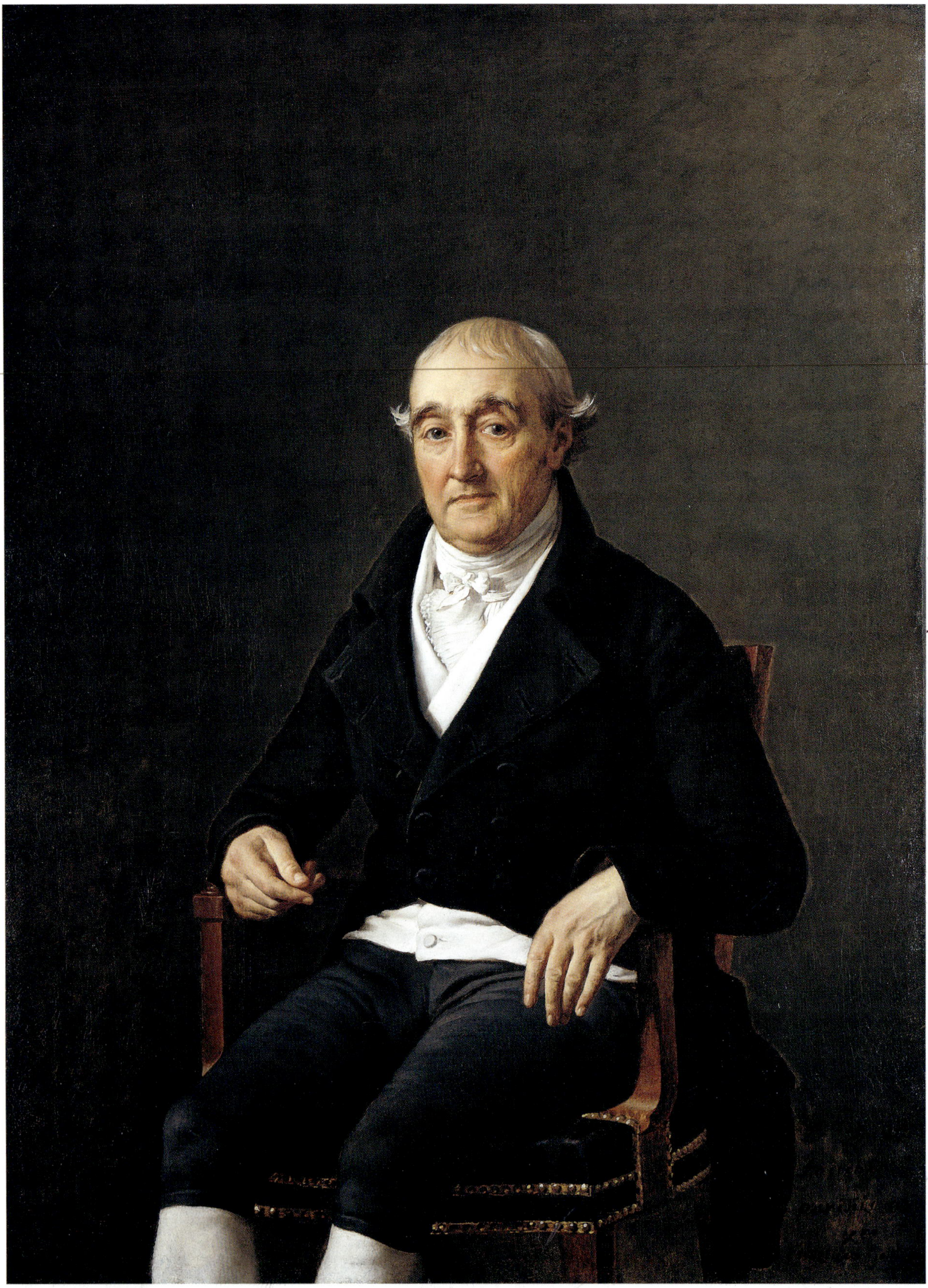

27 *Portrait of Cooper Penrose*, 1802
Oil on canvas, 51⅜ × 38⅜ in. (130.5 × 97.5 cm)
Signed and dated at lower right: *Louis David / faciebat / parisiis anno / Xme / republicae Gallicae*

Although best known for his historical and revolutionary subjects, David was also one of the great portraitists of his age. This straightforward yet powerful likeness of Cooper Penrose exemplifies David's mature portrait style, developed during the early 1790s, when revolutionary fervor was at its height. In those years David had formulated a type of three-quarter-length portrait in which he represented the subject seated before a bare wall. In keeping with the ardent republican beliefs of David and many of his clients at that time, the portraits exhibit an aesthetic austerity in which attributes and accouterments are kept to a minimum. Signs of the sitter's rank and lineage are replaced by a democratic sameness distinguished primarily through the force of individual personality. Although painted during a period when the ideals of the Revolution were undergoing rapid transformation, the Timken's *Portrait of Cooper Penrose* nevertheless follows this pictorial model. In fact, the elaborate Latin inscription at the lower right proclaims the artist's unflagging devotion to the cause of revolutionary France: "Louis David made this in Paris in the tenth year of the Gallic Republic."

Cooper Penrose (1736–1815) was a member of a prominent Quaker family originally from England that in the seventeenth century had immigrated to Waterford, Ireland. One of his uncles founded the famous glassworks there, although Penrose pursued a career as a timber merchant, eventually inheriting the thriving business of his father-in-law. His interests were wide-ranging, however, and he was an avid sportsman and sailor and raised prize cattle. With his wife, Elizabeth, he enlarged and decorated the family estate at Wood Hill, outside Cork, employing Italian artisans to create ceiling paintings, stucco work, and mosaics. He traveled widely in search of art, amassing a large collection of antiquities and porcelain; it was on such a buying trip to Paris in 1802—when the Treaty of Amiens, which temporarily brought an end to hostilities between Britain and France, allowed for easier international travel—that he commissioned his portrait from David.

According to family tradition, Penrose's increasingly worldly interests and lavish tastes reached a point at which he was threatened with expulsion from the Society of Friends. It may well be that the spartan sobriety of David's portrait—in which the sitter is represented utterly without ostentation or pretension—was an attempt to combat this unflattering impression on the part of the Quakers. A letter from David to Penrose reveals that his client sought more in his portrait than a mere likeness: "If Mr. Penrose will entrust himself to me, I shall paint his portrait for two hundred gold louis. I will represent him in a manner worthy of us both. This painting will be a monument that will attest to Ireland the virtues of a good family man and the talents of the painter who has rendered them."[1] The solicitude apparent in this statement is remarkable, coming as it did from the most famous artist in Europe in response to an inconsequential, albeit wealthy, patron, especially considering that—if we are to believe another family anecdote—David initially refused the commission.[2]

Nevertheless, if an image of Quaker asceticism is indeed what Penrose wished to convey, he must have considered the portrait an unassailable success.[3] Few life-size portraits are less assuming: Penrose's austere costume—a black cutaway jacket, white waistcoat and stock, dark gray knee breeches, and white stockings—is matched by the simplicity of the neoclassical armchair in which he sits and the plain brown wall that serves as a backdrop. David positioned the head lower on the canvas than is traditional in French portraiture, so that an open, undifferentiated space surrounds Penrose's smallish form. This has the effect of bringing the sitter down to earth, of making him accessible to the viewer, thus helping to establish an intimate dialogue between the beholder and the beheld. Penrose's portrait has none of the bombast, for example, of Largillierre's extraordinary *Portrait of Barthélemy-Jean-Claude Pupil* (cat. no. 29), where the head is placed higher in the composition and the commanding form fills the space.

The starkness of the conception is matched by its execution, for David restrained his brushwork and color scheme, limiting himself to a muted palette of dark hues sharply offset by lighter passages in the face, hands, and costume. Even the somber background, often enlivened in David's portraits by a rough scumbling technique, here exhibits little painterly flourish. The viewer's attention is instead focused on the head and hands, which form three points of a triangle in the center of the composition. These areas are painted with a fidelity and technical brilliance that give the portrait an unexpected power and visual presence. Whereas earlier artists like Largillierre found inspiration in the high baroque visual rhetoric of Rubens and Van Dyck, in his *Portrait of Cooper Penrose* David drew on the restrained pictorial language of middle-class Dutch art, such as Rembrandt's merchant-portraits of the 1630s. With his relaxed demeanor and good-natured gaze, Penrose nevertheless projects an image of quiet self-assurance.

—R. R.

NOTES

1. The letter, which remained with the Penrose family and is now in the archives of the Timken Museum of Art, goes on to enumerate the payment schedule: "There shall be three payments, 50 louis at the start, 50 louis when the painting is blocked out, and the remaining 100 louis when the work is completed" (Que Monsieur Penrose se fie entièrement à moi, je lui ferai son portrait pour deux cents louis d'or. Je le représenterai d'une manière digne de tous les deux. Ce tableau sera un monument qui attestera à l'Irlande les vertus d'un bon père de famille, et les talens du peintre qui les aura tracées. On s'acquittera en trois payemens. Savoir 50 louis en commenceant, 50 louis quand le tableau sera ébauché, et les 100 louis restans quand l'ouvrage sera achevé).

2. The anecdotes describing Penrose's difficulties with both the Quakers and David are recounted in a typescript history of the Penrose family, in the Timken archives, compiled in August 1966 by Rupert C. Barneby and John Dennis Penrose, both direct descendants of the sitter. According to

Penrose's niece, Julia—a student of David—Penrose sat eighteen times for his portrait, from ten o'clock until four at each sitting (recorded by Joseph Farington in *The Farington Diary,* 2:45).

3. This view was not shared by all at the time. When Joseph Farington—an English painter better known for his chatty diary than his artistic judgment—saw the portrait during a visit to David's studio in October 1802, he proclaimed it to be "painted in a very poor manner having a sort of woolly appearance as if done in Crayons" (ibid.).

PROVENANCE

Cooper Penrose, thence by descent until 1953; Wildenstein & Co., New York; acquired by the Putnam Foundation, 1953.

LITERATURE

Charles Blanc, *Histoire des peintres français au XIXe siècle* (Paris, 1845), p. 211; J.-L. Jules David, *Le Peintre Louis David,* 2 vols. (Paris, 1880), 1:642; Joseph Farington, *The Farington Diary,* ed. James Grieg, 8 vols. (London, 1922–28), 2:45–46; Richard Cantinelli, *Jacques-Louis David* (Paris, 1930), p. 110, no. 100; Klaus Holma, *David: Son Evolution et son style* (Paris, 1940), p. 128, no. 106; Agnes Mongan and Elizabeth Mongan, *European Paintings in the Timken Art Gallery* (San Diego, 1969), pp. 100–101, 132–33, no. 38, ill.; Daniel M. Wildenstein, *Documents complementaires au catalogue de l'oeuvre de Louis David* (Paris, 1973), p. 161, no. 1386, p. 209, no. 1810, p. 226, no. 1938; Antoine Schnapper, *David* (New York, 1982), pp. 208, 210, 211, fig. 121; *Timken Art Gallery: European and American Works of Art in the Putnam Foundation Collection* (San Diego, 1983), pp. 42–43, 118–19, no. 13, ill.; Luc de Nanteuil, *Jacques-Louis David* (New York, 1985), pp. 56, 69, fig. 75; Jean-Jacques Lévêque, *La Vie et l'oeuvre de Jacques-Louis David* (Paris, 1989), p. 212, ill.; Antoine Schnapper et al., *Jacques-Louis David, 1748–1825,* exh. cat., Musée du Louvre (Paris, 1989–90), pp. 19, 21, 375, 601, fig. 93 (in reverse).

EXHIBITED

New York, The Metropolitan Museum of Art, extended loan, 1953–55; Cambridge, Mass., The Fogg Art Museum, extended loan, 1955–65; The Museum of Fine Arts, Houston, 1986–87, *A Magic Mirror: The Portrait in France, 1700–1900,* cat. by George T. M. Shackelford and Mary Tavener Holmes, pp. 78, 131, no. 23, ill.

Jean-Honoré Fragonard

(1732–1806)

Born in Grasse, Fragonard moved to Paris at an early age. There he studied briefly with Jean-Siméon Chardin before entering the studio of François Boucher. Under Boucher's sponsorship Fragonard won the coveted Prix de Rome in 1752. Before leaving for Italy, however, he entered the Ecole des Elèves Protégés in Paris, a school established to train the most promising students of the Royal Academy of Painting and Sculpture. From 1756 to 1761 Fragonard was in Italy, where, under the guidance of the academy's director, Charles-Joseph Natoire, and the Abbé de Saint-Non, an accomplished amateur, he developed an interest in landscape painting and drawing. Back in Paris, he made his public debut at the Salon of 1765 with the monumental *Coresus and Callirhoë* (Paris, Musée du Louvre), which won him probationary acceptance into the academy and was admired by the critic Denis Diderot. Despite his success, Fragonard declined to pursue a public career as a history painter, preferring to work for a private clientele of financiers and courtiers. Over the course of four decades he produced many brilliantly realized easel paintings, like the *Portraits de fantaisie,* and large-scale decorative works, such as the *Progress of Love* (New York, Frick Collection), commissioned by Madame Du Barry for her retreat at Louveciennes. A second trip to Italy in 1773–74 in the company of the financier Bergeret de Grandcourt rekindled Fragonard's interest in landscape and garden imagery, leading to such late masterpieces as the *Fête at Saint-Cloud* (Paris, Banque de France). During the Revolution Fragonard fled to his native Grasse, returning to Paris in 1793, where Jacques-Louis David appointed him a curator at the new National Museum. Fragonard died in Paris in 1806.

28 *Blindman's Buff (Le Colin-Maillard),* ca. 1775–80
Oil on canvas, 24⅝ × 17¾ in. (62.5 × 45.1 cm)

In subject and style *Blindman's Buff* typifies the resplendent pictorial idiom practiced by Fragonard during the height of his artistic maturity in the 1770s. In this intimate and carefully finished painting, a verdant garden provides the backdrop to an amicable gathering of well-dressed men, women, and children. The principal figures in the middle ground, half hidden by a stone wall, prepare to play the familiar game of blindman's buff, in which a player is blindfolded and attempts to capture his or her

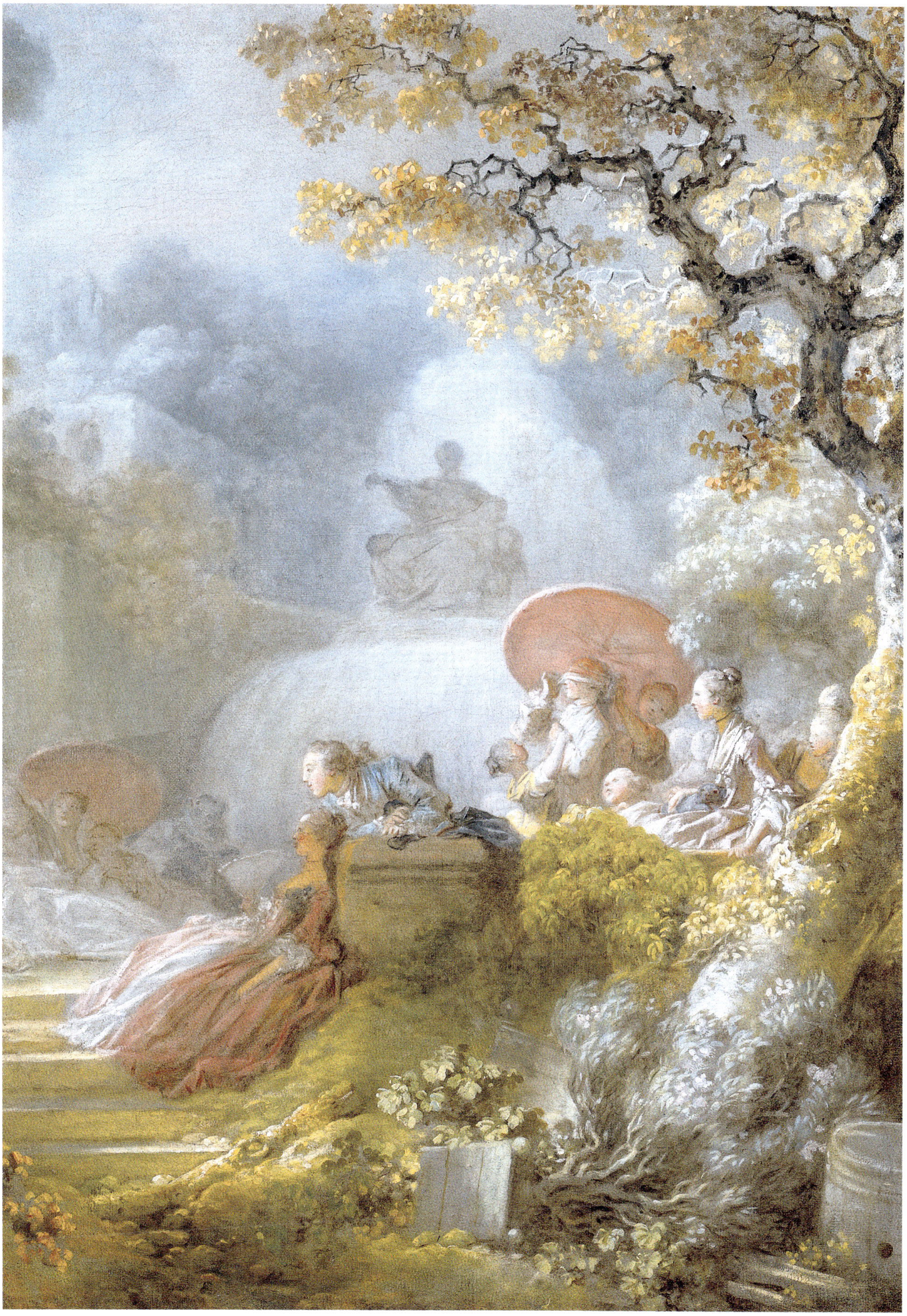

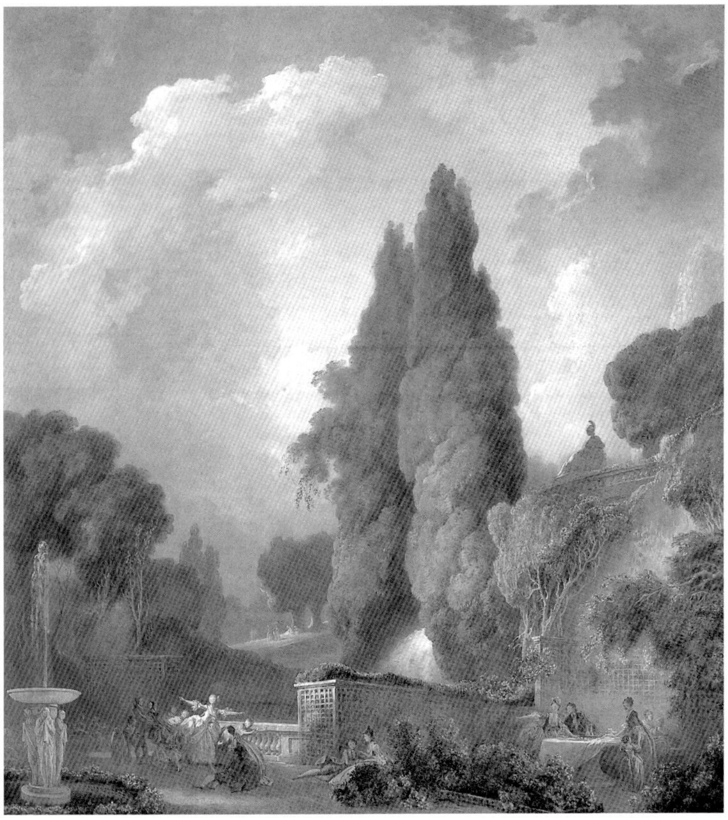

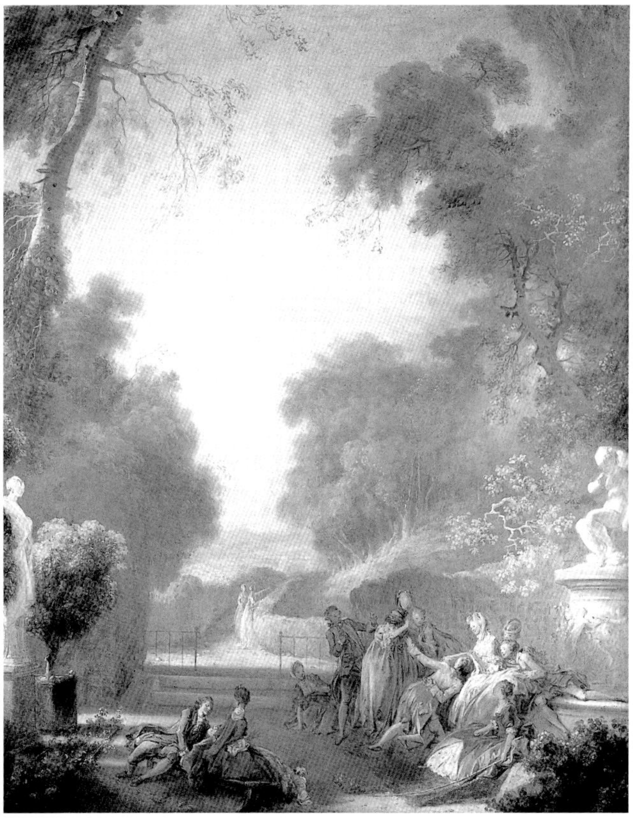

Fig. 1. Jean-Honoré Fragonard, *Blindman's Buff*, ca. 1775–80. Oil on canvas, 85⅛ × 77⅞ in. (216.2 × 197.8 cm). Washington, National Gallery of Art, Samuel H. Kress Collection, 1961.9.16.

Fig. 2. Jean-Honoré Fragonard, *A Game of Hot Cockles*, ca. 1775–80. Oil on canvas, 45½ × 36 in. (115.6 × 91.4 cm). Washington, National Gallery of Art, Samuel H. Kress Collection, 1946.7.6.

companions. Such lighthearted amusements were frequently portrayed by Fragonard and his contemporaries, as were rich and overgrown gardens, and in the Timken painting these two elements are brought into exquisite balance.

Despite some disagreement over its precise date—not unusual in Fragonard's oeuvre—it is generally assumed that *Blindman's Buff* was painted after the artist's second journey to Italy in 1773–74.[1] The painting shows numerous affinities with pictures usually assigned to the second half of the decade, one of the most productive periods in the artist's career. These include the suite of large landscapes now in the National Gallery of Art, Washington, D.C., one of which also shows elegant figures enjoying the game of blindman's buff in a picturesque garden (fig. 1). Leaving aside differences in scale and the proportion of figures to landscape, this work shares with the San Diego *Blindman's Buff* a light pastel color scheme, fluid brushwork, and a vast and misty garden setting punctuated by sculptures, cascades, and artfully arranged masses of foliage. A smaller painting from the Washington group showing a related game, hot cockles (fig. 2), is closer still, remarkably similar in the arrangement and attitudes of the men and women, the treatment of the foliage, and the blue-green garden background. Nevertheless, the Timken painting differs somewhat from these and other works of the late 1770s in the starkness of its forms, which are more thinly painted and less modulated than is Fragonard's usual practice. This is particularly true in the rendering of the figures—which appear almost to be drawn with the tip of the brush—and the gnarled tree branch that fills the upper right corner of the composition. A common enough motif in the artist's repertoire, here the tree's ragged silhouette is emphasized over its three-dimensionality, giving it a sharp calligraphic quality similar to the artist's wash drawings and gouaches.[2] In *Blindman's Buff*, the angular contours of the network of branches add an element of visual drama to the mounting excitement of the participants in the game.

Part of the difficulty in assessing *Blindman's Buff* is a result of its fragmentary condition. The rapt attention with which several of the principal figures stare out of the composition indicates that the picture has been cut at the left and that it originally was considerably wider. This is confirmed by the lack of cusping in the canvas weave along the left edge and the traces (still partially visible to the naked eye) of part of the right leg of a man in knee breeches at the extreme left, near the seated woman with a parasol. Unless more evidence surfaces (such as a reproductive print or related drawing), one can only speculate as to the original appearance of the entire composition. Given the internal dynamics of the remaining picture, which is weighted heavily at the right, it is possible that the painting was originally horizontal in format and that the left side contained several more people who are the focus of the others' attention. Presumably these lost figures were also playing blindman's buff, and the man being blindfolded in the present composition is preparing to join a game already in progress. It is also possible that the left side of the scene showed a different activity altogether, perhaps another amusement or attraction.[3]

Fragonard depicted the subject of blindman's buff and similar activities, such as hot cockles and swinging—one of his favorite subjects—numerous times during his career. Although such amusements undoubtedly were enjoyed in eighteenth-century France, modern scholarship has recognized that their presence in paintings probably carried symbolic meaning, undoubtedly suggesting the game of love.[4] In blindman's buff the player, like love, is blind, and his or her clumsy attempts to locate a lover can be likened to the difficulty of succeeding at courtship. In the Timken painting, Fragonard depicted various stages in this amorous pursuit: at the right sits a woman, a cat in her lap, anticipating her turn to play; in the center the man preparing to enter the game adjusts his blindfold (or is he peeking at the object of his affections?); the couple reclining near the stone abutment have apparently finished playing and, now united, watch their companions enjoy love's progress.

Nearly all Fragonard's depictions of such pastimes take place in the kind of fecund and overgrown picturesque garden that was increasingly popular with the aristocracy at the end of the *ancien régime*.[5] Although Fragonard sometimes drew and painted actual gardens—such as those at Saint-Cloud, outside Paris—his depictions are more often imaginative re-creations of the private retreats enjoyed by his well-heeled patrons and their intimates. Combining as they do luxuriant gardens with figures engaged in amorous dalliance, Fragonard's paintings like the Timken's *Blindman's Buff* extend the tradition of the *fête galante* invented earlier in the century by Antoine Watteau. Yet despite their immense visual appeal, they often lack the enigmatic quality that gives Watteau's creations their elusive mystery and emotional profundity.

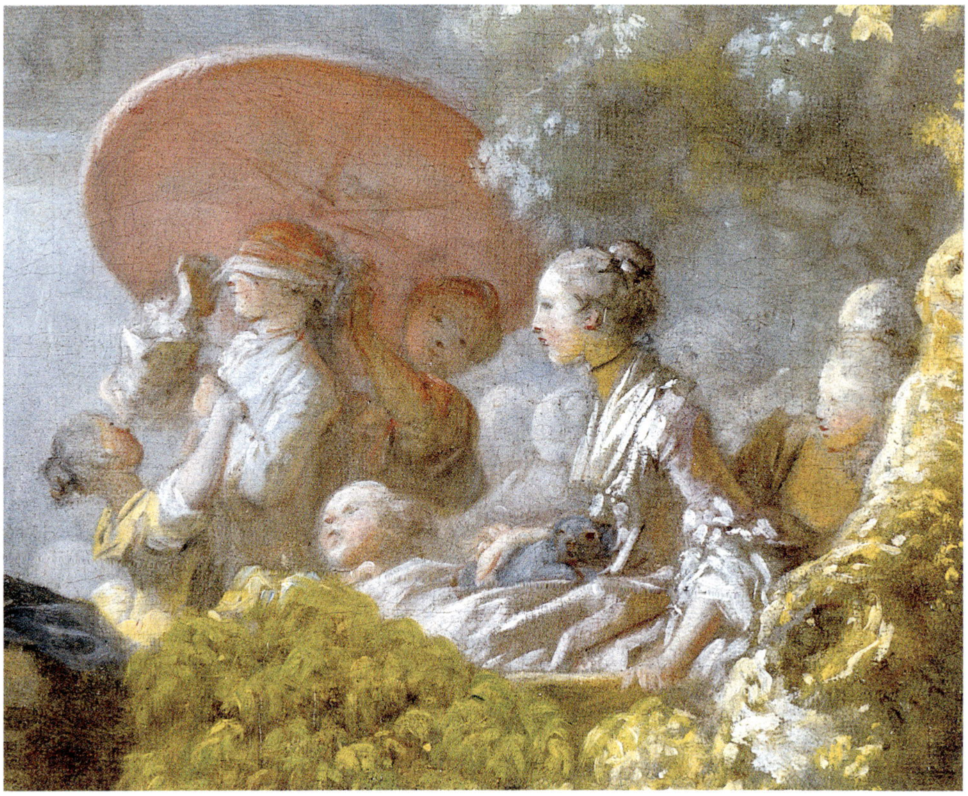

Detail of Plate 28

Indeed, they are closer in spirit to the sprightly pastorals of Fragonard's master Boucher, exemplified in the Timken's *Lovers in a Park* (cat. no. 21). In the increasingly moralizing social and political climate of the 1770s, however, Fragonard's garden scenes were sometimes derided as outdated and frivolous, a fact perhaps recognized by the artist, who rarely exhibited such works in public. At the same time, these pictures still held a strong appeal for private collectors, many of whom created private pleasure grounds similar to the one depicted in *Blindman's Buff*.

Unfortunately, the early history of the Timken's Fragonard is unknown. Given its small size and popular subject, however, it is probable that the picture was painted on speculation rather than on commission. During the 1770s and 1780s Fragonard's cabinet paintings appeared frequently on the art market, and sometimes a single painting changed hands several times over the course of a few years. *Blindman's Buff* was first recorded in the collection of Hippolyte Walferdin, who formed a celebrated collection of works by Fragonard, the public sale of which in 1880 did much to rehabilitate the artist's reputation.[6] It later belonged to Camille Groult, who also owned the large *Blindman's Buff* now in Washington.

—R. R.

NOTES

1. Fragonard's most recent cataloguers (Cuzin 1988 and Rosenberg 1989) date the painting to ca. 1773 (?) and 1775–80, respectively. Such is the difficulty in dating Fragonard's works that one could point out the affinities between the Timken painting and the much earlier *Jeu de la palette* (Cuzin no. 81), datable to 1759–60.

2. It appears, for example, in another of the Washington paintings, *A Game of Horse and Rider* (Cuzin no. 340), as well as in several of the landscapes inspired by Dutch art (Cuzin nos. 136, 137, 191). For drawings with a similar motif, see Rosenberg 1989, nos. 169, 187, 188.

3. It has been suggested that the left side of the picture showed figures gathered around a swing, a pairing that Fragonard repeated in another of the Washington paintings, *The Swing*, the pendant to the *Blindman's Buff* (fig. 1; see Wildenstein and Mandel 1972, pp. 102–3).

4. Donald Posner, "The Swinging Women of Watteau and Fragonard," *Art Bulletin* 64 (March 1982): 75–88. One version of Fragonard's *Blindman's Buff* (private collection, Switzerland; Cuzin no. 326) shows the game played before a statue of Cupid, reinforcing the love theme. For a history of blindman's buff, see Henri René d'Allemagne, *Récréations et passe-temps* (Paris, 1906), pp. 218–30.

5. See Dora Wiebenson, *The Picturesque Garden in France* (Princeton, 1978), and Jean de Cayeux, *Hubert Robert et les jardins* (Paris, 1987).

6. The sale was reviewed by Baron Roger Portalis, "La Collection Walferdin et ses Fragonards," *Gazette des Beaux-Arts* 21 (1880): 295–322.

PROVENANCE

Hippolyte Walferdin, Paris, his sale, Hôtel Drouot, Paris, April 3, 1880, lot 12; bought by Beurnonville, Paris; Camille Groult, Paris, by 1889; Wildenstein & Co., New York, 1954; acquired by the Putnam Foundation, 1955.

LITERATURE

Edmond de Goncourt and Jules de Goncourt, *L'Art du dix-huitième siècle*, 3d ed., 3 vols. (Paris, 1882), 3:335; Roger Portalis, *Honoré Fragonard: Sa Vie et son oeuvre* (Paris, 1889), p. 273; Pierre de Nolhac, *J.-H. Fragonard* (Paris, 1906), p. 150; Georges Grappe, *Fragonard: La Vie et l'oeuvre* (Monaco, 1946), p. 75; Louis Réau, *Fragonard* (Brussels, 1956), p. 158; "Countrywide Loans from California," *Art News* 55 (November 1956): 33; Georges Wildenstein, *The Paintings of Fragonard* (London, 1960), pp. 297–98, no. 446, fig. 188; P. du Colombier, "Nouvelle Jeunesse pour Fragonard," *Connaissance des Arts*, no. 120 (February 1962): 73, ill.; Agnes Mongan and Elizabeth Mongan, *European Paintings in the Timken Art Gallery* (San Diego, 1969), pp. 98, 99, 132, no. 37, ill.; Daniel Wildenstein and Gabriel Mandel, *L'opera completa di Fragonard* (Milan, 1972), pp. 102, 103, no. 379, ill.; Jean-Luc Bordeaux, "Baroque to Neo-Classicism," *Apollo* 115 (June 1982): 454, 456, pl. IV; *Timken Art Gallery: European and American Works of Art in the Putnam Foundation Collection* (San Diego, 1983), pp. 44–45, 119, no. 14, ill.; Jean-Pierre Cuzin, *Jean-Honoré Fragonard: Life and Work* (New York, 1988), p. 310, no. 264, ill.; Dore Ashton, *Fragonard in the Universe of Painting* (Washington, D.C., 1988), p. 172, fig. 41; Pierre Rosenberg, *Tout l'Oeuvre peint de Fragonard* (Paris, 1989), pp. 106–7, no. 316, ill.

EXHIBITED

Paris, Musée du Louvre, 1885, *Exposition de tableaux, statues et objets d'art au profit de l'oeuvre des orphelins d'Alsace-Lorrain*, p. 60, no. 199; Minneapolis Institute of Arts and New York, Wildenstein & Co., 1954, *French Eighteenth-Century Painters*, no. 11; The Art Institute of Chicago, extended loan, 1956–65; Paris, Grand Palais, and New York, The Metropolitan Museum of Art, 1987–88, *Fragonard*, pp. 352–53, no. 166, ill. (exhibited in New York only).

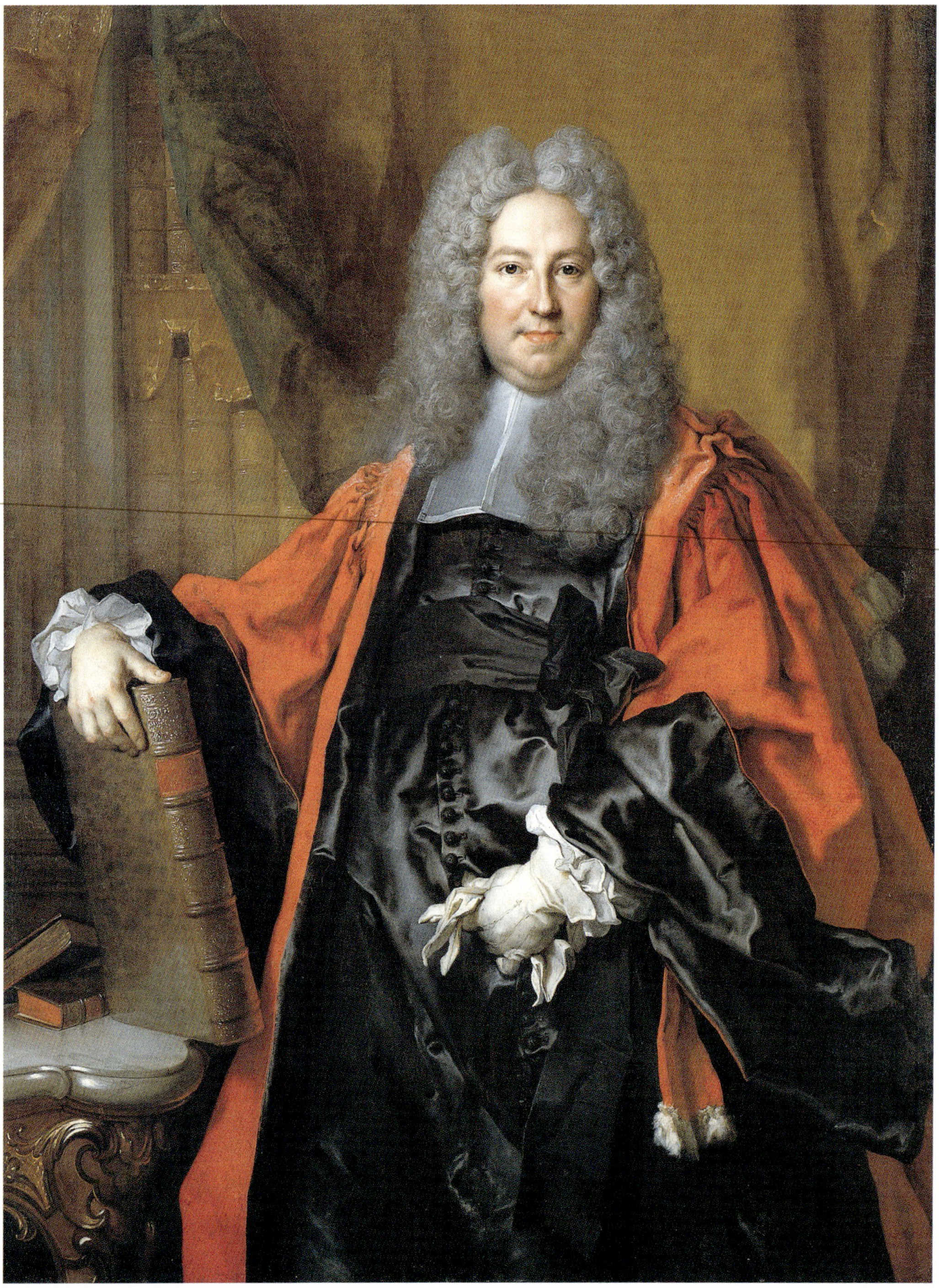

Nicolas de Largillierre

(1656–1746)

Largillierre's early career was exceptional. Born in Paris in 1656, he was brought up at Antwerp, and from 1674 he was an assistant to Sir Peter Lely in England. He was back in Paris in 1682. While his rival, Hyacinthe Rigaud, portrayed the royal family of France, Largillierre had the patronage of the wealthy professional class. He died in Paris in 1746.

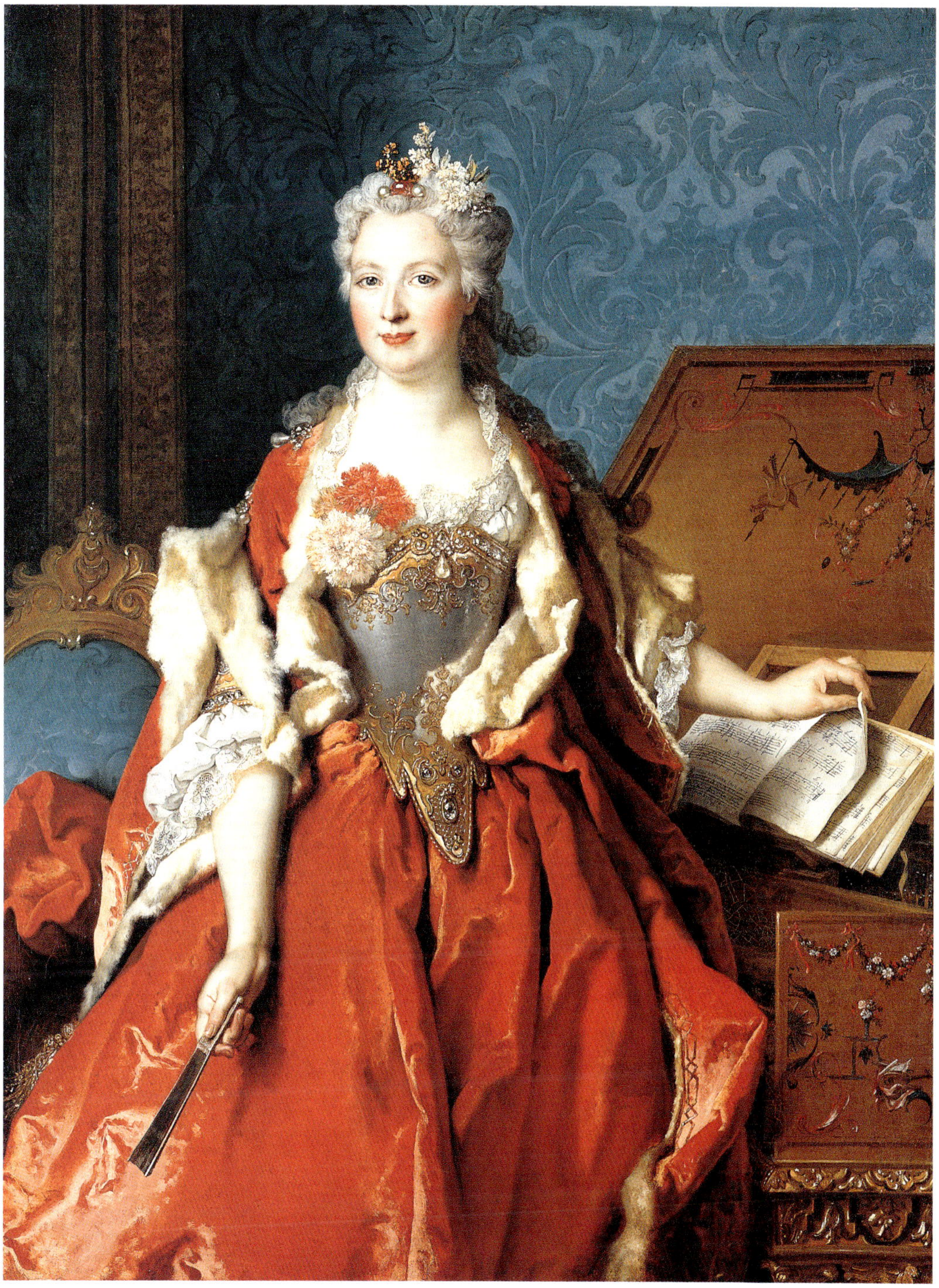

29 *Portrait of Barthélemy-Jean-Claude Pupil*, 1729
Oil on canvas, $54\frac{1}{2} \times 41\frac{7}{8}$ in. (138.4 × 106.4 cm)

30 *Portrait of Marguerite de Sève, Wife of Barthélemy-Jean-Claude Pupil*, 1729
Oil on canvas, $54\frac{1}{2} \times 41\frac{7}{8}$ in. (138.4 × 106.4 cm)

The bewigged sitter is shown at three-quarter length standing in front of a curtain. In his right hand he supports a large book, which rests on a console table. The second compartment from the top of the spine of the book is unornamented, unlike the other

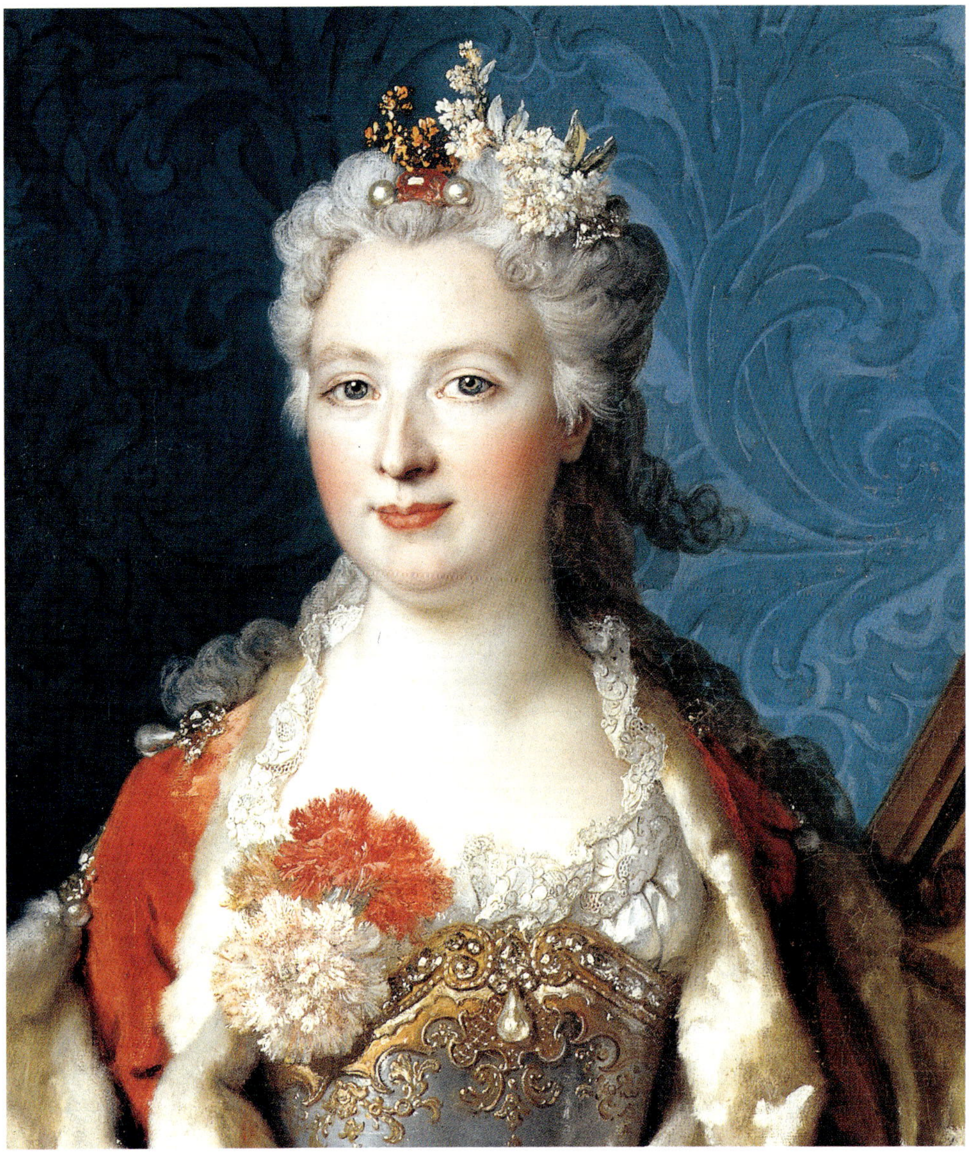

Detail of Plate 30

compartments, and was evidently intended to provide space for the title of the book. But the gilt of the lettering of the title has worn away. Two smaller books lie on the table; others are on the shelves behind.

Inscribed on the lining of the canvas on the reverse, evidently copying an inscription on the back of the original canvas, is the following legend: *peint par / N. de Largillierre. / .1729 / barthelmis. jean. claude. pupil. / chevalier. premier president. / de. la. cour. des monnoyes. / lieutenant. general. de. la. / senchausse. de Lyon.* The sitter is shown in legal robes. The two appointments mentioned in the inscription quoted above, president of the Cour des Monnaies and lieutenant general of the Sénéchaussée of Lyon, were given to him immediately after his marriage in 1722 to Marguerite de Sève, the daughter of Pierre de Sève, who was the former incumbent of the Sénéchaussée of Lyon and whose family had filled this post for more than a century. Both of these offices were judicial. The former exercised jurisdiction concerning financial offenses; the latter was the judicial authority of a more general kind in the Lyon area.

The sitter is mentioned in the royal almanacs of 1742 (p. 213) and 1765 (p. 242). The latter specifies that his son, Barthélemy-Leonard, had succeeded him in the preceding year (1764) as president of the Cour des Monnaies of Lyon.

An engraving by Tardieu of the head and shoulders (in reverse) of what is apparently the present picture specifies the name of the painter as "Grandon." It is assumed that it was Charles Grandon who in the seventeenth century painted the copy of the head and shoulders of the present picture, which was used by Tardieu for his engraving.

The lady is depicted three-quarter-length in front of a keyboard instrument. With her left hand she fingers the musical score that lies on a stand above the keyboard. Her right hand holds a furled fan. Inscribed on the lining of the canvas on the reverse, evidently copying an inscription on the back of the original canvas, appears the following legend: *peint. par / N. de Largillierre. /.1729.*

A peculiarity of the sitter's costume is the embossed and jeweled bodice, which reflects the lining of the sitter's robe, implying that it was made of metal. It has nevertheless been suggested that this effect could alternatively be given if the bodice were made of silk cut on the bias and mounted on molded buckram. It was probably based on the *lorica,* or Roman corselet.

The music on the keyboard instrument on the right of the picture has six, rather than five, stave lines. It is therefore not music intended to be played on a keyboard instrument and appears to be for a lute or theorbo. Underneath, clearly legible, are the words of a drinking song: "Buvons beaucoup mes cher amis. Buvons a la sante . . ." (Drink a lot, my dear friends. Drink to the health . . .). Such songs were fashionable for sophisticated women to sing at an evening gathering at home.

Perez (1980) has pointed out that the sitter's father, Pierre de Sève, had had his portrait painted by Largillierres's great rival, Rigaud.

—C. G.

PROVENANCE

By a series of indirect inheritances to Comte Olivier de la Ferrière, his sale, 1969; acquired by the Putnam Foundation, 1971.

LITERATURE

Marie-Félicie Perez, "Collectionneurs et amateurs d'art à Lyon au XVIIIe siècle," *Revue de l'Art,* no. 47 (1980): 44, 45, 51 n. 19, figs. 1, 2; Jean-Luc Bordeaux, "Baroque to Neo-Classicism," *Apollo* 115 (June 1982): 450, figs. 12, 13; *Timken Art Gallery: European and American Works of Art in the Putnam Foundation Collection* (San Diego, 1983), pp. 52–55, 120, nos. 17, 18, ills.

EXHIBITED

The Montreal Museum of Fine Arts, 1981, *Largillierre and the Eighteenth Century,* cat. by Myra Nan Rosenfeld, p. 245, figs. III, IV.

Camille Pissarro

(1830–1903)

Born in the Danish West Indies of a Jewish family, Pissarro first went to France in 1842 for boarding school. Again in France, in 1855, this time to devote himself to art, Pissarro responded strongly to the work of Camille Corot. Living for many years in Pontoise and Louveciennes, to the northwest of Paris, Pissarro never strayed far from the capital—except for the months he spent in England to avoid the Franco-Prussian War of 1870–71—finding all the inspiration for motifs he needed in the Ile-de-France, the region around Paris. Pissarro joined with Monet, Renoir, Degas, and other artists to exhibit their work to the public directly in what have been called the impressionist group shows. He was the only artist to exhibit in all eight of the showings, from 1874 to 1886. Pissarro's political thinking allied him with anarchists and socialists, yet his faith in the power of human resourcefulness to address social inequalities never undermined his humility before nature and his reliance on the craft of his art. Dedicated and innovative, he was open to new techniques, such as the scientifically based neo-impressionism and various forms of printmaking.

31 *Banks of the Oise at Pontoise*, 1867
Oil on canvas, 18 × 28⅛ in. (45.7 × 71.4 cm)
Signed and dated lower right: *C. Pissarro / 1867*

The simple descriptive title *Banks of the Oise at Pontoise* belies the painting's force and significance. Not merely a view of the banks of the Oise river at Pontoise, fifteen miles northwest of Paris, the painting demonstrates Pissarro's embrace of modernity as it made its way into the French countryside.

Pissarro lived in Pontoise intermittently beginning in early 1866. He and his family moved often during this time. In the spring of 1869 they were in Louveciennes and in September 1870 in Montfoucault, fleeing eventually to London as the Prussians advanced during the Franco-Prussian War. They were back in Louveciennes in late 1871, before returning to Pontoise in August 1872. For four months the Prussians occupied the house the artist had rented in Louveciennes; he estimated that twelve hundred paintings, *études*, and drawings were destroyed in his absence. Therefore this painting is one of the few records remaining of Pissarro's artistic activity during an important phase of his career.

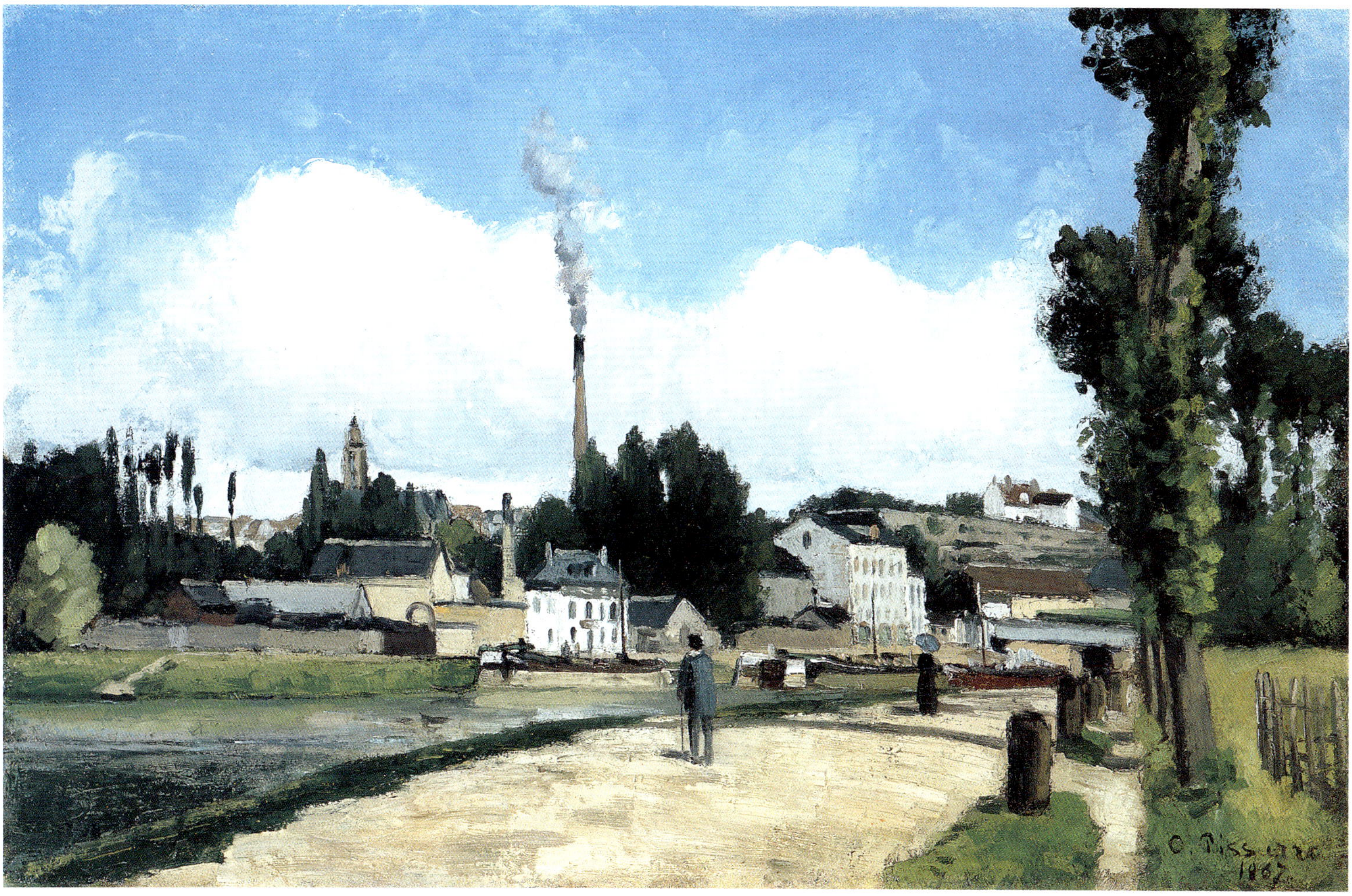

Pontoise, on a plateau rising above the Oise river, had been a market town for centuries. The surrounding countryside was notable, not for its beauty, but for its fertility; the town, for its accessibility. Pontoise was the place where the corn harvest of the Vexin, to the northwest, was transferred to boats on the canalized and navigable Oise. As the painting shows, Pontoise, a river port, did not have a harbor; boats docked along the quays. Pissarro arrived in Pontoise just as that nineteenth-century symbol of modernity, the railroad, entered the town. The railroad had been extended to Saint-Ouen-l'Aumône, across the river, as early as 1843, but not until 1863 did it enter Pontoise proper, over an iron bridge. That particular bridge was short-lived; the Prussians destroyed it in 1870.

The Timken's view of Pontoise was taken from across the river, in Saint-Ouen-l'Aumône, looking upstream. The square, blunt-pointed tower of Saint-Maclou is shown here, to left of center; to its right is the squat tower of the sulphur water factory. However, by late 1867, when Pissarro completed this painting, the structure that dominated the skyline of the town—and that is the focal point of this composition—was the smokestack of the Usine de Gaz, the gasworks, which opened in October of that year.

An X radiograph of the painting reveals a curious fact about this skyline. Although Pissarro blocked in the forms of the trees on the right, the central clump

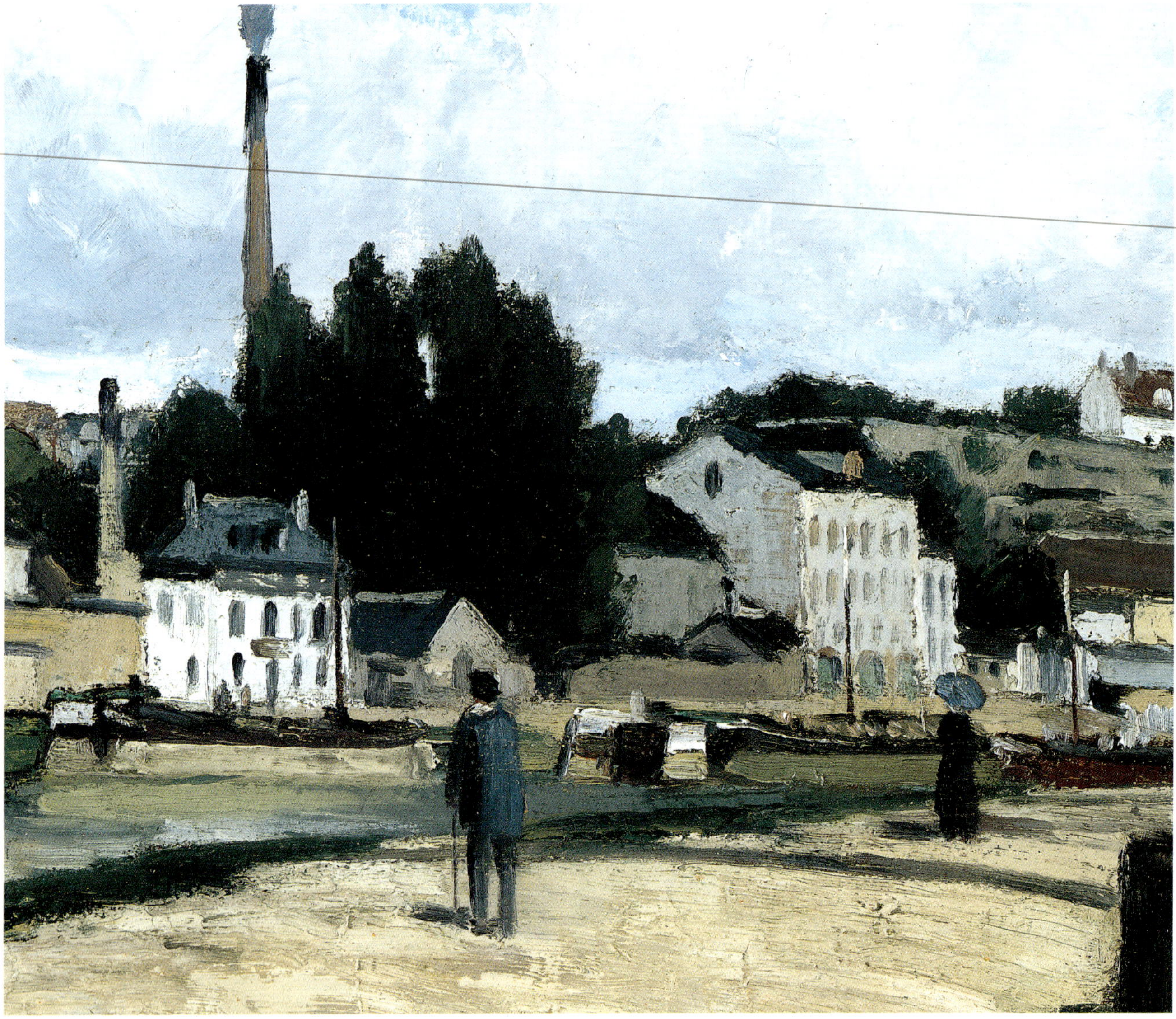

Detail of Plate 31

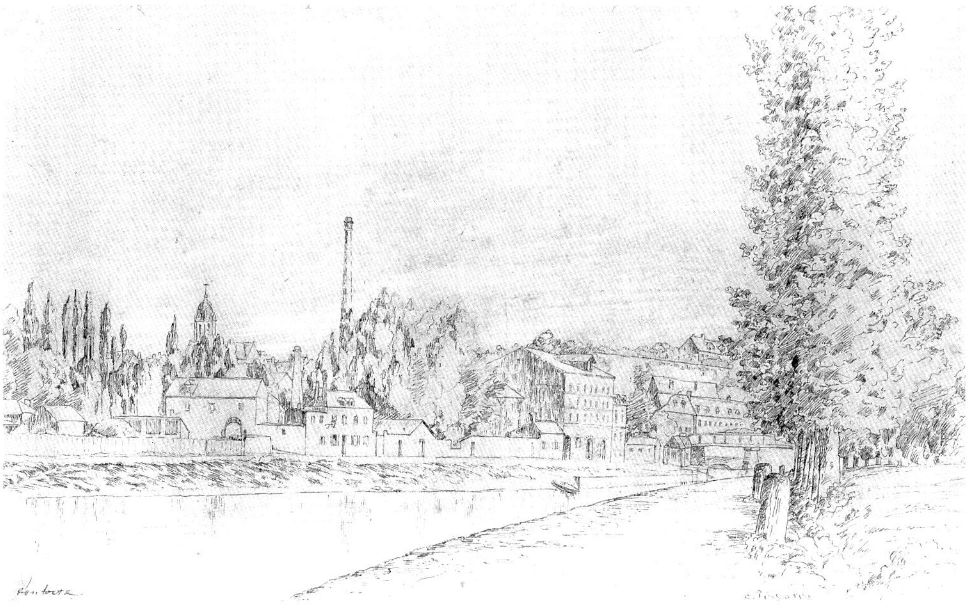

Fig. 1. Camille Pissarro, *Pontoise*, 1867. Pen and ink on paper, 10⅞ × 17¾ in. (27.6 × 45.1 cm). Private collection.

of trees, and the church tower, along with the main forms of the hill and buildings, painting in the sky around them, he did not leave room for the smokestack.[1] We are compelled to consider that the smokestack was added after the painting was conceived. As a later addition, it is evidence of Pissarro's insistence in including a potent symbol of industrial progress in what would otherwise be a prosaic view of a country town. Its central placement is due to its actual location relative to the other structures already built and painted, of course, but it is as if Pissarro were waiting for the smokestack to fit into his tightly composed scene.

Unusually for Pissarro, he made a careful pen-and-ink drawing of the scene (fig. 1), presumably truer to the actual appearance of Pontoise than is the painting. Its slightly different vantage point—along with the wider, narrower proportions—has the effect of straightening out the opposite river bank and thereby emphasizing the horizontal dimension. The little town seems to stretch on indefinitely to the right, past the railroad bridge. The drawing shows a careful looking, a concentration on details that gives it an almost eighteenth-century character. Absent from the drawing are the boats, the two figures walking along the quay, and the smoke—the things that move. The scene shown in the painting is thus more in tune with the contemporary feel of the town. The relationship of the painting and drawing subverts the usual order, however. Traditionally, drawings precede paintings, the easier, more portable, and cheaper medium of pen and ink being used as experimental ground for the more difficult, larger, and historically more valued oil painting. Yet the smokestack, firmly in the central position, indicates that the drawing postdates the painting.

The inclusion of the two figures in the painting demonstrates how Pissarro carefully composed this picture in bands alternately horizontal, vertical, and diagonal. A comparison with the drawing is instructive, for in that image, too, the main lines of the composition form a nexus at the right, at the intersection of the bridge, trees, and bollards. The same nexus is found in the painting, yet any sense of movement, reminiscent of the river's flow, is stopped short by the figures. They are not there for anecdotal interest but for purely formal reasons. They provide vertical accents, stoppages, that echo elements of the built environment: the man makes a pair with the shorter chimney of the sulphur works, and the woman, with the tower of Saint-Maclou. Their combined effect is to focus attention on the smokestack, seen not as an unwelcome intruder but as an integral part of the landscape, its smoke harmonizing with the framing trees.

Pissarro's matter-of-fact inclusion of the signs of industry in Pontoise can be seen in his surviving paintings of the town, but two in particular are related to the Timken's (Mannheim, Kunsthalle; Tel Aviv Museum of Art). Of similar construction, showing a quay on the right with the buildings on the opposite shore closing off the view, they both feature the smokestack of the gasworks in the center. Figures on the quay function as they do in the Timken painting, to lock the various parts of the composition into place. Painted in 1867–68, that is, just after the gasworks was completed and its smokestack became a part of the Pontoise skyline, these three pictures are eloquent testimony not only to Pissarro's enthusiasm for signs of industrial progress but also to his canny pictorial use of a new element in his beloved landscape.[2]

—F. E. W.

NOTES

1. Also missing are the two figures walking on the towpath and the row of spiky poplars at the left. Inserting figures after the composition was completed was standard practice, and the spiky poplars were most likely deemed necessary to balance the final composition.

2. This entry draws heavily on information in Richard Thomson, *Camille Pissarro: Impressionism, Landscape, and Rural Labor* (London, 1990), Richard R. Brettell, *Pissarro and Pontoise: The Painter in a Landscape* (New Haven and London, 1990), Brettell's contributions to the Timken's files, and Pissarro 1993.

PROVENANCE

M. Massion, Paris; bequeathed to his son-in-law, M. Bucaille; private collection, England; private collection, United States; acquired by the Putnam Foundation, 1983.

LITERATURE

Joachim Pissarro, *Camille Pissarro* (New York, 1993), pp. 44–45, fig. 38, as *Landscape with Factory.*

EXHIBITED

Jerusalem, The Israel Museum, and New York, The Jewish Museum, 1994–95, *Camille Pissarro: Impressionist Innovator,* cat. by Joachim Pissarro and Stephanie Rachum, pp. 88–89, no. 26, ill. and detail.

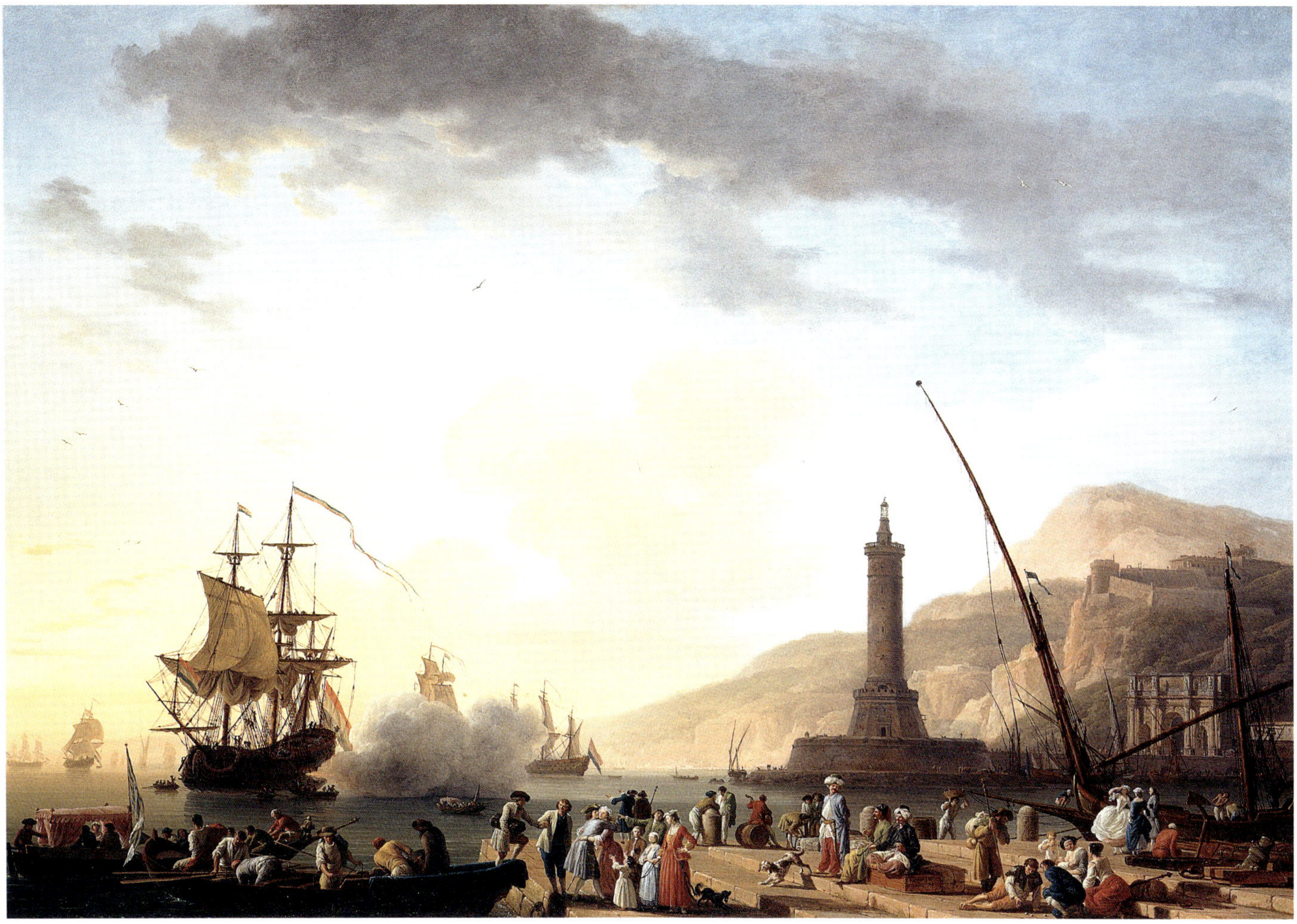

Claude-Joseph Vernet

(1714–1789)

Vernet was born at Avignon in 1714. He went to Rome in 1734, where he married an Englishwoman, Virginia Parker, leading to patronage from rich young English nobles and others who were doing the Grand Tour. Vernet returned to Paris in 1753, where he was commissioned by Louis XV to paint a series of French seaports. He died in Paris in 1789. His father, Antoine, and his son, Carle, were also painters; and the latter's son, Horace Vernet, was, in his day, the most famous of all.

32 *A Seaport at Sunset*, 1749
Oil on canvas, 44⅞ × 64⅝ in. (114 × 164.1 cm)
Signed and dated on the end of the box, below the lighthouse, on which a seated, turbaned figure is smoking: *Joseph Vernet / f.Romae 1749*

On the left is a large warship with one gun firing, presumably as a salute. Many other ships can be seen in the distance. The nearest ship flies no fewer than three

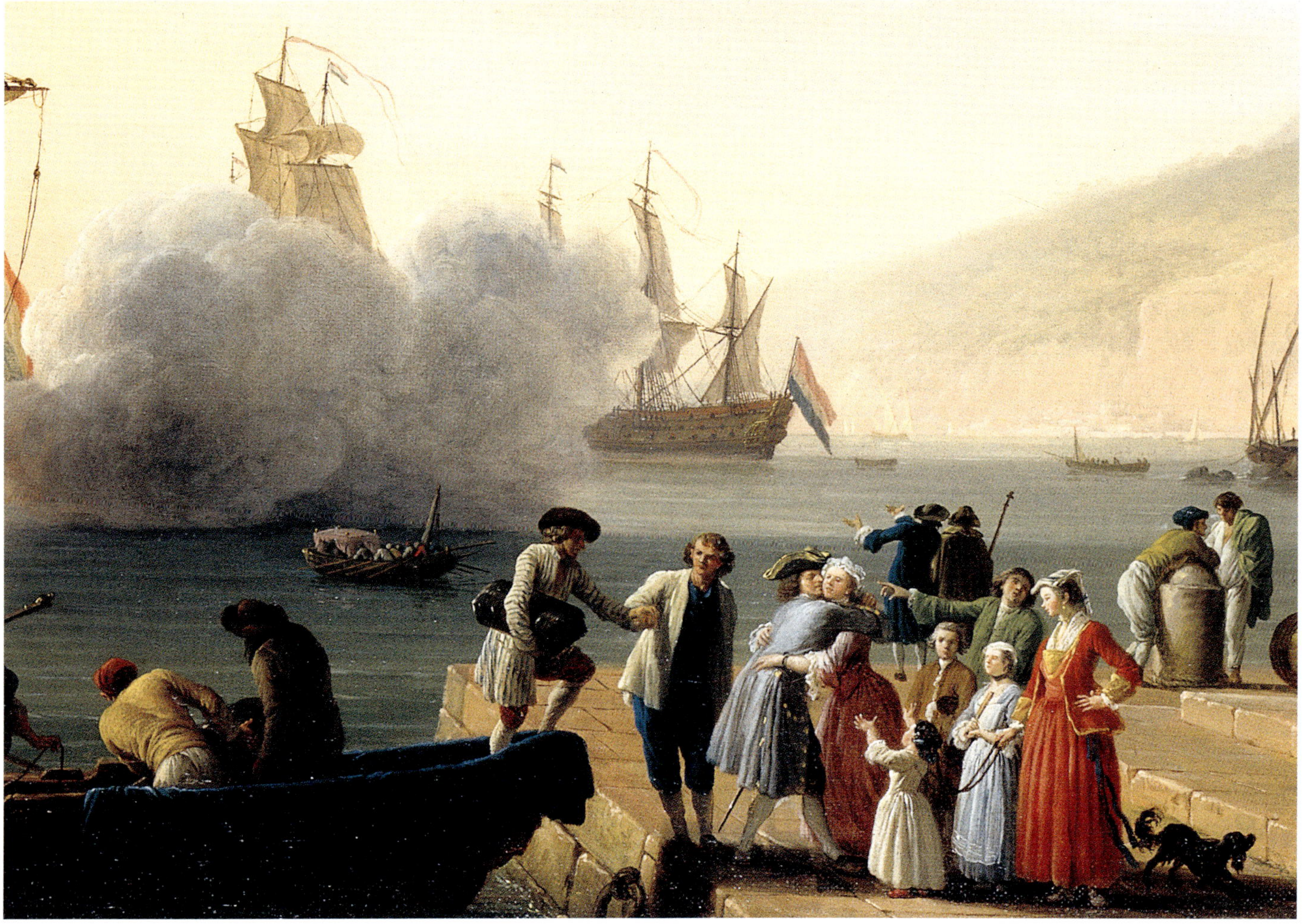

Detail of Plate 32

Dutch flags (horizontal stripes, red at the top, white in the center, blue at the base) and a very long pennant of the same colors that has blown over, so that the order of the colors appears reversed, with blue at the top and red at the base. Four other ships—two on each side of the big one—fly the same flag.

The lighthouse at the right, which recurs, with minor architectural variations, in other pictures by Vernet and other painters, is evidently the ancient lighthouse of Naples, La Lanterna, which existed until the nineteenth century. Certain features of the painting suggest, however, that it was not intended as a specific view either of Naples or of anywhere else, but rather that it was intended to be seen as an ideal Mediterranean seaport, conceived somewhat in the manner of the works of Claude Lorrain. These elements include the mountains seen behind the lighthouse, which are unlike any in the vicinity of Naples; the Arch of Constantine on the extreme right, which is in Rome; and the word *Romae* after the artist's signature, which shows that he was a resident of Rome at the time he painted the picture. Vernet is known to have had a special admiration for Claude, who had himself included the Arch of Constantine as a capriccio in a landscape now belonging to the duke of Westminster (*Liber Veritatis* 115). The inclusion in the present picture of people wearing turbans, seen on the quay below the lighthouse, also occurs from time to time in Claude's seaports as a picturesque detail.

The Timken painting has been identified as one of a pair that figured as lot 22 in the sale catalogue of pictures belonging to the comte de Merle.[1] On the strength of entries in Vernet's notebook,[2] which record his accompanying the count on hunting expeditions in November and December 1748, the present picture, which is dated 1749, has been thought to have been commissioned by de Merle at that time.

Although the details of the picture as given in the sale catalogue do not entirely tally with the present picture, it is possible that the discrepancies are due to haste and carelessness, since the description of a Vernet in the possession of the comte de Merle in 1783[3] corresponds better with the present picture. The comte de Merle was certainly an admirer of Vernet's art, as he commissioned two pictures from him in 1772.[4] But if he owned the present picture, he is likely to have acquired it from a previous owner rather than commissioning it from the painter. This assumption stems from the inclusion and prominence of the Dutch flags. The facts that the figure in the center of the picture, shown being greeted by his family, has just disembarked from one of a fleet of Dutch warships and that he wears a hat trimmed with gold suggest that he is a Dutch naval officer. Mr. E. H. H. Archibald, of the National Maritime Museum, Greenwich, writes that from the second quarter of the seventeenth century the Dutch navy kept a permanent presence in the Mediterranean to protect their merchantmen from the Barbary pirates. He adds that the blue and white stripes, seen in the flag of the barge on the left of the picture, were Barbary colors. A further communication, from Mr. R. M. Vorstmann of the Rijksmuseum Nederlands Sceepvaart Museum, Amsterdam, states that after the conclusion of the Treaty of Aken on October 18, 1748, two Dutch squadrons sailed for the Mediterranean. One squadron was under the command of Rear Admiral H. Linjslager, who arrived at Malta toward the end of November 1748, and then set sail for Constantinople; he was back in Malta in May 1749. The other squadron, commanded by Rear Admiral Alexander Frensel, arrived at Algiers on April 5, 1749.

In view of the closeness between these dates and that of the Timken picture, it does seem a possibility that the painting may have been commissioned to commemorate, in some way, one of these expeditions, and in any case it establishes the probability that it was ordered by a Dutchman. Vernet's notebook of 1766 notes that he painted two pictures in that year for "M. Oudermeulen" of Amsterdam, for whom, at an unspecified previous date, he had already painted a sunset with a lighthouse, a colonnade, and a Dutch warship in the background.[5] The specification of a colonnade, rather than the Arch of Constantine, and of only one Dutch warship militates against identification with the present picture. But at least these notations constitute confirmation that Vernet had Dutch clients and was prepared on occasion to depict Dutch warships.

—C. G.

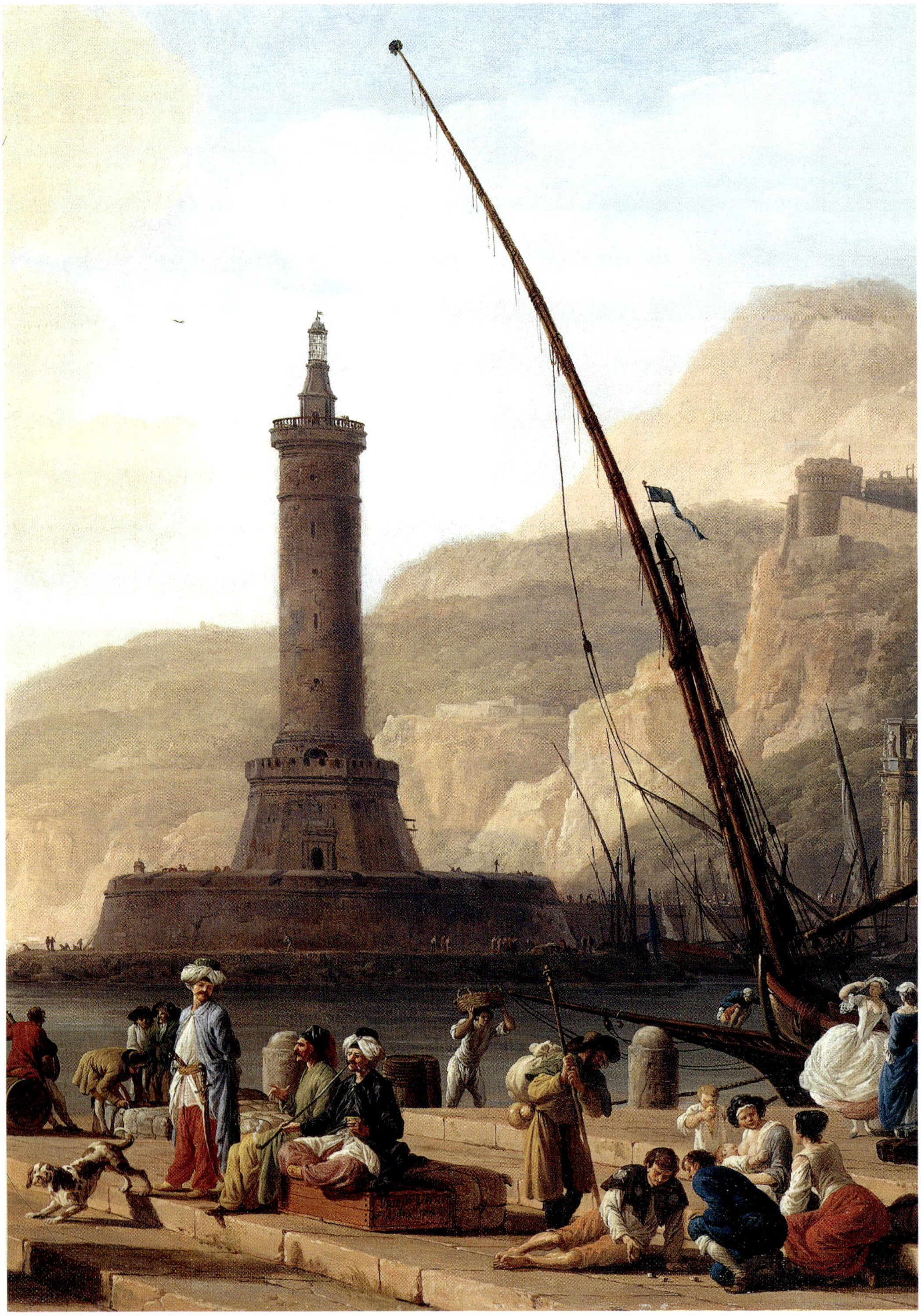

Detail of Plate 32

Albert Bierstadt
(1830–1902)

Albert Bierstadt was born on January 7, 1830, at Solingen, a town near Düsseldorf, Germany. In early 1832 the family moved to New Bedford, Massachusetts. From 1853 to 1857 he studied among the artists associated with the Royal Academy in Düsseldorf and then traveled in Germany, Switzerland, and Italy before returning to New Bedford in 1857. He traveled through the West in 1859 and again in 1863, achieving immense success with the large, impressive paintings that resulted from the experience. Based in New York or nearby, he continued to make frequent, extended trips. Bierstadt died in New York on February 18, 1902.

33 *Cho-looke, the Yosemite Fall,*[1] 1864
Oil on canvas, 34¼ × 27⅛ in. (87 × 68.9 cm)
Signed and dated lower left: *A Bierstadt / 1864* (AB in monogram)

The army surveys that prepared the way for the great westward expansion of the United States following the Mexican-American War of 1848 brought back to eastern cities accounts of unimagined spectacles of nature, which artists and photographers soon set out to capture for a fascinated public. Having already achieved fame as a painter of the western American landscape, Bierstadt set out upon his second western trip in April 1863 with a group of artists, with the principal objective of visiting the valley of Yosemite, which he reached in August of that year. The Timken painting places us at the second camp of the party at the close of a day of sketching, as the six men gather for supper and a comparison of their day's studies, while their boy brings wood from among the grove of oaks and cypresses and their man leads the pack animals down to pasture in the broad meadow bordering the Merced River. Across the valley thunders one of the wonders the group has come to see, the Yosemite Fall, or Cho-looke, to use its Indian name, then thought to be the highest in the United States, with a cataract breaking its double fall.

Although the painting seems to record an actual evening of the party in the Yosemite, its size and degree of finish indicate that it was painted after Bierstadt's return from the West in December 1863. The *New-York Evening Post* of June 9, 1864, recorded that he was at work on the painting then. Bierstadt's characteristic method would have been to base a finished painting such as this not only on detailed oil

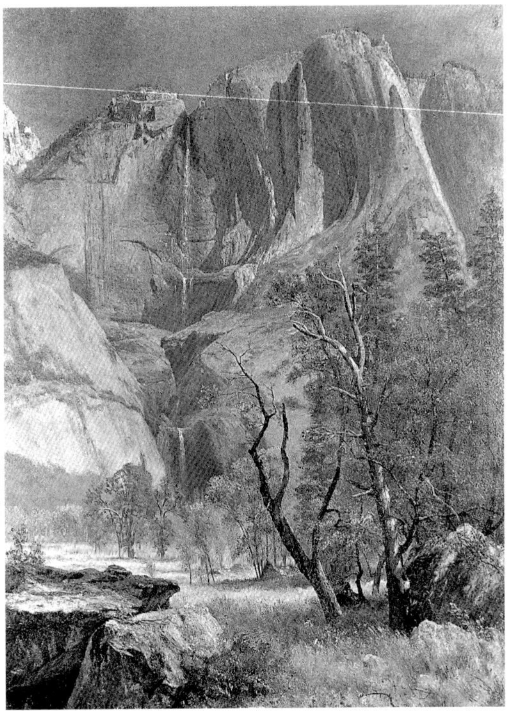

Fig. 1. Albert Bierstadt, *View in the Yosemite, California*, ca. 1863. Oil on paper mounted on canvas, 25¾ × 18¾ in. (65.4 × 47.6 cm). Collection of Dr. Algernon A. Phillips, Jr., Newark, N.J.

studies (such as that in the collection of Dr. Algernon A. Phillips, Jr.; fig. 1), but also on photographs or stereophotographs that he or members of the party had taken. Low clouds have been introduced to enhance the effect of vast distance, and an accident of light adds drama to the spectacle. Bierstadt has also composed the painting as an abrupt jump from a darkened and bulky foreground to a hazy and insubstantial distance. The ultimate objective is an impression of spectacular scale and natural majesty.

Fitz Hugh Ludlow, Bierstadt's companion on the trip, serialized an account of their travels in the *Atlantic Monthly* in 1864, the chapter on Yosemite appearing during June, when the Timken painting was on Bierstadt's easel. The inclusion of the artists' party in the foreground may have been at least partly in response to the topicality of the expedition, although it was also a favorite way of establishing the vast scale of the wonders Bierstadt portrayed. The painting, reproduced in a wood engraving, served as the perfect illustration to Ludlow's *Heart of the Continent*, the book-length account of the journey published in 1870.

—M. Q.

NOTE

1. Having been separated from its original title, the painting was known by at least two other titles by the time it was acquired by the Putnam Foundation. In my entry for the 1983 edition of this collection catalogue, I was able to establish the painting's correct title and early publication history, which have been supported in recent literature.

PROVENANCE

American Insurance Company, Boston; gift to John Ingersoll Bowditch, 1864; to his son, Charles Pinkney Bowditch, 1889; to his son, Harold Bowditch, Brookline, Mass., 1919; acquired by the Putnam Foundation, 1966.

LITERATURE

New-York Evening Post, June 9, 1864, p. 1; Fitz Hugh Ludlow, *The Heart of the Continent* (New York, 1870), ill. opp. p. 438; Richard Shafer Trump, "Life and Works of Albert Bierstadt" (Ph.D. diss., Ohio State University, 1963), p. 218, as *Yosemite Scene of Bridal Veil Falls;* Gordon Hendricks, *Albert Bierstadt: Painter of the American West* (New York, 1973), pp. 132, 155, 326, no. 17, fig. 1 (frontispiece), as *Camping in the Yosemite; Timken Art Gallery: European and American Works of Art in the Putnam Foundation Collection* (San Diego, 1983), pp. 94–95, 125, no. 34, ill.; *American Paradise: The World of the Hudson River School,* exh. cat., The Metropolitan Museum of Art (New York, 1987), pp. 288–89, ill.; Nancy K. Anderson, "The European Roots of Albert Bierstadt: Views of the American West," *Antiques* 139 (January 1991): 220–23, ill. p. 233.

EXHIBITED

San Diego, Timken Art Gallery, 1986, *Albert Bierstadt: "Cho-looke, the Yosemite Fall,"* cat. by Nancy K. Anderson; The Brooklyn Museum; The Fine Arts Museums of San Francisco; National Gallery of Art, Washington, D.C., 1991–92, *Albert Bierstadt: Art & Enterprise,* cat. by Nancy K. Anderson and Linda Ferber, pp. 83–84, 198, ills.

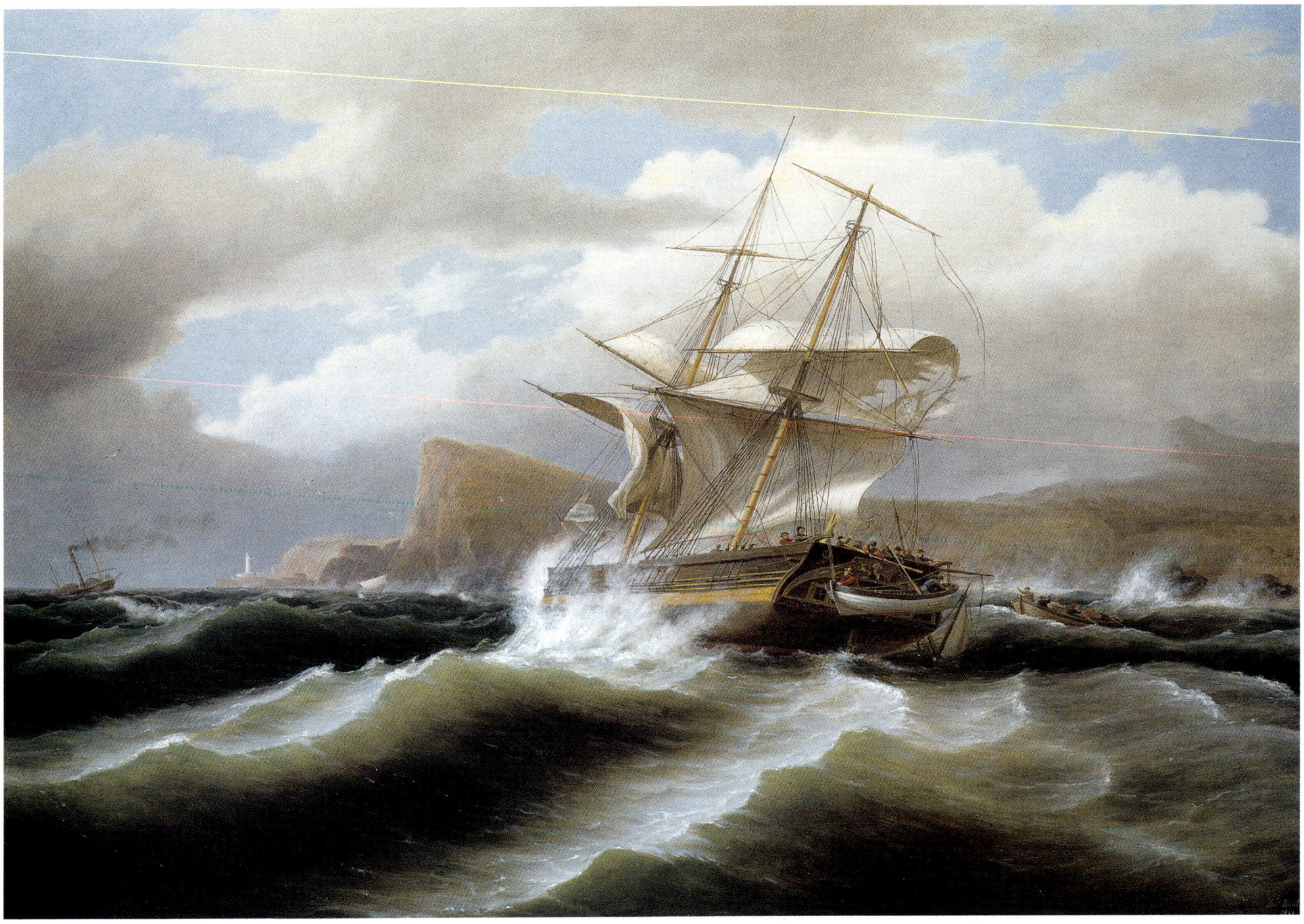

Thomas Birch

(1779–1851)

Thomas Birch was born in Warwickshire, England, in 1779, the son of William Birch, an engraver and painter of portrait miniatures. The family moved to the Philadelphia area in 1794. Thomas began his career as his father's assistant, established himself as a portraitist around 1800, and by 1811 was painting chiefly landscapes and marines. He made his reputation the following year with a series of paintings of naval engagements of the War of 1812. Death in 1851 closed his successful career as America's first marine artist.

34 *An American Ship in Distress*, 1841
Oil on canvas, 36 × 53¾ in. (91.4 × 136.5 cm)
Signed and dated lower right: *Thos Birch / 1841 / Philadelphia*

The violent storm that has torn off the mizzenmast and damaged the mainmast, sails, and rigging of the foreground ship, which still rides a heavy sea, is clearing. Either

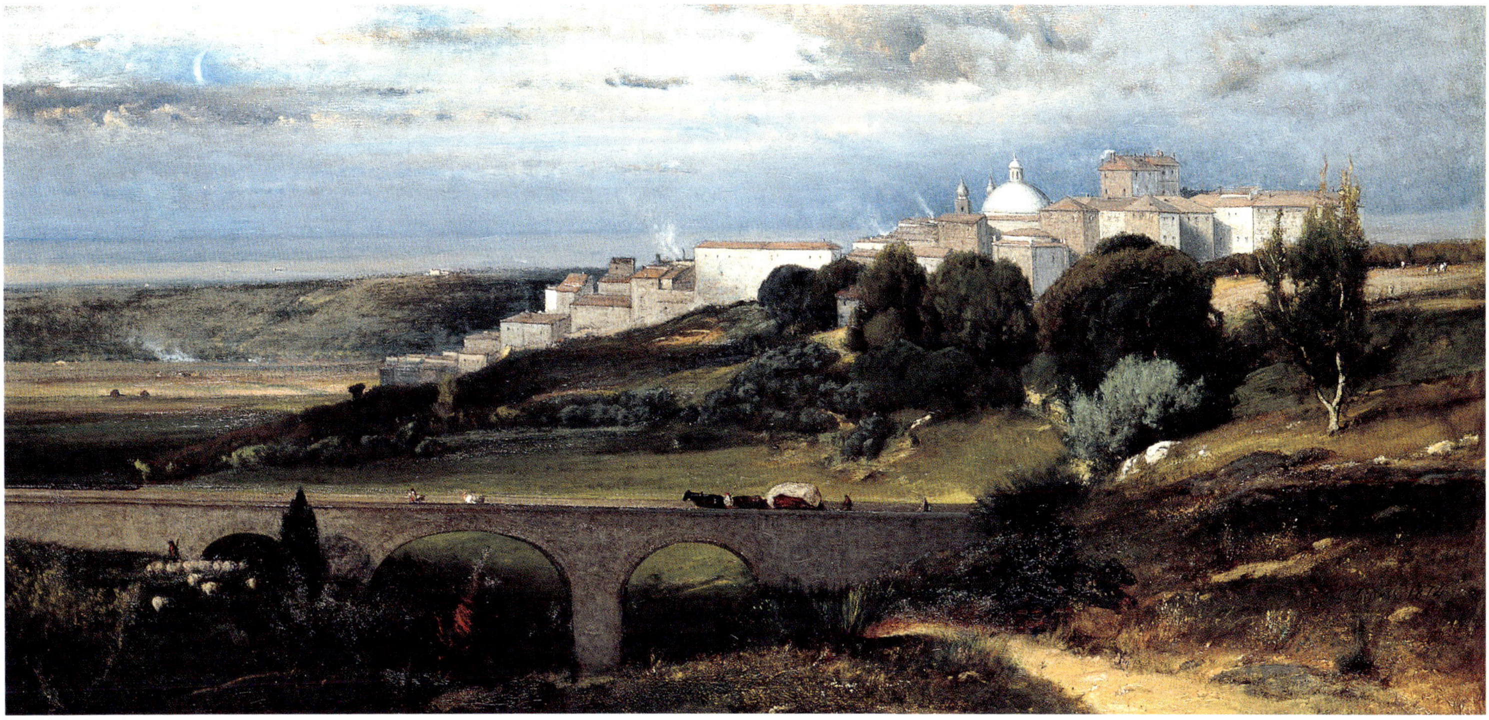

George Inness
(1825–1894)

George Inness was born on May 1, 1825, near Newburgh, New York, and was raised in Newark, New Jersey. He had only very limited training and briefly worked as an engraver before exhibiting his first landscape at the National Academy of Design in 1844. He traveled in Europe in 1851–52, again in 1853–54, and finally during 1870–75. He was elected an associate member of the National Academy of Design in 1853 and a member in 1868. Over the course of his fifty-year career as a painter, he worked and vacationed in several locations but is primarily identified with the New York area. A retrospective exhibition in 1884 established his preeminence in his field, and he enjoyed increasing fame until his death on December 27, 1894.

37 *Ariccia*, 1874
Oil on canvas, 26½ × 56⅞ in. (67.3 × 144.3 cm)
Signed and dated lower right: *G. Inness 1874*

The rosy beige, tan, and white buildings of an Italian town crown a ridge stretching across the middle distance. A valley and answering ridge lie beyond, before a hazy distance. A stone bridge crosses the foreground. The time is very late afternoon, with a crescent moon in the sky on the left.

Inness's stay in Italy during the early 1870s was a time of ripening for his strong landscape vision, leading to the classical style of his middle period. Although he visited other cities, he painted primarily in Rome and its environs, finding many of his

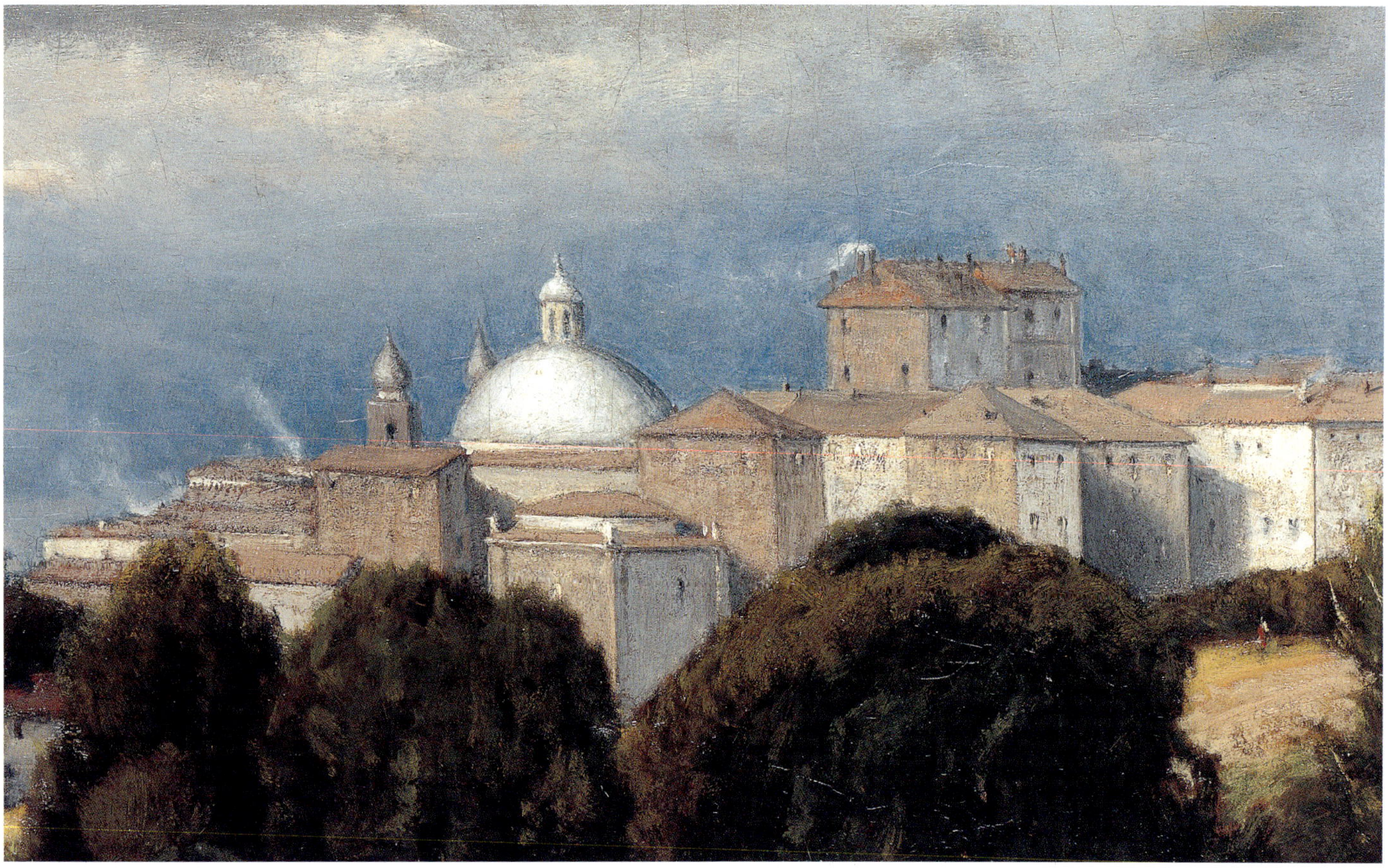

Detail of Plate 37

subjects among the scenic lakes and deep valleys of the Alban Hills and the towns of Genzano, Castel Gandolfo, Ariccia, and Albano, in those days an hour from Rome by train. The region's familiarity to tourists made his paintings more readily salable back home, where they were handled by Inness's Boston agents, Williams and Everett, as the Timken painting was. Views from these hilltop towns also offered him panoramas of mist-filled valleys not unlike the motifs favored by the American landscapists of the Hudson River school and actually sought out in the same area by Sanford Gifford, for instance.

Although the town represented in the Timken painting is identified in the titles of several Inness landscapes as Albano, it clearly is the neighboring town of Ariccia, with the drumless dome and apsidal towers of the church of Santa Maria dell'Assunzione built by Bernini in 1664, facing the Palazzo Chigi with its towers rising above the town. The view seems to be from the east-southeast, looking beyond the Vale of Ariccia to the Roman Campagna lost in the late afternoon haze. The bluer band at the horizon on the left could be the Mediterranean. The towns and hilly countryside were connected by numerous bridges and viaducts which in other paintings seem to have interested Inness as he explored the spatial complexity of the area. The unusually wide Timken painting, related to an even more panoramic oil study (fig. 1), uses the long bridge as the first of three parallel horizontal elements, continued in the actual horizon and the strata of thin clouds, and balanced by the upthrusting geometry of the town.

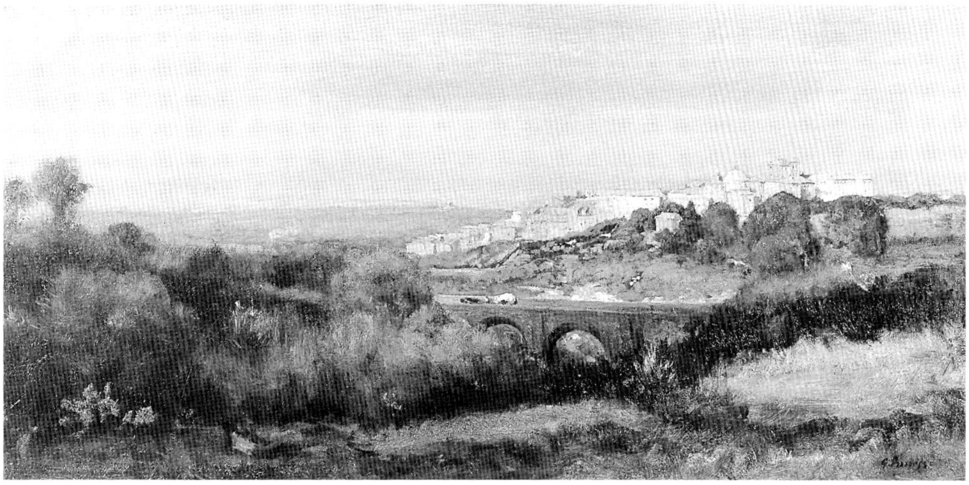

Fig. 1. George Inness, *Ariccia*, ca. 1870–74. Oil on canvas, 12⅝ × 25¾ in. (32.1 × 65.4 cm). Collection of Paulsen K. Bailey, Vienna, Austria.

The best Innesses of these years go beyond mere scenery to offer a poetic sentiment of the most delicate kind. Color is a large part of it—the rich and varied greens of the foreground and middle distance and the sky and distance entirely in pink and blue—but another part is the capturing of the characteristic light of a particular time of day. In the Timken painting it is that transitional moment at the end of the day, as the warm light fades upon the land, a brief time of stillness and tender melancholy to which Inness often returned in his later work.

—M.Q.

PROVENANCE

Williams and Everett Art Gallery, Boston; Arthur Hunnewell; his daughter, Jane B. Hunnewell, Wellesley, Mass.; Vose Galleries, Boston; acquired by the Putnam Foundation, 1972.

LITERATURE

Timken Art Gallery: European and American Works of Art in the Putnam Foundation Collection (San Diego, 1983), pp. 102–3, 125, no. 38, ill.

EXHIBITED

Museum of Fine Arts, Boston; The Cleveland Museum of Art; and The Museum of Fine Arts, Houston, 1992–93, *The Lure of Italy*, cat. by Theodore E. Stebbins, Jr., et al., pp. 314–15, no. 70, ill.

Eastman Johnson

(1824–1906)

Eastman Johnson was praised in his day as being among the most American of American painters. Son of a public figure active in Maine and Washington, D.C., Johnson (who did not use his given name, Jonathan) started his career making charcoal, crayon, and chalk drawings of the nation's leading citizens, among them John Quincy Adams, Dolley Madison, Henry Wadsworth Longfellow, and Ralph Waldo Emerson. His formal training, aside from a brief stay in a Boston lithography shop, began later, when in 1849 he traveled to Düsseldorf and enrolled in the Royal Academy, subsequently working in the studio of the American Emanuel Leutze. Johnson went to Holland in late 1851, achieving such competence that he was reportedly offered the position of court painter in The Hague. He declined this honor, instead moving to Paris in 1855 to study with Thomas Couture. He returned to the United States on his mother's death later in the year.

Like other foreign-trained artists of his generation, once home Johnson set out to find a demonstrably American subject matter that would yet allow him to reveal his European technical achievements. He traveled first, in the summers of 1856 and 1857, to Wisconsin, where he made sketches toward a never-fulfilled project devoted to Chippewa life. His first public success came with *Negro Life at the South* (1859, The New-York Historical Society), based on observations of his family's Georgetown (District of Columbia) neighborhood. On the strength of this work, he was elected associate of the National Academy of Design (elevated to academician in 1860) and came to immediate and consistent public attention. For the next two decades, Johnson sustained his reputation as the foremost American figure painter through a series of domestic-scaled genre scenes, portraits, and—something of an innovation of his to American art—conversation pieces that combined group portraiture with a detailed interior setting and hint of quiet narrative (see, for example, *The Hatch Family* [1871, New York, The Metropolitan Museum of Art]). Increasingly after 1880 he turned his focus to portraiture; many of the generation's political leaders, academics, financiers —in short, the leaders of East Coast society—were painted by the man who was himself a leader in that society, serving in many official capacities, including that of a founding trustee of the Metropolitan Museum of Art.

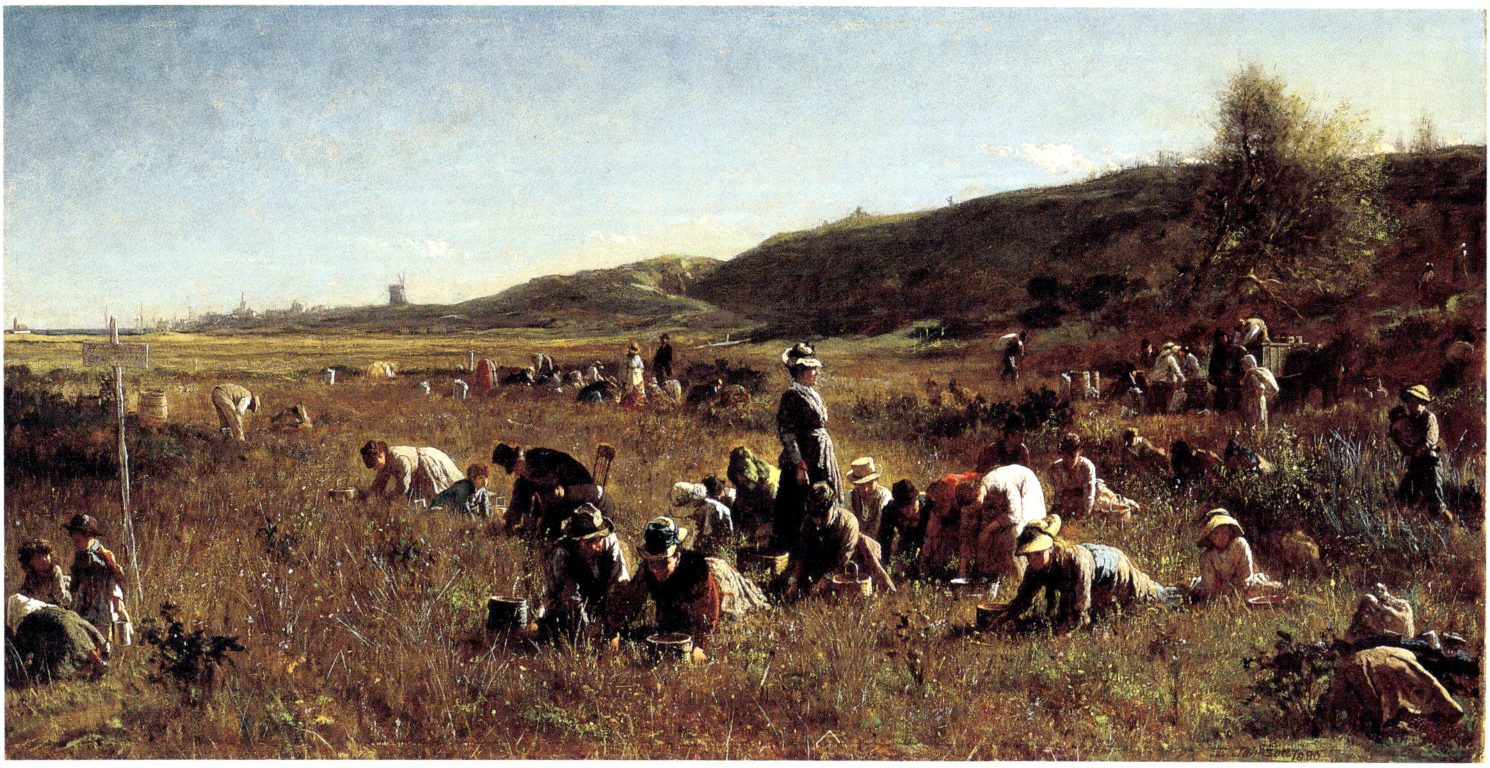

38 *The Cranberry Harvest, Island of Nantucket,* 1880
Oil on canvas, 27⅜ × 54½ in. (69.5 × 138.4 cm)
Signed and dated lower right: *E. Johnson 1880.*

In the early 1860s, during the years of the Civil War, Johnson searched for celebratory moments of American rural life that he could convert to ambitious paintings. He wrote in 1864:

> I hope in the next year to do something more considerable than I have yet done, to paint two or three larger and more *pretentious* pictures. . . . In furtherance of one of these I am about starting for the country to make studies for a month or six weeks. This will be my fourth annual trip for the same purpose to the wilds of the State of Maine—The scene is a Down-east *Sugaring,* a picturesque & to me very interesting one, partly perhaps on account of its being associated with my pleasantest early recollections.[1]

The sugaring-off project failed to materialize in a finished work, although around thirty studies—at least one of grand scale (Providence, Rhode Island School of Design)—testify to the seriousness of Johnson's enterprise.

Starting about 1870, the year of his marriage, Johnson began to draw inspiration for his genre scenes from the island of Nantucket, Massachusetts, where he and his young family regularly thereafter spent their summers.[2] The Timken Museum's painting, *The Cranberry Harvest, Island of Nantucket,* is the culmination of Johnson's Nantucket work, as well as the fruition of his two-decades-long effort to paint a celebration of New England outdoor life. After this he never again, so far as we know,

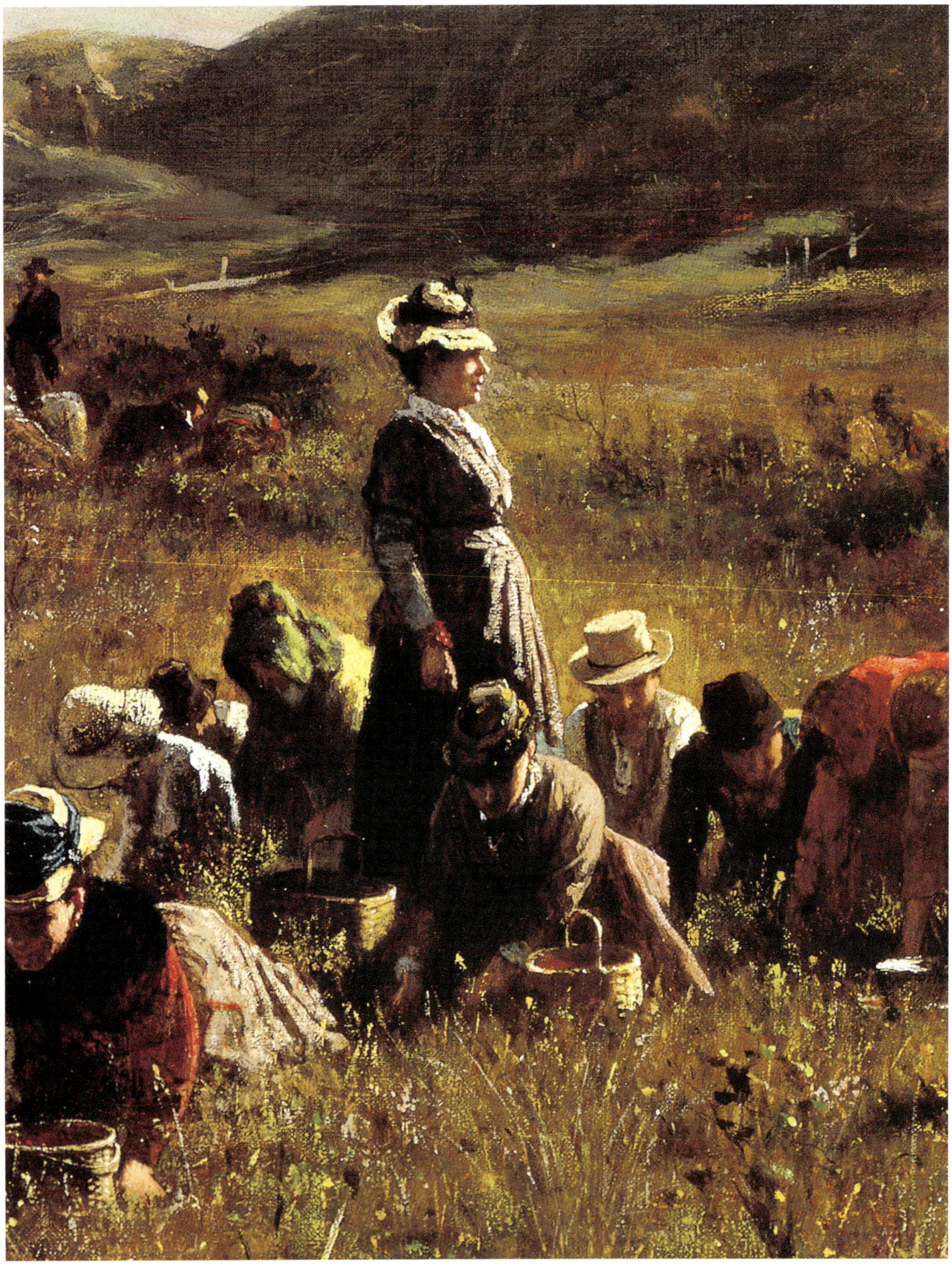

Detail of Plate 38

attempted any comparably ambitious outdoor genre project. More than simply a personal milestone, moreover, *The Cranberry Harvest* marks a significant achievement in the history of American art.

The Cranberry Harvest, Island of Nantucket shows a bog on the north shore of the island, along the region known as the Cliff. The bog, its brown and dried grasses enlivened by wildflowers and the red berries, holds over forty people—mostly women, children, and old men. Off to the right the picked berries are loaded onto a wagon, while in the distance, singly and in pairs, figures climb the Cliff toward North Road. In this work more than anywhere else in his oeuvre, Johnson has lavished attention on the landscape, truly trying to capture the sense of a specific place. From the dry grasses of the foreground to the distant (but accurately depicted) view of Nantucket's spires, lighthouse, and shipping, he has created a vivid and recognizable setting for his figures. He has even taken the trouble to paint a windmill on the horizon left of center, helping further to identify the island for his New York audience (although the island's remaining windmill was, in fact, located elsewhere and would not have been visible from the bog). Late afternoon light washes over the scene, with a pink glow at the horizon to tell of the day's fast-approaching end.

And yet, in spite of Johnson's loving attention to the site, the pickers are the painting's principal focus. Their brightly colored clothes, partially glimpsed glances and gestures, and seemingly random groupings provide the canvas with its animation and sense of vast scale. Near the painting's center a woman stands and pauses, looking toward a boy who carries an infant to her. While nearly everyone around her —children, courting couples, old men—looks down to the ground, her gaze bridges the space of the painting, marking her as the protagonist of Johnson's restrained narrative.[3] One of the work's signal innovations is the way in which the artist is able to suggest anecdote but at the same time subsume it within his appreciation of the landscape and the atmosphere of the whole. This emotional restraint, combined with his evocative (rather than descriptive) technique, imposes a neutrality on the scene, lending it an air of spontaneous truth and asking us to believe that it is a transcription actually witnessed and captured by the artist. It is this relative neutrality that distinguishes *The Cranberry Harvest* from the French paintings of harvesting workers by such late-nineteenth-century artists as Jules Breton. As one writer of the day noted, Johnson

> preaches no ugly gospel of discontent, as does so much of the contemporary French and Flemish art of this genre; his Nantucket neighbors know nothing of the *"protestation douloureuse de la race asservie à le glebe"*; there is no *"cri de la terre"* arising from his cranberry marshes or his hay-stuffed barns.[4]

In fact, however, the apparent spontaneity of *The Cranberry Harvest* is an illusion; the Timken painting stands at the end of a long and complicated artistic campaign. The earliest dated reference to Johnson's work on the theme is contained in a letter the painter wrote from Nantucket to his artist-friend Jervis McEntee on October 12, 1879. McEntee was expected on a visit:

> I shall have precious little to show you tho. I have been industrious enough since here. I was taken with my cranberry fit as soon as I arrived (some people have rose fever yearly—I have the cranberry fever) as they began picking down in the meadow a day or two after we arrived and I have done nothing else since I have been here *not a thing*.[5]

Although they are not dated and so cannot be definitely linked to the fall of 1879, it seems likely that most if not all of the seventeen paintings (two on either side of one panel), one watercolor, and two drawings (one on the back of a painted panel) of the cranberry harvest now recorded are from the 1879 bout of cranberry fever.[6] This group includes rough jottings of posture and evocations of atmosphere, fairly detailed working-ups of a few figures (what Johnson called "finished studies"), and compositional overviews at various scales. Six of the paintings clearly relate to the large canvas now at Yale University. This work seems to hold great promise, with figural interest divided mainly between the cluster of people at the right foreground and the much-studied figure of the woman at the center middle ground who bears her full bucket toward us. Johnson worked hard at these two spots, experimenting and developing them through several variants. For some reason we shall probably never know, he did not finish this canvas, instead abandoning it and its series of preparatory works. We do know that as late as mid-November the artist had complained of frustration, writing: "I am trying to get some work done. The harder I try the more I cant."[7]

Yet in December—still on the island to his considerable surprise—he writes of contentment:

> I am staying here to get through with things begun, not much, you will be surprised at how little I can dawdle over so long a time, but then the models are here and whatever materials I require, and that is all there is of the pictures, so of course I cant do them elsewhere. . . . There is something very peaceful and satisfactory in our life here.[8]

One possible explanation of Johnson's change from frustration to satisfaction is that he got a fresh start on the theme. Drawing inspiration, perhaps, from such a "finished study" as *In the Fields* (fig. 1), he seems to have worked quickly through a series of compositional studies (including *Cranberry Pickers* [fig. 2]) to the finished work.

Johnson submitted *The Cranberry Harvest* and another Nantucket work, *The Reprimand* (1880, private collection), to the National Academy of Design spring exhibition. Both were received with enthusiasm, but *The Cranberry Harvest* was the star of the show:

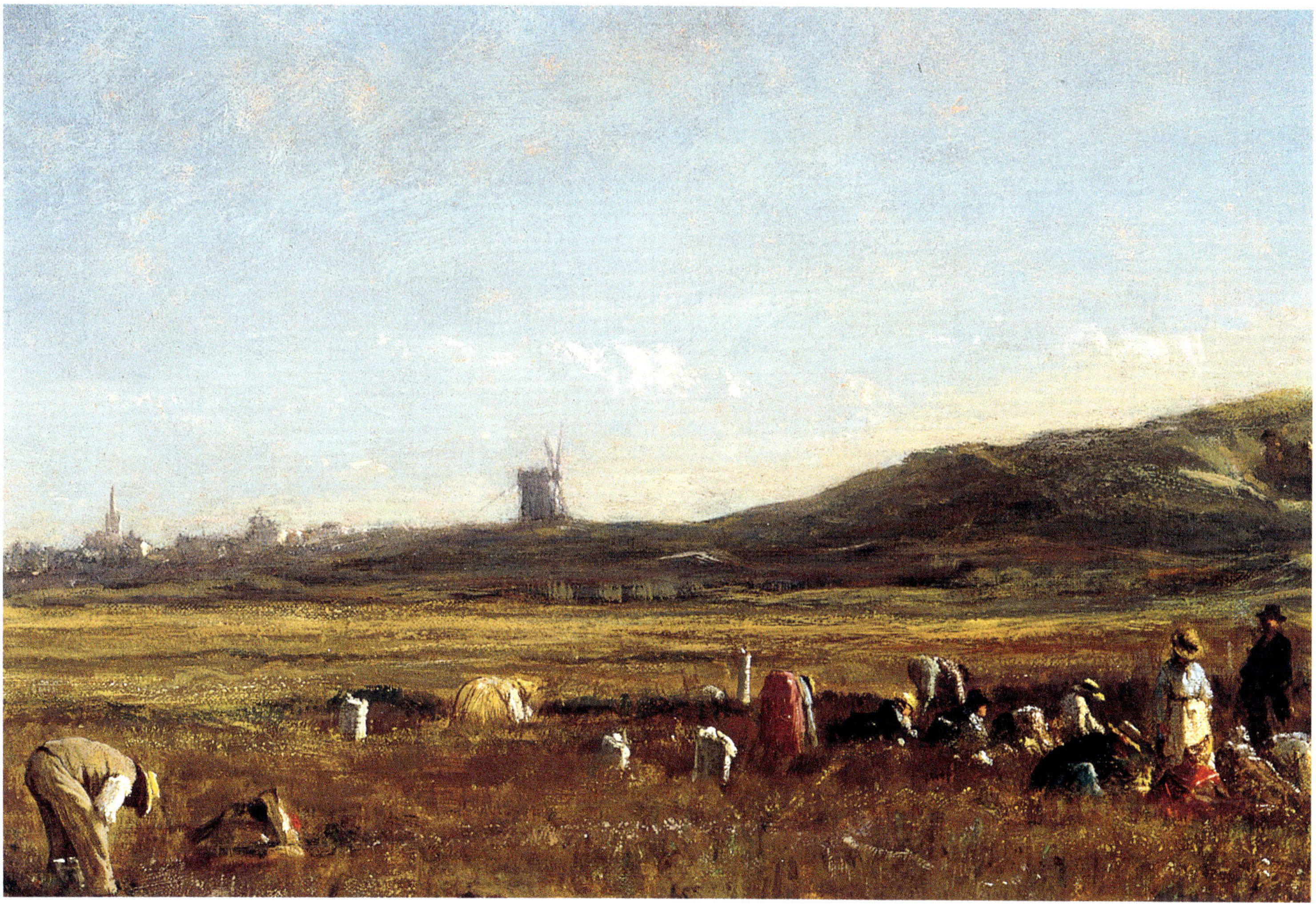

Detail of Plate 38

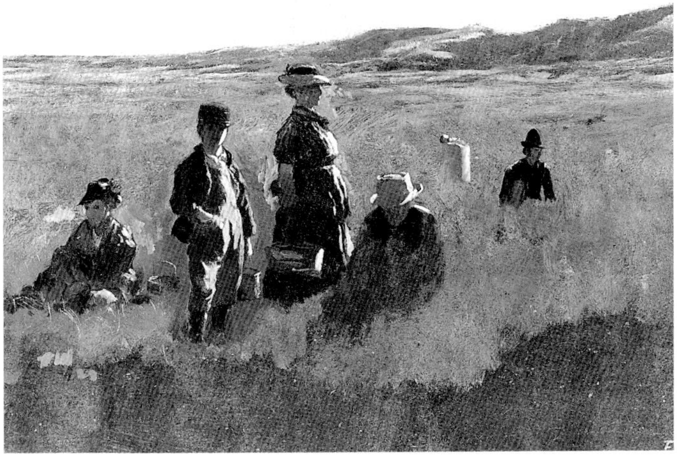

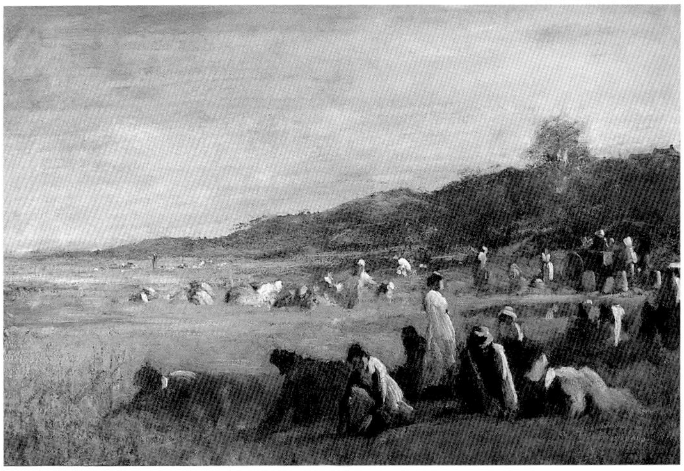

Fig. 1. Eastman Johnson, *In the Fields*. Oil on board, 17¾ × 27½ in. (45.1 × 69.9 cm). The Detroit Institute of Arts, Founders Society Purchase, Dexter M. Ferry Fund, 38.1.

Fig. 2. Eastman Johnson, *Cranberry Pickers*. Oil on board, 19¾ × 30 in. (50.2 × 76.2 cm). Private collection.

> Among the over seven hundred works hung one of the very best and most creditable to American art is Eastman Johnson's scene on a cranberry patch, which has deservedly been given the position of honor in the centre of the southern wall of the south gallery. . . . It is an excellent work and a credit to American art.[9]

The critic's words were apt in 1880 and during the next several years, when the painting was on public view at the newly opened uptown galleries of the Metropolitan Museum of Art, and later, in 1893, at the World's Columbian Exposition in Chicago. For over seventy years afterward, however, the painting was unrecorded. Its reemergence in 1969 and subsequent inclusion in exhibitions and American art surveys as one of the finest of Johnson's works has done much to rejuvenate the artist's current reputation.[10]

—M. S.

NOTES

1. Eastman Johnson to [John F.] Coyle, New York, March 13, 1864; Archives of American Art, Smithsonian Institution (hereafter AAA), Misc. MSS: Eastman Johnson, roll D10, frames 1371–73.

2. For a review of Johnson and the island of Nantucket, see Marc Simpson, "Taken with a Cranberry Fit: Eastman Johnson on Nantucket," in San Diego et al. 1990–91.

3. In the Timken's 1983 catalogue, Michael Quick pointed out that the figures form an *X* over the field, with the standing woman at the center; this *X* opens the space of the painting.

4. William Walton, "Eastman Johnson, Painter," *Scribner's Magazine* 40 (September 1906): 270–71.

5. Johnson to Jervis McEntee, October 12, 1879, AAA, Misc. MSS: Jervis McEntee, Gift of Charles E. Feinberg, roll D30, frame 517.

6. See Sally Mills, " 'Right Feeling and Sound Technique': French Art and the Development of Eastman Johnson's Outdoor Genre Paintings," in San Diego et al. 1990–91, pp. 52–75.

7. Johnson to Jervis McEntee, November 17, 1879, AAA, Misc. MSS: Jervis McEntee, Gift of Charles E. Feinberg, roll D30, frame 457.

8. Johnson to Jervis McEntee, December 13, 1879, AAA, Misc. MSS: Jervis McEntee, Gift of Charles E. Feinberg, roll D30, frames 460–62.

9. "Fifty-fifth Annual Exhibition of the National Academy of Design," *New York Herald*, March 27, 1880.

10. In preparation for the 1990 exhibition *Eastman Johnson: The Cranberry Harvest,* which celebrated the twenty-fifth anniversary of the Timken Museum of Art, David Bull (the museum's consulting conservator) undertook a conservation treatment of *The Cranberry Harvest*. In consultation with a group of American art scholars, Bull rectified three areas of concern: the slightly yellowed surface varnish; the twentieth-century addition of light green paint over significant portions of the middle ground; and the modern addition of a bending figure in blue, placed just right of the standing female figure. The latter, in particular, had disturbed writers on the painting since the late 1960s (see, for example, Carol Troyen's entry on the work in Boston 1983).

PROVENANCE

Auguste Richard, 1880–at least 1893; with Bernard Bivall, London, 1969; with Peter Tillou, Inc., Litchfield, Conn., and Vose Galleries, Boston; acquired by the Putnam Foundation, 1972.

LITERATURE

S. G. W. Benjamin, "The Exhibitions. V.—National Academy of Design," *American Art Review* 1 (1879–80): 309; "The Academy Exhibition," *The Evening Post,* March 26, 1880; "National Academy of Design," *New York Commercial Advertiser,* March 27, 1880; "Fifty-fifth Annual Exhibition of the National Academy of Design—Private View Day—First Article," *New York Herald,* March 27, 1880; "The Academy Exhibition," *The New-York Times,* March 27, 1880; "The Academy Exhibition," *The World,* March 27, 1880; "Fifty-fifth Annual Exhibition of the National Academy—Opening Reception—in the South Gallery—Second Notice," *New York Herald,* March 30, 1880; "National Academy of Design Exhibition. First Notice," *Art Interchange* 4 (March 31, 1880): 54–55; "The New York Spring Exhibitions. I. The National Academy Exhibition," *Art Journal* (New York) 6 (1880): 154; "National Academy of Design. Fifty-fifth Annual Exhibition (Third Article)," *The New-York Daily Tribune,* April 18, 1880; *Inquirer and Mirror,* April 24, 1880; "Exhibition of the Academy of Design," *Art Amateur* 2 (May 1880): 112; M[ariana] G[riswold] van Rensselaer, "Spring Exhibitions and Picture-Sales in New York.—II," *American Architect and Building News* 7 (May 8, 1880): 201; S. G. W. Benjamin, "A Representative American," *Magazine of Art* 5 (1882): 489, ill., and reprinted in Wilfrid Meynell, ed., *Some Modern Artists and Their Work* (London, 1883), pp. 153–59, ill., and id., *The Modern School of Art,* 3 vols. (London, n.d. [probably 1886–88]), 1:225–32, ill.; Clarence Cook, *Art and Artists of Our Time,* 3 vols. (New York, 1888), 3:245, 263, ill.; William A. Coffin, "*The Century*'s American Artist Series. Eastman Johnson," *Century Magazine* 48 (October 1894): 958; Sadakichi Hartmann, "Eastman Johnson: American Genre Painter," *International Studio* 34 (April 1908): 109, ill.; Patricia Hills, *The Genre Painting of Eastman Johnson: Sources and Development of His Style and Themes* (New York, 1977), pp. 151–54, 724, ill.; Hermann Warner Williams, Jr., *Mirror to the American Past* (Greenwich, Conn., 1973), pp. 149–50, fig. 139; Clay Lancaster, *Nantucket in the Nineteenth Century* (New York, 1979), p. 15; Robert A. di Curcio, *Art on Nantucket: The History of Painting on Nantucket Island* (Nantucket, Mass., 1982); *Timken Art Gallery: European and American Works of Art in the Putnam Foundation Collection* (San Diego, 1983), pp. 104–5, 125–26, no. 39, ill.

EXHIBITED

New York, National Academy of Design, 1880, *Fifty-fifth Annual Exhibition of the National Academy of Design,* no. 382; New York, The Metropolitan Museum of Art, November 1881–April 1882, *Loan Collection of Paintings and Sculpture in the West Galleries and the Grand Hall,* no. 10, and May–October 1882, no. 174; Chicago, World's Columbian Exposition, 1893, no. 621; Atlanta, The High Museum of Art, 1971, *The Beckoning Land,* no. 44; New York, Whitney Museum of American Art, 1972, *Eastman Johnson,* cat. by Patricia Hills, pp. 92, 97, 101, no. 97, ill.; Washington, D.C., National Gallery of Art, 1980, *American Light: The Luminist Movement,* pp. 48, 49, 146, fig. 46; Evanston, Ill., Terra Museum of American Art, 1981, *Life in Nineteenth-Century America,* p. 35, no. 2, frontispiece; Museum of Fine Arts, Boston, 1983, *A New World: Masterpieces of American Painting, 1760–1910,* pp. 270–72, no. 60, ill.; San Diego, Timken Art Gallery; The Fine Arts Museums of San Francisco; New Haven, Conn., Yale University Art Gallery; and New York, National Academy of Design, 1990–91, *Eastman Johnson: "The Cranberry Harvest, Island of Nantucket,"* cat. by Marc Simpson, Sally Mills, and Patricia Hills.

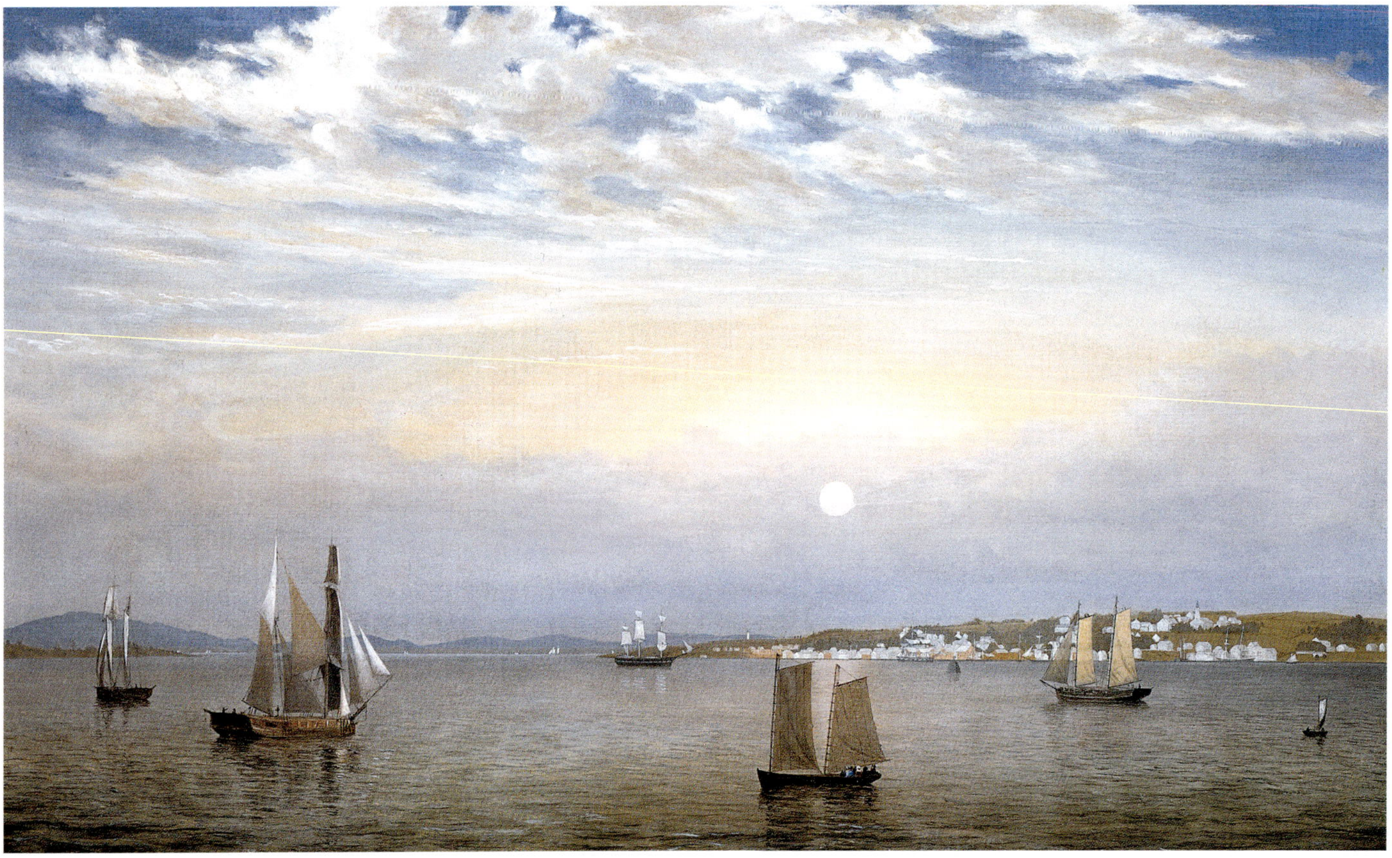

Fitz Hugh Lane
(1804–1865)

Nathaniel Rogers Lane was born in Gloucester, Massachusetts, on December 19, 1804. The family soon changed the child's given names to Fitz Hugh, which they and he used consistently afterward. When Lane was two, he suffered partial paralysis in his legs (the family believed by eating tomatoes, although recent scholars have speculated that he contracted infantile polio[1]). After a brief stint working as a shoemaker, Lane took an apprenticeship in 1832 with the Boston lithographer William S. Pendelton. Lane remained in Boston, working as both a lithographer (of topographic views, trade cards, and especially sheet-music covers) and, after 1840, a marine painter, until 1848. Soon after his return to Gloucester in that year,[2] Lane purchased property, designed and built (with a sister and brother-in-law) a seven-gable granite house on Duncan Street, participated actively in the civic life of the community, traveled (south to New York and Baltimore and perhaps as far as San Juan, Puerto Rico, and frequently north to Maine), and taught local artists. During these years Lane attained a respected position among New England artists and collectors; although he exhibited in New York, he was not well known there or elsewhere in the country.[3] His last dated drawings were done in July 1864. He suffered a bad fall on August 6, 1865, and, after either a stroke or a heart attack, died a week later on August 12.

39 *Castine Harbor and Town*, 1851
Oil on canvas, 20 × 33¼ in. (50.8 × 84.5 cm)
Signed and dated lower right: *F. H. Lane / 1851*

Fitz Hugh Lane's work grows from the topographic view: a depiction of a real place portrayed with extreme clarity and order. Lane's earliest training as an urban-scene lithographer and ships' portraitist, fields in which accuracy (at least to the extent of ready identification) and legibility are criteria of success, would predispose him in this direction. Indeed, in many instances Lane's urge for order seems extreme. Even in crowded harbor views, for instance, he positions craft and props as if there were a measured grid laid out before the viewer to which all the objects simply and directly relate, not unlike such quattrocento artists as Uccello who baldly show their wonder at the development of systematic linear perspective.

The sense of a controlling intelligence ordering Lane's scenes imposes a stillness and artificiality over the landscape. What prevents this order from devolving into a toylike miniature view is his rhapsodic evocation of real light and palpable air. Over a full range of atmospheric effects—sunlit glare to nocturne, placid calm to storm—the artist observes and transfers to his canvas individual skies and light effects, whose subtleties shatter the simplified patterns that his boats, buildings, land forms, and occasional people would otherwise establish. The end result of this disjunction between Lane's presentation of the material and the immaterial worlds is his consistent establishment—in his best, generally later, works—of an intensely poetic mood. Nowhere is this feeling more apparent than in his views of the relatively untraveled coves near his native Gloucester and in his paintings of Maine, such as the Timken's exceedingly handsome *Castine Harbor and Town*.

Lane first traveled to Maine in 1848 and returned at least five more times: during the summers of 1850, 1851, 1852, and 1855 he explored Penobscot Bay and Mount Desert Island, slightly more than halfway up Maine's Atlantic coast; in 1863 he traveled at least as far north as Portland. The state's landscape was a revelation and inspiration to him; he drew from his on-site sketches for much of his most memorable studio work throughout the 1850s until his death.[4]

Lane's companion on a number of the northern journeys was his young friend Joseph L. Stevens, Jr., secretary of the American Art Union.[5] Stevens's family lived in Castine, a small town south of Bangor, where the Penobscot River empties into its eponymous bay. Stevens's father wrote the artist in January 1851, thanking Lane for a painting and a drawing he had just received. He encouraged the artist to make another visit:

> There are several points of view, which you did not see, and to which it will be my pleasure, next summer to carry you. . . . Our house we shall expect to be your home, and if as you suggested in Gloucester, you should come in your Boat, this place could be made the rendezvous, from whence you could start to anyplace that convenience and inclination might dictate.[6]

And, indeed, Castine apparently served thereafter as a home base for Lane during his extended fishing, sailing, and hiking expeditions in the state. A friend on one of these outings recounted the artist's pluck: "we had to wait once in a while for Lane who with his crutches could not keep up with us—but got along better than we thought possible—the climb up after we left the path was somewhat severe . . . Lane got up about an hour after the rest of us."[7] Over the years Lane drew various sites around the town, which in turn served as guides for a series of later paintings, such as *Castine, Maine* (1850, Museum of Fine Arts, Boston), *Penobscot Bay from the Southwest Chamber Window* (1850, Rockland, Maine, William A. Farnsworth Library and Art Museum), and *Old Stevens Homestead* (1859, Andrew Wyeth), as

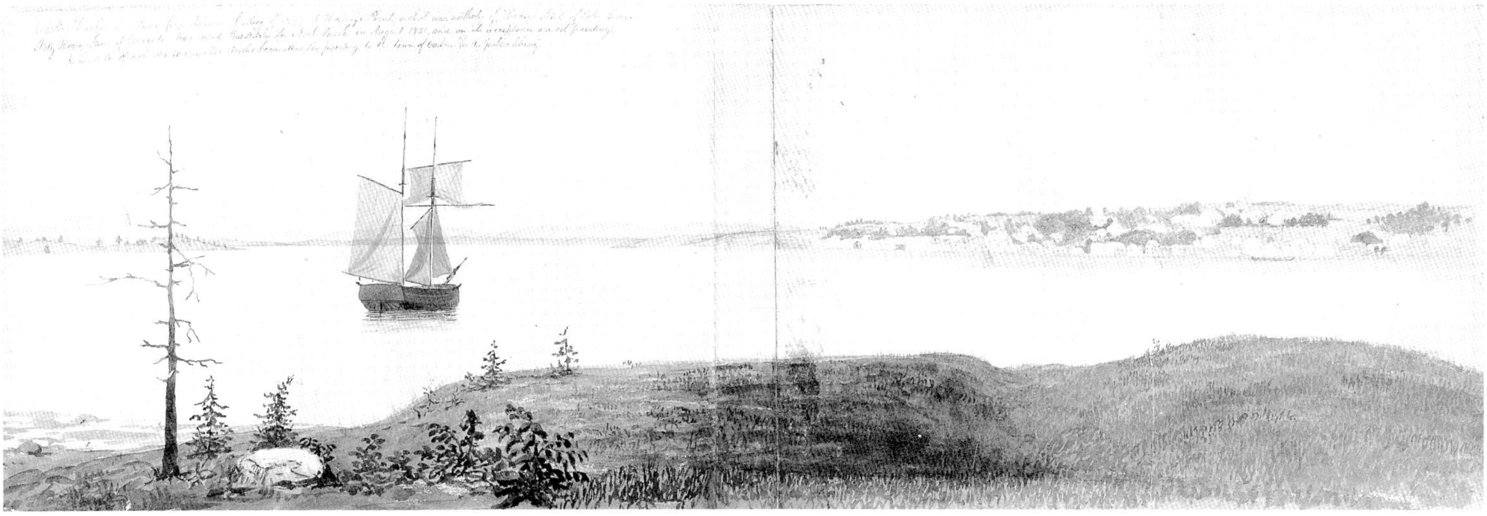

well as the basis of his most accomplished color lithograph, *Castine from Hospital Island*—which was published in 1855 by the younger Stevens.

Among the sites that Lane apparently visited in 1851 was Hainey's Point. There he made the drawing (fig. 1), looking across the water toward Castine, that is the basis for the Timken painting.[8] In its complexity and finish, the drawing is rare, if not unique, among Lane's work. Most of his on-site studies are pencil on paper, recording the barest outlines of topography and noteworthy characteristics of a given spot. Here, by contrast, he has worked the sheet up in light washes of green, blue, and pink watercolor and included a sailing ship—all indicating a more deliberate, extensive purpose for the study than mere record keeping. An inscription on the drawing, probably in the younger Stevens's hand, provides the story:

> Castine harbor and town from American battery of 1779 at Hainey's Point, a short way northerly of Henry's Point of later time. Fitz Henry *[sic]* Lane of Gloucester, Mass., made this sketch for Noah Brooks in August 1851, and on its acceptance an oil painting. In his will of date Nov. 30 1900 Mr. Brooks bequeathed the painting to the town of Castine "for the public library."[9]

Lane evidently made the pencil drawing on site, creating a panoramic view with two sheets pasted together, as was customary for his drawings, to give him sufficient breadth. Alphabetic or verbal color notations (e.g., R=red) indicate that Lane did not have colors with him outdoors but later added the delicate washes, and probably the ship, to make a more compelling presentation to his prospective patron, Noah Brooks (1830–1903).[10]

The genesis of the painting *Castine Harbor and Town* from the middle band of the drawing's right-hand section is clear, especially in the distant view of the town, details of the hill's foliage, and the topography of the general scene. The differences between the two works, however, are far more striking. Chiefly, of course, Lane has removed the solid ground of Hainey's Point—the detailed rendering of its grasses, bushes, and leafless tree dominate the drawing—and has instead suspended the

Fig. 1. Fitz Hugh Lane, *Castine Harbor and Town*, 1851. Watercolor, 10⅛ × 31⅛ in. (25.7 × 79.1 cm). Courtesy, Museum of Fine Arts, Boston, M. and M. Karolik Collection, 54.1727.

viewer from some elevated, but unspecified, vantage over the water. This opens up the expanse of the harbor, emphasizing the maritime nature of the scene and suggesting that the viewer is surveying the port from, perhaps, the rigging of a ship. Psychologically, this directs the viewer's attention to Castine as a goal—as either last glimpse of home or a welcome end of the journey—rather than as merely part of the landscape. The little town serves as a beacon of humanity, the order of its repeated right angles (echoed in the marine architecture of the boats and sloops in the harbor) contrasting with the rolling, irregular landscape in the distance.

The other principal distinction between the drawing and the painting is Lane's choice to emphasize the painting's sky. Above the quiet of town and harbor in the later work play a variety of cloud types and light effects, splendid in their color and effulgence. The perfect orb of the sun, low in the sky and turned pink by veils of low-lying fog, is the painting's focal point.[11] An aureole of warm yellow light glows upward, while a steady stream of clouds streaks the darkening blue heavens. The near theatricality of the sky commands attention, enlivening the otherwise placid view of the town and its busy shipping. The changes from drawing to painting transform a topographic account of Castine to a compelling vision that testifies both to Lane's great skill as a delineator of light and to mankind's harmonious and orderly life within the dramatic spectacle of nature.

—M. S.

NOTES

1. See Wilmerding 1971, pp. 17–18, and Washington 1988, p. 9.

2. Some sources say 1849 (Theodore E. Stebbins et al., *A New World: Masterpieces of American Painting 1760–1910*, exh. cat., Museum of Fine Arts [Boston, 1983], p. 234).

3. The New York critic Clarence Cook claimed that Lane "ought to be known from Maine to Georgia," in *The Independent* (September 7, 1854), but such was not the case. See William H. Gerdts, "'The Sea Is His Home': Clarence Cook Visits Fitz Hugh Lane," *American Art Journal* 17 (Summer 1985): 47.

4. See especially Frederic Allan Scharf, "Fitz Hugh Lane: Visits to the Maine Coast, 1841–1855," *Essex Institute Historical Collections* 98 (April 1962): 111–20; and John Wilmerding, "The Lure of Mount Desert and the Maine Coast," and Franklin Kelly, "Lane and Church in Maine," both in Washington 1988, pp. 107–26, 129–56.

5. For Stevens and his relationship to Lane, see Wilmerding 1971, pp. 50–51, which quotes a long letter by Stevens of October 17, 1903, recounting their friendship and activities. Lane appointed Stevens the executor of his will; it was Stevens who, in carrying out that responsibility, made the many annotations on Lane's drawings that have proven helpful to scholars concerning the site, date, and circumstances surrounding many of Lane's works.

6. Joseph L. Stevens, Sr., to Lane, January 29, 1851; quoted in Wilmerding 1971, pp. 57–58.

7. William Howe Witherle, diary manuscript quoted in Wilmerding 1988, pp. 125–26.

8. The fullest examination of the drawing to date is Carol Troyen's entry in Reed and Troyen 1993, pp. 27–28.

9. Quoted in Reed and Troyen 1993, p. 27. Troyen notes that the historic battery, which is not vis-

ible in either watercolor or painting, was not successful; the British prevailed in 1779 and occupied Castine for four years.

10. Brooks led a fascinating life. Famed as a journalist and author, the Castine-born youth had traveled to Boston when he was eighteen to study art, but soon turned instead to writing. In 1855 he traveled across the continent, ending up in California, where he wrote for the *Overland Monthly*. After the death of his wife and infant son, he went to Washington, D.C., as correspondent for the *Sacramento Union* in 1862. There he formed a fast friendship with Abraham Lincoln and the First Family; reportedly, only a severe cold kept the journalist at home rather than in the presidential box at Ford's Theater the night Lincoln was assassinated. In 1866 he was again in California as editor of *Alta California*. He moved to New York in 1871, working as editor at the *New York Tribune*, the *New-York Times*, and the *Newark Daily Advertiser*. Brooks retired from journalism in 1892 and, after traveling to the Holy Land, returned to Castine to write his memoirs. He died while on a futile trip to Pasadena undertaken to restore his health *(Dictionary of American Biography)*.

11. The painting was, in fact, at one point catalogued as a moonlight scene (see Salem 1964, p. 58, no. 52).

PROVENANCE

Witherle Memorial Library, Castine, Maine, ca. 1915; Hirschl & Adler Galleries, New York, 1978; private collection; acquired by the Putnam Foundation, 1986.

LITERATURE

John Wilmerding, *Fitz Hugh Lane* (New York, 1971), pp. 58, 182; William Nathaniel Banks, "Castine, Maine, and St. Andrews, New Brunswick, Canada," *Antiques* 118 (July 1980): 107, ill.; Sue Walsh Reed and Carol Troyen, *Awash in Color: Homer, Sargent, and the Great American Watercolor*, exh. cat., Museum of Fine Arts (Boston, 1993), pp. 27–28.

EXHIBITED

Salem, Mass., Essex Institute, 1964, *Fitz Hugh Lane, 1804–1865: American Marine Painter*, cat. by John Wilmerding (reprint, Gloucester, Mass., 1967), p. 58, no. 52; Rockland, Maine, William A. Farnsworth Library and Art Museum, 1974, *Fitz Hugh Lane*, no. 24, ill.; New York, Hirschl & Adler Galleries, 1979, *Recent Acquisitions of American Art, 1769–1938*, no. 21, ill.; Portland, Maine, Museum of Art, 1983, *State of Maine Collection: Grand Opening;* Washington, D.C., National Gallery of Art, 1988, *Paintings by Fitz Hugh Lane*, cat. by John Wilmerding et al., pp. 146–47, no. 59, ill.

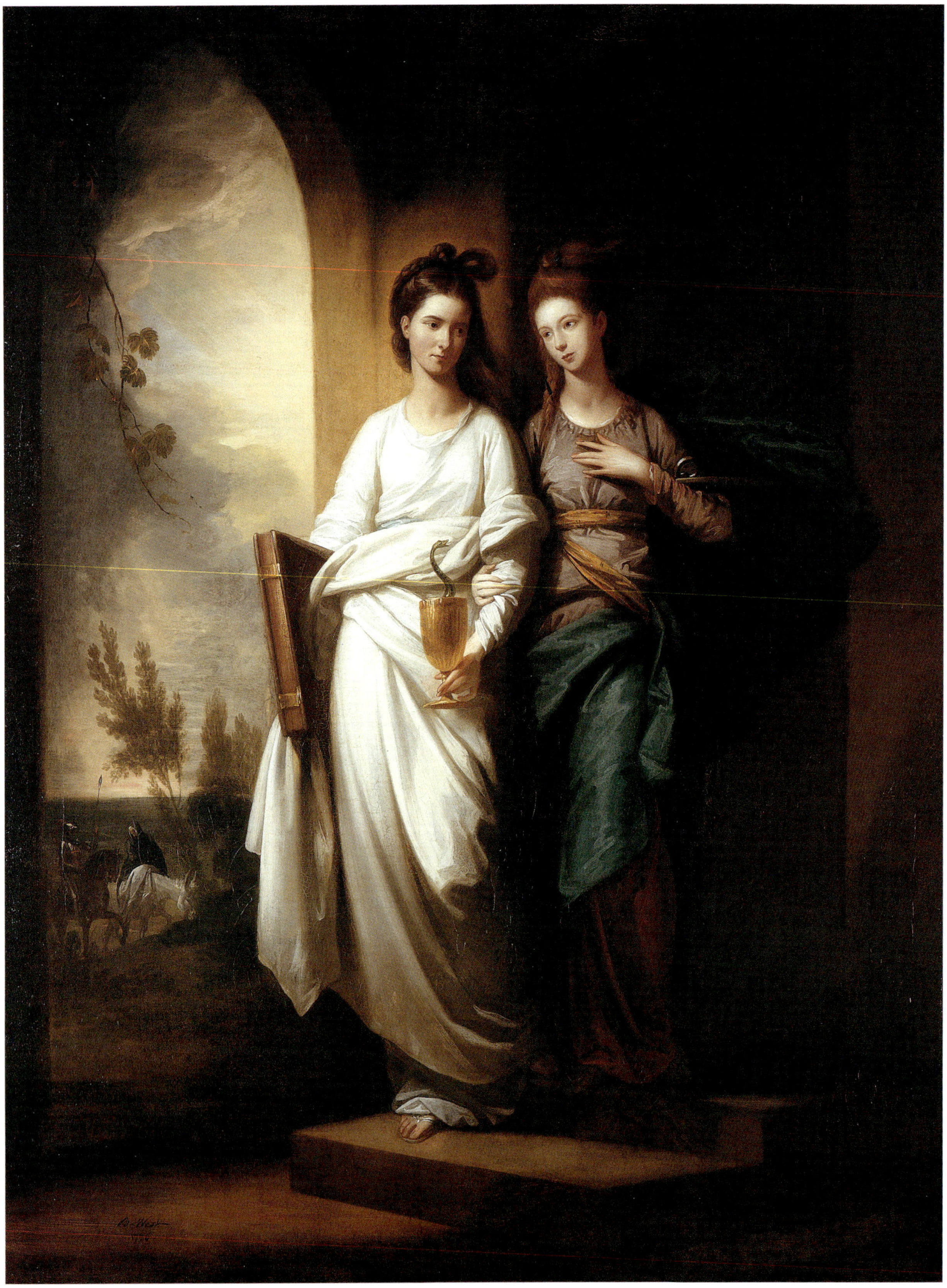

Benjamin West

(1738–1820)

Benjamin West was born on October 10, 1738, in Springfield, Pennsylvania. At a very early age he received some instruction from the English portrait painter William Williams and by the age of eighteen had set up as a portraitist in Philadelphia. Impressed by his precocious gifts, patrons enabled him to travel to Italy in 1760. In 1763 he went to England, where he was to spend the rest of his life. His neoclassical style of history painting met with warm success, and in 1772 he was appointed Historical Painter to the King. One of the original members of the Royal Academy, in 1792 West was elected its second president, a position he held, with a brief interruption, until his death in 1820. An artist of considerable international influence, he welcomed a generation of American art students to his studio.

40 *Fidelia and Speranza*, 1776
Oil on canvas, 53¾ × 42⅝ in. (136.5 × 108.3 cm)
Signed and dated lower left: *B. West / 1776*

Fidelia, dressed in white, advances down a short flight of steps, carrying in her right hand a large brown book with gold clasps and in her left a gold chalice, from which a green snake emerges. Showing no fear of the creature, she looks downward and to the side. A faint radiance surrounds her head. Speranza is clad in a mauve dress partly covered by a blue-green mantle and bound with an orange sash. Sad in expression, she takes her sister's arm with her right hand and places her left hand upon her heart, while carrying a short brown anchor in the crook of her left arm. To the left a large arch opens upon a stormy landscape, in which Una and the Red Cross Knight can be seen approaching.

West's subject closely follows stanzas twelve through fourteen of book 1, canto 10 of *The Faerie Queen* by Edmund Spenser, the Elizabethan poet. The passage occurs after Una (Truth) brings the sinning knight from the House of Pride and the Cave of Despaire to the House of Holiness, where his healing and conversion take place. The first to teach him are Fidelia (Faith) and Speranza (Hope), whom Spenser described with their traditional attributes as cardinal virtues. Fidelia bears the book of the New Testament and the communion chalice of wine and water, which in this case is the chalice of St. John from which the poison meant to kill him was driven off in the

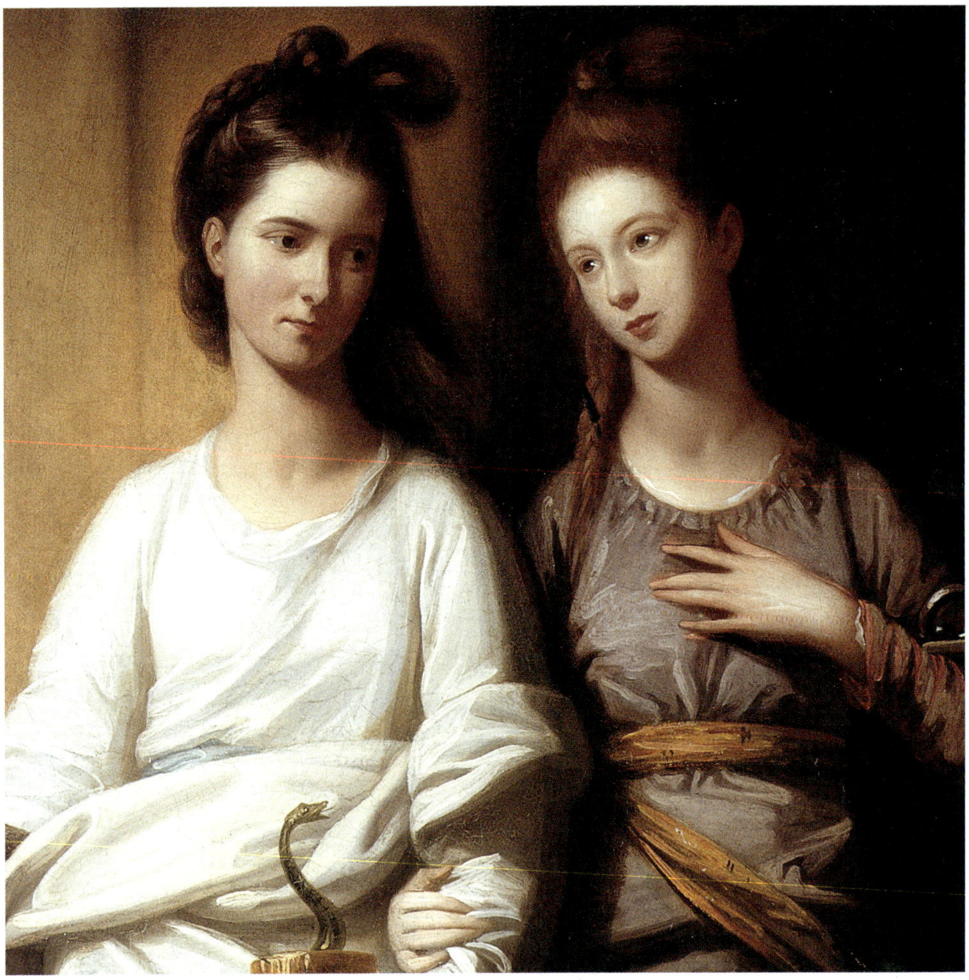

Detail of Plate 40

form of a snake. Hope is likewise traditionally associated with an anchor and the color blue and is shown looking heavenward. Spenser describes them as walking arm-in-arm because they are closely linked in Christian theology.

Besides *Fidelia and Speranza,* West painted two other subjects from *The Faerie Queen, Una and the Lion* (1771, Hartford, Conn., Wadsworth Atheneum) and *The Cave of Despaire* (1772, New Haven, Conn., Yale Center for British Art), responding to a widespread interest in subjects from the poem, particularly the more imaginative "Gothik" passages that the emerging romantic movement characterized as sublime. West's *Cave of Despaire* was meant to be horrific in this sense, but *Una and the Lion* and *Fidelia and Speranza* are both in his "stately mode," the decorous neoclassical style that West was influential in establishing in England and on the Continent. A preparatory pen-and-ink drawing for *Fidelia and Speranza* (Sotheby's, London, March 22, 1979, lot 6), in fact, is cast in a fully neoclassical manner with columns and planar presentation. The final version of both paintings has been softened by elements of the new romantic style—in *Fidelia and Speranza* specifically by the stormy sky and the enveloping darkness—as well as by the diagonal recession. Still, West departs from Spenser in using classical dress, the proper costume for ideal subjects in the art theory of West's period. It is the very heavy drapery West used in the

1770s, and the figures display the graceful contrapposto and elegant gestures that he also learned from his models in classical sculpture and the old masters he admired.

Smith (1883) has suggested that Fidelia may be a portrait of a Miss Hall, whom he identifies as the model for West's Una. She was born in Jamaica, married Richard James Laurence of that place, and died in London on January 20, 1815, aged sixty-six. Allen Staley, in his catalogue raisonné, advances this theory of allegorical portraits, presumably of sisters. Such portraits were common during the period, particularly in the work of Reynolds, and West is thought to have done several during the 1770s. Since West generally idealized the features of all his portrait subjects, identifications are often far from certain, but there is a resemblance between Fidelia and Una, which seems to be even more marked in the finished drawing West executed after the Timken painting in 1784 (fig. 1). It is the kind of drawing with an emphasis on facial features that itself suggests a portrait use. The Timken painting was exhibited at the Royal Academy in 1777, and John Boydell published, on November 9, 1778, a mezzotint by Valentine Green after the painting. However, the painting does not appear in the early lists of West's work, which is again characteristic of his portraits. It is interesting to note that John Singleton Copley's painting *The Red Cross Knight* (1793, Washington, D.C., National Gallery of Art) contains portraits of his own daughters as Fidelia and Speranza.

—M.Q.

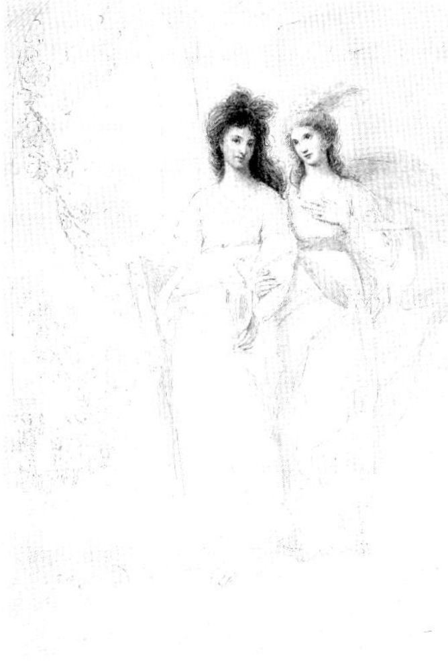

Fig. 1. Benjamin West, *Faith and Hope*, 1784. Brown ink and watercolor on cream antique laid paper with watermark, 21 × 16 in. (sight) (53.3 × 40.6 cm). Cambridge, Mass., The Harvard University Art Museums, Bequest of Grenville L. Winthrop, 1943.329. © President and Fellows, Harvard College, Harvard University Art Museums.

PROVENANCE

Acquired by the Putnam Foundation, 1969.

LITERATURE

John Chaloner Smith, *British Mezzotinto Portraits*, 4 vols. (London, 1883), 1:249–50, 2:598; John Dillenberger, *Benjamin West: The Context of His Life's Work with Particular Attention to Paintings with Religious Subject Matter* (San Antonio, Tex., 1977), pp. 25, 192, 211; Laurel Bradley, "Eighteenth-Century Paintings and Illustrations of Spenser's *Faerie Queen:* A Study in Taste," *Marsyas* 20 (1979–80): 51; William H. Gerdts, "*Hermia and Helena* by Washington Allston," *Christie's Review of the Season, 1982* (London, 1982), pp. 39, 40, fig. 4; *Timken Art Gallery: European and American Works of Art in the Putnam Foundation Collection* (San Diego, 1983), pp. 110–12, 126, no. 42, ill.; Helmut von Erffa and Allen Staley, *The Paintings of Benjamin West* (New Haven and London, 1986), pp. 209, 269, 279–80, 502, no. 222.

EXHIBITED

London, Royal Academy of Arts, 1777, no. 364; Cambridge, Mass., The Fogg Art Museum, 1969, *Grenville L. Winthrop: Retrospective for a Collector*, p. 132, ill.

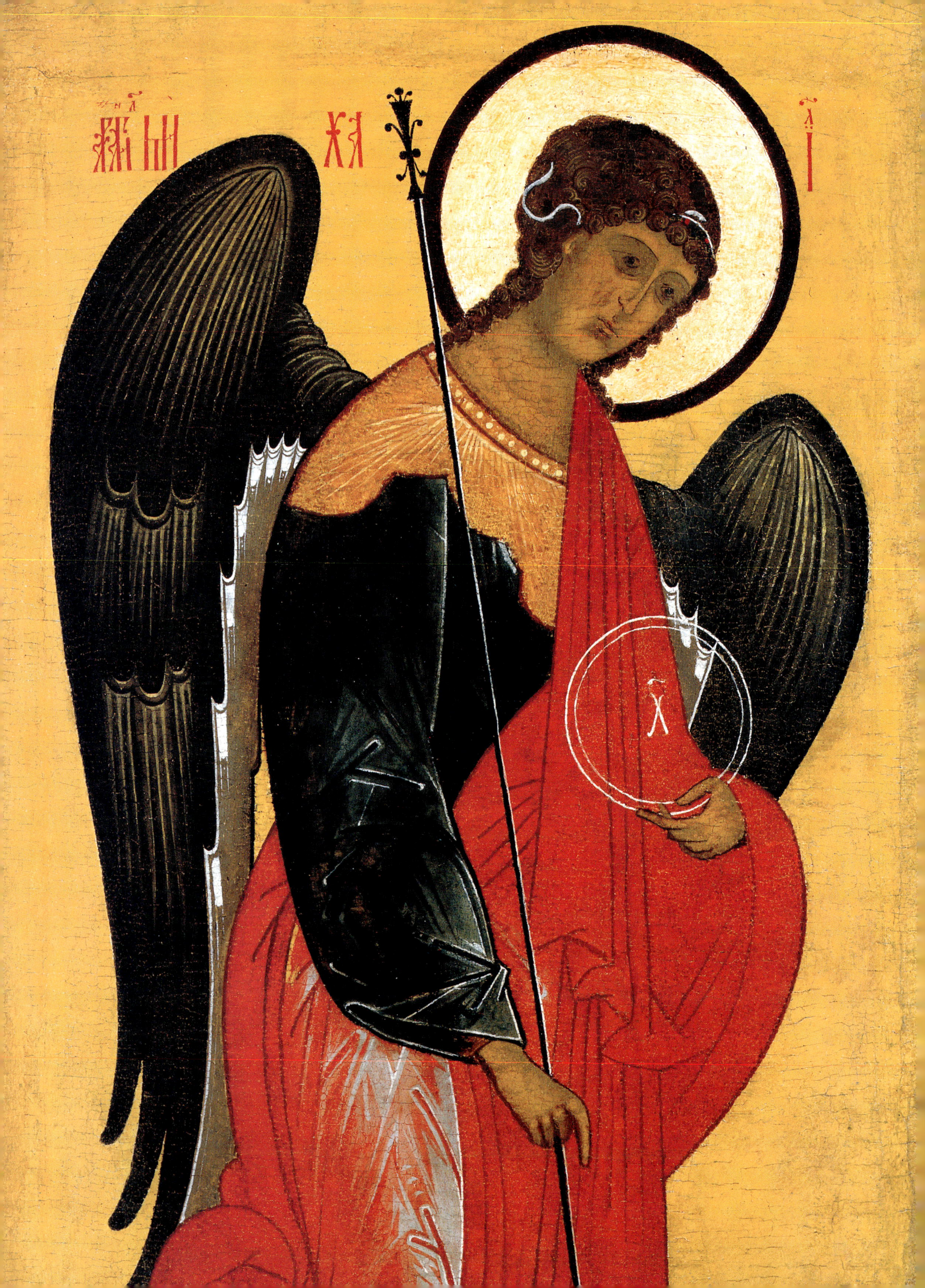

Russian Icons

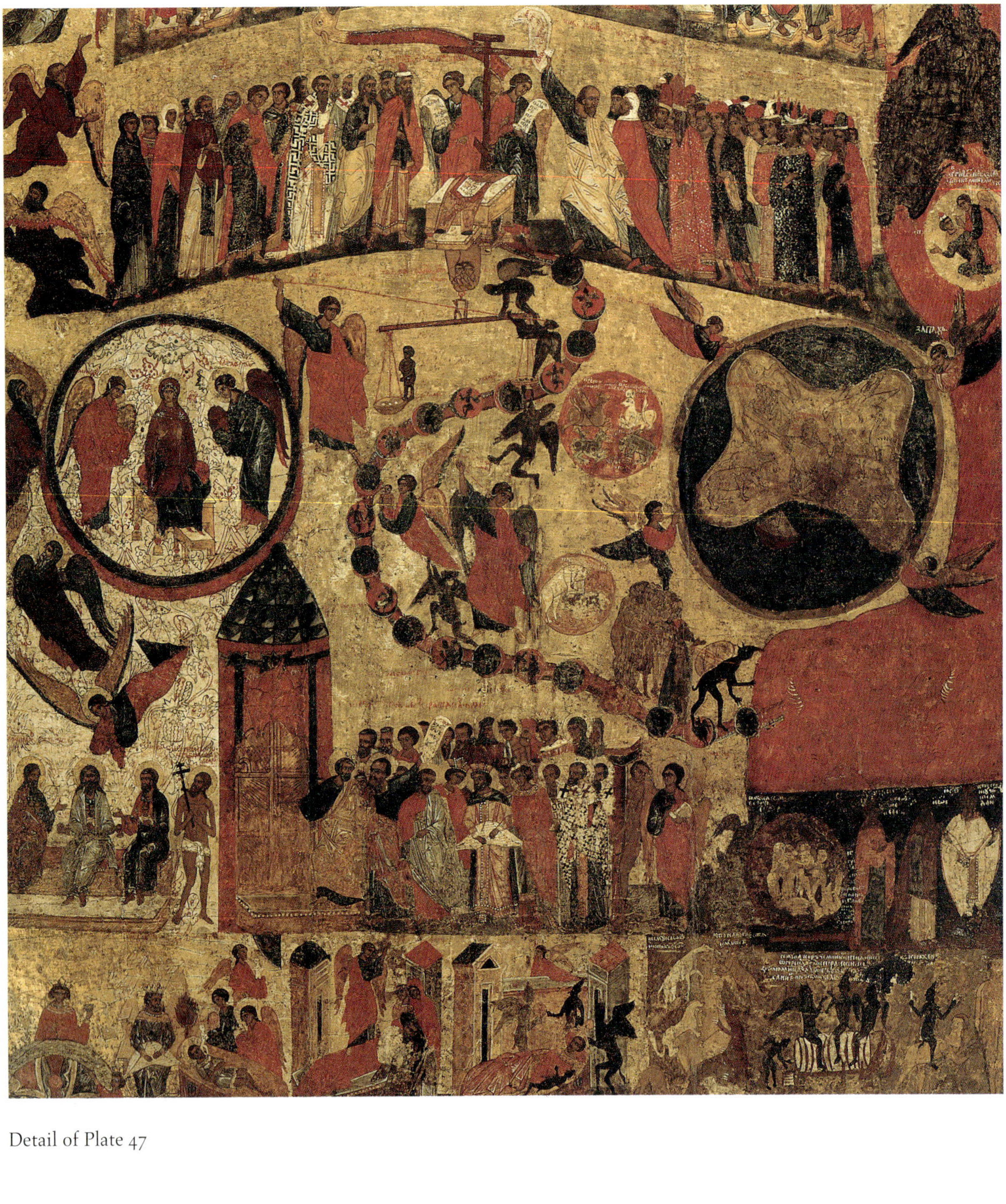

Detail of Plate 47

Russian Church Icons in the Putnam Foundation Collection

The Russian Orthodox Church is symbolized by its icons, whose function and message are elements of its very essence. The life of a church revolves around the liturgy and images of Jesus Christ, the Virgin Mary, saints, and special feast days. The congregation lights candles near the icons, kisses them, and makes profound bows in reverence and veneration. Priests and bishops cense the icons, and aromatic smoke ascends heavenward carrying prayers and petitions of the faithful.

The Putnam Foundation Collection features a select group of church icons. Within the traditional church setting these icons occupied specific places, either on the lectern, in the *iconostas'*—the screen that symbolically divides the human and divine worlds—or on the walls of the nave. Following the Communist Revolution, icons such as these were stripped from their traditional settings. Some, including those now in the Putnam collection, were sent abroad, where over the ensuing decades they were to enter private and public collections.

The Lectern

Small icons representing feast days or patron saints of the church are set on a cloth-draped lectern, or *analoy*. The faithful venerate icons on an *analoy* by making the sign of the cross, kissing the icon, and lighting beeswax candles near it. The Timken *tabletka* is a particularly interesting icon of this type (cat. no. 41a–b). This double-faced "tablet" icon is made of glued linen, gesso, and tempera paints. Originally produced as samples, from which orders could be taken, they were called *palatentzi*, or towels, and often depicted feast days. Tablets of this type are rare, and only a few dozen remain in Russia.

The Timken *tabletka* is typical of icons produced in Novgorod, south of St. Petersburg, at the end of the fifteenth century, when white was frequently used for the clothing, and figures were often painted out of proportion. This *tabletka* depicts the Forty Martyrs of Sebaste, the forty Roman soldiers who were martyred for their Christian beliefs under orders of Emperor Licinius in the fourth century. The men were forced to stand barefoot in a freezing lake near the town of Sebaste. One of the men recanted and entered a shelter on the lakeshore. A tormentor was so impressed with the faith of the remaining thirty-nine that he removed his warm clothing and joined the martyrs to bring the count once more to forty. Christ and the crowns of martyrdom hover above the Christians. The other side of the icon shows Four Men in the Fiery Furnace, the story from the third chapter of Daniel, where Shadrach, Meshach, and Abednego refuse to worship the golden idol erected by King Nebuchadnezzar. After they were thrown into the fiery furnace, an angel appeared to them.

At this the king said, "I see four men, unbound, walking around in the fire, and they are not even hurt by the flames! And the fourth looks like a god!" The king then released the three and gave them promotions, and Shadrach, Meshach, and Abednego prospered greatly in the province of Babylon.

The *Iconostas'*

Larger icons of a special type are displayed on an *iconostas'* (Russian for a sanctuary screen with icons) symbolizing the boundary between the divine world and the human world. The *iconostas'* physically separates the nave, where the congregation stands, from the sanctuary, where the sacrament of the Eucharist is celebrated. The Timken collection includes several icons from an *iconostas'*. *The Royal Gates* (cat. no. 42), or Czar's Doors, set in the center of the *iconostas'*, were so-called because Christ, the King of Glory as represented by his priests, enters the Royal Gates that lead to the altar. No one, other than clergy, is allowed to pass through the Royal Gates. A curtain hung on the inside is drawn or opened during various parts of the divine service. In addition, an *iconostas'* will have a northern and a southern door, to the right and left of the Royal Gates, known as "deacons' doors" because deacons use them during services. The Timken's Royal Gates were made in Novgorod in the fifteenth century of wood carved with three registers on each half. Placed together, the doors depict the Annunciation (April 7)[1] at the top, where the Archangel Gabriel announces to the Virgin Mary that she is to become the mother of Jesus, the Son of God. The other four panels show the evangelists, Matthew (November 29), Mark (January 17), Luke (January 17), and John (May 21). The architectural features and red pigments are also typical of Novgorod.

By tradition, an icon of the Virgin Mary and Christ Child is on the first register of the *iconostas'* to the left of the Royal Gates as one faces them, and an icon of Jesus is to the right. The Timken's seventeenth-century icon of the Moscow school (cat. no. 43), *The Jerusalem Mother of God* (October 25), is of the size that could flank the Royal Gates. The Mother of God is depicted in the traditional pose of the *Hodigitria*, Greek for "pointer of the way." This is an icon of the Virgin pointing with her right hand to the Christ Child as being "the Way, the Truth, and the Life."

This icon first appeared in the Sofia cathedral in Novgorod as a gift from Prince Vladimir Sviatoslavich, and the prototype gained great popularity in Novgorod. Ivan the Terrible transferred the icon to the Dormition cathedral in the Moscow Kremlin and placed it on one of the pillars. The iconography is unusual in that Jesus offers his mother a small sheaf of wheat, a traditional symbol of the bread of the Eucharist. As a rule, the fingers of Christ's right hand are usually folded in a gesture of blessing. In his left hand he holds a scroll of his teachings. The letters on either side of the Virgin's head mean "Maria, Mother of God," and the letters above Christ's halo, *IC XC*, stand for Jesus Christ. The three stars on Mary's *maphorion*, or garment, signify her virginity before, during, and after the birth of Christ. The dozens of nail holes in a right-angle pattern indicate that the background of the icon had once been overlaid with a *bas'ma oklad* (cover). *Bas'ma* is very thin, gilded silver stamped with an ornamental design and usually made in small squares or long strips to cover the background of an icon. *Bas'ma* was usually attached with very small, thin silver nails. A similar sixteenth-century Novgorodian icon of Our Lady of Jerusalem (but without traces of *bas'ma*) in the Nationalmuseum in Stockholm is called the *Vadstena-madonnan,* or the Madonna of Vadstena, after the town of that name in southern Sweden. This Jerusalem Mother of God iconography, a favorite of Georgian Christians, was often referred to as the Georgian Mother of God in eighteenth- and nineteenth-century Russia.

In addition to other traditional and specially placed icons, the *iconostas'* may have several horizontal rows of icons, sometimes reaching up to the high ceiling of a very tall church. *Iconostases* in smaller churches may have only a few rows of icons, but the order of images in each row is governed by tradition. The first row above the Royal Gates incorporates the Deisis *tchin* (prayer order). Representing the fulfillment of the New Testament church, it is the center of the *iconostas'*. Icons of the full-length figures of the Mother of God and St. John the Baptist standing before Jesus Christ as the Savior Enthroned together form the *Deisis*, meaning "prayer." An icon of the Savior Enthroned, such as the Timken's fifteenth-century example from Novgorod, would be the center of the Deisis *tchin* (cat. no. 44). This iconography depicts the Savior as the King of Glory seated on a carved throne with the church fathers shown in much smaller scale standing three to each side at the upper edge of the panel. His left hand holds a closed Gospel and his right hand is raised in blessing.

The saints arranged on either side are in an orderly succession with prayerful movement toward the Lord sitting on his throne. The saints are depicted without any evidence of their earthly service. Here Mary is shown without Christ Emmanuel, but she again points to Christ as the Savior and wears a blue robe and a burgundy mantle. To the left of Mary is an icon of the Archangel Michael (November 21, with All Angels), holding a transparent globe in his right hand and a scepter in his left. St. Peter (July 12) stands next to the Archangel Michael and is shown as an elderly man with gray hair and a beard. His right hand points to the Savior, and his left holds a scroll and a key on a string. The key signifies the keys of the Kingdom of Heaven as told in the book of Matthew (16:18–19): "You are Peter, a stone; and upon this rock I will build my church; and all the powers of hell shall not prevail against it. And I will give you the keys of the Kingdom of Heaven; whatever doors you lock on earth shall be locked in heaven; and whatever doors you open on earth shall be open in heaven!"

An icon of St. John the Baptist (July 7) stands to the right (proper left) of Christ with his hands extended to the Savior against a ground patterned in stripes of green and gold. Next to St. John is an icon of the Archangel Gabriel (November 21), holding a transparent globe in his right hand and a scepter in his left. The Apostle Paul

(July 12), next to the Archangel Gabriel, wears a green robe and a brown cloak with his right hand upraised and a book in the left. All the icons for this *tchin* are identified with their titles in Old Church Slavonic and are from fifteenth-century Novgorod, although the style of the St. John the Baptist and the Archangel Gabriel is slightly different from that of the other four.

The next higher register is made up of icons illustrating the holy days, or feast days of the Church. The Timken has only one icon from this row, that of *The Ascension of Our Lord Jesus Christ* (cat. no. 45). This feast day is always celebrated on the fortieth day after Easter (*Pascha* in Russian). The iconography shows the Mother of God flanked by two angels dressed in white, accompanied by the twelve apostles. Christ, in a mandorla with his right hand raised in blessing, is carried heavenward by two angels. An account of the Ascension is given briefly in Luke (24:46–51). A more detailed description is in Acts (1:1–3, 9–11), a continuation of the Gospel of Luke written about 65–70, which begins:

> Dear friend who loves God: In my first letter I told you about Jesus' life and teachings and how He returned to heaven after giving His chosen apostles further instructions from the Holy Spirit. . . . It was not long afterwards that He rose into the sky and disappeared into a cloud, leaving them staring after Him. As they were straining their eyes for another glimpse, suddenly two white-robed men were standing there among them, and said, "Men of Galilee, why are you standing here staring at the sky? Jesus has gone to heaven, and some day, just as He went, He will return!" . . . They were at the Mount of Olives when this happened, so now they walked the half mile back to Jerusalem and held a prayer meeting in an upstairs room of the house where they were staying.

Icon artists depicted this scene showing the rocky height of the Mount of Olives with four olive trees as the background and the two white-robed men as angels of the Lord.

The Timken *Ascension* is a product of the Moscow school of the sixteenth century. Originally rectangular, this icon was refashioned into a circular shape. Circular icons became popular at the beginning of the eighteenth century, when Peter I began his Westernization of Russia. At a later time, the round icon was restored to its present rectangular shape by a new addition, probably cut from an old icon. This could possibly have been in the mid-nineteenth century or later, when Russia began to turn once more to its own cultural heritage.

The Nave

The biographical icon of *St. Basil with Scenes from His Life* (cat. no. 46) is from the Moscow school of the sixteenth century. Because of its large size, it might have hung on a wall in the nave of a church. St. Basil (January 14) was a fourth-century archbishop who, aside from being a prolific writer and doctor of the church, was active in helping the sick and the poor. He built a hospice and a huge complex to minister to the sick and attracted huge crowds with his preaching. Basil became the leader of the orthodox believers against Arianism, the heresy that threatened to destroy the church in the East. Arianism (from Arius, a priest in Alexandria) maintained that the Son was inferior to the Father, a created being instead of "begotten not made, one in essence with the Father." St. Basil's work was continued by the second Ecumenical Council in Constantinople in 381, which expanded and adapted the Nicene Creed. St. Basil established the basis of monastic life in the East, was involved in works of charity, instituted clerical discipline, and fought against the widespread prostitution traffic in Cappadocia.

St. Basil stands full length with the Gospel in his left hand, while his right is raised in a two-fingered blessing. A three-quarter-length figure of Christ is depicted in a roundel above his right hand and a similar one of the Blessed Mother appears in a roundel above the Gospel. Fourteen scenes of St. Basil's life surround the saint. The icon was once covered with strips of *bas'ma* nailed to the background. An X radiograph shows hundreds of nails still imbedded in the icon, although the holes they made in the surface have been filled and in-painted. Some nails are still visible on the edges.

The monumental *Last Judgment* is six feet tall and is said to be from the Stroganoff school (cat. no. 47). Following a traditional composition, the icon is divided into five uneven, horizontal zones. In the uppermost zone, which is made up of several parts, in the left corner, is Heavenly Jerusalem with figures of the fathers of the church. Within the open gates, three angels receive seven ascetics who are flying one by one to heaven. This scene represents the vision of St. John Kolov: "Those who lived with God and disdained the beauty of the world, have wings of fire, so that they might ascend to Heavenly Jerusalem." At the top center, two angels unfold a scroll upon which are represented the sun, the moon, and the stars. Below the scroll sits God the Father in an aureole surrounded by seraphim and cherubim. On the right is Christ, being blessed by God the Father. To the right of that, Christ, against a red background, stands before the throne of God the Father. Farther to the right, Christ is placed to the right of God the Father, there to reign eternally. Below them, the Archangel Michael smites the devils who fall headlong from heaven.

In the next zone, Christ sits in judgment, flanked by the Virgin Mary and St. John the Baptist (the traditional Deisis), pleading for humanity. To the left and right are rows of apostles. Behind them are rows of angels. The books of the Last Judgment lie open on tables.

In the third zone is the throne of the millennium attended by two angels. On the left are prophets, martyrs, and saintly women. On the right, Moses, having descended from heaven, leads those who do not recognize Christ—Jews, Muslim warriors, and, last, heathens in Western garb, wearing jabots and high hats, recalling the Dutch merchants of the sixteenth century. Moses points out the figure of Christ in Judgment to all these people.

In the fourth horizontal zone, beneath the throne, are the scales on which angels and devils weigh the deeds of a man standing before them. Emerging from the jaws of hell is the wriggling serpent symbolizing evil. Its fangs touch the heels of Moses, and devils are seated on its body. Numerous angels and winged devils are placed in this zone. Angels carry the righteous souls or pitch sinners into eternal fire. Some of the devils pursue the angels, trying to pluck the saved souls from them. To the left is a large roundel containing the *Theotokos:* the Virgin enthroned in paradise with two attending angels. Below, in paradise, are Abraham, Isaac, and Jacob. In the large roundel to the right, angels indicate the coming of Christ to the prophet Daniel. In the center are two ovals representing the beasts of the Apocalypse, symbolizing the kingdoms of Greece, Rome, Babylon, and Persia. In the center of the zone, the righteous are led by St. Paul to the gates of paradise. An angel indicates a picture of the Last Judgment to a naked man tied to a column. On the right, on a red ground, the kingdom of hell is represented by a large two-headed beast on which the devil rides, surrounded by his court of sinners and cohorts. Various scenes of the tortures of hell are represented on the fifth level as well as scenes of death in which the forces of good and evil vie for the souls of the dying.

—V. B. E.

NOTE

1. The date in parentheses indicates the saint's or event's feast day in the Russian Orthodox Church according to the Old Style, Julian calendar.

GENERAL REFERENCES

L. Ouspensky and V. Lossky, *The Meaning of Icons* (Basel, 1952); V. I. Antonova and M. E. Mneva, *Katalog drevnerusskoi zhivopisi,* 2 vols. (Moscow, 1963); Victor N. Lazarev, *The Novgorod School of Icon Painting* (Moscow, 1969); id., *The Moscow School of Icon Painting* (Moscow, 1971); Richard E. Ahlborn and Vera B. Espinola, eds., *Russian Copper Icons and Crosses from the Kunz Collection: Castings of Faith* (Washington, D.C., 1991).

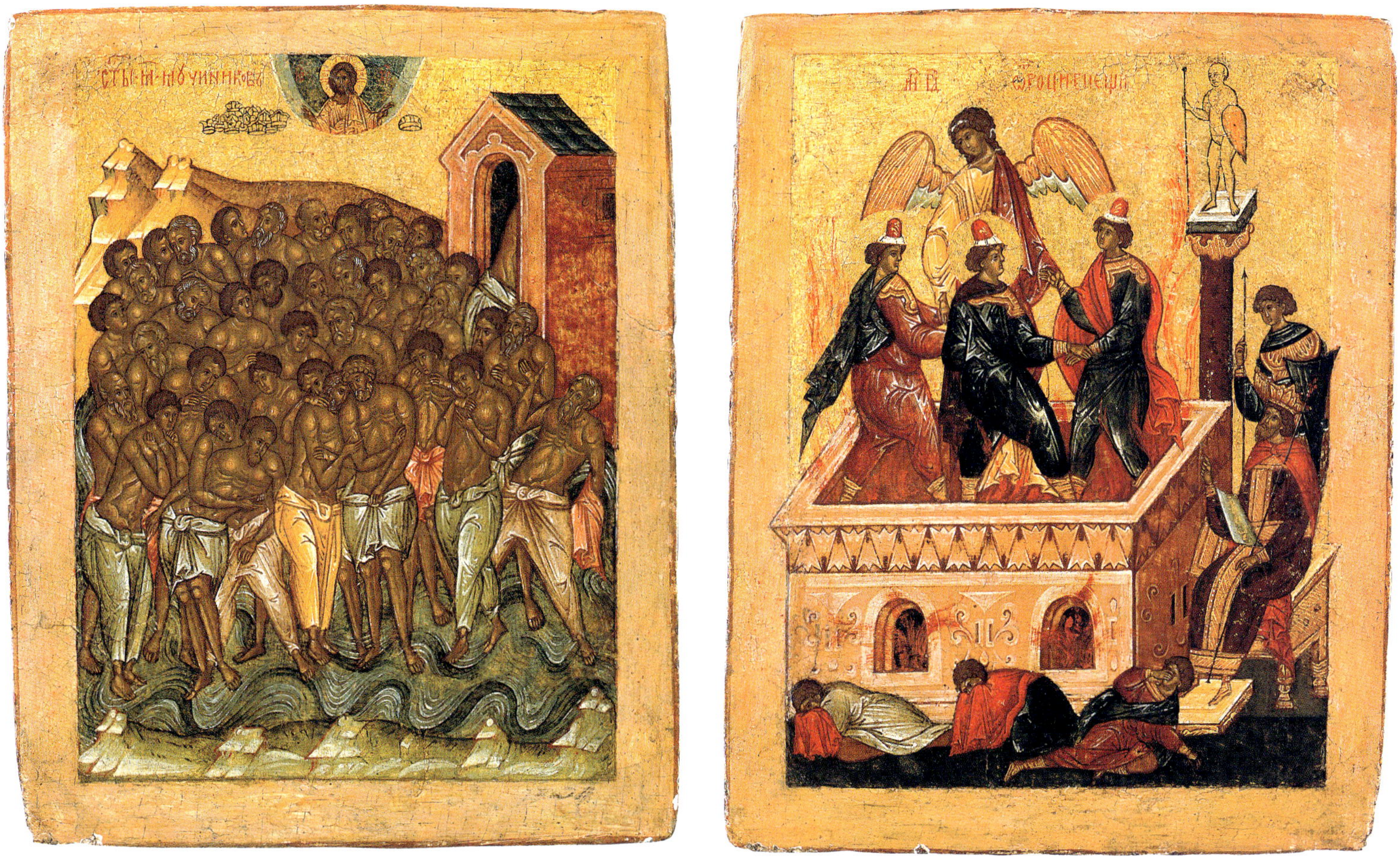

41a–b *The Forty Martyrs of Sebaste* and *Four Men in the Fiery Furnace,*
15th century, Novgorod school
Tempera and gesso on linen, $9\frac{5}{8} \times 7\frac{7}{8}$ in. (24.4 × 20 cm)

PROVENANCE

The de Wijenburgh collection, Netherlands; Temple Gallery, London; acquired by the Putnam Foundation, 1979.

EXHIBITED

London, Temple Gallery, 1979, *Byzantine and Russian Icons,* cat. by Richard Temple, pp. 32–36, no. 23, ill.

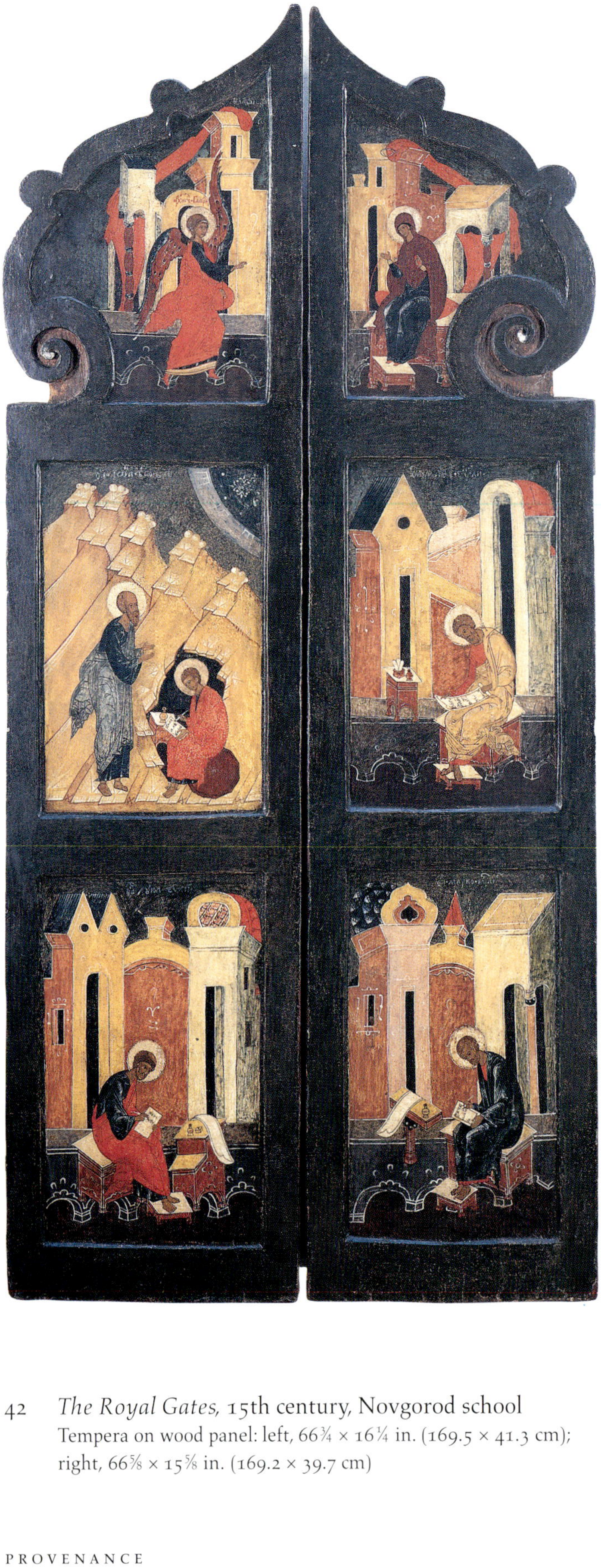

42 *The Royal Gates,* 15th century, Novgorod school
Tempera on wood panel: left, 66¾ × 16¼ in. (169.5 × 41.3 cm); right, 66⅝ × 15⅝ in. (169.2 × 39.7 cm)

PROVENANCE
A la Vieille Russie, New York; acquired by the Putnam Foundation, 1968.

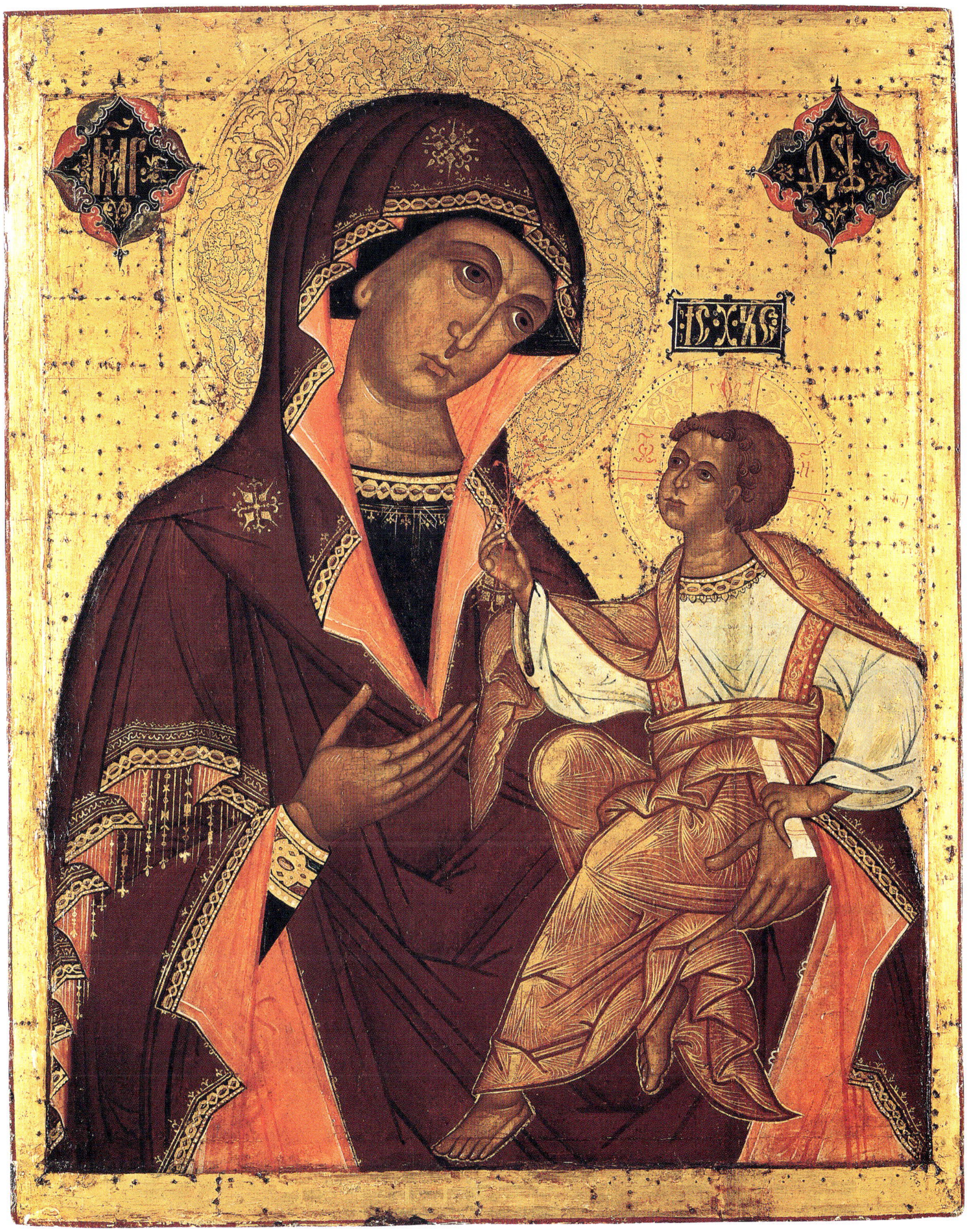

43 *The Jerusalem Mother of God*, 17th century, Moscow school
Tempera on wood panel, 51⅝ × 42 in. (131.1 × 106.7 cm)

PROVENANCE
A la Vieille Russie, New York; acquired by the Putnam Foundation, 1956.

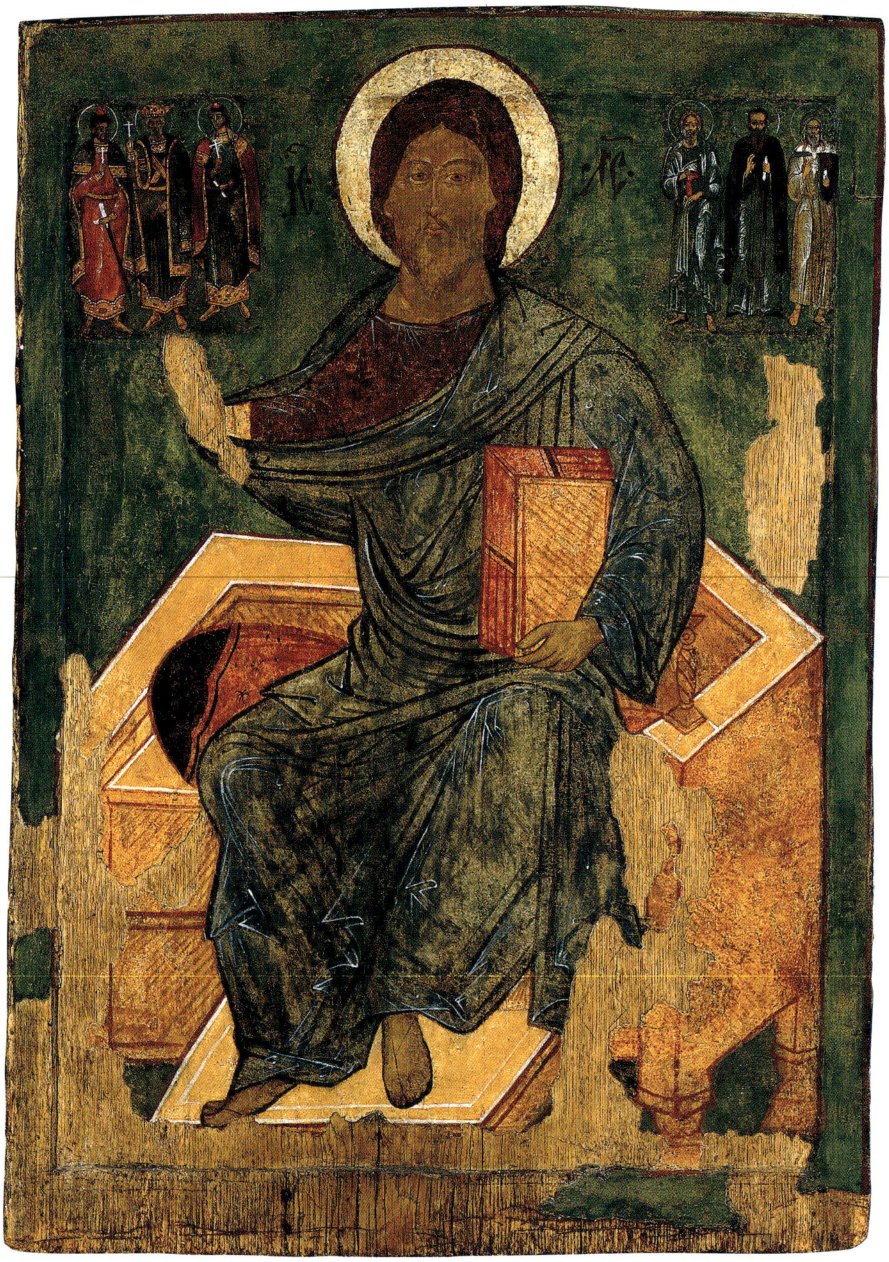

44 *Deisis: The Savior Enthroned, the Virgin Mary, the Archangel Michael, the Apostle Peter, St. John the Baptist, the Archangel Gabriel, the Apostle Paul,* 15th century, Novgorod school

Tempera on wood panel: Savior, 35¾ × 25¾ in. (90.8 × 65.4 cm). Top row: Peter, 34½ × 13 in. (87.6 × 33 cm); Michael, 34½ × 16¾ in. (87.6 × 42.5 cm); Virgin, 34⅜ × 14 in. (87.3 × 35.6 cm). Bottom row: John, 34⅜ × 16¼ in. (87.3 × 41.3 cm); Gabriel, 34¼ × 16⅞ in. (87 × 42.9 cm); Paul, 34½ × 13 in. (87.6 × 33 cm)

PROVENANCE

A la Vieille Russie, New York; acquired by the Putnam Foundation, 1964.

EXHIBITED

New York, A la Vieille Russie, 1962, no. 9.

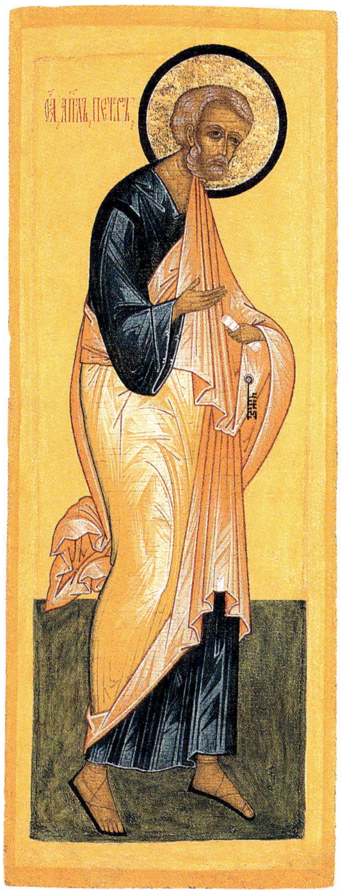
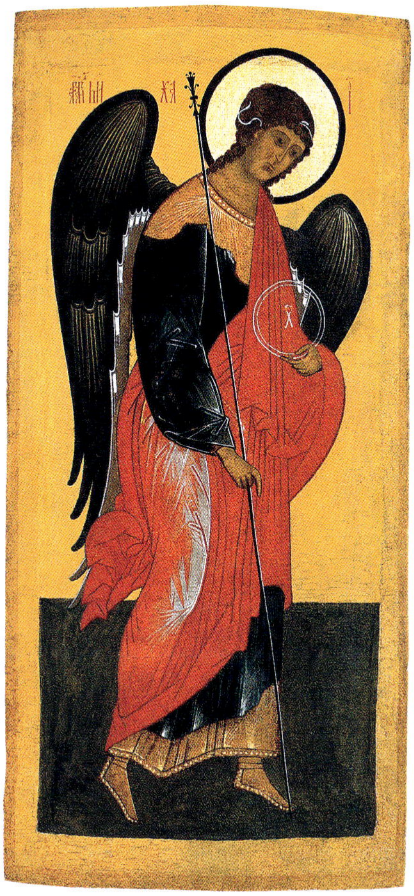
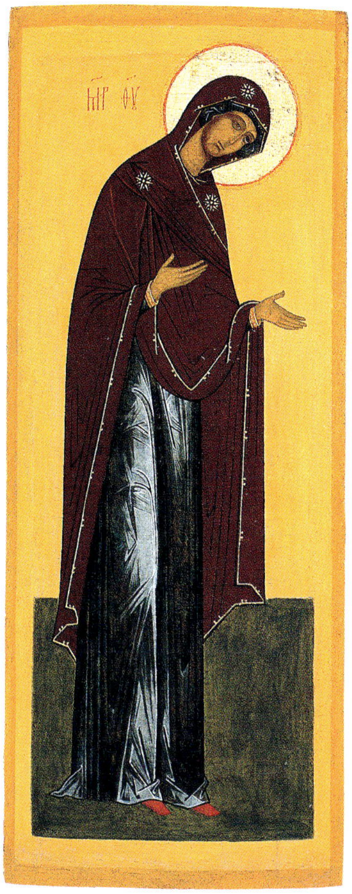
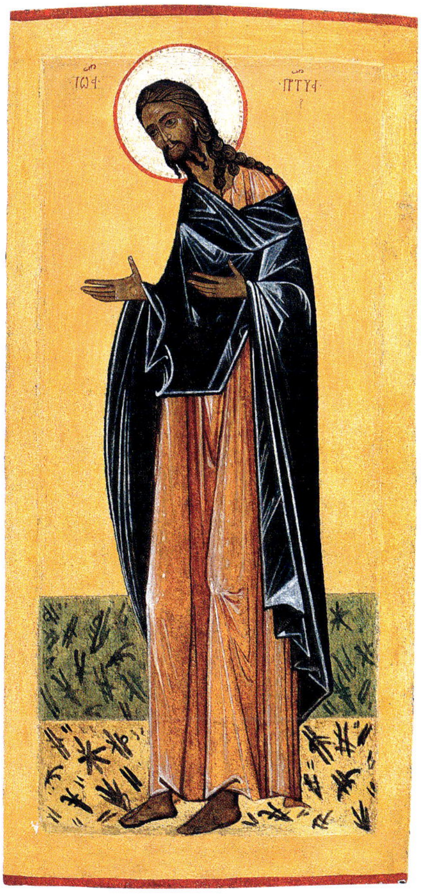
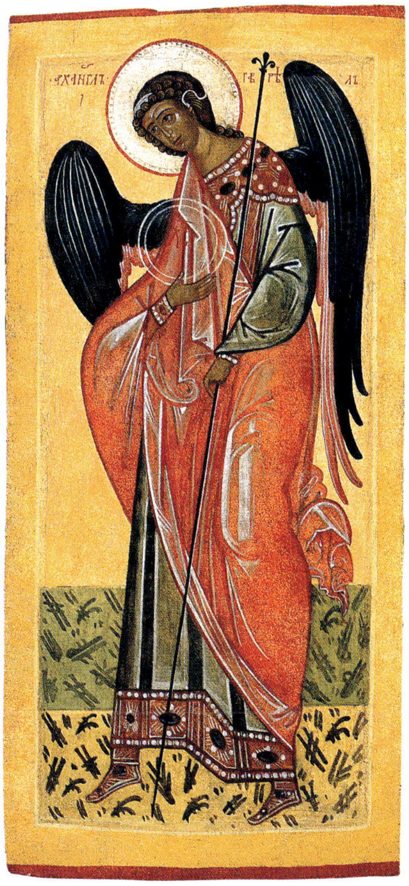
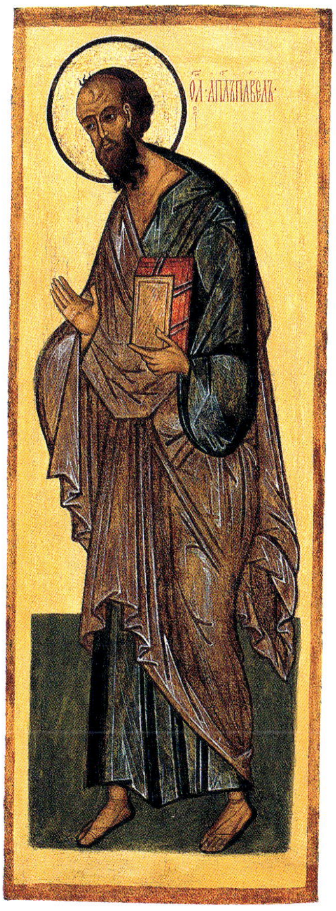

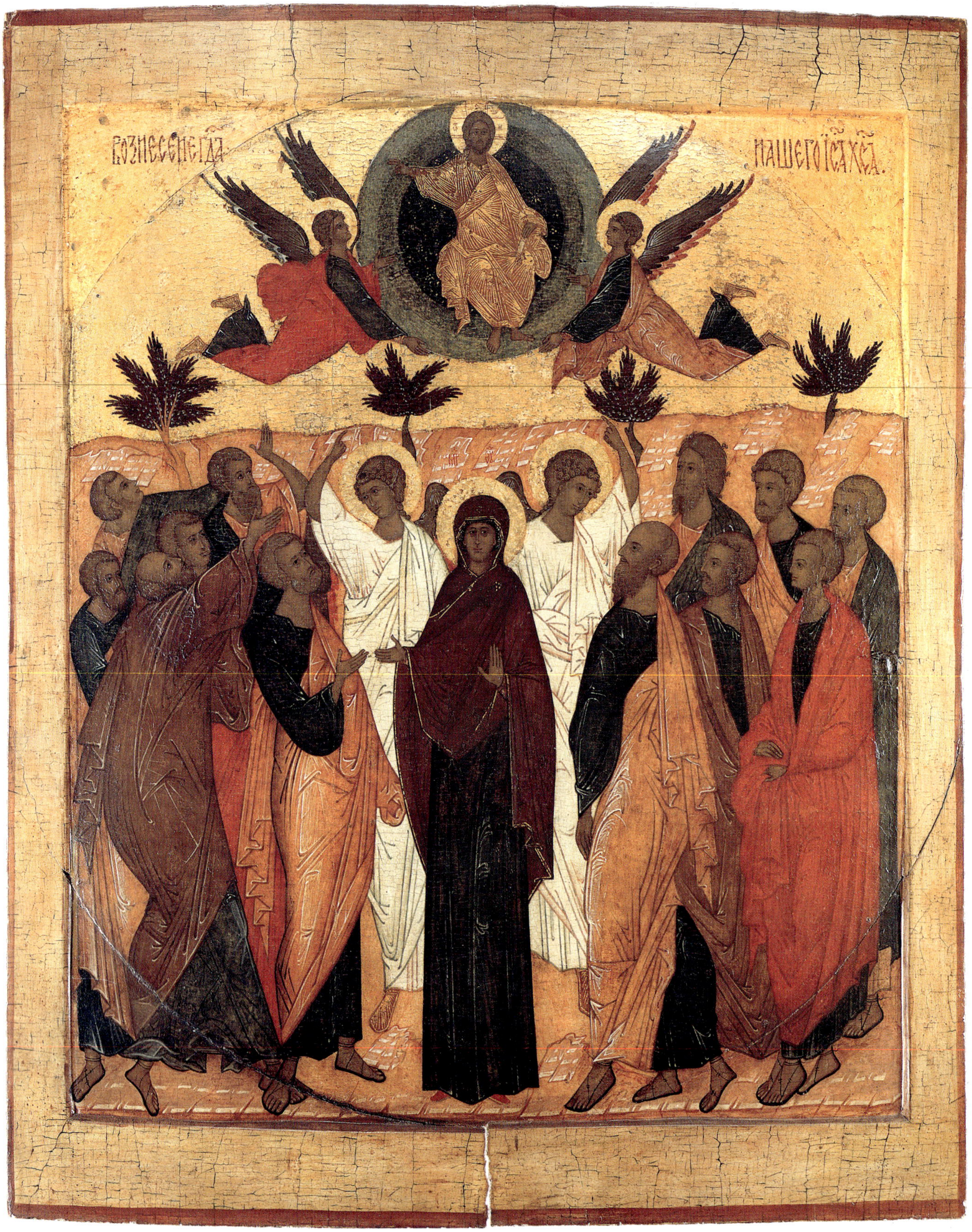
ВОЗНЕСЕНЕ ГДА
НАШЕГО ІСА ХСА.

45 *The Ascension of Our Lord Jesus Christ,* 16th century, Moscow school
Tempera on wood panel, 32⅞ × 26¾ in. (42.9 × 35.2 cm)

PROVENANCE

Tretyakov Gallery, Moscow; U.S.S.R. Central Art Collection Warehouse, 1936; George R. Hann, Sewickley Heights, Pa., his sale, Christie's, New York, April 15, 1981, lot 56; acquired by the Putnam Foundation, 1981.

LITERATURE

Russian Icons, intro. by Phillipp Schweinfurth (New York and London, n.d.), p. 45, ill.; Heinz Skrobucha, *Meisterwerke der Ikonenmalerei* (Recklinghausen, 1961), pl. p. 233; Robert Wallace et al., *Rise of Russia* (New York, 1967), pl. p. 109; *The Horizon Book of the Arts of Russia* (New York, 1970), pp. 72, 73, ill.

EXHIBITED

Pittsburgh, Carnegie Institute, 1944, *Collection of George R. Hann,* no. 68; Syracuse, N.Y., Syracuse Museum of Fine Arts; Columbus, Ohio, Columbus Gallery of Fine Arts; Indianapolis, John Herron Art Museum; and Oberlin, Ohio, Allen Memorial Art Museum, 1944–45, *Collection of George R. Hann,* no. 33; The Art Institute of Chicago, 1944–45, *Art of the United Nations;* The Saint Louis Art Museum, 1945, *Russian Icons and Objects of Ecclesiastical and Decorative Arts.*

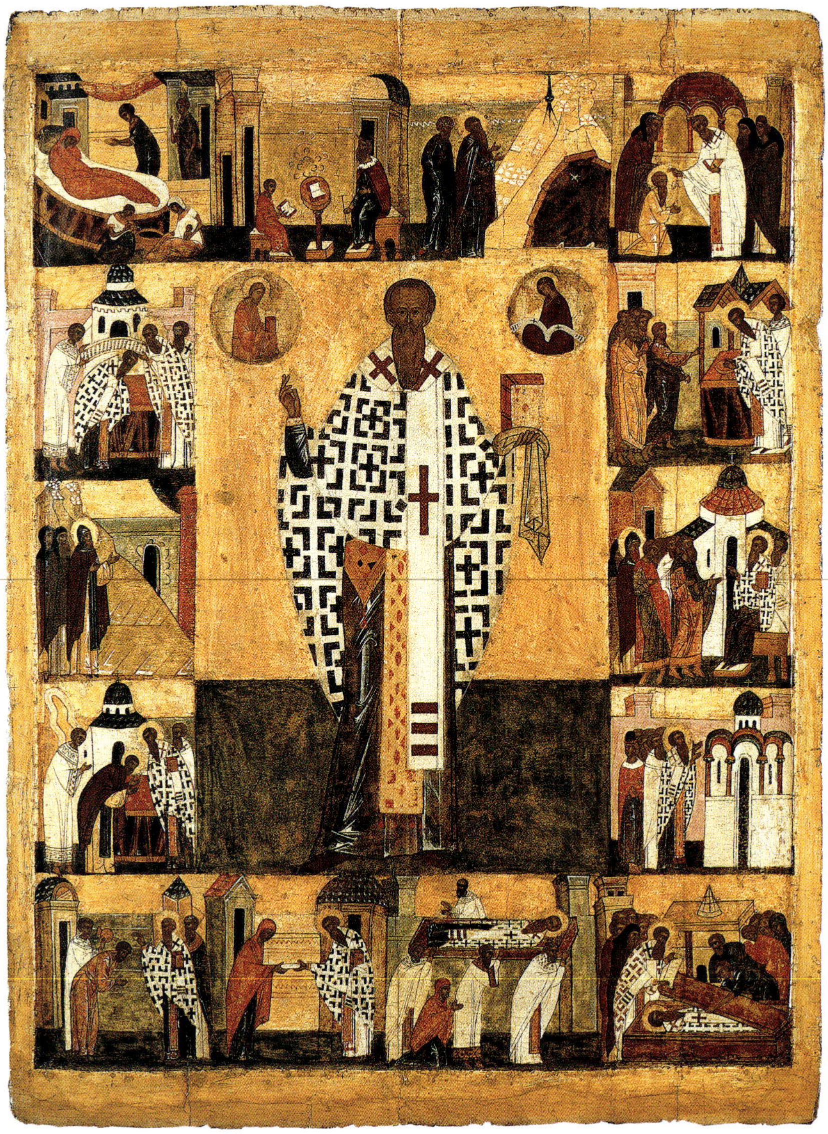

46 *St. Basil with Scenes from His Life,* 16th century, Moscow school
Tempera on wood panel, 42⅝ × 32½ in. (108.3 × 82.6 cm)

PROVENANCE

George R. Hann, Sewickley Heights, Pennsylvania; acquired by the Putnam Foundation, 1980.

LITERATURE

George Every, *Christian Mythology* (London, 1970), p. 69, ill.; Tamara Talbot Rice, *Russian Icons* (London, n.d.), pp. 34, 35, pl. 28; Jerry E. Patterson, "Russian Icons from the Hann Collection," *Connoisseur* 213 (April 1980): 242, ill.

EXHIBITED

Pittsburgh, Carnegie Institute, 1944, *Collection of George R. Hann,* no. 65; New York, The Metropolitan Museum of Art, 1944; Syracuse, N.Y., Syracuse Museum of Fine Arts; Columbus, Ohio, Columbus Gallery of Fine Art; Indianapolis, John Herron Art Museum; Oberlin, Ohio, Allen Memorial Art Museum, 1944–45, *Exhibition of Russian Icons from the Collection of George R. Hann,* no. 33; The Saint Louis Art Museum, 1945, *Russian Icons and Objects of Ecclesiastical and Decorative Arts.*

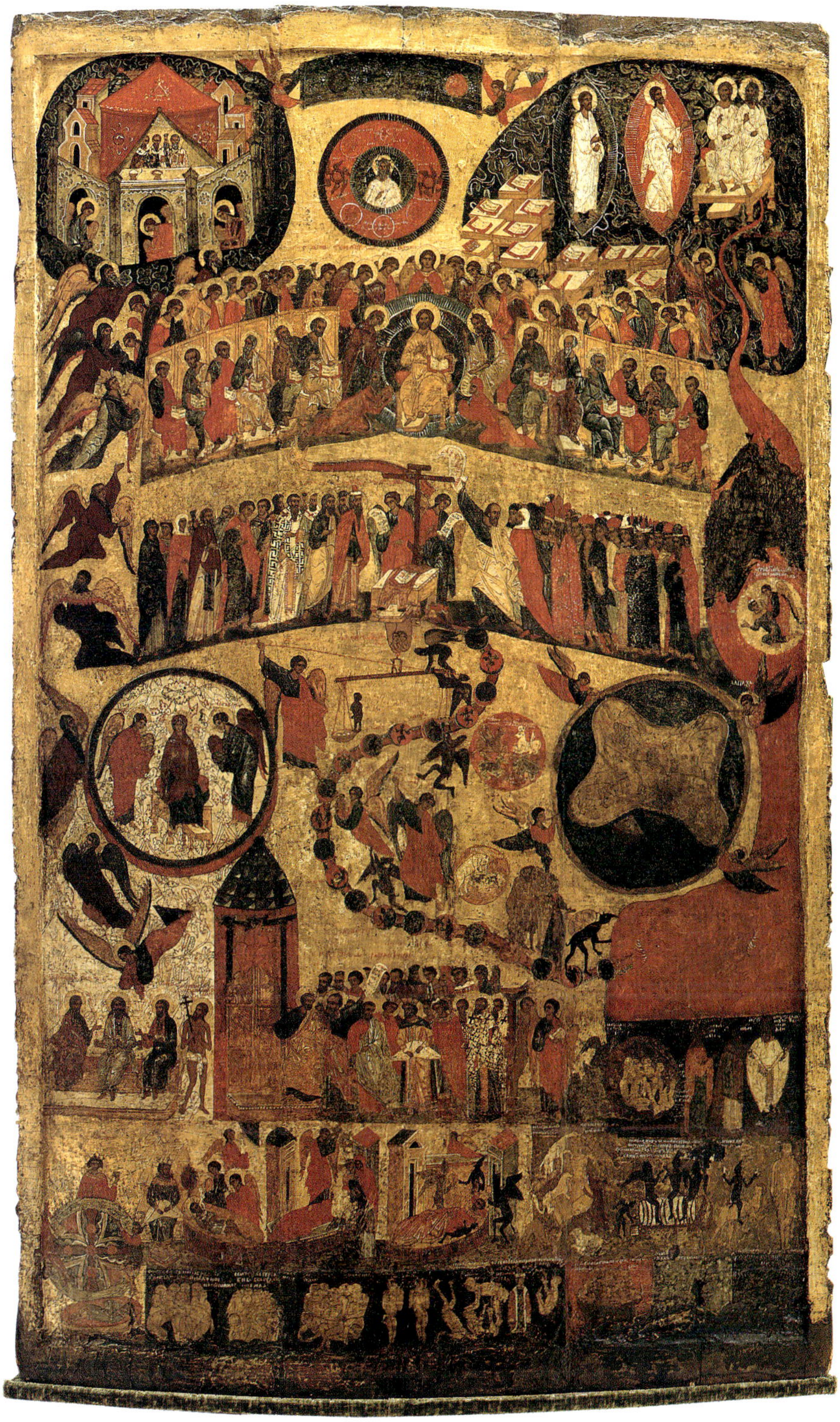

47 *The Last Judgment,* 16th century, Stroganoff school
Tempera on wood panel, 72 × 44⅝ in. (182.9 × 113.3 cm)

PROVENANCE
A la Vieille Russie, New York; acquired by the Putnam Foundation, 1967.

Appendix

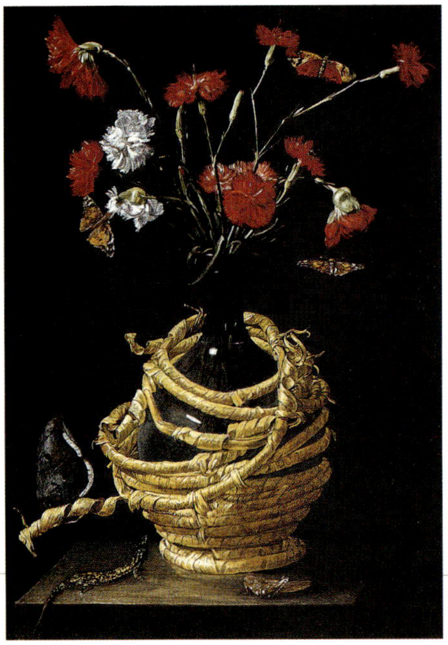

Anonymous
(Italian, act. first quarter 17th century)

Still Life
Oil on canvas, 25⅞ × 19 in. (65.7 × 48.3 cm)

> A flask, filled with red and white carnations, rests on a pedestal. Its raffia wrap uncoils; a moth has alighted on a wayward strand. A second moth and two painted lady butterflies, wings spread, are poised near the blossoms. A rock lizard and a migratory locust can be seen at the base of the flask.
>
> The fact that the straw is broken, that the flowers are withering, and that butterflies are notoriously short-lived may indicate a moral on the brevity of life in general. Such an allegorical reading could be considered confirmed by the fact that the livestock depicted are mutually destructive: the locust, and probably also the moths and butterflies, would eat the flowers, but the lizard would eat the locust. (Gould, in *Timken Art Gallery* 1983)

Comparable pictures showing a bouquet of flowers in a Chianti bottle with an unraveling raffia wrap are in the museum at Forlì, Italy, and in the Museum of Fine Arts, Boston. In 1959 Francesco Arcangeli attributed the Boston picture to Guido Cagnacci, based on its similarity to the picture in Forlì. In 1964, when the Forlì and Boston pictures were hung together in an exhibition of Italian still life, the Boston picture was given to an anonymous follower of Caravaggio. While certain aspects of the San Diego picture are closer to the Forlì picture, most notably the inclusion of the insects and lizard and the tight arrangement of the flowers and neat coil, scholarship does not support attribution of the San Diego picture to Cagnacci.

PROVENANCE

Acquired by the Putnam Foundation, 1971.

LITERATURE

Timken Art Gallery: European and American Works of Art in the Putnam Foundation Collection (San Diego, 1983), pp. 22, 23, 116, no. 4, ill., as Guido Cagnacci, *Still Life;* Pier Giorgio Passini, *Guido Cagnacci, pittore (1601–1663)* (Rimini, 1986), p. 277; Karyn Esielonis, *Still-Life Painting in the Museum of Fine Arts, Boston* (Boston, 1994), pp. 63–64, no. 2.

Anonymous
(Flemish, act. last quarter 15th century)

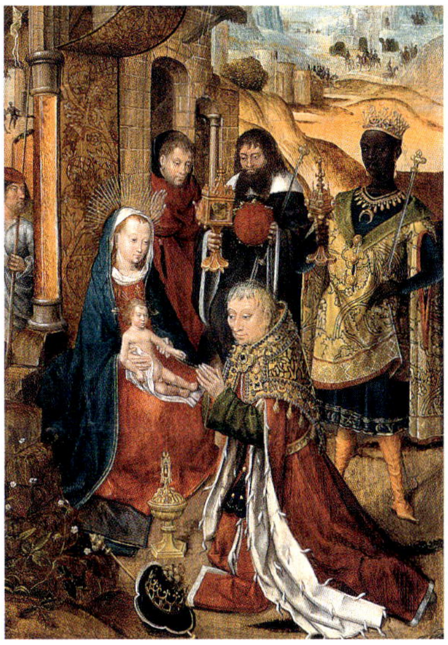

Adoration of the Magi
Oil on oak panel, 22⅞ × 17 in. (58.1 × 43.2 cm)

This Flemish version of the Adoration of the Magi is thought to have been painted in Bruges toward the end of the fifteenth century. Following the practice of several centuries, the Wise Men are not represented as the Magi of the Gospels, but as earthly kings who would lay the symbols of their temporal reigns before a heavenly ruler. The three kings were intended to symbolize the three known continents and the three ages of man. Caspar, the old king, traditionally kneels to make the first offering; Melchior stands in the center; and to the right is Balthasar, who came to be represented as a black man during the course of the fifteenth century.

The painter of this work was probably familiar with Hans Memling's *Adoration of the Magi*, now in the Prado, Madrid. As noted by Elizabeth and Agnes Mongan in the 1969 Timken catalogue: "The position of the Madonna, the personalities of the Magi, and even the characterization of St. Joseph, a civilized gentleman rather than a rustic, are very close to Memling's exposition." They note, however, that the painter of this picture has his own talents: "They are to be felt in the general composition of the picture: his placing the principal participants in a narrow space near the front of the picture plane; his bold juxtaposition of color, for example, green against bright blue; and the introduction of large areas of black for dramatic effect."

Friedländer attributed this picture to the Master of the St. Lucy Legend. In an addendum to the 1983 catalogue entry, Cecil Gould noted that the attribution was provisional at best, and that "not all scholars might agree, for example, that the San Diego picture is by the same hand as *The Saint Lucy Legend* triptych in Bruges, or that all of the pictures attributed to the unnamed painter of the latter by Friedländer are by the same hand."

PROVENANCE

M. Chillingworth, Nuremberg, sale, Galeries Fischer, Lucerne, September 5, 1922, *Catalogue de la collection Chillingworth: Tableaux anciens XIII à XVII siècles*, p. 9, no. 9, ill.; Albert J. Kobler, New York; Mrs. Edward A. Westfall, New York; acquired by the Putnam Foundation, 1955.

LITERATURE

Max J. Friedländer, *Die altniederländische Malerei*, 14 vols. (Berlin and Leiden, 1924–37), 6:140, no. 144; "Countrywide Loans from California," *Art News* 55 (November 1956): 33; Agnes Mongan and Elizabeth Mongan, *European Paintings in the Timken Art Gallery* (San Diego, 1969), pp. 50, 51, 115–16, no. 16, ill., as by Master of the St. Lucy Legend; *Timken Art Gallery: European and American Works of Art in the Putnam Foundation Collection* (San Diego, 1983), pp. 60–61, 121, no. 21, ill., as attributed to the Master of the St. Lucy Legend.

EXHIBITED

New York, F. Kleinberger Galleries, 1929, *Catalogue of a Loan Exhibition of Flemish Primitives*, cat. by Harry G. Sperling, pp. 126–27, no. 40, ill.; New York, Duveen Art Galleries, 1946, *Catalogue of Exhibition of Flemish Paintings*, no. 2, ill.; New York, The Metropolitan Museum of Art, extended loan, 1956–65.

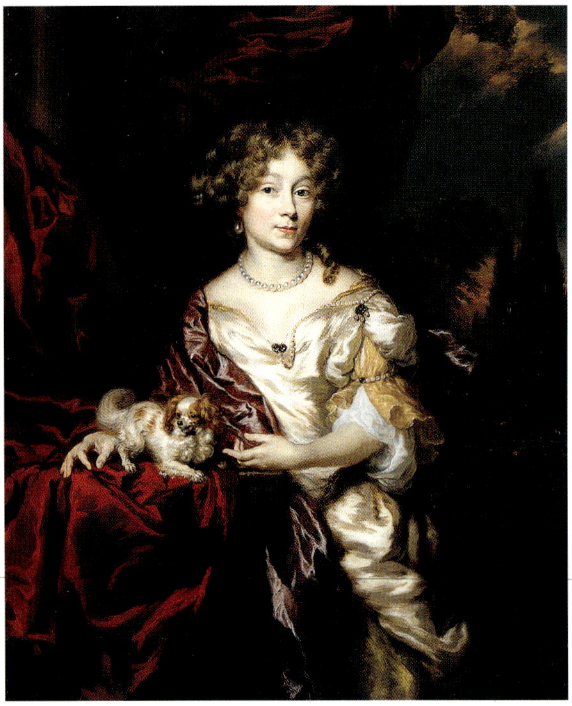

Nicolaes Maes
(Dutch, 1634–1693)

Portrait of a Lady, 1677
Oil on canvas, 26⅝ × 22¼ in. (67.6 × 56.5 cm)
Signed and dated lower right: *Maes 1677*

A native of Dordrecht, by the mid-seventeenth century Nicolaes Maes was in Amsterdam, where he was to become Rembrandt's best-known pupil. Maes's early paintings are very much in the tradition of Dutch genre painting, but by 1660 he had developed a more fluid style that readily lent itself to portraiture.

It has been suggested that this portrait is of Mary Stuart, daughter of James, duke of York, and Anne Hyde. In 1677, the year this work was painted, the fifteen-year-old Mary Stuart married William of Orange, the Stadholder of the United Provinces of the Netherlands. She later became Mary II when he became William III. They ruled England, popularly known as William and Mary.

PROVENANCE

Lord Northwick, Thirlestane House, Cheltenham; Massey-Mainwaring collection, sale, Christie's, London, March 16, 1907, lot 17; Rosenberg Gallery, New York; Henry A. Butler, Youngstown, Ohio; Noortman & Brod, New York; Alan Mark Levenson; acquired by the Putnam Foundation, 1986.

LITERATURE

Cornelis Hofstede de Groot, *Holländische Maler des XVII. Jahrhunderts*, 10 vols. (Esslingen and Paris, 1907–28), 6: no. 223.

EXHIBITED

London, Royal Academy, 1884, no. 120, as by G. Netscher; San Francisco Museum of Art, 1920, *Loan Exhibition of Paintings by Old Masters*, p. 26, no. 54, ill.

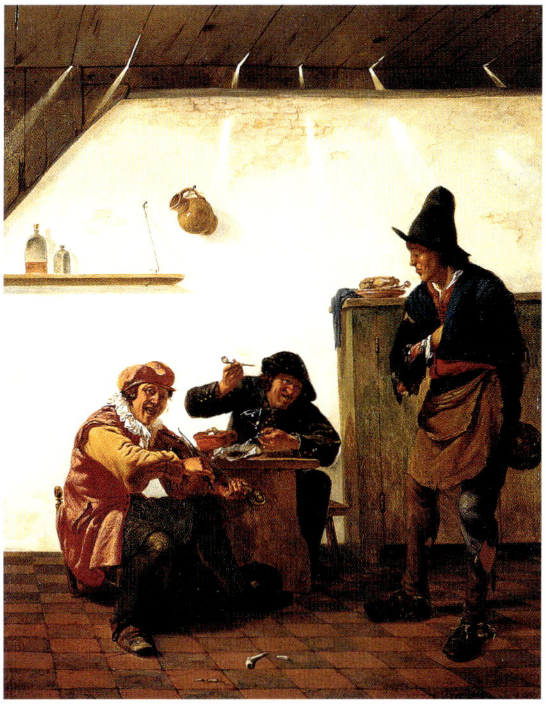

Johannes Natus
(Dutch, act. second half 17th century)

Three Peasants in an Inn, 1660
Oil on panel, 20⅜ × 16⅛ in. (51.8 × 41 cm)
Signed and dated lower right: *Natus 1660*

Johannes Natus was active in Middelburg about 1662. He is probably identical with Anton Natus, whose signature is very similar. Natus's genre paintings most often depict scenes of peasant life, such as weddings, dances, and boys playing cards. His landscapes are Italianate, with genre figures playing an important role, and have strong contrasts of light and dark.

PROVENANCE
Sotheby's, Amsterdam, May 4, 1976, lot 40; acquired by the Putnam Foundation, 1976.

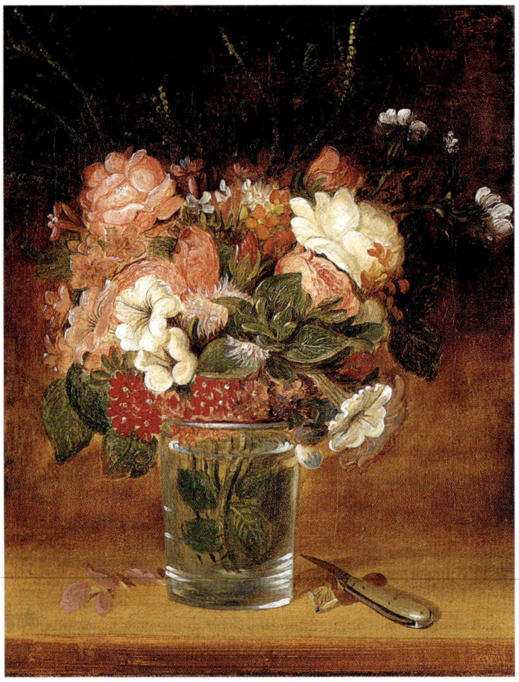

Anonymous
(American, 19th century)

Mixed Flowers in a Tumbler
Oil on canvas, mounted on board, 12½ × 10¼ in. (31.8 × 26 cm)

This unsigned still life depicts a glass tumbler with cut flowers and greenery. A small pearl-handled penknife rests on the table next to the tumbler.

PROVENANCE
Acquired by the Putnam Foundation, 1979.

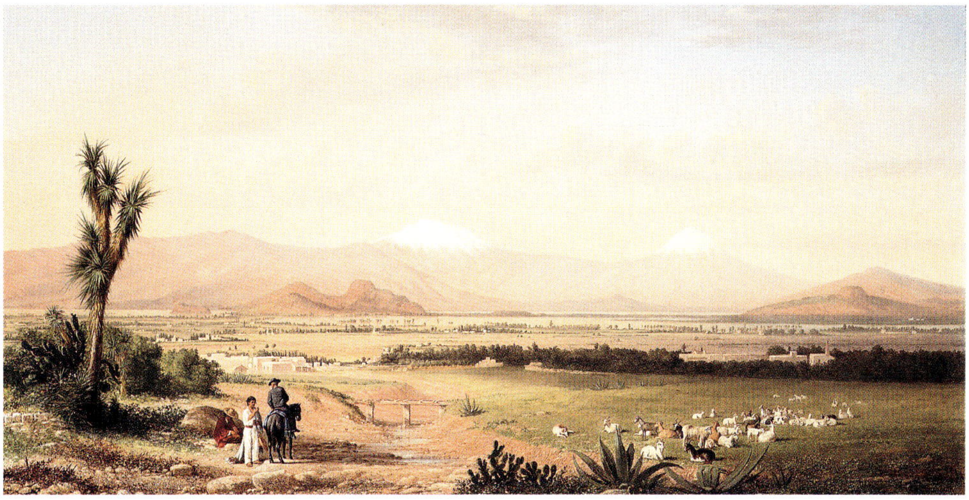

Conrad Wise Chapman
(1842–1910)

View of the Valley of Mexico, 1894
Oil on canvas, 24⅞ × 49⅝ in. (63.2 × 126.1 cm)
Signed and dated lower right: *CWChapman Mexico 1894*

The son and pupil of the painter John Gadsby Chapman, Conrad Wise Chapman established his professional reputation as a painter of war scenes at Charleston. At the close of the Civil War, with no money to return to Italy, where he had lived before the war, and no desire to settle in Virginia, which despite years of living abroad was still considered the family home, Chapman traveled to Mexico and took up residence in Mexico City. He traveled to Europe in 1866, living in Rome, London, and Paris. From 1883 through the late 1890s Chapman resided for varying periods of time in Mexico. At the outbreak of the Spanish-American War, he returned to the United States. At the close of the war Chapman once again took up residence in Mexico. In 1909 he returned to North America, settling in Hampton, Virginia, where he died the following year.

In the background of the painting are the peaks of Popocatepetl and Ixtaccihuatl, their snowy tops rising above the Lake of Texcoco. To the right, beyond the herd of goats, stands the tile factory of W. R. Jolly of Manchester, England. The San Diego picture is a later version, in smaller format, of a painting of the Valley of Mexico with the tile factory that Mr. Jolly had commissioned Chapman to paint in 1865. Chapman painted numerous views of the Valley of Mexico, a subject that proved popular throughout his career. A number of oil studies and sketches are in the Valentine Museum, Richmond, Virginia, acquired through Chapman's association with Granville G. Valentine and a donation made by his widow, Laura Seager Chapman. An inscription on the reverse states: *Valle de Mexico / desde la Hacienda de Los Olivares de los Padres / Hecho para el Senor Don Alejandra Najera / por CWChapman Mexico 1894*. The provenance of the picture is unknown; however, it is reported to have come from Mexico. It surfaced in Southern California in 1968.

PROVENANCE
Acquired by the Putnam Foundation, 1968.

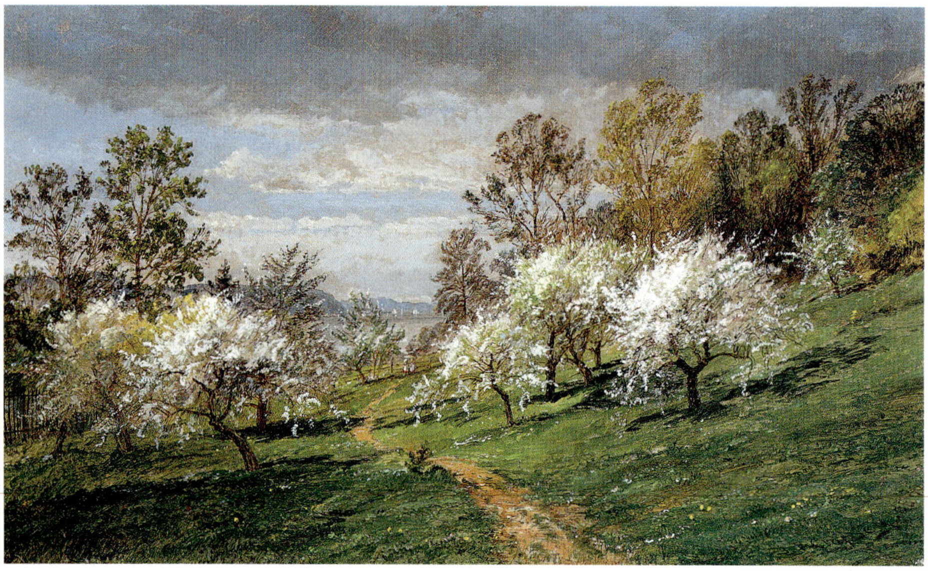

Jasper F. Cropsey
(1823–1900)

Apple Blossoms, 1887
Oil on canvas laid on panel, 12⅛ × 20⅛ in. (30.8 × 51.1 cm)
Signed and dated lower right: *J.F. Cropsey 1887*

The trees in this rural apple orchard are shown in springtime blossom. A path leads through the center of the composition. In the distant background two women are visible on the path. A river view with sailboats appears on the horizon.

PROVENANCE
Acquired by the Putnam Foundation, 1978.

EXHIBITED
New York, Berry-Hill Galleries, 1993, *The Apple of America: The Apple in Nineteenth-Century American Art,* p. 33, no. 30, ill.

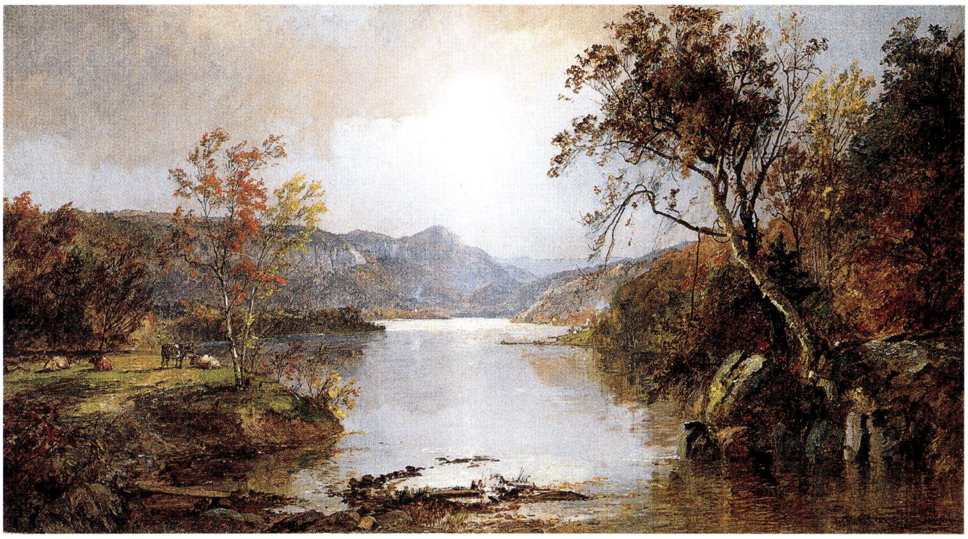

Fall Landscape, 1895
Oil on canvas, 16¼ × 30 in. (41.3 × 76.2 cm)
Signed and dated lower right: *J.F. Cropsey 1895*

Although Jasper Cropsey received his professional training in architecture, his painterly abilities were recognized and encouraged at an early age. In 1843 his work was exhibited at the National Academy of Design. Two extended trips to Europe and the writings of philosophers and aestheticians such as Ralph Waldo Emerson and Sir Joshua Reynolds influenced his mature painting style. By the 1850s Cropsey was painting what was to become the specialty of his half-century career as a landscape painter—the New England autumn with its glorious and brilliant color.

PROVENANCE
Acquired by the Putnam Foundation, 1978.

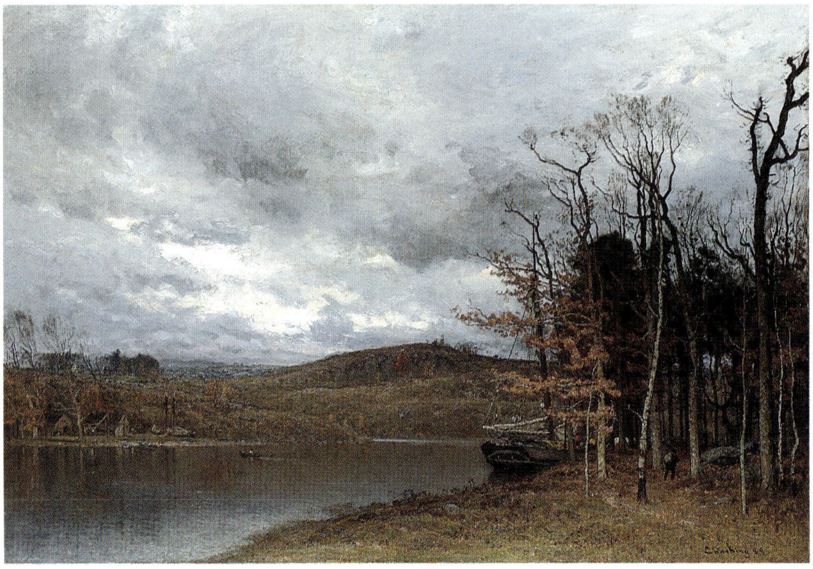

John Joseph Enneking
(1841–1916)

Coaster's Retreat, 1889
Oil on fabric, 42¾ × 63½ in. (108.6 × 161.3 cm)
Signed and dated lower right: *Enneking '89*

As with so many artists of his generation, John Enneking combined an early training in lithography with later study in Europe. In 1872 Enneking left the United States for four years abroad. He studied landscape painting at the Munich Academy and figure painting in Paris. He also worked with the French landscape painters Charles-François Daubigny and Eugène Boudin.

In this painting a coaster, a vessel used in coastal trade, is moored in an estuary along the Maine shoreline. The water reflects the cold, gray light of Enneking's favorite season—late November in New England.

PROVENANCE
Acquired by the Putnam Foundation, 1975.

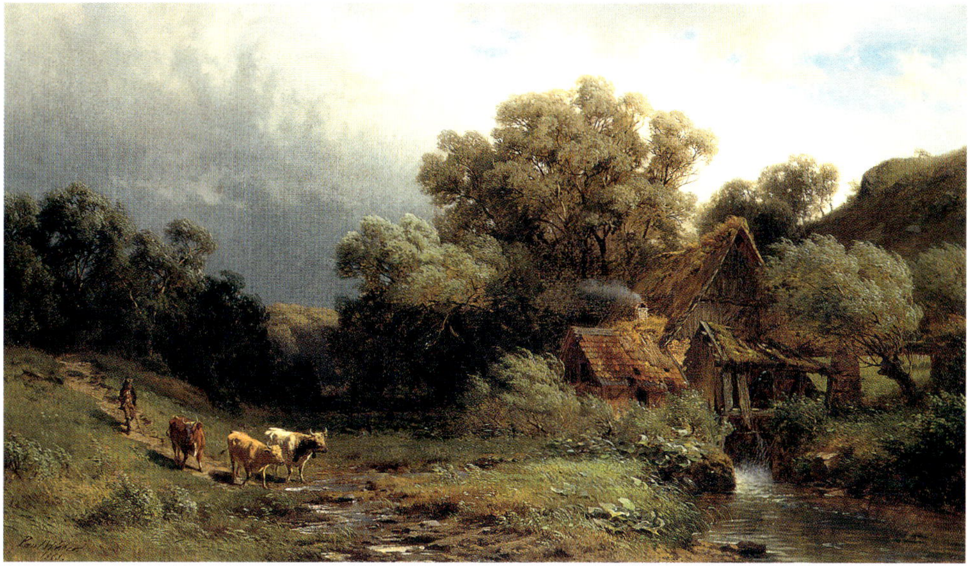

Paul Weber
(1823–1916)

The Mill, 1868
Oil on canvas, 31½ × 55 in. (80 × 139.7 cm)
Signed and dated lower left: *Paul Weber, 1868*

Born in Darmstadt, Germany, Weber came to the United States in 1848 and settled in Philadelphia. The following year he began exhibiting at the Pennsylvania Academy of the Fine Arts. He returned to Darmstadt in 1858 and was appointed court painter. His American work was generally pure landscape; his later work was devoted primarily to animal life. Weber spent his last years in the United States and died in Philadelphia.

PROVENANCE
Acquired by the Putnam Foundation, 1978.

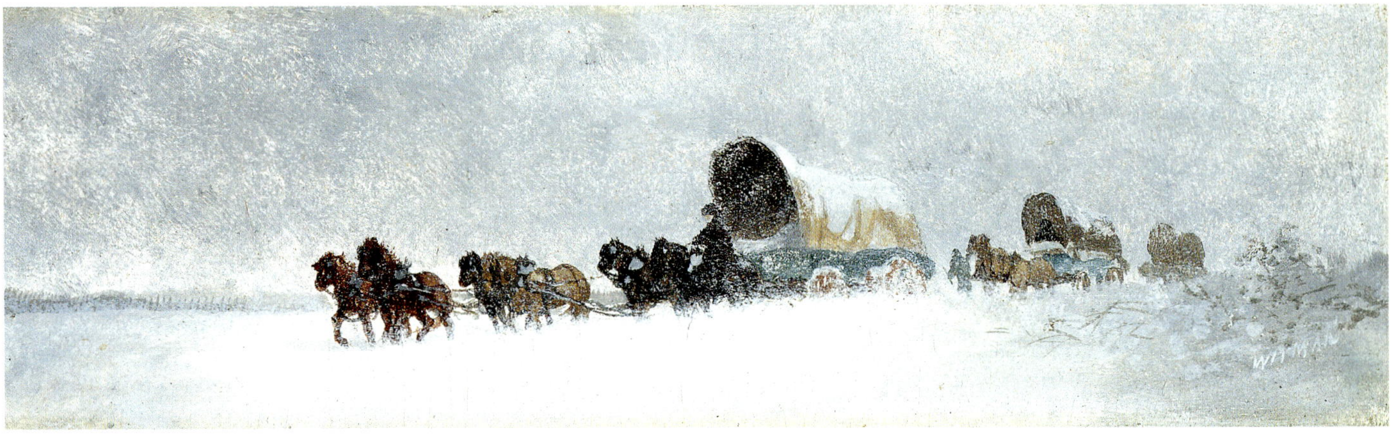

C. F. Witman
(act. late 19th–early 20th century)

On the Plains
Oil on panel, 4⅛ × 13¼ in. (10.5 × 33.7 cm)
Signed lower right: *Witman*

A group of three covered wagons is shown crossing a snow-covered landscape. On the reverse is affixed the business card of C. F. Witman and a handwritten inscription, in ink: *Painted by C. F. Whitman* [sic] *presented to S. F. Southerland by C. W. Snow.*

PROVENANCE
Acquired by the Putnam Foundation, 1978.